Kirtley Library
Columbia College
8th and Rogers
Columbia, MO. 65201

THE MARCH OF JOURNALISM

THE MARCH OF JOURNALISM

The Story of the British Press from 1622 to the Present Day

by
HAROLD HERD

GREENWOOD PRESS, PUBLISHERS
WESTPORT, CONNECTICUT

Library of Congress Cataloging in Publication Data

Herd, Harold, 1893-
  The march of journalism.

  Reprint of the 1952 ed. published by Allen & Unwin,
London.
  Bibliography: p. 328-
  1. Journalism--Great Britain--History. I. Title.
[PN5112.H4 1973]   072   73-722
ISBN 0-8371-6788-4

This book is copyright under the Berne Convention. Apart from any fair dealing for the purposes of private study, research, criticism or review, as permitted under the Copyright Act, 1911, no portion may be reproduced by any process without written permission.

First published in 1952 by George Allen & Unwin Ltd, London

Reprinted with the permission of George Allen & Unwin Ltd

Reprinted by Greenwood Press,
a division of Williamhouse-Regency Inc.

First Greenwood Reprinting 1973
Second Greenwood Reprinting 1976

Library of Congress Catalog Card Number 73-722

ISBN 0-8371-6788-4

Printed in the United States of America

INTRODUCTION

WITHIN the compass of a single volume it is not possible to give a detailed history of British journalism. To accomplish that task adequately—and no one has ever attempted it—would require a whole shelf of volumes. What this book aims to do is to provide an outline of the main developments in journalism, traced through the newspapers that chiefly influenced them, during three centuries—to describe the stages of evolution from the crude newsbooks of the seventeenth century to the modern newspapers and from the two-page essay papers and simple miscellanies of the eighteenth century to the reviews and magazines of today. If it has not been possible to give as much space as I should like (as a provincial-bred journalist) to provincial journalism, the reasons for compression will be obvious.

Journalism for the purpose of this volume comprehends both newspapers and periodicals. For the greater part of the time they have grown up together, and they have largely borrowed from each other. The serious daily newspaper of today publishes long authoritative articles of a type that once were to be found only in the monthly and quarterly reviews; the modern popular daily, and even more so the popular Sunday journal, is a combination of newspaper and magazine. The story of British journalism and of the prolonged struggle for freedom of expression cannot be properly told without describing the parallel development of the newspaper, the review and the magazine.

The distinction between a newspaper and a periodical is generally agreed to be impossible of completely exclusive definition. I have followed the broad definition commonly accepted—that a newspaper is a journal appearing at frequent intervals (usually daily or weekly) that is *primarily* devoted to reporting news. In borderline cases—as, for instance, Theodore Hook's *John Bull*, which I have treated as a periodical—I have been guided by the main intention of the journal. Such weeklies as the present *Spectator* described themselves as newspapers originally and gave much space to current news items, but gradually evolved into the review form. For convenience I have included them as periodicals throughout.

The materials available to historians of the Press are so abundant that a thorough study of them would absorb the attention of a team of research workers for years. In the first place there is the British Museum Library, which in addition to having a vast collection of periodicals and pre-nineteenth-century newspapers, contains the remarkable Burney Collection of newsbooks and newspapers covering the seventeenth and eighteenth centuries (including the only known copy of No. 1 of *The Times*) and the valuable Thomason Collection of newsbooks and pamphlets of the Civil War period (22,000 items in all). Then there is the Newspaper Library at Colindale, which houses nineteenth- and twentieth-century journals—a gigantic storehouse of national and local history and a formidable accumulation of material for the student of journalistic progress. These are the main sources that I have investigated. Other collections include the representative one at the Press Club, which contains several newspapers that are not filed at the Newspaper Library. I have personally examined nearly every publication of which more than a simple mention is made in this book.

Some individual histories of newspapers have been written, but there are many serious gaps. The only work of this type which has been designed to give a complete, detailed and objective picture is the official history of *The Times*. Three volumes have already been issued, and the fourth and final volume will carry the story up to 1935, the 150th anniversary of the founding of the journal. My indebtedness to this work will be apparent and is gratefully acknowledged. Mr. Stanley Morison's *The English Newspaper: 1622–1932*, with its informative text and its wealth of illustration, is the outstanding work on the technical evolution of the newspaper, and contains a great deal of fresh material about the history of journalism; and his interesting monographs on John Bell and Ichabod Dawks throw much new light on the

INTRODUCTION

developments with which they were associated. J. B. Williams's *A History of English Journalism to the Foundation of the Gazette* is the most exhaustive book on the period covered and gives a useful catalogue of publications from 1641 to 1666. J. B. Williams is a pen-name of J. G. Muddiman, who under his own name is the author of *The King's Journalist* (the only full study of Henry Muddiman, one of the principal journalists of the Restoration) and compiler of the *Tercentenary Handlist of English and Welsh Newspapers, Magazines and Reviews.*

Several histories of journalism were published in the nineteenth century, the latest—and most comprehensive—being H. R. Fox Bourne's *English Newspapers: Chapters in the History of Journalism* (two volumes, 1887). Anyone writing on the history of the newspaper owes much to Fox Bourne for his spadework. Various shorter works have appeared in the meantime, but none of these has given a complete survey. A list of the principal historical and biographical works that I have consulted is given at the end of this book. Part of the material in the chapters dealing with modern journalism has appeared in the *Fleet Street Annual.*

Some new facts about "firsts" have come to light in the course of my research. The *Morning* (1892) was not, as is usually stated, the first London halfpenny morning newspaper. Several journals at that price appeared long before—the *London Morning Mail* (1864), the *Morning Latest News* (1870) and others. There is a general belief that the *Echo* (1868) was the first London halfpenny evening, but it was preceded by the *London Daily Mercury* (1862) and the *Evening Mercury* (which was started two months before the *Echo* and lived only a fortnight). The *Evening Illustrated Paper* (1881), mentioned by Mr. Stanley Morison but not elsewhere, was the first pictorial daily—not the *Daily Graphic* (1890). The *Review of Reviews* (1890) was anticipated by so many types of periodical, ranging back from *Public Opinion* (1861) to the *Magazine of Magazines* (1750) and earlier, that a whole chapter could be devoted to these precursors of W. T. Stead's magazine and the modern "digests." Because of the immense field for investigation, as well as the incompleteness of even the greatest of the collections, the difficulty of determining "firsts" in any branch of journalistic enterprise is obvious.

Journalism has been transformed since Fox Bourne's history was published, and the time has come to bring the story up to date and to record, among other things, the effect of the Northcliffe revolution. Once-famous journals have disappeared in the meantime and, on the other hand, several leading newspapers have gained fresh vitality and prosperity. New dailies and weeklies and new magazines have sprung up in astonishing profusion in the two-thirds of a century that have elapsed since Fox Bourne wrote his last chapter. The beginnings of the New Journalism, though perceptible in the experiments of W. T. Stead, were not then decisively apparent. Traditional journalism, with its limited public of leisured readers, seemed firmly entrenched; newspapers were still set by hand; and T. P. O'Connor, Alfred Harmsworth and others, with their visions of a journalism designed to interest everyman, were still waiting in the wings. The process of evolution, long halted, was about to receive a tremendous jolt. The New Journalism has culminated in the mass circulations of today and made newspapers an indispensable part of the everyday life of almost every man and woman in the country. It has been a powerful creative force, but one day it will be supplanted in its turn, for the law of journalism—like the law of life—is one of endless change, and new generations with new ideas will demand fresh types of newspapers and magazines.

I should like to express my thanks to the staffs of the British Museum Reading Room and Newspaper Library and to Mr. Andrew Stewart, hon. librarian of the Press Club, for their helpful co-operation, and to Mr. Cecil Hann for many valuable suggestions.

H. H.

CONTENTS

INTRODUCTION		page 5
I.	The Newsbooks	11
II.	The First Newspaper	27
III.	The Advent of the Daily	39
IV.	The Rise of the Periodical	46
V.	The Developing Newspaper	64
VI.	New Men at the Head	78
VII.	The Rebels	97
VIII.	The Independent Newspaper Emerges	128
IX.	End of the "Taxes on Knowledge"	147
X.	The Age of Expansion	160
XI.	Nineteenth-Century Periodicals	188
XII.	The New Journalism	222
XIII.	Newspaper Developments in the Twentieth Century	252
XIV.	The Changing Magazine	284
XV.	The Press in the Second World War	301
XVI.	Parliament and the Press	312
XVII.	The Daily Miracle	322
BIBLIOGRAPHY		328
APPENDIX		331
INDEX		337

LIST OF ILLUSTRATIONS

		facing page
1.	FORERUNNER OF THE NEWSPAPER	12
2.	A DIURNAL WITH A PICTORIAL TITLE	16
3.	TWO FAMOUS "FIRSTS"	32
4.	STEELE'S "TATLER"	48
5.	MID-VICTORIAN HEADLINES	176
6.	THE FIRST OF THE LITERARY EVENINGS	224
7.	"THE TIMES" THEN AND NOW	272
8.	THE EVOLUTION OF MODERN HEADLINES	304

CHAPTER ONE

The Newsbooks

BRITISH journalism as we know it today is the product of a slow-moving evolution in the seventeenth and eighteenth centuries—a development that was watched with unfriendly eyes by kings and Parliament alike. There has never been a period in our history when authority has genuinely liked the idea of full publicity for its activities and unchecked criticism of its conduct, though in modern times it has come to be recognized that democracy cannot survive without freedom of expression; but in the seventeenth century the dislike of journalism was violent and unconcealed and took the form of repressive measures varying from censorship to suppression and from fines to imprisonment for those engaged in writing, printing and distributing news of, and comment on, public affairs.

When, in 1680, the judges held "that his Majesty may by law prohibit the printing of all newsbooks and pamphlets of news whatsoever not licensed by his Majesty's authority as manifestly tending to the breach of the peace and disturbance of the kingdom" their ruling merely confirmed on behalf of Charles II a privilege that was constantly—and sometimes brutally—asserted by Parliament in the Cromwellian period. Sir Roger L'Estrange, Surveyor of the Press in 1663 and the sole person then authorized to write and publish newsbooks, expressed this characteristic seventeeth-century viewpoint somewhat naïvely when he rejected the idea of issuing any sort of what he called Public Mercury (the contemporary equivalent of a newspaper) on the ground that it made the multitude too familiar with the actions and counsels of their superiors and "gives them not only an Itch but a Colourable Right to be Meddling with the Government."

Over a hundred years of trial and error preceded the emergence of the English newspaper proper. Several generations of enterprising spirits who were variously known to their contemporaries as authors, curranters, mercurists, newsmen, newsmongers, diurnalists, gazetteers and (eventually) journalists, experimented with modes of communicating news and opinions. The forerunners of the newspaper were the newsbooks of the seventeenth century. They appeared under many different names, several of which have survived in the titles of modern newspapers—Courant, News (then spelt Newes), Mercury, Post and Gazette. Others were called Corantos, Intelligencers, Diurnal(l)s, Occurrences, Passages, Accounts, Proceedings, etc. Pioneer enterprise was circumscribed by slow communications and by the chill hand of authority, which forbade the publication of home news in the early newsbooks.

First to appear was *Weekly Newes from Italy, Germanie, Hungaria, translated out of the Dutch copie*, published by Nicholas Bourne and Thomas Archer on May 23, 1622, but it was not the originator of newsbooks in Europe, being preceded some years by Continental publications.[1] Other pamphlets containing the word "Newes" in the title had appeared earlier in this country, but since these were single productions recording particular events they cannot be accepted as forerunners of the newspaper, the essential characteristic of which is continuity. The initial attempts at journalism were pamphlets of eight, sixteen or twenty-four pages that adhered to the technique of the book in size and appearance. The layout of the first page was in the current style for a book, the only difference being that the exact date of publication was incorporated—and, presently, the serial number too. Though the first newsbooks could claim continuity, they did not yet possess the other characteristic of the newspaper—

[1] J. B. Williams, in *A History of English Journalism to the Foundation of the Gazette*, quotes from a draft memorandum found in the State Papers, probably written in 1621, which put forward a proposal for an official newsbook to report "occurrents." The writer said that he had heard Britain "reproved in foreign parts for the negligence herein. From Antwerp, Brussels, Hague, Bulloyn, Frankfort, Prague, Vienna, Gratz, Venice, Florence, Rome, Naples, Genoa, Spain, Paris, and Lyons we have the occurrents every week."

The 23. of May.
VVEEKELY
Nevves from Italy,
GERMANIE, HVNGARIA,
BOHEMIA, the PALATINATE,
France, and the Low Countries.

Translated out of the Low Dutch Copie.

LONDON,
Printed by *I. D.* for *Nicholas Bourne* and *Thomas Archer*, and are to be sold at their shops at the Exchange, and in *Popes-head Pallace.*
1622.

FORERUNNER OF THE NEWSPAPER
The first dated newsbook

regularity of publication. They appeared at intervals ranging from a week to several weeks, but the very fact of reappearance denotes that a public demand for news had been found to exist.

Quick to recognize the significance of this new development was Nathaniel Butter, a freeman of the Stationers' Company, who had already made several experiments in this field—among others, a published account of two recent murders in Yorkshire (1605) and a single number of *Newes from Spain* (1611).[1] He engaged in rivalry with Bourne and Archer by publishing the grandiloquently titled *Newes from Most Parts of Christendom* and presently entered into partnership with Bourne and issued newsbooks frequently. Archer continued to publish independently for some years, and in 1625 he brought out the first newsbook with a title in the modern sense—*Mercurius Britannicus*. (The first publication to use Mercury in its title appears to have been *Mercurius Gallobelgicus*, a record of events printed at Cologne and published at infrequent intervals, in the form of a bound book, from 1594 to 1635. Written in Latin, it had a European circulation and was well known in England.) Earlier productions by various publishers had changed the name with each issue, either by specifying the nature of the contents (the title beginning with "A Coranto," "A Relation," "A True Relation" or "Weekly Newes") or by the simple device of calling the pamphlet "Continuation of Our Weekly Newes"

---

[1] Reports of murder cases in pamphlet form found a ready sale. Examples:
THREE BLOODIE MURDERS, The First Committed by Francis Cartwright upon William Storre, . . . the second committed by Elizabeth James on the body of her Mayde, . . . the third committed upon a Stranger, neere High-gate, very strangely found out by a Dogge, 2 July, 1613.

NATURES CRUELL STEP-DAMES; or, Matchless Monsters of the Female Sex, Elizabeth Barnes and Anne Willis, who were executed 26 April, 1637, at Tyburne, for the unnaturall murthering of their owne children.

NEWS FROM FLEETSTREET; or, The Last Speech and Confession of the Two Persons Hanged there for Murther. With an exact Account of all the Circumstances of their Murthering the Knight for which they Dyed. (1675.)

Many of these pamphlets have survived. The above examples are taken from a list of forty-eight that recently appeared in a catalogue issued by a well-known London bookseller.

and giving the period covered. Newsbooks were commonly known as "corantos" at this time.

Nathaniel Butter was the outstanding figure in the earliest days of journalism. Ben Jonson's play *The Staple of News*, printed in 1631, contains an obvious topical allusion by the Register of the Staple (or Office) of News:

> *Reg.* Dispatch; that's news indeed, and of importance.
> *Enter* a Countrywoman.
> What would you have, good woman?
> *Wom.* I would have, sir,
> A groatsworth of any news, I care not what,
> To carry down this Saturday to our vicar.
> *Reg.* O! you are a butter-woman; ask Nathaniel,
> The clerk there.
> *Nath.* Sir, I tell her she must stay
> Till emissary Exchange, or Paul's send in,
> And then I'll fit her.

A groat was fourpence; later newsbooks were usually sold at a penny or twopence each. Though tedious to read as a whole, *The Staple of News* reflects contemporary public interest in "Coranti and Gazetti," in printed news and views. As one character says:

> See divers men's opinions: unto some
> The very printing of 'em makes them news;
> That have not the heart to believe any thing,
> But what they see in print.

Butter also produced half-yearly volumes of collected news, e.g., the *German Intelligencer* (news of the war in Germany being one of the mainstays of early journalism).

A candid student of the early newsbooks cannot escape the impression that their contents were mostly a rough blend of fact, conjecture and transparent sensationalism. As yet the news was limited to happenings abroad and consisted largely of translations from Continental newsbooks or a rehash of their most interesting items, and either because some of it was too shrewdly accurate or because the blend did not suit the palate of his master, the Spanish ambassador complained about the newsbooks and the Star Chamber in 1632 ordered them to cease publication. Six years later Nathaniel Butter and Nicholas Bourne were allowed to resume their activities—Charles I gave them a monopoly of printing news for the term of twenty-one years on payment of a yearly rent of £10 towards the repair of St. Paul's—but as before they confined themselves to reporting foreign news. They carried on their work under the shadow of the licensees of the Press who were appointed in 1638. Butter soon got into trouble with the censorship and his publications appeared irregularly.

When the Star Chamber was abolished in 1641 and the Press freed—but only temporarily—new men came forward and, stimulated by the removal of the ban on the publication of home intelligence, brought fresh vitality to the writing of newsbooks. The first publication to print home news contained only Parliamentary intelligence. Entitled *The Heads of Severall Proceedings in this Present Parliament*, it was started in November 1641 by a printer named J. Thomas, and had eight pages. Subsequent issues were to be variously described; Nathaniel Butter was a partner in the enterprise for a short time and then appears to have retired from journalism. The title evolved into *A Perfect Diurnall of the Passages in Parliament* in 1642, and the diurnalist —to use the contemporary term—was Samuel Pecke, a scrivener who produced diurnals and other newsbooks at intervals up to 1655, and who like many other early pioneers of journalism suffered imprisonment. *A Perfect Diurnall* was not a daily, as its title suggests to modern ears, but a weekly summary of the daily proceedings in Parliament. Interest in the proceedings of the Commons was, for obvious reasons, at a high point in those days, and other publishers took advantage of this by producing diurnals of their own. Some of these productions were distinguished by pictorial devices ranging from symbols to illustrations of the Commons in session.

The scope of the newsbook was widened in 1642, which saw the appearance of several publications that contained "passages"

—favourite term in the sixteen-forties—from various parts of the country. Technical innovations that contain hints of modern journalistic practice were introduced. In April 1643, for instance, Walter Cook and Robert Wood's newsbook *A Continuation of certaine Speciall and Remarkable Passages from both Houses of Parliament, and other parts of the Kingdom* had on its title-page a numbered list of contents containing fourteen items and in addition employed the new device of setting out three italicized headlines in the top left-hand corner. *Mercurius Civicus*, which began publication in the following month, made regular use of this method, having four headlines in the same position. Examples:

The KING *and* QUEENE *conjoyned,*
The Kentish news related,
Our Forces are united,
A publique Fast appointed.

The last news from Gloucester related.
Oxford Occurrences imparted.
The Cornish Forces from Exeter repulsed.
Monuments of Idolatry to be defaced.

Mercury—first used in England, as we have seen, in 1625—formed part of the title of several publications that were issued in 1643 and continued to be a popular name for the purpose, the word becoming a synonym for newsbook. *Mercurius Civicus*, which had the sub-title "LONDONS INTELLIGENCER, or, Truth impartially related from thence to the whole Kingdome, to prevent mis-information" (the first use of London in a title), is of special interest because, in addition to using headlines, it originated the practice of putting the date between rules below the title and had illustrations on the front page, e.g., portraits of King Charles and the Queen or a pictorial device such as the figure of Mercury poised on the globe. Its new-style front page makes *Mercurius Civicus* interestingly noticeable among the newsbooks of the time.

Numb. 15

A PERFECT DIVRNALL OF THE PASSAGES IN PARLIAMENT.

From Munday the 17. of Aprill till Munday the 24. Aprill.

Collected by the same hand that formerly drew up the Copy for William Cooke *in Furnivals Inne. And now Printed by* I. Okes *and* F. Leach *and are to be sold by* Francis Coles *in the Old Baily.*

Note that here is also a true and punctuall relation of the whole proceedings of the siedge at Reading for all the last weeke unto this present.

Munday the 17. of Aprill 1643.

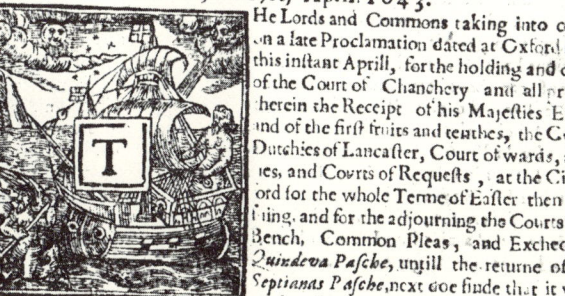

THe Lords and Commons taking into consideration a late Proclamation dated at Oxford the first of this instant Aprill, for the holding and continuing of the Court of Chancery and all proceedings therein the Receipt of his Majesties Exchequer, and of the first fruits and tenthes, the Court of the Dutchies of Lancaster, Court of wards, and Liveries, and Courts of Requests, at the City of Oxford for the whole Terme of Easter then next ensuing, and for the adjourning the Courts of Kings Bench, Common Pleas, and Exchequer from *Quindeva Pasche*, untill the returne of *Quinque Septianas Pasche*, next doe finde that it will much end to the prejudice of the Common-wealth to have the said Courts and Receipts held and continued at Oxford where great part of an

Army

British Museum

A DIURNAL WITH A PICTORIAL TITLE

THE NEWSBOOKS

Sixteen forty-three brought a great increase in the number of newsbooks. Several new names emerged, including *Weekly Account*, *Weekly Post*, *Scout* and *Intelligencer* (the *Kingdomes Weekly Intelligencer*, a newsbook designed to be "sent abroad to prevent misinformation," which survived until 1649). To modern eyes the news they printed was often vague and scrappy, but allowance must be made for the meagre resources of the producers of newsbooks and the slowness of communications at a time when there was only one post (later two) a week. The *Parliament Scout*, written by John Dillingham—a leading news writer who was formerly a tailor—began the issue for August 10 to 17, 1643, with this announcement: "Our Scout is returned very empty of newes this weeke, and that little that he brings is very uncertaine, he tells us that Gloucester hath been several times assaulted by the enemy, and that most furiously. . . ." The last paragraph of this issue stated: "The Oxford Scout whispers up and downe that Gloucester is taken." The *Scotish Dove* (*sic*), started in 1643, printed a rhymed list of contents on the right side of a woodcut title that showed a dove in flight. The number dated June 28, 1644, gave the news at a glance in these lines:

> London hath Oxford *Aulicus* reviv'd,
> A Massacre Virginia hath contriv'd.
> Sir Thomas *Fairfax Rupert* will defeat,
> Colonell *Charles Fairfax* made Montrosse retreat.
> In Weymouth store of Armes and poders (*sic*) found.
> Brave *Waller's* Royall Chase is related.
> The King to *Rupert* is about to flye,
> The Earle of Dinbigh hath tooke Auswostrey.

One newsbook—or leaflet, for it consisted of four small pages only—was printed in French and designed to be sent abroad by "all merchants and others that are desirous weekely to impart beyond seas the certain condition of affairs here and of the proceedings of the war." *Le Mercure Anglois*, as it was called, appeared regularly from 1644 to 1648. A similar paper, *Nouvelles Ordinaires de Londres*, which was started in 1650, ran for many years, the latest issue known to have survived being No. 567, printed in 1663: it appears to have been the longest-lived newsbook.

Now and again a vivid piece of reporting stands out of the mass of news items, rumours, invective and ponderous articles that formed the main content of the newsbooks in that troubled decade. Three centuries later the account of the execution of Charles I printed in *A Perfect Diurnall of Some Passages in Parliament and the Daily Proceedings of the Army under His Excellency the Lord Fairfax* (January 29 to February 5, 1649) still moves the reader by its graphic simplicity, as this extract shows:

Tuesday, January 30. This day the King was beheaded, over against the Banquetting house by Whitehall. The manner of Execution, and what passed before his death take thus. He was brought from Saint *James* about ten in the morning, walking on foot through the Park, with a Regiment of Foot for his guard, with Colours flying, Drums beating, his private Guard of Partizans, with some of his Gentlemen before, and some behind bareheaded, Doctor *Juxon* late Bishop of *London* next behinde him, and Col. *Thomlinson* (who had the charge of him) to the Gallery in Whitehall, and so into the Cabinet Chamber, where he used to lye, where he continued at his Devotion refusing to dine (having before taken the Sacrament) onely about 12, at noone, he drank a Glasse of Claret Wine, and eat a piece of bread. From thence he was accompanyed by Dr. *Juxon*, Col. *Thomlinson*, Col. *Hacker* and the Guards before mentioned through the Banquetting-house adjoyning, to which the Scaffold was erected, between Whitehall Gate, and the Gate leading into the Gallery from Saint *James*: The Scaffold was hung round with black, and the floor covered with black, and the Ax and Block laid in the middle of the Scaffold. There were divers companies of Foot and Horse, on every side the Scaffold, and the multitudes of people that came to be Spectators, very great. The King making a Passe upon the Scaffold, look'd very earnestly on the Block, and asked Col. *Hacker* if there were no higher; and then spake thus directing his speech to the Gentlemen upon the Scaffold. [Report of speech follows.] Then the King took off his cloak, and his George, giving his George to Dr. *Juxon*, saying Remember, (it is thought for the Prince,) and some other small ceremonies past: after which the king stooping down laid his neck upon the blocke, and after a little pause stretching forth his hands, the Executioner at one blow severed his head from his Body. Then his Body was put in a coffin covered with black Velvet and removed to his lodging chamber in White hall.

Note the inconsistency in the spelling of several words and in the use of capitals. Lack of uniformity in style is constantly noticeable in the newsbooks, as in other printed matter of the period.

The outstanding personalities in the journalism of the sixteen-forties were two young men—Sir John Birkenhead (or Berkenhead) who in 1643, at the age of 27, founded *Mercurius Aulicus* ("Communicating the Intelligence and affaires of the Court, to the rest of the Kingdome"), the first newsbook to support the Royalist cause, and Marchamont Nedham (or Needham), who, in 1644, at the age of 24, became the principal writer of *Mercurius Britanicus* [sic]—founded in 1643 by Captain Thomas Audley to oppose *Mercurius Aulicus*—and was to be the subject of many satires provoked by his venomous journalism between 1644 and 1660. One of the most notorious time-servers in history, Nedham supported in turn Cromwell, King Charles and Cromwell again until by the time of the Restoration he was completely discredited. Birkenhead was his exact opposite—a man of principle who stuck to the Royalist cause throughout and a writer with a sense of responsibility.[1]

Something like two score newsbooks had appeared before the Royalists realized the need for a journal of their own. A foreword to No 1 of *Mercurius Aulicus* (printed at Oxford) thus proclaimed its purpose: "The world hath long enough beene abused with falshoods: And there's a weekly cheat put out to nourish the abuse amongst the people, and make them pay for their seducement. And that the world may see that the Court is neither

---

[1] "The Malignants do pay sometimes as deare for that pamphlet as for a psalm book, one of the last was sold for 18 pence a peece. We know say the Malignants that what Aulicus writeth is true."—From a pamphlet, *The True Character of Mercurius Aulicus*, published in 1645.

so barren of intelligence, as it is conceived; nor the affaires thereof in so unprosperous a condition, as these Pamphlets make them: it is thought fit to let them truly understand the state of things that so they may no longer pretend ignorance, or be deceived with untruthes: which being premised once for all, we now go into the business; whereas we shall proceed with all truth and candor." After the Restoration Birkenhead served as a member of Parliament, withdrawing from public life two years later on his acceptance of a knighthood and his appointment as Master of Requests.

Nedham's reckless pen made him the most formidable and the most bitterly hated journalist of his time; and, it should be added, the most feared—in which fact surely lies the explanation of his journalistic survival after a double apostasy. The man who in 1645 wrote in this manner of the King

> Where's King Charles? What's become of him? it were best to send Hue and cry after him. If any man can bring any tale or tiding of a wilful King, which hath gone astray these four yeares from his Parliament, with a guilty conscience, bloody hands, a heart full of vowes and protestations. . . . Then give notice to *Britanicus* and you shall be well paid for your paines. . . .

two years later sought and obtained the royal pardon and kissed the King's hand and then started *Mercurius Pragmaticus*, in which paper he bespattered the enemies of Charles with characteristic abuse: Cromwell, for instance, was nicknamed "Copper-Nose." The Government, deciding to suppress this newsbook, imprisoned the printer, and Nedham—who in 1646 had made a brief stay in the Fleet and had his paper (*Mercurius Britanicus*) suppressed for making mischief between the two Houses of Parliament—prudently went into hiding. In 1649 he was arrested and sent to Newgate; three months later he gained his release on the undertaking to write for the Commonwealth. A considered statement of *The Case of the Commonwealth*, published in 1650, brought him as a reward a gift of £50 and a pension of £100. In the same year he took charge of a new weekly,

Mercurius Politicus (which continued publication for a decade), and for a time John Milton was responsible for the supervision of this paper and may have written for it. Among his other journalistic activities in this decade Nedham was associated with the *Publick Adviser* (1657), the first all-advertisement weekly, which in the inaugural issue contained brief announcements under such headings as "Houses to be Let or Sold," "Persons Wanting Houses," "Persons Wanting Imployment," "Accommodation of Lodging and Board" and "Stage-Coaches," as well as this remarkable early specimen of advertisement copy-writing:

In Bartholomew Lane on the back side of the Old Exchange, the drink called Coffee, (which is a very wholsom and physical drink, having many excellent vertues, closes the Orifice of the Stomack, fortifies the heat within, helpeth Digestion, quickneth the Spirits, maketh the heart lightsom, is good against Eye-sores, Coughs, or Colds, Rhumes, Consumption, Head-ach, Dropsie, Gout, Scurvy, Kings Evil, and many others) is to be sold both in the morning, and at three o'clock in the afternoon.

The close of Nedham's career was brusquely announced by an advertisement in the *Parliamentary Intelligencer* (March 26 to April 2, 1660) notifying that "Marchemont Nedham, the Author of the Weekly News books, called *Mercurius Politicus*, and the *Publique Intelligencer*, is, by order of the Council of State, discharged from Writing or Publishing any Publique Intelligence." Note that the term journalist is not yet in use, Nedham being described as an author. A further official announcement ordered the Stationers' Company to take care that no books of intelligence were printed and published on Mondays and Thursdays other than those put forth by Henry Muddiman and Giles Dury, "who have an allowance in that behalf from the Council of State." Muddiman, as writer of newsletters and newsbooks, and as the first to produce a newspaper—the *Oxford Gazette* (afterwards *London Gazette*)—was a leading figure in post-Cromwellian journalism, and an outline of his career will be given in the next chapter.

If Muddiman and Dury, the choice of the Council of State,

discharged their functions in the spirit of over-eager partisans rather than as objective recorders we need not judge them too harshly. England had lived through two decades of civil war and political and sectarian bitterness, and there were many who saw in General Monk, who is fulsomely portrayed by the new official news writers, a strong and honest man who would bring peace to a distracted land; and it can now be seen that his intervention in the early months of 1660 was decisive and shrewdly attained its purpose without armed conflict. In the *Parliamentary Intelligencer* (April 9 to 16, 1660) we find these references:

On Tuesday, His Excellency, and the Council of State, and several Officers of the Army, dined at Goldsmiths Hall, where they were received with very great demonstrations of joy and respect; after Dinner there was an handsome Enterlude, after which they were entertained with a costly Banquet.

From *Exon.*

The affections and respects of this County for his Excellency the Lord General, is very remarkable, for as if they had intended an expression equal to the high merits of so eminent a Patriot, they met in such numbers as were never known before on such occasion, and did with one voice in a full Election, *nemine contradicente*, choose him for Knight of the Shire, which we hope he will be pleased to accept of, it being the place of his Nativity.

His Excellency the Lord General Monck, and the Council of State, dined at Vintners Hall on Thursday April 12. on Friday the 13 at Fishmongers Hall, where they were treated with such demonstrations of joy, as did sufficiently speak the high honour they did bear him. . . .

Other items of home news in the same issue included this paragraph: "From Norwich we are informed by Letter, that a soulder of Colonel *Evelins* Regiment is secured in the Goal [*sic*] there, for speaking dangerous and seditious words: His Examination is sent up to his Excellency; the rest of the Regiment are in very good order."

A year later (April 22–29, 1661) the same paper, now renamed the *Kingdomes Intelligencer*, devoted several pages to a report of the coronation of Charles II. In the companion newsbook, *Mercurius Publicus*, issued the previous Friday, Muddiman gave this brief but ecstatic account of the ceremony:

> ... we now proceed to the Narrative of *His* Sacred MAJESTIES Coronation, which because it exceeded even the Expectation of all Beholders (whether Forainers or Natives) as well as the example of all his Glorious Ancestors, we shall give it at large in the News-Book on Monday, the Officers and others employed in that great and matchless Solemnity, having not yet fully brought in their Particulars, and it would ill become us to divide or mangle any thing so illustrious, or cheat you with fictions (as some late Pamphlets crept abroad have lately endeavoured, whose boldness hereafter will be more severely handled) especially since both Heaven and Earth conspired to make it glorious; the weather itself (as once the sun) standing still on purpose, that not one drop of rain durst ever to fall till the Solemnity was full over; so as those giddy Bretheren (who would all be Rulers, and would have no other) are forced to confess, that as we *never had such a King, so there never was such a Coronation*.

Nearly forty years had passed since the advent of the newsbook. During the first half of that period the publication of home news had been prohibited; from 1641 to 1660 home news, especially Parliamentary intelligence, became the main content, and some of the essential features of the modern newspaper emerged—editorial comment, articles on questions of the day, special correspondence, headlines, illustrations, advertisements. There were even crude attempts at humorous journalism, including *Mercurius Jocosus; or the Merry Mercurie* (1654), a tame little pamphlet that promised to give its readers "the best concets from the most refined fancies," together with "the heads of all the Remarkable News" but ran out of material and left its eighth page blank—and ceased publication after a few issues. No. 1 contained an attack in verse on "Mercurius Fumigosus, or the Smoking Mercurie; alias the froth and scum of the TIMES." *Mercurius Fumigosus* (1654–1655) and its predecessor, the *Laughing Mercury* (previously called *Mercurius Democritus*;

or, a True and Perfect Nocturnall) were vulgar publications conducted by John Crouch. This was a lamentable falling-off for the man who had written with so much vigour *The Man in the Moon* (1649–1650). In No. 2 of this Royalist newsbook he led off with verse that was exceedingly topical, as these two stanzas show:

> O wond'rous *thing*! is it not strang
> In this *madd, frantick* Land,
> That *Knaves* and *Fools*, by a *change*,
> Have all things at *command*?

> The *law* lies murder'd with the *King*,
> The *Gospel* overthrown;
> Great *Summes* they still are *Leavying*,
> And no man *knows* his *own*.

The liberty to print—sometimes, it must be said, violently abused—was never conceded for long, the newsbooks being subjected to licensing for the greater part of the time. Individual publications that offended Parliament were suppressed; many authors and printers were fined and imprisoned; and the mercuries or hawkers (including "women mercuries") who sold them in the street were at times treated by authority as common rogues and whipped or sent to gaol. Oliver Cromwell suppressed the licensed Press from October 1649 to June 1650, and again from September 1655, and for a time (as later under Charles II) the only newsbooks issued were official journals. Altogether journalism from 1641 to 1660 was a dangerous trade, but a surprising number of men braved the risks, scores of different newsbooks being produced, of which a few continued publication for years. Suppression was not always complete, certain Royalist publications evading at one time the vigilance of Parliament—early examples of what we now call underground newspapers.

"What a pannique fear possesses the soule of the Universe when the hawkers come roaring along the streets like the religious singers of Bartholomew Fayre," wrote Samuel Sheppard in depicting the effects on seventeenth-century Londoners of "the mysterie of a little inck and paper." Sheppard, a clergyman, who had been associated at various times with several newsbooks—including the Royalist *Mercurius Pragmaticus*—and been imprisoned, proclaimed himself in 1652 the scourge of the Mercuries. In *Mercurius Mastix*, published in that year, he announced his purpose as that of "Faithfully Lashing All Scouts, Mercuries, Posts, Spyes, and others; who cheat the Commonwealth under the name of Intelligence."

No rest day nor night with these cursed *Caterpillars, Perfect Passages, Weekly Occurrences, Scout, Spye, Politicus, Diurnal*, the devil and his dam. . . . But the cream of the jest is, how they take their times and rises; one upon Munday, t'other on Tuesday, a third on Wednesday; and so come over one anothers backs, as if they were playing at Leap-frog. Nay, it's fine to see how authentically and positively these Caytiffs obtrude their parboyl'd Non-sense; with what impudence they'll rout you an Army at five hundred leagues distance, and with one dash of a pen piece it up again, and make it as whole as ever it was. . . . These fellows come flurting in, and style themselves by new names; they flie up and down a week or two, and then in a moment vanish. Seriously I could wish it were enacted, that whosoever did betake himself to this Lying trade, should be bound at least seven years to it.

This, the last journalistic appearance of Samuel Sheppard, must be partly discounted as the swan song of an embittered Royalist, written three years after the execution of the king to whose cause he had devoted his pen; but his attack, though splenetic, had some shrewd thrusts. It was perhaps the unhappiest age through which the English people have ever lived, an age in which two philosophies were so sharply opposed that for either side compromise was synonymous with treachery and tolerance with shameful weakness: obviously not an atmosphere favourable to the development of a calm, objective attitude on the part of the newly emerged Press. In the modern phrase there were no neutrals in that struggle, and the newsbooks of the period reflect—often crudely—the sombre hatreds of the Civil War. Badgered by authority and handicapped by inexperience and meagre resources, the newsbooks lived from hand to mouth and the majority did not survive for more than a few issues.

Scholars, printers, booksellers, politicians, scriveners and tradesmen, honest men and knaves—the pioneers of journalism appear a motley collection. They were very human in their faults; many of them were unscrupulous in controversy, and there is no evidence that any of the newsbook writers had a vision of a journalism that would be something more than an instrument of faction; but they cannot be denied courage. These bold and sometimes truculent pioneers, who lived under the constant menace of imprisonment and suppression, must be given credit for one great service to their country. They opened the windows and gave thoughtful men and women their first glimpse of the wider freedoms that could be secured by the liberty to print—but it was still only a glimpse, for two centuries were to pass before this basic freedom was firmly established.

CHAPTER TWO

The First Newspaper

THE day of the newsbooks was nearly over. From 1660 to 1665, when the first newspaper appeared, they were never more than few in number and a Parliamentary enactment robbed them of what had constituted their main interest for the public.

The proceedings of Parliament had provided the most important content of the newsbooks. When, therefore, the Commons passed a resolution on June 25, 1660—a few weeks after the return of Charles II—"that no person whatsoever do presume at his peril to print any votes of proceedings of this House without the special leave and order of this House" the chief source of intelligence was cut off and the appeal of the newsbooks much diminished. Shortly before this Oliver Williams, previously known as the conductor of six short-lived "Offices of Intelligence" (which charged fees for registering public wants, services, etc., and were in effect advertising centres), made a bit of journalistic history by publishing a daily newsbook—a report of the proceedings of the House of Commons from February 21 to March 16, 1660, when the Long Parliament was dissolved. He followed this up by reviving Nedham's newsbooks, *Mercurius Politicus* and the *Publick Intelligencer*, in a slightly different form, from his "Office of Intelligence near the Old Exchange"; and several other newsbooks—including one written by Henry Walker, a former bookseller who had been a prominent figure in journalism since 1647—also made their appearance. All these books were suppressed after a brief run, and the *Kingdomes Intelligencer* and *Mercurius Publicus* of Henry Muddiman held the monopoly until 1663.

Of Giles Dury, whose name was linked with that of Muddiman as a writer of these newsbooks, we know little; he appears to have been simply an assistant for a short time. But Muddiman, as newsbook writer, as editor of the first newspaper and as a prolific author of newsletters, was to become one of the two most important figures in journalism from 1660 to 1690: the other was Sir Roger L'Estrange. Pepys met Muddiman shortly before the dramatic appearance of General Monk on the London scene and has left us an unfavourable portrait (January 9, 1660): "I found Muddiman a good scholar, an arch rogue: and owns that though he writes newsbooks for the Parliament, yet he did declare that he did it only to get money; and did talk very basely of many of them." The newsbook mentioned was the *Parliamentary Intelligencer*—published by the Council of State from the fourteenth issue—and its scope was defined as "comprising the sum of forraign intelligence with the affairs now in agitation in England Scotland and Ireland"; and, as Muddiman's biographer fairly points out, as it "advocated a free Parliament, Pepys must soon have discovered his mistake in thinking that he wrote newsbooks for the Rump."[1] Muddiman was then just over thirty years old, and since leaving Cambridge he had worked as a schoolmaster. The publication of the *Parliamentary Intelligencer* marked the beginning of his work as a journalist.

Muddiman was replaced in 1663 as a writer of newsbooks by L'Estrange, who had given zealous service to the Royalist cause as a Cavalier and as a pamphleteer (and was constantly reminding people of the fact) and had been imprisoned four years in Newgate after a reprieve from a death sentence. L'Estrange had hoped to become the chief journalist at the Restoration, and the choice of Muddiman to succeed Nedham was a heavy blow to him; but he had a vigorous pen as a pamphleteer and his writing kept his name to the forefront, and he lost no opportunity of pressing his claims on authority. In February 1662 he received a notable mark of official favour, being granted a general warrant that empowered him to seize seditious books and their writers—a congenial task for one who notoriously regarded toleration as a danger to the State. Three months later the Licensing Act,

[1] *The King's Journalist* (J. G. Muddiman).

designed to prevent any abuses in printing and limiting the number of master printers to twenty, was passed and he was requested to draw up proposals for the regulation of the Press. One of his suggestions was that printing employees found guilty of taking part in the publication of offensive works should be sentenced to wear some badge of ignominy. When as a reward for his services he asked to be given the right to publish news and all bills and advertisements, he got nearly everything that he specified in his application: he was made Surveyor of the Press and granted as remuneration for this work "the sole privilege of writing, printing and publishing all narratives, advertisements, mercuries, intelligencers, diurnals and other books of public intelligence"; and simultaneously he was granted the power to seize "unlicensed and treasonable schismatical and scandalous books and papers." At last he had achieved the position that had eluded him in 1660. Muddiman's newsbooks had to cease publication in 1663, and in their place L'Estrange issued the *Intelligencer* and the *Newes*, published on Mondays and Thursdays respectively. In the first number of the *Intelligencer*—which had a line below the title proclaiming that it was "Published for Satisfaction and Information of the PEOPLE"— we get a hint of the official nervousness about the activities of newsbook hawkers that recalls the suspicious attitude in Cromwell's day:

> The *Way* (as to the Vent) that has been found Most *Beneficiall* to the *Master* of the *Book* has been to *Cry*, and *Expose* it about the Streets, by *Mercuries* and Hawkers; but whether that *Way* be advisable in some *other respects*, may be a *Question*; for under Countenance of that Imployment, is carried on the *Private Trade* of *Treasonous* and *Seditious Libels*, (nor, effectually, has anything considerable been dispersed, against either Church, or State, without the *Aid*, and *Privity* of this sort of *People*).

There was one vital omission from the comprehensive powers granted to L'Estrange, for he was not given the authority he had asked for to control written news. This left a loophole for

Muddiman, who already had the valuable privilege of free postage for his letters and who was now to become the principal writer of newsletters. The newsletter appears to have had its origin in the sixteenth century, when the Fuggers of Augsburg, a banking house that had connections abroad, arranged for information on current happenings to be regularly transmitted to them by their agents in London, Paris and other foreign centres.[1] Newsletters had been a valuable means of conveying intelligence in England ever since the establishment of the weekly public post in 1637—especially valuable because being written they were exempt from licensing, which applied to printed matter only. They were reporting domestic news several years before the newsbooks had permission to do so, and they were much in demand during the period when newsbooks were prohibited from recording the proceedings of Parliament. The high cost of subscription—Muddiman's fee, for instance, was £5 a year, probably equivalent to £40 or £50 in present-day values—limited their circulation to coffee-houses and persons of means, and it was assumed that their readers were responsible persons as distinct from those who bought the penny and twopenny newsbooks. Newsletters were to continue to flourish until the beginning of the eighteenth century, when the fuller service given by the newspapers, at a relatively low charge, brought their career to an end. Between the First and Second World Wars the newsletter, in printed and duplicated form, was revived in Britain and the United States, and a number of these private information services are still in existence; of the British newsletters only one —conducted by the *Economist*—is associated with a newspaper or periodical. The reason assigned for this revival is basically the reason for the special periods of prosperity enjoyed by the seventeenth-century newsletters—that at a time of political crisis they publish information that, it is claimed, cannot be found elsewhere (such information now chiefly taking the shape of forecasts of how world events are expected to develop).

[1] A selection of these letters, covering several decades, was issued by the Bodley Head in 1924.

Muddiman embarked on his long and successful career as newsletter writer with several great advantages—he already had a newsgathering organization and enjoyed access to people of influence, he was able to publish reports of Parliament, the postal service had been improved and he scored over his rivals by having the privilege of free postage. At his office at the "Seven Stars," near the New Exchange in the Strand, he kept a staff of clerks to copy the letters, which were sent out with the heading "Whitehall" and the date.

L'Estrange's apparently profitable monopoly did not turn out satisfactorily to himself. His newsbooks were thin in content and were restricted in appeal by the ban on Parliamentary reports; and eventually they were taken from him and he was compensated with a sum of £100 a year charged on their profits plus £200 a year for his work as Surveyor of the Press. He discharged his official duties with fanatical conscientiousness and let it be known that informers would be suitably rewarded at his offices at the "Gun" in Ivy Lane. The most unfortunate of the many victims of his zeal was a printer named John Twyn. When his home in Cloth Fair was raided in October 1663, he had not time to destroy all the incriminating material, which included printed sheets that contained the argument that the execution of justice was the people's as well as the magistrates' duty and that "if the magistrates prevent judgment, the people are bound by the law of God to execute judgment without them and upon them." He was tried and found guilty and sentenced to be hanged, disembowelled and quartered—a judgment delivered in precise and obscene wording, part of this barbarous formula being omitted by judges of later generations. When Twyn appealed for intercession with King Charles for mercy, the judge retorted: "I would not intercede for my own father in this case if he were alive."

After losing the newsbooks L'Estrange resumed his pamphleteering and wrote with a bitterness that infuriated his opponents: once he was burned in effigy. "From the malice of L'Estrange the grave was no hiding place, and the house of mourning no sanctuary," declared Macaulay. In later life, from 1681 to 1687, L'Estrange published the *Observator*, a political periodical in dialogue form whose avowed intention was "to encounter the faction and to vindicate the government." He discontinued the paper when he found himself unable to support James the Second's policy of toleration. In 1688, at the Revolution, he lost the office of licenser. The new political climate after the Revolution was unfavourable to a man with his views and he was accused of fomenting trouble and twice went to prison. Energetic, intolerant and a convinced enemy of free discussion, Sir Roger L'Estrange was a turbulent figure throughout the second half of the seventeenth century. He died in 1704, at the age of 88, sixty years after being reprieved by Parliament. As seen through the eyes of posterity he is a repellent personality, but Pepys found him "a man of fine conversation . . . most courtly" and Evelyn "a person of excellent parts," and Clarendon describes him as "a man of a good wit and a fancy very luxuriant, and of an enterprising nature."

The title *Observator* was revived in L'Estrange's lifetime by John Tutchin, who as a youth had been sentenced by Judge Jeffreys at the Bloody Assizes (1685) to seven years' imprisonment for sedition and to be whipped once a year during this sentence through all the market towns in Dorset. "They tell me you are a poet," sneered the judge. "I'll cap verses with you." Tutchin published the new *Observator* (1702), a little weekly paper, in partnership with John How, a printer, and he adopted the technique of L'Estrange—though not his opinions—by presenting his views in the form of a series of dialogues between an outspoken Whig and a countryman. These views did not commend him to authority, and in January 1704 the House of Commons passed a resolution declaring "that the Observator from December 8 to 12 contains matter scandalous and malicious, reflecting on the proceedings of the house, tending to the promotion of sedition in the kingdome, and that Tutchin, the author, How, the printer, and Bragg, the publisher of that paper, should be taken into custody by the sergeant-at-arms." Tutchin

TWO FAMOUS "FIRSTS"

The first newspaper and the first daily paper

was tried in the Queen's Bench Court in the following November and found guilty, but because of an error in the indictment the judges ordered a new trial. This did not take place and Tutchin continued to publish the *Observator*, but private enemies were said to have taken the law into their own hands, attacking him one night and inflicting injuries from which he died.[1]

The Great Plague of 1665 drove the Court to take refuge in the purer air of Oxford, and this fact suggested to Joseph Williamson, Under-Secretary of State, the idea of starting another official paper, the *Oxford Gazette*, to be published twice a week. After twenty-three issues it became the *London Gazette* and has continued publication under that title ever since. In the history of journalism its significance lies in the fact that its single-leaf form (technically a half sheet in folio), with its pages divided into two columns, broke away from the news-pamphlet form to a style that is a recognizable link with the newspaper as we know it today. The *London Gazette* of the present time contains only official announcements and is not a newspaper in the true sense of the word, but in 1665 and for long afterwards it published news. The two-column layout which it inaugurated became the standard for the new publications of the next few decades. Pepys noted the first number of the *Oxford Gazette* with this comment: "Very pretty, full of news, and no comment in it," and added—incorrectly—"Wrote by Williamson." The writer was Henry Muddiman, and he was almost certainly responsible for the choice of size, identical with that of his newsletters, with which he sent it by post.

The first page of No. 1 began with a four-line announcement of the appointment of a new Bishop of Oxford, and was followed by a list of sheriffs "pricked" for the succeeding year. The remainder of the two-page paper consisted of paragraphs, ranging

---

[1] This story is reproduced by H. R. Fox Bourne, but Mr. Winston Churchill, in *Marlborough: His Life and Times* (Harrap), points out: "In fact Tutchin, after being flogged, died in the Queen's Bench Prison at the Mint in September 1707."

from three lines to a little more than half a column, headed usually by the place of origin of the news and the date—a journalistic practice which was to have a strangely long life (for even after American newspapers introduced bold and numerous headlines in the nineteenth century they long continued to lead off with the name of the town from which the news had emanated). Most of the news came from abroad and was concerned with fighting on land and at sea. A grim two-line item at the very end of the paper was the only reference to the biggest news story of 1665: "The accounts of the weekly Bill at London, runs thus: Total, 1359. Plague, 1050. Deceased, 428." The imprint read: "*Oxon*, printed by *Leonard Litchfield*, and Re-printed at *London*, for the use of some Merchants and Gentlemen who desired them." This is the first known occasion on which a newspaper or periodical was printed in more than one city; the next was in 1832, when *Chambers's Journal* was printed in three different centres; seventy years later a daily newspaper—the *Daily Mail*—began the simultaneous publication of a duplicate edition (at Manchester); and in 1925 the idea was applied to evening newspaper production by the *Yorkshire Evening Post* and the *Yorkshire Evening News* of Leeds, duplicate plants being established at Doncaster.

To return to the *Oxford Gazette*: No. 1 had no date, which was evidently overlooked in the hurry of getting out the first issue; the second number had the date under the "Printed by Authority" line—"*From* Thursday November 16. to Monday November 20. 1665." Muddiman broke off relations with Williamson when he found that the latter was trying by underhand means to get control of his newsletter, take the profits for himself and pay Muddiman a salary. After the twenty-fifth issue Muddiman ceased writing for the *Gazette* and attached himself to Sir William Morice, the first principal Secretary of State. He secured authority to issue another official paper, which he named the *Current Intelligence*. It had the same format as the *Gazette*, and in No. 1 the news was headed "Beginning June 4. 1666." The copy of No. 26 in the Burney Collection has this written endorsement:

"No. 26 was the last number published in consequence of the Great Fire of London." All the London printing offices were destroyed by fire.

The *Current Intelligence* did not reappear, though the same title—with the difference that the adjective was spelt "Currant" —was to be used by others about fifteen years later: one publisher changed the name to *Smith's Currant Intelligence* (the first use of a personal name as part of a title) to distinguish his paper from a competitor's imitation. Titles in use about this time included the *London Mercury*, the *Loyal London Mercury; or The Moderate Intelligencer* and the *Loyal Impartial Mercury* (started within three months in 1682, in the order named), the *Impartial Protestant Mercury*, *Mercurius Anglicus*, the *Domestick Intelligencer, or News both from City and Country Impartially Related*, and *Heraclitus Ridens: or, A Discourse between Jest and Earnest*. The last-named was not a humorous paper, as its title has suggested; it was a news-sheet whose purpose was defined in the continuation of the title—"where many a True Word is spoken in opposition to all Libellers against the Government." Another paper issued in the same year (1681) had the rather lugubrious title of *The Weekly Visions of the late Popish Plot*.

After 1666 Muddiman limited his activities to the writing of newsletters, which because of their inclusion of Parliamentary news adversely affected the sales of the *London Gazette*, and he continued to issue them for more than a score of years. In 1696, four years after the death of Muddiman, Ichabod Dawks, a London printer, introduced a striking innovation in the production of newsletters by printing them in an appropriate script type, with an attractively designed headpiece. The initial subscription for the three weekly numbers was ten shillings a quarter. As shown by copies that have survived, *Dawks's News-Letter* was still being published in 1716.[1] Another well-known news-

---

[1] Mr. Stanley Morison's *Ichabod Dawks and His News-Le ter* reproduces a complete specimen, gives examples of the headpieces and contains facsimiles of the front page of two issues of *Jones's Evening News-Letter* (also printed in script type).

letter of William the Third's reign was the one published by a printer called Dyer, whose Jacobite sympathies gave offence. He was twice sent to prison for issuing seditious publications, and in December 1694 he was brought before the House of Commons and reprimanded for "his great presumption" in taking notice of the proceedings of Parliament. The Commons at the same time passed a resolution warning newsletter writers not to "presume to intermeddle" with the debates or any other proceedings of Parliament. Shortly afterwards Lord Mohun, meeting Dyer in a coffee-house, thrashed him for mentioning his name in one of his newsletters. Macaulay (*History of England*) gives this picture of the work of a writer of newsletters:

> The newswriter rambled from coffee room to coffee room, collecting reports, squeezed himself into the Sessions House at the Old Bailey if there was an interesting trial, nay, perhaps, obtained admission to the gallery of Whitehall, and noticed how the King and Duke looked. In this way he gathered materials for weekly epistles destined to enlighten some county town or some bench of rustic magistrates. Such were the sources from which the inhabitants of the largest provincial cities, and the great body of the gentry and clergy, learned almost all that they knew of the history of their own time.

Imitation of the new form originated by the *Gazette* continued for about thirty years. The word newsbook went out; readers now referred to the paper or newspaper (the earliest recorded use of the term goes back to 1670). There was no development of interest until 1695, when Parliament declined to renew the Licensing Act and a great revival of journalistic enterprise was seen. At this period there was a special liking for the word Post in newspaper titles: the *London Post*, the *Flying Post*,[1] the *Post Boy* and the *Post Man* were among the new papers. (Another favourite title was News Letter, e.g., the *Weekly News Letter*.) All these papers had a symbolic woodcut either above

---

[1] The first use of this title was in 1644, when a single issue was published of the *Flying Post*. Both this and the *Kingdomes Weekly Post* (1643) had a woodcut of a man on horseback blowing a horn.

THE FIRST NEWSPAPER

or on both sides of the title, a mounted postman being a favourite idea, and this style of title can be found in many newspapers up to the nineteenth century. Competition stimulated the use of what may be described as a contemporary equivalent of the stop-press device in the insertion of late news, first written in the margins and subsequently printed on separate sheets, and known as Postscripts. The news of the Battle of Ramillies (1706) was thus announced by the *London Gazette* and the *Flying Post*, but the former did not use the word Postscript as the title of any of the four special slips which it issued within a fortnight. (A later employment of this idea was seen when *The Times* produced an "Extraordinary" issue on Sunday, November 3, 1805.) The stop-press device (or fudge) was not introduced until 1889.

The limited reading public of those days had the choice of a number of papers published three times a week—very much alike in appearance and for the most part wretchedly produced. They were cautious politically, not being sure of the limit set by authority to the freedom of the Press. "It is a remarkable fact that the infant newspapers were all on the side of King William and the Revolution," says Macaulay. "This fact can be partly explained by the circumstance that editors were, at first, on their good behaviour. . . . There is much invective: it is almost all directed against the Jacobites and the French." The news provided by these papers was wider in range than that contained in the *London Gazette*, and they scored over that paper by printing articles on current topics; but many of the news items were of the vague "it's said" type characteristic of the old newsbooks. Reporting was still a haphazard affair, with the distinction between fact and rumour not clearly drawn. The efficient organization of newsgathering and the evolution of a technique of news writing were to be the work of later generations of journalists.

The newspapers of the early eighteenth century were still in the rough pioneer stage—inadequate, poorly written and lacking any professional standards. Addison, writing in the *Tatler* (May 21, 1709), was gaily satirical about the prodigies of

... the ingenious fraternity of which I have the honour to be an unworthy member: I mean the news-writers of Great Britain, whether Postmen or Postboys, or by what other name or title so ever dignified or distinguished. The case of these gentlemen is, I think, more hard than that of the soldiers, considering they have taken more towns and fought more battles. They have been upon parties or skirmishes where our armies have lain still, and given the general assault of many a place where the besiegers were quiet in their trenches. They have made us masters of several strong towns many weeks before our generals could do it, and completed victories when our courageous captains have been content to come off with a drawn battle. Where Prince Eugene has slain his thousands, Boyer[1] has slain his ten thousands. This gentleman can, indeed, never be enough commended for his courage and intrepidity during the whole war. He has laid about him with inexpressible fury, and, like an offended Marius of ancient Rome, made such havoc among his countrymen as must be the work of two or three ages to repair.

The occasional illustrations in early eighteenth-century newspapers took the form of maps or plans to depict the scene of battles or sieges, crude pictorial representations of remarkable events, and—very rarely—a caricature. The problem of adequately illustrating the news was not to be solved until the twentieth century.

[1] Proprietor of the *Post Boy*.

CHAPTER THREE

The Advent of the Daily

THE first English daily newspaper was a half sheet printed on one side of the paper only. Except for a lack of headlines, it looked not unlike some of the small-size emergency issues of newspapers with only a single page of news that appeared during the General Strike of 1926.

This pioneer of daily journalism was the *Daily Courant*, which was born on March 11, 1702, and had the imprint: "LONDON. Sold by *E. Mallet*, next Door to the *King's-Arms* Tavern at *Fleet-Bridge*." (From the tenth issue a change in the imprint revealed that the paper was now printed and sold by "Sam Buckley at The Dolphin in Little Britain." Buckley was also the publisher of the *Spectator*, which started in 1711.) Remarkably, it contained not a single item of home news. Apart from the fact that it appeared daily the paper had no original feature. Its two columns resembled the make-up of the *London Gazette*, and its news consisted solely of translations from two Dutch papers and one French journal, so that in this respect it had advanced no farther than the newsbooks of eighty years earlier. To be precise, the first issue contained ten paragraphs and a total of 104 lines of news. An editorial "Advertisement" thus stated the aims of the new journal:

It will be found from the Foreign Prints, which from time to time, as Occasion offers, will be mention'd in this Paper, that the Author has taken Care to be duly furnish'd with all that comes from Abroad in any Language. And for an Assurance that he will not, under Pretence of having Private Intelligence, impose any Additions of feign'd Circumstances to an Action, but give his Extracts fairly and Impartially; at the beginning of each Article he will quote the Foreign Paper from whence 'tis taken, that the Publick, seeing from what Country a piece of News comes with the Allowance of that Government, may be better able to Judge of the Credibility and Fairness of the Relation: Nor will he take it upon himself to give any Comments or Conjectures of his own, but will relate only Matter of Fact; supposing other People to have Sense enough to make Reflections for themselves.

This Courant (as the Title shews) will be Publish'd Daily: being design'd to give all the Material News as soon as every Post arrives: and is confin'd to half the Compass, to save the Publick at least half the Impertinences, of ordinary News-Papers.

In the following month the *Daily Courant* began printing on both sides of the sheet. At the end of the year the two-page paper (December 31, 1702) had a page and a half of news translated from Dutch and French newspapers, four items of shipping news and nearly half a column of small advertisements. It developed into a four-page newspaper and at times published six-page issues. The *Daily Courant* continued publication for over thirty years, the latest issue which has survived having appeared in June 1735.

The now familiar word "Evening" first appeared in a newspaper title in August 1706, when the *Evening Post*, published at "Six at Night," came into existence; but it was not an evening newspaper in the modern sense, for it was published on Tuesdays, Thursdays and Saturdays only and timed to catch the principal country mails that left London on those nights. These mails had been established in the late seventeenth century and thrice-weekly papers which took advantage of this service had already appeared (there were, in addition, a number of thrice-weekly morning journals); but the *Evening Post* was the first journal to proclaim itself an evening paper. Other thrice-weekly evening journals followed—the *Evening Courant* and the *Night Post* (1711) and the *St. James's Evening Post* (1715). The last-named was issued from the same office as the *St. James's Post*, a thrice-weekly morning paper started a few months earlier, and both papers are noteworthy for their introduction of a new style of title incorporating the Royal Arms—a device that was to be widely adopted later. An everyday evening paper was not to appear until nearly the end of the century.

The second English daily to appear, Steele and Addison's *Spectator* (1711), was not a newspaper but a literary journal and as such will be treated in the next chapter, which describes the beginnings of periodical journalism. The next daily newspapers to be published were the *Daily Post* (1719), whose contributors included Daniel Defoe, and the *Daily Journal* (1720), both of which were modelled on the *Daily Courant*. Far more notable was the first publication—on February 3, 1730—of the *Daily Advertiser*, which was to develop from a purely commercial sheet into a comprehensive newspaper that long set the standard in daily journalism. In the first number of the *Daily Advertiser* (Matthew Jenour, Queen's Head Court, Giltspur Street), a two-page paper somewhat larger than the *London Gazette*, the upper half of the front page was devoted to this announcement, which was set in italics to the full width of the page:

This Paper will be given Gratis to Coffee-Houses Four Days Successively, and afterwards Printed every day, Sundays excepted, and deliver'd to any Person within the Bills of Mortality at One Penny per single Paper, or Six Shillings per Quarter. It is requested of all Persons who will please to take in this Paper, that they Book the same, as they usually do other Papers. All Advertisements of moderate Length will be taken in at Two Shillings each, and the most easy advances for those of greater Length. And the Publick is hereby assur'd, that neither the Paper, (although the same should amount to one or more Sheets) or Advertising therein, will ever be raised in Price, on any Account whatsoever, except in the manner before mention'd. This Paper is intended to consist wholly of Advertisements, together with the Prices of Stocks, Course of Exchange, and Names and Descriptions of Persons becoming Bankrupts. . . .

The lower half of the front page, divided into three columns (at this time the usual make-up for dailies and weeklies), gave commercial information on the lines specified; the back page, also set in three columns, consisted entirely of advertisements, four of which had small pictorial devices. These announcements included one inserted by "Mr. Weston, *at the Hand and Pen, over against* Norfolk Street *in the* Strand," who "Continues to teach expeditiously, at Home or Abroad, his New Method of SHORT-HAND, (Authorized by his Majesty). . . . He can teach at any Distance, by conveying Instruction, from Time to Time, by the General or Penny Post"—one of the earliest advertisements of tuition by post. An editorial note in No. 22 stated that in order to render the paper "equally useful and acceptable, as well as to entertain readers," in future the *Daily Advertiser* would publish

the best and freshest Accounts of all Occurrences Foreign and Domestick. . . . And for the better Dispersing and Publishing the Usefulness of this Undertaking, This Paper will be left Gratis for some Days at most of the Houses of the Nobility and Gentry, and the Coffee-Houses; and such who are pleased to approve thereof are humbly desired to signify the same to the Person who leaves it.

In addition to commercial and financial news, this issue contained a column and a half of items from abroad and over a column of paragraphs simply headed "LONDON. Feb. 27" in the current journalistic style. The sixteen untitled items under this heading included a brief note of an inquest "upon the Body of Mr. Delicate, who cut his Throat at his Brother's House in Spittlefields on Wednesday last" and a twelve-line account of the marriage of two sisters, of whom one was described as "a young Gentlewoman of great Merit and ample Fortune" and the other as possessing a fortune of £3,000.

The starting of dailies and tri-weeklies was not the only journalistic development of interest in the first thirty years of the eighteenth century. New weeklies also appeared in London, and the contribution they made to the evolution of journalism will be considered in Chapter V. Many provincial weekly newspapers were founded (but no dailies until the nineteenth century), among them being the *Norwich Post* (1701), *Norwich Postman*[1]

[1] The price was one penny, "but a halfpenny not refused." Fox Bourne mentions two early eighteenth-century London newspapers with the title *Halfpenny Post*. The Burney Collection contains a single issue, dated December 13, 1738, of a two-page paper called the *London Farthing-Post*.

THE ADVENT OF THE DAILY

(1706), *Nottingham Journal* (1710), *Newcastle Journal* (1711), *Liverpool Courant* (1712), *Bristol Times & Mirror* and *Hereford Journal* (1713), *Norwich Mercury* (1714), *Salisbury Postman* and *York Mercury* (1715), *Kentish Gazette* (1717), *Leeds Mercury* (1718), *Northampton Mercury* (1720), *Gloucester Journal* (1722), *Reading Mercury* (1723), *Salisbury & Winchester Journal* (1729), *Manchester Gazette* and *Chester Courant* (1730). Scotland had several weeklies in the first decade of the eighteenth century—the *Edinburgh Courant* (1705), *Scots Courant* (1706), *Edinburgh Flying Post* (1708), *Scots Postman* (1709) and *Northern Tatler* (1710). But these were not the first papers to be started outside London. There is some dispute about which was the earliest provincial journal—the *Lincoln, Rutland & Stamford Mercury* (1695) or *Berrow's Worcester Journal*, which is held to date back to a newspaper known to have existed in 1690. These two journals are the oldest newspapers in the country; the oldest London paper, *The Times* (1785), is their junior by nearly a century. The *Edinburgh Gazette* appears to have been first published in 1699, but did not assume its present form as a Goverment publication until July 2, 1793.

In 1712, seventeen years after the lapse of the Licensing Act, Parliament again laid its hand on journalism. This time the attack was in the form of a stamp tax—a halfpenny apiece if printed on a half sheet or less and a penny if on a whole sheet—which was inspired not by the idea of raising revenue but of using the most "effectual way for suppressing libels"—and simultaneously a tax of a shilling was imposed on every advertisement in papers issued weekly or oftener. Parliament had become jealous of the increasing popularity of the Press and thought that it could restrict its activities by putting a tax on it. An oversight in the drafting of the Act allowed six-page papers (a sheet and a half) to evade the tax. The Act provided for the stamping only of half-sheet and one-sheet papers. One consequence was a stimulus to the production of six-page weeklies. Later the provisions of the Act were more precisely worded.

Swift painted a lively picture of the effects of the tax. "Do you know that Grub Street is dead and gone last week?" he wrote to Stella. "No more ghosts or murders now for love or money.... The *Observator* is fallen; the *Medleys* are jumbled together with the *Flying Post*; the *Examiner* is deadly sick; the *Spectator* keeps up and doubles its price—I know not how long it will hold. Have you seen the red stamp the papers are marked with? Methinks the stamping is worth a halfpenny." Addison accepted the new impost with an air of cheerfulness, not foreseeing the suspension of the *Spectator* a few months later. "I consider that the tax on papers was given for the support of the government.... I shall glory in contributing my utmost to the public weal, and if my country receives five or six pounds a day by my labours, I shall be very well pleased to find myself so useful a member." A few days later he was rebuking scurrility in the Press:

Should a foreigner who knows nothing of our private factions, or one who is to act his part in the world when our present heats and animosities are forgot—should, I say, such an one form to himself a notion of the greatest men of all sides in the British nation who are now living from the characters which are given them in some or other of those abominable writings which are daily published among us, what a nation of monsters we must appear!

What was the size of this giant that a jealous Parliament wanted to curb? According to a statement prepared by the Treasury in 1711 the total sale of the papers then published was 44,000 weekly, or two and a quarter million copies a year. The tax did not have the results that were expected. It was certainly ruinous to a few publications and imposed a temporary check on the progress of the Press, but after a time new papers appeared and the total circulation resumed its growth. When the regulations for the collection of the tax were strengthened in 1724 and a list was compiled of all the printers in London, it was revealed that there were three daily papers, ten thrice-weekly journals and five weeklies. The tax was doubled in 1757 (in the meantime newspaper sales had grown until they were about eightfold those of 1712) and raised to three-halfpence in 1776, at which date London had fifty-three papers.

Taxation of the Press in various forms was to continue for another three-quarters of a century after this date, and the abolition of what by then had come to be known as "taxes on knowledge" marked the most important turning-point in the history of journalism.

CHAPTER FOUR

The Rise of the Periodical

THE early eighteenth century, which saw the publication of the first daily newspapers, also witnessed the rise of the periodical. Though it was not to come to full stature for another hundred years, the periodical made a vigorous and interesting start because the men chiefly associated with the invention and development of this new form were writers of personality.

In L'Estrange's *Observator* and one or two other seventeenth-century journals[1] may be seen foreshadowings of the review and the essay paper; but the beginnings of the periodical as we know it can be more confidently dated from the publication of Daniel Defoe's *Review* in 1704 and Sir Richard Steele's *Tatler* in 1709. The familiar description of Defoe as "The Father of English Journalism" is roughly accurate, for unquestionably he was the first professional journalist of major standing, being a regular contributor to principal journals for many years as well as an industrious pamphleteer. His contemporaries regarded him as a journalistic hireling, a man of no principle, and there are chapters in his career that defy any other explanation; but after exploring

---

[1] A tame anticipation of the popular periodical—say, the early *Tit-Bits* and *Answers*—is discernible in the *Athenian Mercury*, published by John Dunton from 1690 to 1696. It usually consisted of two pages in question-and-answer form, and at the best was only moderately entertaining.

From 1691 to 1694 appeared the *Gentleman's Journal*, an octavo-sized monthly miscellany in the form of a "Letter to a Gentleman in the Country," edited by Peter Anthony Motteux, a Huguenot. The verse that it published—by Prior, Sedley and others—made livelier reading than the medley of anecdotes, essays, history, philosophy and miscellaneous information written in a tedious, affected style. An original feature was the publication of the words and music of new songs. With all its defects, it was an enterprising production for those early days of periodical journalism, and was a forerunner of the eighteenth-century miscellanies.

the many ups and downs of his crowded, energetic life it is difficult not to view the faults rather more charitably than they deserve. At the outset of his career as a commentator on public affairs he gained popular sympathy as a victim of official persecution. For writing a savagely ironical pamphlet, *The Shortest Way with Dissenters*—so outrageous in its suggestions that the irony was missed—he was arrested and imprisoned in Newgate. He pleaded guilty at the trial some weeks later (1703), his friends advising him not to attempt a defence, and was sentenced to stand three times in the pillory, to pay a fine of a hundred marks, to remain in prison during the Queen's pleasure and to find sureties for his good conduct during the next seven years. The sentence was clearly excessive, and this probably explains the popular reaction in his favour. He had dreaded the pillory, but what promised to be an ordeal turned into a triumph. His satirical *Hymn to the Pillory*—of no literary merit but remarkably bold in its wording[1]—was hawked in the streets, his pillory was covered with flowers and men drank his health.

After a few months in prison Defoe was released,[2] at the instance of Robert Harley, and in February 1704 he issued the first number of *A Weekly Review of the Affairs of France: Purg'd from the Errors and Partiality of News-Writers and Petty-Statesmen, of all Sides*. It began as a small eight-page weekly and was shortly afterwards reduced to four pages; after a time it was issued twice a week, and from the second year it appeared thrice a week. The paper lasted for nine years and throughout Defoe wrote it single-handed. The editorial content soon ranged beyond the confines of the original title, which was shortened to *The Review*. Articles on social and commercial topics were printed in addition to those on political subjects, and Defoe experimented

---

[1] "Tell them, the men that placed him here,
Are scandals to the Times,
Are at a loss to find his guilt,
And can't commit his crimes."

[2] He was pardoned in November 1703. The commonly accepted idea that he edited the *Review* while in prison—that he was not released until August 1704—appears to be legendary.

with supplements designed to entertain the reader—the monthly "Advices from the Scandal Club," which ran for five issues, and a twice-a-week four-page supplement, "The Little Review," of which twenty-three numbers were published. Six years later another political journal came into the field—the *Examiner: or, Remarks Upon Papers and Occurrences*. Started on August 3, 1710, and published weekly it was edited by Dr. William King and had Matthew Prior, poet and diplomatist, and Francis Atterbury, later Bishop of Rochester, as its chief writers. A more powerful pen joined them from the fourteenth issue, when Swift became a regular contributor. The *Examiner* was bitterly controversial, and after some months Swift retired on the ground that the enmities he had provoked made his life unbearable. Political hatreds raged fiercely in those days, and Swift—who had notoriously a venomous pen—probably did not exaggerate when he said that it had become dangerous for him to go about after dark. The *Examiner* was under the patronage of Henry St. John (afterwards Lord Bolingbroke), the chief instigator of the stamp tax and sixteen years later, as will be told, the most formidable contributor to the *Craftsman*. Another writer for the *Examiner*, said to have succeeded Swift as editor, was Mrs. Mary de la Rivière Manley, possibly the first woman journalist, who was already known for her work on the *Female Tatler*, a paper started three months after Steele's *Tatler*, and as the author of a notorious book, *Secret Memoirs and Manners of Several Persons of Quality, of both Sexes. From the New Atalantis*. She was arrested in October 1709 for libelling public men in this work, and discharged in the following February. Swift, in urging upon Lord Peterborough that she should have some reward for her services to the Tory cause, described her as a woman of "very generous principles for one of her sort, and a great deal of sense and invention; she is about forty, very homely and very fat."

To return to Defoe. It was quickly noticed that the views expressed in his review corresponded with the policy of Robert Harley, and though for long he posed as an independent writer Defoe years later made this candid avowal: "Let any one put

Numb. 1

The TATLER.

By *Isaac Bickerstaff* Esq;

Quicquid agunt Homines nostri Farrago Libelli.

Tuesday, April 12. 1709.

THO' the other Papers which are publish'd for the Use of the good People of England have certainly very wholesom Effects, and are laudable in their particular Kinds, they do not seem to come up to the main Design of such Narrations, which, I humbly presume, should be principally intended for the Use of Politick Persons, who are so publick-spirited as to neglect their own Affairs to look into Transactions of State. Now these Gentlemen, for the most Part, being Persons of strong Zeal and weak Intellects, It is both a Charitable and Necessary Work to offer something, whereby such worthy and well-affected Members of the Commonwealth may be instructed, after their Reading, what to think: Which shall be the End and Purpose of this my Paper, wherein I shall from Time to Time Report and Consider all Matters of what Kind soever that shall occur to Me, and publish such my Advices and Reflections every Tuesday, Thursday, and Saturday, in the Week, for the Convenience of the Post. It is also resolv'd by me to have something which may be of Entertainment to the Fair Sex, in Honour of whom I have taken the Title of this Paper. I therefore earnestly desire all Persons, without Distinction, to take it in for the present Gratis, and hereafter at the Price of one Penny, forbidding all Hawkers to take more for it at their Peril. And I desire all Persons to consider, that I am at a very great Charge for proper Materials for this Work, as well as that before I resolv'd upon it, I had settled a Correspondence in all Parts of the Known and Knowing World; and forasmuch as this Globe is not trodden upon by mere Drudges of Business only, but that Men of Spirit and Genius are justly to be ejected as considerable Agents in it, we shall not upon a Dearth of News present you with musty Foreign Edicts, or dull Proclamations, but shall divide our Relation of the Passages which occur in Action or Discourse throughout this Town, as well as elsewhere, under such Dates of Places as may prepare you for the Matter you are to expect, in the following Manner:

All Accounts of Gallantry, Pleasure, and Entertainment, shall be under the Article of White's Chocolate-house; *Poetry, under that of* Will's Coffee-house; *Learning, under the Title of* Grecian; *Foreign and Domestick News, you will have from* St. James's Coffee-house; *and what else I shall on any other Subject offer, shall be dated from my own Apartment.*

I once more desire my Reader to consider, That as I cannot keep an Ingenious Man to go daily to Will's, under Two-pence each Day merely for his Charges; to White's, under Sixpence; nor to the Grecian, without allowing him some Plain Spanish, to be as able as others at the Learned Table; and that a good Observer cannot speak with even Kidney at St. James's without clean Linnen. I say, these Considerations will, I hope, make all Persons willing to comply with my Humble Request (when my Gratis Stock is exhausted) of a Penny a Piece; especially since they are sure of some Proper Amusement, and that it is impossible for me to want Means to entertain 'em, having, besides the Helps of my own Parts, the Power of Divination, and that I can, by casting a Figure, tell you all that will happen before it comes to pass.

But this last Faculty I shall use very sparingly, and not speak of any Thing 'till it is pass'd, for fear of divulging Matters which may offend our Superiors.

White's Chocolate-house, April 7.

THE deplorable Condition of a very pretty Gentleman, who walks here at the Hours when Men of Quality first appear, is what is very much lamented. His History is, That on the 9th of *September,* 1705. being in his One and twentieth Year, he was washing his Teeth at a Tavern Window in *Pall-Mall,* when a fine Equipage pass'd by, and in it a young Lady who look'd up at him; away goes the Coach, and the young Gentleman pull'd off his Night-Cap, and instead of rubbing his Gums, as he ought to do, out of the Window till about Four a Clock, he sits him down, and spoke not a Word till Twelve at Night; after which, he began to enquire, If any Body knew the Lady — The Company ask'd, What Lady? But he said no more, till they broke up at Six in the Morning. All the ensuing Winter he went from Church to Church every Sunday, and from Play-house to Play-house all the Week, but could never find the Original of the Picture which dwelt in his Bosom. In a Word, his Attention to any Thing, but his Passion, was utterly gone. He has lost all the Money he ever play'd for, and been confused in every Argument he has enter'd upon since the Moment he first saw her. He is of a Noble Family, has naturally a very good Air, is of a frank, honest Temper: But this Passion has so extremely maul'd him, that his Features are set and uniform'd, and his whole Visage is deadened by a long Absence of Thought. He never appears in any Alacrity, but when rais'd by Wine; at which Time he is sure to come hither, and throw away a great deal of Wit on Fellows, who have no Sense further than just to observe, That our poor Lover has most Understanding

himself in my stead! and examine upon what principles I could ever act against either such a Queen, or such a Benefactor! ... Let any man who knows what principles are, what engagements of honour and gratitude are, make this case his own! and say what I could have done less, or more, than I have done." He never forgot the injustice of his sentence for writing an ironical pamphlet; he remembered equally the man through whose intervention an indeterminate prison sentence was brought to an end. When Lord Haversham, in the course of a controversy in 1705, haughtily disdained the idea of entering upon the lists with "such a mean and mercenary prostitute" as the author of *The Review*, claiming that he was answering those from whom he received "both his encouragement and his instructions," Defoe's retort was caustic.

Fate, that makes footballs of men, kicks some up stairs and some down; some are advanced without honour, others suppressed without infamy; some are raised without merit, some are crushed without crime; and no man knows by the beginning of things whether his course shall issue in a PEERAGE or a PILLORY; and time was, that no man should have determined it between his Lordship and this mean fellow except those that knew his Lordship's merit more particularly than outsides would have directed.

Publication of three pamphlets on the Succession Question in 1713 led to the arrest of Defoe. He might have avoided any penalty but for the indiscretion of commenting on the case in his review, which resulted in a brief imprisonment for contempt of court (though one of the judges warned him that he might come to be hanged, drawn and quartered for his writings). Next year he was in trouble again with the authorities. A letter that he wrote to the *Flying Post*, held to be a libel on the Earl of Anglesey, one of the Lords Regent, brought about his arrest. He was released and not tried until 1715, when he was found guilty. Sentence was deferred until the following term—and that was the last to be heard about the prosecution. Either before or after his trial Defoe approached the Lord Chief Justice and through him convinced the ruling Whigs that henceforth he would be on his good behaviour and would make himself very useful to them. Probably Defoe was by this time a badly frightened man: that is the only explanation that can be given for the career of journalistic double-dealing which he pursued for several years. He became in effect a Government spy. Ostensibly a Tory, he secretly worked for the other side, attaching himself to Tory journals with the object of moderating their contents and acquainting his employers with anything that might be embarrassing or objectionable to them. The newspaper for which he chiefly wrote was *Mist's Weekly Journal*, whose lively, irresponsible editorial style made it one of the most successful of the weeklies.

Nathaniel Mist, the publisher of the journal that bore his name, had several brushes with authority before his journalistic activities led to his being imprisoned. Found guilty of scandalously reflecting on the King's interposition in favour of the Protestants abroad, he was sentenced in February 1721 to stand in the pillory at Charing Cross and the Royal Exchange, to pay a fine of £50, to be imprisoned for three months and to give security for good behaviour for seven years. He was not able to pay the fine and remained in prison, and in May he was brought before the House of Commons for publishing an article that reflected upon the King and the Duke of Marlborough and committed to Newgate because he would not give up the names of the writers. After some months he was discharged because of illness and the proceedings against him were dropped. In 1724 a libel on the Government was punished by a fine of £100, twelve months' imprisonment and an order to find sureties for good behaviour during life. Three years later he was tried for publishing a libel on George I and this time was fined £100, again directed to give security for good behaviour during life, and ordered to be kept in prison until the sentence was fulfilled. In January 1728 he took refuge in France, and when in the following August steps were taken to prosecute those responsible for a long letter hostile to the Government which had appeared in his paper, over twenty persons were arrested, but Mist himself was stated to be in Rouen. The next month the press of *Mist's Weekly Journal* was destroyed and the paper, which had been conducted by his friends, nominally came to an end. A week later it reappeared in the same form but with a new title, *Fog's Weekly Journal*, and continued publication until Mist died in 1737. The leading article in No. 1 of the new series was signed "N. Mist" and began: "Dear Cousin Fog, The Occasion of my present Address to you, is to acquaint you, that I was lately seiz'd with an Apoplectic Fit, of which I instantly died...."

Defoe's contributions to the weeklies, written in racy, popular style, mainly took the form of essays on the lighter topics of the times. He was the first journalist to make a popular appeal, and he defined his own mode of writing when he said: "If any man was to ask me what I would suppose to be a perfect style or language, I would answer, that in which a man speaking to five hundred people, of all common and various capacities, idiots or lunatics excepted, should be understood by them all." *Mist's Weekly Journal*, *Read's Weekly Journal*[1] (a more reputable paper, which deservedly outlived by many years its boisterous rival) and one or two other newspapers similar in design usually gave up at least half of the front page to a leading article or essay, devoting the rest of their four-page issues to paragraphs headed "Foreign Affairs" and "Home Affairs" (the latter had now become the more important news source) and about two pages of advertisements. A rather similar publication, though more literary in its interests, was the *Grub-street Journal*, whose first issue on January 8, 1730, had this imprint: "Printed and Sold by J. Roberts in *Warwick-Lane*, and at the Pamphlet-Shops of *London* and *Westminster*, also at the *Pegasus* (vulgarly called the *Flying-Horse*) in Grubstreet. (*Price Two Pence*.)" It continued until 1738 and reappeared the following year, in quarto form, with the new title of *Literary Courier of Grub-street*. The *Miscellany* (1732)— afterwards the *Weekly Miscellany*—also had a bookish flavour.

[1] Robert Mawson started a paper called the *Weekly Journal* in 1713, and its success led to the production of imitations by Nathaniel Mist and others, which later incorporated the names of their publishers to avoid confusion.

The most influential political journal of the age was the *Craftsman*, started in 1726 by "Caleb D'Anvers, of Gray's-Inn, Esq." (Nicholas Amhurst), to oppose the policy of Sir Robert Walpole. Later it was renamed the *Country Journal: or, the Craftsman*. At the peak of its success it had for those days the large circulation of 10,000 a week. It was the vigour of its political criticism—especially the bitter and forceful contributions from the pen of Bolingbroke—that made the *Craftsman* such a powerful organ. Pulteney was another frequent contributor. To Amhurst must be given the credit, however, for the creation and the effective direction of the *Craftsman*, and when eventually he had served his purpose because they had made a compromise with the Government, his political friends had no further use for him and he ended his days in poverty.

Defoe was a robustious and versatile writer, who lived a life of extraordinary activity against a background of political intrigue and of partisan journalism precariously conducted under the hostile scrutiny of Governments that roughly classified journalists as impudent fellows or servile tools; Steele and Addison, the creators of the literary periodical, were the embodiment of a new and more polite society that was slowly emerging as a reaction from the excesses of the post-Restoration period.

When two years after his appointment as gazetteer (writer of the *London Gazette*), which gave him valuable access to political news, Sir Richard Steele founded the *Tatler* in 1709 he invented a new kind of periodical journalism that was to develop into the modern weekly review, and in page size as well as layout there is an obvious resemblance between the new and the old. The *Tatler* was a two-page thrice-weekly paper intended to reflect in particular the more urbane outlook and interests of those who frequented the coffee-houses, and like its successor the *Spectator* it became the favourite periodical of those who enjoyed civilized discussion, and appealed to women as well as to men. No. 1, published on April 12, 1709, contained seven short articles, including a notice of a new comedy; later issues were to consist of an essay lightly commenting on the modes and manners and the intellectual interests of the day. Steele's friend Joseph Addison began to contribute from the eighteenth number and was to give a new charm and finish to the essay form; but the *Tatler* was Steele's invention and Addison wrote only forty-two out of the 271 issues that were published between 1709 and 1711, when the paper ceased publication. Political and other reasons have been suggested for the stoppage of the *Tatler*, but a likelier explanation is that Steele and Addison had conceived a more ambitious project. Two months later they jointly founded the *Spectator* as a daily, and in No. 10 Addison, writing on "The Spectator and Its Purpose," said that already 3,000 copies were being sold every day.

> It was said of Socrates, that he brought philosophy down from heaven, to inhabit among men; and I shall be ambitious to have it said of me, that I have brought philosophy out of closets and libraries, schools and colleges, to dwell in clubs and assemblies, at tea-tables and in coffee-houses.
>
> I would therefore in a very particular manner recommend these my speculations to all well-regulated families, that set apart an hour in every morning for tea and bread and butter; and would earnestly advise them for their good to order this paper to be punctually served up, and to be looked upon as a part of the tea equipage.

Addison wrote 274 out of 555 papers. He was superior to Steele in the grace and the range of his writing, but the *Spectator* was essentially a joint enterprise for which both must have the credit. Together they gave fresh vitality and lucidity to the essay form, and all the modern essayists are lineal descendants of this unique partnership. In an age of small circulations they daily reached a wide audience—every copy had many readers, and these were multiplied by the sale of bound volumes—and they accomplished this feat by means of a new and enlightened type of journalism that revealed keen observation of the contemporary scene. They were essentially moralists, but since their instruction was agreeably blended with wit and shrewd insight their writings were read with constant delight; and because the rich legacy of their enterprise has come down to us intact we can appreciate the pleasure they gave to the many thousands of their readers who found in the *Spectator* a wise and pleasantly satirical commentary on the follies as well as the civilized interests of the times. And it was this paper, the forerunner of the more serious type of periodical journalism, that was the chief victim of the ill-conceived stamp tax, whose avowed intention was to curb "abuse of the liberty of the Press."

Steele later conducted on his own the *Guardian* (1713), a daily that started as a non-political paper with a moral purpose, lightly treating the topics of the hour, but eventually became controversial. The paper ran for 176 issues and was followed a few days later by the *Englishman*, of which Steele, who had now become a member of Parliament, declared that its purpose was to deal as a patriot with the present state of the world. It was issued three times a week, and ceased publication after fifty-seven issues. The Government took exception to part of the contents of two issues and ordered Steele to attend in his place in the House of Commons. Despite a powerful defence by Walpole, who urged that the liberty of the Press was unrestrained and that a part of the legislature should not dare to punish as a crime that which was not declared to be so by any law passed in Parliament, the House of Commons decided by 245 votes to 152 that Steele should be expelled. Other journals that he started were the *Plebeian*, the *Reader*, *Theatre*, *Town Talk*, *Chit Chat* and *Tea Table*: none of them had a long life. Addison also engaged in political journalism for a time. As chief secretary to the Earl of Sunderland, Lord Lieutenant of Ireland, he was given the task of supporting the Government journalistically, and from December 1715 to June 1716 conducted the *Freeholder*, in which he argued the legality and the expediency of the Hanoverian succession.

The only periodical of those days to establish itself firmly was the *Gentleman's Magazine*, founded in 1731, which survived well into the following century. A monthly miscellany, it was stated to be written by "Sylvanus Urban, Gent."—an obvious copy of the style that Steele employed from the first number of the *Tatler*, under the title of which appeared the line "By Isaac Bickerstaff Esq." One of the stated purposes of the *Gentleman's Magazine* was to print extracts from the newspapers of the preceding month for the convenience of the busy reader; other material in the early issues included a summary of home and foreign news. Five years later Edward Cave, the founder of the magazine, boldly introduced reports of Parliament—a practice that had been expressly forbidden by the House of Commons—and the list of contents of the 1736 volume reveals this as the leading feature, and at the same time shows that the magazine was still mainly a kind of literary and news digest (later it was to publish more original matter):

I. Proceedings and Debates in Parliament.
II. Essays, Controversial, Humorous and Satyrical; Religious, Moral and Political: Collected Chiefly from the Publick Papers.
III. Dissertations and Letters from Correspondents.
IV. Select Pieces of Poetry.
V. A Succinct Account of the most remarkable Transactions Foreign and Domestick.
VI. Births, Marriages, Deaths, Promotions and Bankrupt.
VII. The prices of Goods and Stocks, Bills of Mortality, and Register of Books.

The brief reports of Parliament indicated the speakers by the first and last letters of their names—which was, of course, no disguise at all. Presently a rival periodical, the *London Magazine*, followed Cave's example, and the only surprising fact about this episode, having regard to the known attitude of the House of Commons, is that no action was taken in the matter until April 1738, when a warning was issued that such publication was a notorious breach of the privilege of the House and that offenders would be proceeded against with the utmost severity. Cave felt that he had a moral right to acquaint his fellow-countrymen with the doings of their rulers and he found an ingenious way of continuing his Parliamentary reports. From June 1738 he introduced what purported to be an account of the debates in the Senate of Great Lilliput, and in this form he reported the chief Parliamentary speeches, the speakers being readily identifiable under the fictitious names that were assigned to them. The House made no move in the matter, and fourteen years later Cave threw off this transparent disguise and resumed the publication of reports that gave the first and last letters of the speakers' names—again without interference by Parliament. How were the reports obtained? Most of them were written by William Guthrie, and for more than two years—from November 1740 to February 1743—they were prepared by Dr. Johnson. When at a later date friends with whom he was dining expressed admiration of a certain speech made by William Pitt, Johnson told them that he wrote the speech in Exeter Street.

I never had been in the gallery of the House of Commons but once. Cave had interest with the doorkeeper. He and the persons employed under him gained admittance: they brought away the subjects of discussion, the names of the speakers, the sides they took, and the order in which they rose, together with notes of the arguments adduced in the course of the debate. The whole was afterwards communicated to me, and I composed the speeches in the form which they now have in the "Parliamentary Debates," for the speeches of that period were all printed in Cave's magazine.

According to Sir John Hawkins, from whose *Life of Johnson* the account of this incident is taken, Cave thought that the success of his magazine was due to its other features and "was scarcely able to see the causes that at this time increased the sale of his pamphlet from ten to fifteen thousand copies a month." This is improbable on the face of it: Cave took plain risks as well as considerable trouble to get the reports of Parliament and obviously believed that the results would justify his boldness and enterprise.

Dr. Johnson did a good deal of miscellaneous literary journalism, contributing to various newspapers and periodicals and conducting a periodical of his own. Many attempts were made from time to time to repeat the success of the *Spectator*; the only one that possessed character was Johnson's *Rambler*, which he started in 1750 and continued until the death of his wife in 1752. Published twice a week, at twopence, it was only a *succès d'estime* in periodical form, not more than 500 copies of each issue being sold: "I have never been much a favourite with the public," he declared in the last issue. However, when the essays were published in volume form they had a considerable sale, a number of reprints being required to meet the demand in his lifetime. Nearly all the papers published in the *Rambler* were written by Johnson. Boswell thought that in no writings could be found "more bark and steel for the mind," but Johnson's style appears heavily moralistic to a modern reader. He used a less ponderous style when, at the invitation of the publisher of the *Universal Chronicle, or Weekly Gazette,* he became a regular contributor, writing a weekly essay under the general title of "The Idler." These essays, which also sold well in volume form, were more acceptable to the readers of a weekly journal than those written in the *Rambler* manner. In one of his early essays (May 27, 1758) Johnson revealed that he was in two minds about the merits of contemporary journalism. As on a later occasion reported by Boswell, he referred to the diffusion of knowledge among our people by the newspapers—which, according to foreigners (he said), was superior to the knowledge of the common people in other countries. But he found the newspapers repetitive and was not satisfied with the quality of the material they contained. "The compilation of newspapers is often committed to narrow and mercenary minds, not qualified for the task of delighting or instructing, who are content to fill their paper with whatever matter is at hand, without industry to gather or discernment to select. . . . The tale of the morning paper is told in the evening, and the narratives of the evening are brought out again in the morning." In a later issue (November 11, 1758) he was bluntly condemnatory. Quoting Sir John Wotton's definition of an ambassador as a man of virtue sent abroad to lie for the advantage of his country, he wrote: "A news-writer is a man without virtue who writes lies at home for his own profit. To these compositions is required neither genius nor knowledge, neither industry nor sprightliness, but contempt of shame and indifference to truth are absolutely necessary."

An earlier critic of eighteenth-century journalism was Henry Fielding, who prefaced his own journal, the *True Patriot* (1745), with an article that exposed what he considered to be the "imperfections" of the contemporary newspapers, that they contained little truth and no sense: "there is in reality nothing at all in them." The *True Patriot*, despite Fielding's belief that the public would prefer something better and would find it in his periodical, lasted only a few months. Earlier he had been connected for a time with the *Champion*, a thrice-weekly newspaper which he started in 1739 in partnership with James Ralph. Political articles purporting to be contributed by Captain Hercules Vinegar—surely one of the most striking pen-names in the history of journalism—were the principal feature of the journal. In his *Covent-Garden Journal*, a threepenny bi-weekly with a reformist tone issued for eleven months from January 1752, Fielding engaged in a paper war with various writers. The contents included essays, articles, verse and general news, together with a column of news from the Bow Street Court, where Fielding served as magistrate. One of the writers Fielding crossed swords with was Dr. John Hill (self-styled Sir John Hill by virtue of having received the Order of Vasa from the King of Sweden), who conducted the *British Magazine* from 1746 to 1750 and afterwards wrote a daily letter, "The Inspector," for the *London Advertiser, and Literary Gazette* (later the *London Daily Advertiser*). With a handsome carriage and a reputed income of £1,500 a year from his miscellaneous writing, the foppish but resourceful Dr. Hill was one of the most flamboyant literary personalities of the time. "An ingenious man, but had no veracity"—such was Dr. Johnson's judgment. David Garrick coined this epigram:

> "For physics and farce, his equal there scarce is;
> His farces are physic, his physic a farce is."

THE RISE OF THE PERIODICAL

Another novelist who became a leading figure in the periodical journalism of the time was Tobias Smollett. At the invitation of Archibald Hamilton, an enterprising printer, he became head of a syndicate, grandly styled "The Society of Gentlemen," formed to conduct the *Critical Review*, a monthly literary periodical that started publication in 1756. He had a taste for pungent criticism, and one or two of the writers he criticized in the pages of the review made savage retorts. Reflections on the personal courage of Admiral Sir Charles Knowles led to the trial of Smollett in 1759 for defamation of character, and he was fined £100 and sent to prison for three months. In 1760 he was appointed editor of the *British Magazine; or Monthly Repository for Gentlemen and Ladies*, and serialized in it one of his novels—a new idea in the magazine form but not a journalistic innovation, Defoe's *Robinson Crusoe* having been serialized many years before (from October 7, 1719, to October 19, 1720) by the *Original London Post, or Heathcote's Intelligence*. In 1762 Smollett edited for some months a pro-Bute organ called the *Briton*, which could not thrive in the enormous shadow cast by the provocative anti-Bute *North Briton* of John Wilkes.

Octavo-size monthly magazines of the literary miscellany type, illustrated with engravings and sometimes with political cartoons, were a favourite journalistic form in the eighteenth century. Among them were the *Universal Magazine*, 1747; the *Political Register and Impartial Review of New Books*, 1767; the *Oxford Magazine*, 1768 ("Embellished with Copper-plates Satirical, Political, and Scientifical"); the *Town and Country Magazine; or Universal Repository of Knowledge, Instruction and Entertainment*, 1769; and the *London Museum*, 1770.

The popular digests of the twentieth century are generally held to be an adaptation of the idea which W. T. Stead employed successfully for many years in his *Review of Reviews*. But Stead was not the first in the field. The *Gentleman's Magazine*, as we have seen, published extracts from other publications, and this policy was carried a stage farther in the *Magazine of Magazines* (1750) and the *Grand Magazine of Magazines* (1758). The contents of the February 1751 issue of the *Magazine of Magazines* included Gray's *Elegy*.[1] The full title of its rival was the *Grand Magazine of Magazines or Universal Register*, "comprising all that is curious, useful or entertaining in the magazines, reviews, chronicles . . . at home and abroad."

No other writers for eighteenth-century periodicals were able to achieve the lightness and the felicity of invention that distinguished the *Spectator*; none of the essay papers modelled on it made any noteworthy contribution to journalism. Not until the beginning of the nineteenth century, when the great quarterlies came along, was any further significant development to be seen in the periodical form, and later a new *Spectator* and other weekly—and monthly—reviews further expanded the vision that came to Steele when in 1709 he modestly set out on his immortal adventure.

Towards the end of the eighteenth century a sixpenny political journal appeared that published only thirty-six numbers, and yet had a tremendous effect on contemporary public opinion and seventy years later was to influence the shaping of the *Pall Mall Gazette*. Designed to combat the revolutionary ideas from France that found many sympathizers on this side of the Channel, the *Anti-Jacobin; or, Weekly Examiner* (November 20, 1797, to July 9, 1798) was established by George Canning, the 27-year-old Under-Secretary for Foreign Affairs, and a group of his political friends and associates. Canning, who wrote the prospectus, gave the first sample of the clear, vigorous and satirical writing that was to be the special characteristic of the *Anti-Jacobin* and to make it outstanding in British political journalism.

It may be thought a narrow and illiberal distinction—but We avow ourselves to be *partial* to the COUNTRY *in which we live*, notwith-

[1] Mentioned in Walter Graham's *English Literary Periodicals*. The British Museum copies of the *Magazine of Magazines* and the *Grand Magazine of Magazines* were destroyed during the air raids on London in the Second World War.

standing the daily panegyricks which we read and hear on the superior virtues and endowments of its rival and hostile neighbours. We are *prejudiced* in favour of *her* Establishments, civil and religious; though without claiming for either that ideal perfection, which modern philosophy professes to discover in the other more luminous systems which are arising on all sides of us. . . .

We do not dissemble,—that We reverence Law,—We acknowledge USAGE,—We look even upon PRESCRIPTION without hatred or horror. And We do not think these, or any of them, less safe guides for the moral actions of men, than the new and liberal system of ETHICS, whose operation is not to bind but to loosen the bands of social order; whose doctrine is formed not on a system of reciprocal duties, but on the supposition of individual, independent, and unconnected rights; which teaches that all men are pretty equally honest, but that some have different notions of honesty from others, and that the most received notions are for the greater part the most faulty. . . .

Of all these and the like principles,—in one word, of JACOBINISM in all its shapes, and in all its degrees, political and moral, public and private, whether as it openly threatens the subversion of States, or gradually saps the foundation of domestic happiness, We are the avowed, determined, and irreconcileable enemies. We have no desire to divest ourselves of these inveterate prejudices; but shall remain stubborn and incorrigible in resisting every attempt which may be made either by argument or (what is more in the charitable spirit of modern reformers) by force, to convert us to a different opinion.

The most important feature of the plan of the *Anti-Jacobin*, as defined by Canning, was to expose "Lies of the Week," "Misrepresentations" and "Mistakes," and the paper claimed the support of all who thought "that the PRESS has been long enough employed principally as an engine of destruction." This task was pursued week by week throughout the sitting of Parliament—it was not intended to continue the paper longer—and the *Morning Chronicle*, the *Morning Herald*, the *Morning Post* and the *Courier* were repeatedly pilloried. Two extracts from the *Morning Post*, for instance, were reproduced in the second issue with the blunt note: "These two paragraphs require no comment. They are direct falsehoods, and were known to be such by the Writer."

Articles on current events were a regular feature of the *Anti-Jacobin* and were written with pungent effectiveness. The poetry section had a grand finale in the last issue with an untitled poem (afterwards called "New Morality")—four and a half pages in length—attacking the French terrorists and British sympathizers. Canning was the chief author, and his share in it included this verse:

> "Much may be said on both sides."—Hark! I hear
> A well-known voice that murmurs in my ear—
> The voice of CANDOUR—Hail! most solemn Sage,
> Thou driv'ling Virtue of this Moral Age,
> Candour, which softens Party's headlong rage,
> Candour—which spares its foes—nor e'er descends
> With bigot zeal to combat for its friends,
> Candour—which loves in see-saw strain to tell
> Of acting foolishly, but meaning well:
> Too nice to praise by wholesale, or to blame,
> Convinc'd that all men's motives are the same;
> And finds, with keen discriminating sight,
> BLACK'S not *so* black—nor WHITE *so very* white.

In addition to Canning, the contributors included William Pitt, John Hookham Frere, George Ellis and the 41-year-old editor, William Gifford, who had triumphed over an unfortunate start in life. He was left an orphan at an early age, and his godfather, to save himself the expense of fees, removed him from school and placed him on a farm. He was not strong enough for this work and suffered an accident that left him with a permanent injury. For a year, from the age of 13, he worked on a Brixham coaster, and after another brief spell at school he was apprenticed to a shoemaker. A local surgeon was impressed by his promise, and raised a subscription to buy him out of his apprenticeship and to cover the cost of his education. Through the help of these friends he was enabled to proceed to the university, where he graduated B.A. His later career, as editor of the *Quarterly Review*, is described in Chapter XI.

How the *Anti-Jacobin* influenced the editorial plan of the *Pall*

Mall Gazette (founded 1865) was explained by its first editor, Frederick Greenwood. One day he happened to buy in Holborn Bars a complete set of the paper and "was taken by its originality, incisiveness, wit, literary character and appearance. . . . How fresh and pleasing seemed not only the high spirits and downrightness but the type and headlines, the wide double columns and the easily-held size of page of the *Anti-Jacobin!*"[1] He linked it in his mind with the new and brilliant *Saturday Review.* "Make as good a combination of the two as the current supply of mind allows, throw in a scrap or two of novel feature, mix with an eye to the needs and demands of the hour, publish every day, and you will have a new thing that ought to be a power and a glory." Such was Greenwood's vision, as described in his own words: how far he achieved it is a story that belongs to a later chapter.

[1] *The Story of the Pall Mall Gazette* (J. W. Robertson Scott) devotes a chapter to Greenwood's own *Anti-Jacobin* (sub-titled "A Review of Politics, Literature and Society"). A twopenny (afterwards sixpenny) weekly, started in 1891, it was handicapped by what Greenwood himself admitted to be a "dangerous and ambitious title," but survived for seven years.

CHAPTER FIVE

The Developing Newspaper

DR. JOHNSON's dual view of the Press of his time was not essentially contradictory. On the one hand he recognized that newspapers had a valuable informative function and that they did enable people to take an interest in the affairs of the day, to know something about what was happening in the world; on the other hand, he knew that function was not being properly discharged and that journalism taken as a whole was superficial, ill-conducted and lacking in integrity. It was not that he objected to its being fiercely partisan. He was not a man who took his politics mildly, and on the occasion already mentioned, when he told a company of his friends how he wrote the Parliamentary debates for the *Gentleman's Magazine*, he almost gleefully refuted the suggestion that he had been impartial in his reports and had dealt out reason and eloquence with an equal hand to both parties. "That is not quite true," he said. "I saved appearances well enough, but I took care that the Whig dogs should not have the best of it."

The economic position of the newspaper was still precarious. Circulations were small and the revenue from sales and advertisements was insufficient to cover the cost of production and provide a reasonable return to the proprietor. How was the difference met? Usually by Government subsidy, as Treasury records show in revealing detail; sometimes by dubious practices for which a more precise word is blackmail. Eighteenth-century Governments regarded newspapers as a nuisance whose power for mischief must be restricted by legislation (so often disappointing in its results), by intimidation or persecution or by the use of corruption to ensure editorial support for the party in office. Sir Robert Walpole systematically employed bribery to secure a favourable Press:

during the last ten years of his administration over £50,000 of public money was paid to newspapers and pamphleteers. This practice of bribing newspapers continued until the early part of the nineteenth century. At the time of the French Revolution, for instance, a number of leading newspapers were in receipt of a regular allowance—among others, the *Morning Herald* and the *World* received £600 a year each and *The Times* £300. The Press was not able to gain its independence until the growth of commercial prosperity consequent on the Industrial Revolution brought a large and increasing revenue from advertisements, and enabled the newspaper to stand on its own feet financially. The story of this transition to independent and responsible journalism will be told in a later chapter.

Notwithstanding the financial hazards and personal dangers attendant on newspaper publishing in the eighteenth century—and contrary to the expectations of the politicians who devised the stamp tax—there was a continual increase in the number of journals and in their aggregate sale. In 1753 over 7,000,000 copies a year were being sold, and within a quarter of a century this total was doubled. The news service was being developed despite limited resources. The dailies published at mid-century tended to concentrate on commercial and financial news; the weeklies of the period had more general news and regularly published a political article or an essay on the front page; but it is indicative of the growing stature of the newspaper that both types of journal were beginning to cover important events adequately. One of the major news stories about that time was the great earthquake at Lisbon. The daily *Public Advertiser* for November 28, 1755, which had four folio pages of three columns each, gave over a column of earthquake news from various sources. *Read's Weekly Journal, or British Gazetteer* for December 6, 1755, devoted two and a half columns to an article entitled "An Account of Earthquakes," describing former disasters. A vivid account of the earthquake at Lisbon appeared in the foreign intelligence.

Our freshest advices from Lisbon are of the 5th, on which day the flames had completed the destruction of the buildings whose solidity had resisted the shocks. These advices increase the number of lives lost to 100,000; the shocks that happened after the 1st having thrown down many buildings that were shatter'd or rent before, and buried a great number of persons in the ruins.

The fields round the town are filled with inhabitants, who ran thither when the first shocks were felt but having carried nothing away with them, they are in the most deplorable situation. . . .

The best contemporary account traced was the one printed by the *London Gazette* in its eight-page issue published on December 13, 1755. Most of page 1 and half of page 2 were occupied by a letter received from "Abraham Castres, Esq., His Majesty's Envoy Extraordinary to the King of Portugal," written from Lisbon on November 6th. The opening, unconsciously journalistic, summarized the awful event in one graphic sentence:

You will, in all likelihood, have heard before this, of the inexpressible Calamity befallen the whole Maritime Coast, and in particular this opulent City, now reduced to a Heap of Rubbish and Ruins, by a most tremendous Earthquake, on the 1st of this Month, followed by a Conflagration which has done ten Times more Mischief than the Earthquake itself.

The news of the capture of Quebec (September 13, 1759) reached London five weeks later. A half-column account in the *Public Advertiser* (October 18, 1759) began: "Tuesday in the evening arrived Express from General Townshend and Admiral Saunders at Quebec, the Captain Brett-Douglas, to Mr. Secretary Pitt, with Advice of the Taking of Quebec, by a Coup de Main, on the 18th of September. . . ." In the next day's issue several columns were devoted to dispatches, a casualty list and details of the guns, etc., found in the city of Quebec, and the date of the capture was correctly given this time as September 13th.

The newspapers published in early June, 1780, gave considerable space to reports of the Gordon riots, which lasted several days. The *Morning Chronicle* for Monday, June 5th, had a report of the proceedings in the House of Lords extending to seven and a half columns, with three headlines (a remarkable display for those days):

HOUSE OF LORDS
Some Account of Saturday's Business
PUNISHMENT OF THE RIOTERS

Forming part of the latest report of the riots in this paper was half a column of editorial comment that referred to Lord George Gordon's "very extraordinary" conduct and the menacing attitude of the mob to Parliament, pointing out that there would be an end of free discussion if such methods were to succeed.

Though only a few hundred miles separate London and Paris the news of the fall of the Bastille on July 14, 1789, was not published here until six or seven days later. The newspaper was now living up to its name more fully, professional alertness and method having been substituted for the vague, haphazard reporting of the past. When reading the many contemporary accounts of the taking of the Bastille one gets the authentic thrill of great events. The newspapers devoted a large amount of space to the news and showed quick recognition of its significance. The *London Chronicle* of July 21, 1789, which had eight quarto pages (three columns to the page), printed this headline on page 5:

Postscript
CIVIL WAR IN FRANCE

But it was a very modest headline, being set in small capitals. No fewer than seven columns—more than one quarter of the total issue—were occupied by descriptions of what was happening in France. Next came a short article headed "Bastile" [*sic*], which began: "In consequence of the destruction of this dreadful fortress, the grave of many miserable thousands or rather millions of French subjects, such horrid scenes are come to light as must make human nature even shrink at itself." The afterthought "or rather millions" is suggestive of the "literally decimated" mode of reporting. The *Public Advertiser* of the day before—which, despite its name, had only two columns of advertisements in a sixteen-column issue—used this top-of-column headline on page 3:

FRENCH REBELLION

The importance of the dispatch (about five inches in length) that followed was emphasized by leading. On the back page of the *St. James's Chronicle: or, British Evening-Post*[1] (published three times a week), of the same date, a column of news about the fall of the Bastille and other events in France was headed:

POSTSCRIPT
FRENCH COMMOTIONS

The *London Gazette*, still a newspaper as well as an official organ, had a front-page dispatch from Paris about the fall of the Bastille and other news of what was happening in France which ran over to the second page—about two columns in all.

The foreign news no longer consisted entirely of translations from Continental newspapers, but was supplemented by first-hand accounts received from correspondents on the spot. One of the most graphic accounts of the destruction of the Bastille and the execution of the officers was printed in the *Morning Post*, which announced, with a not-too-sensitive choice of adjective, that it had received "interesting detail of the recent convulsions in Paris . . . from our correspondent in that capital."

The French Revolution gave a big impetus to the development of foreign news services. Though lamenting the expense, John Walter of *The Times* took steps to strengthen this part of his paper; his son, John Walter II, was later to show great enterprise in this direction and to appoint Henry Crabb Robinson as a travelling war correspondent in 1807. *The Times* of May 21,

---

[1] Thrice-weekly newspapers maintained their popularity throughout the eighteenth century. Several had a long life, surviving into the nineteenth century, e.g., the *Whitehall Evening Post* (founded 1716), *General Evening Post* (1733), *London Evening Post* (1737), *London Chronicle: or, Universal Evening Post* (1757). Longest-lived was the *St. James's Chronicle*, which continued until 1866.

1792, announced with some satisfaction that it had established a new correspondence "at Brussels and Paris, which we trust will furnish us with the most regular and early intelligence that can possibly be obtained. Our communications will not be confined to the ordinary conveyance by the foreign Mails only, as we have taken such measures as will enable us to receive Letters from abroad on those days when the Foreign Mails do not become due." The arrangements did not work as smoothly as had been anticipated: a few months later *The Times* informed its readers that it had been "subject to daily disappointments" because of delays occasioned by the circuitous channels through which the news came and by the frequent stoppage of correspondence from France.

Since 1750 the scope of the newspaper had been greatly extended. The news was more fully and more seriously reported; the literary side of the paper now included reviews, theatrical notices and light verse; articles on political and other subjects were numerous, but the leader had not yet become a regular feature; "Letters to the Printer" (still to the public mind the central person in a newspaper organization) were frequently published. Crabbe, in his poem *The Newspaper*, poked fun at the earnestness of the readers who voluntarily engaged in controversy:

> Now puffs exhausted, advertisements past,
> Their correspondents stand exposed at last:
> These are a numerous tribe, to fame unknown,
> Who for the public good forego their own;
> Who, volunteers in paper war engage
> With double portion of their party's rage:
> Such are the Bruti, Decii, who appear,
> Wooing the Printer for admission here;
> Whose generous souls can condescend to pray
> For leave to throw their precious time away.

Now and again a writer of the first rank would appear pseudonymously in the pages of a newspaper. Dr. Johnson, as we have already seen, wrote "The Idler" essays weekly. The most formidable of these special contributors was "Junius" (a name that is generally held to have disguised the identity of Sir Philip Francis), whose letters to the *Public Advertiser* (formerly the *London Daily Post and General Advertiser* and before that the *Daily Post*) were sharply controversial and at times contemptuously defiant. He wrote under various signatures, but the best-known letters are those that he signed "Junius." Even at this distance of time it is easy to imagine the fury which they kindled in political circles; what is surprising, having regard to the bitterness of the invective, is that the letters should have involved the printer (Henry Sampson Woodfall) in only a single prosecution. It was Letter XXXV (December 19, 1769), addressed to King George the Third, that led to the printer's trial at the Guildhall before Lord Mansfield. The jury[1] returned an ambiguous verdict of "Guilty of printing and publishing only," and Woodfall was acquitted.[2] The opening of the letter that led to this prosecution was anything but ambiguous, and this extract may be taken as a fair sample of the whole:

SIR,
It is the misfortune of your life, and originally the cause of every reproach and distress which has attended your government, that you should never have been acquainted with the language of truth, until you heard it in the complaints of your people. It is now, however, too late to correct the error of your education. We are still inclined to make an indulgent allowance for the pernicious lessons you received in your youth, and to form the most sanguine hopes from the natural benevolence of your disposition. We are far from thinking you capable of a direct, deliberate purpose to invade those original rights of your subjects, on which all their civil and political liberties depend. Had it been possible for us to entertain a suspicion so dishonourable

---

[1] A 30-year-old coal merchant named John Walter, who founded the *Daily Universal Register* (afterwards *The Times*) sixteen years later, was a member of this jury.

[2] About a fortnight before John Almon, publisher of a monthly magazine called the *London Museum*, had been tried before Lord Mansfield for reprinting the letter, found guilty and fined ten marks (£6 13s. 4d.).

to your character, we should long since have adopted a style of remonstrance very distant from the humility of complaint.

A more notorious letter was the one addressed to Lord Mansfield (November 14, 1770). It attacked him in his capacity as judge as well as for his conduct in public life and takes rank as one of the most ferocious and wounding attacks ever printed. Such a letter if published in a newspaper today would result in immediate legal proceedings. "Junius" tauntingly challenged his victim to take action, probably confident that a jury would not convict—for the Woodfall case was not the only instance of frustration by jury. Minor offenders were prosecuted relentlessly in the eighteenth century, but "Junius" was so much feared because of his deadly malice that after one futile attempt to strike at him he was left alone. No modern newspaper would consider for a moment printing such a savage onslaught as the one that is typified by these extracts:

You will not question my veracity, when I assure you that it has not been owing to any particular respect for your person that I have abstained from you so long. Besides the distress and danger with which the press is threatened, when your Lordship is party, and the party is to be judge, I confess I have been deterred by the difficulty of the task. Our language has no term of reproach, the mind has no idea of detestation, which has not already been happily applied to you, and exhausted. Ample justice has been done by abler pens than mine to the separate merits of your life and character. Let it be *my* humble office to collect the scattered sweets, till their united virtue tortures the sense. . . .

The injustice done to an individual is sometimes of service to the public. Facts are apt to alarm us more than the most dangerous principles. The sufferings and firmness of a printer have roused the public attention. You knew and felt that your conduct would not bear a parliamentary inquiry, and you hoped to escape it by the meanest, the basest sacrifice of dignity and consistency, that ever was made by a great magistrate. Where was your firmness, where was that vindictive spirit, of which we have seen so many examples, when a man, so inconsiderable as Bingley, could force you to confess, in the face of this country, that, for two years together, you had illegally deprived an English subject of his liberty, and that he had triumphed over you at last? Yet I own, my Lord, that yours is not an uncommon character. Women, and men like women, are timid, vindictive, and irresolute. Their passions counteract each other, and make the same creature, at one moment hateful, at another contemptible. I fancy, my Lord, some time will elapse before you venture to commit another Englishman for refusing to answer interrogatories. . . .

Your charge to the jury, in the prosecution against Almon and Woodfall, contradicts the highest legal authorities, as well as the plainest dictates of reason. In Miller's cause, and still more expressly in that of Baldwin, you have proceeded a step further, and grossly contradicted yourself. You may know perhaps, though I do not mean to insult you by an appeal to your experience, that the language of truth is uniform and consistent. To depart from it safely, requires memory and discretion. . . . In public affairs, my Lord, cunning, let it be ever so well wrought, will not conduct a man honourably through life. Like bad money, it may be current for a time, but it will soon be cried down. It cannot consist with a liberal spirit, though it be sometimes united with extraordinary qualifications. When I acknowledge your abilities, you may believe I am sincere. I feel for human nature, when I see a man, so gifted as you are, descend to such vile practice. Yet do not suffer your vanity to console you too soon. Believe me, my good Lord, you are not admired in the same degree in which you are detested. It is only the partiality of your friends, that balances the defects of your heart with the superiority of your understanding. No learned man, even among your own tribe, thinks you qualified to preside in a court of common law. . . .

Here, my Lord, it may be proper for us to pause together. It is not for my own sake that I wish you to consider the delicacy of your situation. Beware how you indulge the first emotions of your resentment. This paper is delivered to the world, and cannot be recalled! The persecution of an innocent printer cannot alter facts, nor refute arguments. Do not furnish me with farther materials against yourself. An honest man, like the true religion, appeals to the understanding, or modestly confides in the internal evidence of his conscience. The impostor employs force instead of argument, imposes silence where he cannot convince, and propagates his character by the sword.

In "A Dedication to the English Nation," written for the

collected letters, "Junius" stated the case for a free Press and popular control of the government of the country with powerful clarity:

> Let it be impressed upon Your minds, let it be instilled into Your children, that the liberty of the press is the *palladium* of all the civil, political, and religious rights of an Englishman, and that the right of juries to return a general verdict, in all cases whatsoever, is an essential part of our constitution, not to be controuled or limited by the judges, nor in any shape questionable by the legislature. The power of King, Lords, and Commons is not an arbitrary power. They are the trustees, not the owners of the estate.

The sturdily independent attitude of the *Public Advertiser*, which continued to print the letters of "Junius" for several years, was something new in journalism, and one consequence was that many correspondents favoured this paper for the expression of their views on matters of public interest. For a time it was the most influential newspaper in the country. Henry Sampson Woodfall, who controlled the paper from 1758 to 1793, had succeeded his father, Henry Woodfall, in the management. Another member of this notable journalistic family was William Woodfall, his younger brother, who conducted the *Morning Chronicle* for twenty years up to 1789 and afterwards started another daily, the *Diary*, which was unsuccessful. William Woodfall is better remembered under the name of "Memory" Woodfall. He would listen to a long debate in the House of Commons and afterwards, without the use of notes, he would write for the *Morning Chronicle*, from memory, a report extending to as much as seven columns. But men with phenomenally retentive memories are rare, and now that Parliament had abandoned its attempts to suppress the publication of accounts of its proceedings, as will be told later, newspapers in the late eighteenth century began to organize the reporting of debates in a more systematic manner, employing several reporters on their Parliamentary staff.

Another important characteristic of the eighteenth-century

newspaper has still to be mentioned. When the *Daily Universal Register* appeared in 1785 it closely followed what had become the established make-up of the morning newspaper. Two columns of advertisements on the front page began with theatre announcements; three years later, when the title was shortened to *The Times*, all four columns of the front page were occupied by advertisements, with the theatres again to the forefront. For a considerable time newspapers paid for the privilege of inserting playbills, as they were called: many years before *The Times* appeared this feature was costing the *Public Advertiser* £200 a year. For a long time now these announcements have occupied in many dailies another preferential position—the first column of the leader page—and although they have to be paid for as advertisements they are inserted at a favourable rate, for the excellent reason that the information they contain is regarded as an essential part of the service given by the newspaper.

The first evening newspaper appeared towards the end of the century. It was preceded by a noon paper, the *Noon Gazette and Daily Spy*—"Published at Twelve o'Clock, and contains all the actual News of the Nine Morning Papers"—about which little is known. Of the two issues that have survived the one for December 10, 1781 (there is no serial number but the paper had been running for at least a few months, the printer having been fined and imprisoned the previous July) is of considerable interest, having a page-wide block, just below the date-line, of the Rock of Gibraltar and the bay, showing Spanish gunboats firing on the town. It is also a noticeably clean and attractive-looking paper. A selection of news from the same day's morning papers occupies over two columns, and the journals quoted from are the *Daily Advertiser, Gazetteer, Public Advertiser, Public Ledger, Morning Chronicle, Morning Post, General Advertiser, London Courant* and *Morning Herald*. On May 3, 1788, the first evening paper was published—the *Star and Evening Advertiser*—and like the *Noon Gazette* it sold for threepence. It was conventional in make-up, the front page being devoted to advertisements, with the playbills taking first place. Peter Stuart, the main projector, quarrelled with his partners (chief of whom was William Lane, a bookseller) after a time, and in February 1789 he broke away from them and produced his own evening paper—*Stuart's Star and Evening Advertiser*. After sixty-four issues, having failed to supplant the *Star* (which, in fact, continued for over forty years), he turned his paper into the *Morning Star*, but was not able to keep it going for long. A month before the *Star* appeared Mrs. Elizabeth Johnson, publisher of the first Sunday paper (*E. Johnson's British Gazette, and Sunday Monitor*), had brought out the *Evening Star, And Grand Weekly Advertiser*—a contradictory title for a weekly—and when Stuart and his partners produced their evening paper she renamed her journal *The Original Star*. In 1789 John Walter started the *Evening Mail*, but this was published three times a week. The paper changed its title to the *Mail* in 1868 and was eventually absorbed by *The Times Weekly Edition*.

Statesmen such as Edmund Burke and Charles James Fox—the latter, after some preliminary doubts, being converted by the reasoning of a brilliant young lawyer who was to become Lord Erskine—recognized the perils inherent in a direction given by Lord Mansfield in the Woodfall case that it was the function of the Crown or the Government, not of a jury, to decide whether any published matter complained of was a libel and that all a jury had to do was to ascertain whether the accused person had published it. This ruling placed a dangerous weapon in the hands of authority, and as Lord Camden declared, it was contrary to the law of England; but more than twenty years passed before Parliament could be persuaded to pass legislation that put an end to the Mansfield doctrine.

"A man had better make his son a tinker than a printer," said John Almon, who was several times prosecuted. "The laws of tin he can understand, but the law of libel is unwritten, uncertain, and undefinable. . . . It is sometimes what the king or queen please; sometimes what the minister pleases; sometimes what the attorney-general pleases." As interpreted it had become arbitrary and tyrannical, a savage instrument for bludgeoning the Press.

There was one notorious series of prosecutions in 1781 which resulted in heavy punishment for six newspapers which had published a single paragraph that offended the Russian ambassador. The printer of the *London Courant*, who first published the item, was sent to prison for a year and had to stand in the pillory before the Royal Exchange for an hour; the printer of the *Noon Gazette*, who was held to have published it in aggravated form, went to prison for eighteen months and was fined £200; the publisher of the *Morning Herald* and two printers of the *Middlesex Journal* received sentences of twelve months' imprisonment and were fined £100 each; Mary Say, the printer of the *Gazetteer*, had her punishment cut by half because of her sex—six months' imprisonment and a fine of £50; and the printers of the *St. James's Chronicle* escaped with a fine of £100 each.

After two attempts a motion for a Bill to amend the law of libel, proposed by Fox and seconded by Erskine, was passed by both Houses in 1792. Pitt supported the proposal on the ground that it was expedient to regulate the practice of the courts and make it "conformable to the spirit of the Constitution." The Libel Act secured a fair and honest trial before juries for accused persons and swept away the pernicious doctrine of Lord Mansfield.

Though Pitt had adopted a reasonable attitude on the question of the libel law, he was no friend of the Press. He several times raised the stamp duty and he increased the advertisement tax, and he went to the length of making it a legal offence for persons to hire out the newspapers whose selling prices this taxation had forced up. It was enacted that hawkers of newspapers and others who let out newspapers for small sums to be read by different persons, instead of selling the copies, "whereby the sale of newspapers is greatly obstructed," should be liable to a penalty of £5 for each offence.

The development of the newspaper in the eighteenth century was achieved in face of largely hostile administrations. A few enlightened statesmen saw that the liberty of the Press was essential to the healthy expression of public opinion; most eighteenth-century politicians would have rejected with contempt and loathing the vision that Sheridan unfolded in a speech delivered in the House of Commons in 1810.

> Give me but the liberty of the Press, and I will give the minister a venal House of Peers, I will give him a corrupt and servile House of Commons, I will give him the full swing of the patronage of office, I will give him the whole host of ministerial influence, I will give him all the power that place can confer upon him to purchase submission and overawe resistance, and yet, armed with the liberty of the Press, I will go forth to meet him undismayed, I will attack the mighty fabric he has reared with the mightier engine, I will shake down from its height corruption, and lay it beneath the ruins of the abuses it was meant to shelter.

Even in 1810 that must have seemed to many of Sheridan's hearers an alarming prospect; in the previous century it would have bordered upon criminal heresy. But however theatrical the language, it embodied a hope that was closer to realization than was then suspected. Parliament had already lost the first round when the Press successfully asserted its right to keep the nation fully informed of what was being done in its name, to report the debates and keep the proceedings of both Houses under the searchlight of public opinion; Parliament would eventually abandon, after a stubborn fight, the prolonged attempt to throttle the development of the Press by means of punitive taxation; but years before the last of the "taxes on knowledge" was removed it would encounter a new and (at first) disconcerting spirit in the Press—the lively, bracingly controversial voice of the independent newspaper. How all this came about, how the newspaper attained maturity and ultimately achieved its freedom, will be told in succeeding chapters.

CHAPTER SIX

New Men at the Head

For, soon as morning dawns with roseate hue,
The HERALD of the morn arises too;
POST after POST succeeds, and all day long
GAZETTES and LEDGERS swarm, a noisy throng.

   * * * *

When evening comes, she comes with all her train
Of LEDGERS, CHRONICLES, and POSTS again,
Like bats appearing, when the sun goes down,
From holes obscure, and corners of the town.[1]

THE late eighteenth century was a time of intense activity in journalism. The daily paper, which had started unimpressively at the beginning of the century as a sheet of second-hand foreign news printed on one side only, was now evolving into a comprehensive journal comparable with the modern newspaper. New men were emerging who were to give a more decisive character to journalism, and the tremendous impact of the French Revolution powerfully stimulated the development of newsgathering. The booksellers and the printers who had been chiefly responsible for the direction of newspapers up to now began to recede into the background as the importance of the editorial side steadily increased. It was a period in which the morning newspaper came to adult growth and able editors—James Perry of the *Morning Chronicle* and Daniel Stuart of the *Morning Post*—demonstrated by the measure of their success that the prosperity of a newspaper fundamentally depends upon its journalistic quality.

 The most versatile of the newspaper-makers who came on the

---

[1] *The Newspaper*, George Crabbe (1785).

scene at this time was John Bell (1745–1831), whose many-sided career has no parallel in the history of journalism. He was the originator or part-owner of three morning newspapers, a successful weekly and several magazines; he was an editor and probably the first war correspondent; he was a publisher of taste and enterprise, issuing several distinguished series of books; he was a printer and a typefounder, and his books, newspapers and advertisements alike showed the impress of his skill in typography; and he was also a leading bookseller. Yet he was one of the least-known figures in the history of journalism until Mr. Stanley Morison's memoir appeared in 1930 and revealed the extraordinary range of his achievement.

John Bell, already established as a bookseller, was 27 at the time of his first newspaper venture. He was one of a remarkable group of twelve men who jointly founded the *Morning Post* in 1772. Among his partners were the founders of Christie's and Tattersall's, the Rev. Henry Bate ("The Fighting Parson") and the Rev. Dr. Trusler, a lively personality who had earlier started the Literary Society, which had the declared purpose of suppressing booksellers. Most of the partners were business men, and their primary object was to establish a sound advertising organ. The first number bore the title *The Morning Post; And Daily Advertising Pamphlet*; after some issues the name was changed to *The Morning Post; or, Cheap Daily Advertiser*; later it became *The Morning Post, and Daily Advertiser*. It began as an eight-page pamphlet half the usual newspaper size, and it escaped duties on the early issues through a mistaken ruling by the Stamp Office and was thus able to publish at three-halfpence. After a fortnight, when the Stamp Office notified that duty would be payable, the paper changed to the standard newspaper form of those days—four pages size $18\frac{3}{4}$ inches $\times$ $12\frac{1}{4}$ inches—and the price went up to twopence. There was a good show of advertisements, including announcements of Bell's books and Christie's sales by auction. Among the advertisements in the first issue was one that was conspicuously frank even for those non-prudish days—the offer for sale of a list of addresses of the "ladies of the town" who lived in Piccadilly.[1] Under Henry Bate, who edited it for the first eight years (afterwards founding the *Morning Herald*), the *Morning Post* was conducted with more liveliness than dignity. "The Fighting Parson" was the inevitable nickname for a man who engaged in duels and even fought with his fists (as reported with vivid detail in his own paper). The contents of the *Morning Post* were often scandalous—hence the duels—and it was a reckless libel that brought Bate's editorship to an end. It was alleged in the issue of February 25, 1780, that the Duke of Richmond was in treasonable correspondence with the French, who were at that time suspected of planning an invasion of England. Bate declared that the libel, which came from a Plymouth correspondent, was inserted without his knowledge, but a prosecution followed and he was sentenced to twelve months' imprisonment. A few years later he inherited property and adopted the name of Dudley, and a respectable old age was crowned by the conferment on him of a baronetcy (after which he became Sir Henry Bate Dudley) for "uncommon merits" as a magistrate. One other fact about the early history of the *Morning Post* must be mentioned here: the publication for a few months in 1776–1777 of a counterfeit edition[2] of the paper by George Corrall, who had been dismissed from his employment as publisher, and Edward Cox, the printer. In a vicious attack on their former employers they referred to them as "reverend parsonical banditti."

John Bell sold his shares in the *Morning Post* in 1786—about two years before the Prince of Wales (afterwards George the Fourth) was to acquire an interest in the paper at a time when he was

[1] *The Morning Post: 1772–1937* (Wilfrid Hindle).
[2] "The newspaper of a hundred years ago was sold to a great extent by hawkers, and the proprietors of the *Morning Post* employed boys in livery, who blew a postman's horn at the corners of the most popular thoroughfares and sold the papers to all who would buy them. The proprietors of the 'spurious' paper referred to, not content with pirating the title, employed a corps of boys arrayed in uniform similar to those of the original journal, in order to dispose of their paper."—*Morning Post*, November 2, 1872 (Centenary Number).

embarrassed by the references in its columns to Mrs. Fitzherbert, with whom he had recently gone through a form of marriage—and for a time he was associated with a thrice-weekly evening paper, the *English Chronicle; Or, Universal Evening-Post*. He wanted to start another daily and was able to interest Captain Edward Topham in the project, the agreement providing that they should have one-third and two-thirds interest respectively. On New Year's Day, 1787, the first number appeared of *The World, Fashionable Advertiser*, with Topham as editor and Bell as printer. In a memoir of his former partner which appeared in 1820, Bell lightly alluded to the origin of the paper in the phrase, "Love first created the world," the allusion being to the common belief that Topham had in view that he could help to advance the theatrical fortunes of Mary Wells, an actress who bore him four children; and it did not escape remark that the notices of her performances which appeared in the *World* were highly favourable. Bell gave particular attention to the typography and set a new standard for the daily Press in the quality of appearance and production.[1] The paper did well, and when the partners disagreed in the following year Bell received £4,000 for his interest. A few months later he started yet another daily, having previously informed the public through the columns of the *Morning Star* that he was no longer interested in the *World* and that Captain Topham had "rashly and unhandsomely" withdrawn the printing from him. On June 1, 1789, appeared the first issue of the *Oracle, Bell's New World*, which he was to conduct with success for a few years. As before Bell kept a close eye on the printing of the paper, with excellent results. In 1792 he got into difficulties at a time when he was heavily involved in his book-publishing ventures. A charge of libelling the foot-guards led to proceedings against him by the Crown, and when he failed to appear for judgment early in the following year a process of the court was

---

[1] The *Morning Herald*, an enterprisingly conducted paper—it was one of the first journals to give a liberal amount of space to Parliamentary reports—followed Bell's example on January 1, 1789, when it announced with pride the use of an "entire *New Type*" and "a superior *Paper*."

taken out against him and his stock was sold at Doctor's Commons six months later. But Bell, though financially embarrassed, put on a bold front to the world and re-established his fortunes within three years. In 1794 he was vigorously active on behalf of the *Oracle* (now, as the result of amalgamation, the *Oracle and Public Advertiser*, thus incorporating the once-famous journal that had published the letters of "Junius"), acting as his own war correspondent on the Continent at a time when the British Army was fighting the French in Flanders, though his chief aim in going to "the field of contention," as he wrote from Ostend, was to establish "the REGULAR CORRESPONDENCE of some ACTIVE and WELL-INFORMED PERSONS in DIFFERENT PARTS of the CONTINENT, for the purpose of furnishing the fair Representation of Proceedings and Events as they occur...." Unfriendly references by other newspapers to this tour included a description of him by *The Times* as "a vagabond Jacobin." Energetic though he was in schemes for promoting circulation, Bell found the competition of his many rivals (including the dominant *Morning Chronicle* and the now developing *Morning Post*) increasingly troublesome and sold the copyright of his paper to Peter Stuart. In 1798 the *Oracle* was absorbed in the *Daily Advertiser*.

Meanwhile he had started, in 1796, a weekly which was to have a long run of success and which was to be one of the most imitated journals ever known—*Bell's Weekly Messenger*, an eight-page folio. The first page of No. 1, divided into three columns, led off with a calendar for the week and a list of fairs. The second column was headed by a personal statement signed "John Bell" referring to litigation with a former partner over the printing of *The British Theatre* (one of Bell's book-publishing ventures), and promising that his experience would be "actively employed to render the MESSENGER hereafter a welcome visitor at the SUNDAY Breakfast-table of every Person who wishes to be informed or amused." In the lower half of this column was a short description of the "Admiralty Telegraph" headed by a crude woodcut, and the third column had a turnover article giving a retrospect of political events since the beginning of the year. Within a few years the paper achieved great prosperity, and Bell—now in his early fifties—became an outstanding and somewhat envied figure in journalism. His name was felt to have a magic potency in gaining public favour for a journal, and acting on this belief a succession of newspaper publishers blatantly added it to the titles of their papers and sometimes imitated the format. The *Weekly Dispatch*, which had been started in 1801, changed its title some years later to *Bell's Weekly Dispatch*[1] at a time when it was "printed, published and edited by Robert Bell" —an Irish barrister and no relation of John Bell. Not content with this misleading use of the name, Robert Bell also copied the style of *Bell's Weekly Messenger*. There was an ironical sequel. In 1822 another Robert Bell started a new Sunday paper with the title *Bell's Life in London, and Sporting Chronicle* ("combining, with the News of the Week, a rich Repository of Fashion, Wit, and Humour, and interesting Incidents of High and Low Life"), which led Robert Bell of *Bell's Weekly Dispatch* to issue a circular in which he referred to "certain piratical attempts made by the conductors of a lately established journal to impress on the public that the two Papers belong to the same parties." *Bell's Weekly Dispatch* later reverted to its original title. *Bell's Life in London* survived until the 'eighties, when it was incorporated in *Sporting Life* (formerly the *Penny Bell's Life, or Sporting News*—a title that the publishers, against whom action was taken, changed to *Sporting Life* at the judge's suggestion). Sunday papers had become an established feature of English life by the first quarter of the nineteenth century. The first one—started about 1780 by Mrs. E. Johnson—was *E. Johnson's British Gazette, and Sunday Monitor* (later shortened to *Sunday Monitor*) and continued for many years. In appearance it was modelled on the daily newspapers of the period, and the contents included, in addition to the

---

[1]Among the contributors to *Bell's Weekly Dispatch* was Pierce Egan, a popular writer on sport. He was also the author of *Life in London*, depicting the "fast" life of the period—a book which has since, mainly because of its coloured illustrations, become a sort of raffish classic.

latest news, a summary of the week's events, a religious article and advertisements. Of the many Sunday papers that sprang up in the next forty years three still survive—the *Observer*[1] (1791), the *Weekly Dispatch* (1801) and the *Sunday Times* (1822). The *News of the World* was not started until 1843, and its founder was John Bell's son, John Browne Bell, who had vigorously reacted to disinheritance under his father's will fifteen years earlier by bringing out *The Bell's New Weekly Messenger* and contemptuously disclaiming any connection with what was alleged to be known as "My Grandmother's Newspaper."

Some years before he started his successful weekly newspaper John Bell embarked on an interesting magazine venture. It was in 1790 that he began publication of *La Belle Assemblée, or Bell's Court and Fashionable Magazine addressed particularly to the Ladies*, an octavo-size magazine which, in addition to a coloured fashion plate and notes on fashions and other feminine interests, contained a variety of general reading matter.[2] He obviously found stimulating exercise for his talents in producing the magazine, which continued under his direction until he sold it in 1821, and he took especial pride in later years in the engraved portrait that served as a coloured frontispiece to each number. Another and more ambitious periodical, *British Academy*—designed to give "engravings in outlines after the principal works of painting, sculpture, and architecture, ancient and modern"—ceased publication after a few issues.

In his autobiography Leigh Hunt gives this picture of John Bell in the days when he was best known as the proprietor of the *Weekly Messenger*:

Bell was upon the whole a remarkable person. He was a plain man, with a red face, and a nose exaggerated by intemperance; and yet there

[1] In 1820 the *Observer* struck a blow for the freedom of the Press, when it defied the law which forebade the publication of reports of trials in progress. For this offence it was fined £500, which it did not pay—and thus an obsolete regulation perished.
[2] Described in *John Bell* (Stanley Morison). The British Museum copies were destroyed during the bombing of London in the Second World War.

was something not unpleasing in his countenance, especially when he spoke. He had sparkling black eyes, a good-natured smile, gentlemanly manners, and one of the most agreeable voices I ever heard. He had no acquirements, perhaps not even grammar; but his taste in putting forth a publication, and getting the best artists to adorn it, was new in those times, and may be admired in any; and the same taste was observable in his house. . . . Unfortunately for Mr. Bell, he had as great a taste for neat wines and ankles as for pretty books; and, to crown his misfortunes, the Prince of Wales, to whom he was bookseller, once did him the honour to partake of an entertainment at his house. He afterwards became bankrupt. He was one of those men whose temperament and turn for enjoyment throw a grace over whatsoever they do, standing them in stead of everything but prudence, and sometimes supplying them with the consolations which imprudence itself has forfeited.

A frank portrait but a friendly one; and those who have had occasion to study the typography of John Bell will agree that he had a taste in design that will be admired in any age.

The beginnings of many great human enterprises appear curiously accidental when we examine them. John Walter (1739–1812) had no belief that he was founding a national institution when he started *The Times* on January 1, 1785. He had been a leading coal merchant and an underwriter at Lloyd's, and because of reverses was compelled to look round for a new source of income. He happened to meet one Henry Johnson who held the patents for the logographic process—a method of setting up type by logotypes or combinations of several letters in one piece. He bought the patents and improved the process, and in May 1784 he issued an announcement from the "Logographic Office, Blackfriars" stating that he had bought the printing house near Apothecaries' Hall—at one time the King's printing house—for the purpose of printing by the new process. The present offices of *The Times* stand on this site.

John Walter embarked on logographic printing with the conviction that it was quicker and cheaper than the usual method, but he found that his enthusiasm was not shared either by the trade or by the public. How was he to break down this apathy? He decided that a daily newspaper offered the best way of demonstrating the superiority of this process. Thus *The Times* came into existence chiefly as a means of advertising a new method of printing, so that the manner of its birth was doubly accidental. With eight morning papers "already established and confirmed in the public opinion," to quote from the long signed foreword in No. 1, to bring out a new one was clearly "an arduous undertaking," the more so as Walter embarked on it without any experience to guide him. He told his readers that a newspaper ought to be

the Register of the times, and faithful recorder of every species of intelligence; it ought not to be engrossed by any particular object; but, like a well covered table, it should contain something suited to every palate; observations on the dispositions of our own and foreign courts should be provided for the political reader; debates should be reported for the amusement or information of those who may be particularly fond of them; and a due attention should be paid to the interests of trade, which are so greatly promoted by advertisements.

The new journal, a four-page paper, began with the handicap of a cumbrous title. Walter named it the *Daily Universal Register* ("Printed Logographically by His Majesty's Patent"), but its readers called it "The Register," which led to confusion with several publications which had that word in their title. Exactly three years later he changed the title to *The Times or Daily Universal Register*, and in the following March he dropped the alternative title and at last attained a simple, apt and dignified name for his newspaper—*The Times*. The germ of the title is to be found in Walter's declaration in No. 1 that a newspaper should be a "Register of the times." The usual price for a daily newspaper in the seventeen-eighties was threepence. Walter issued his journal at twopence-halfpenny, which he knew was an uneconomic price, but he hoped to make up the difference by the profit from a good volume of advertisements. After three months he raised the price to threepence. Walter discovered that logographic printing was not cheaper and gradually the use of logotypes was discontinued.

Though he was not an independent journalist, since he regularly accepted Government subsidies, John Walter could be bluntly candid in print, especially when referring to the family of George the Third, and this imprudence brought sharp punishment. He was several times in trouble in the early days. A libel against the Lord Chief Justice cost him a fine of £150 in the second year of *The Times*. A harsher penalty followed his indiscretion in allowing the publication of a statement that the Dukes of York, Gloucester and Cumberland were insincere in their expression of joy at the King's recovery after his attack of 1788; he was tried for libel and sentenced to a fine of £50 and a year's imprisonment in Newgate. These were the chief penalties imposed, and he appears to have been let off one part of the sentence which commanded that he should stand in the pillory at Charing Cross for an hour. But that was not the end. During his imprisonment he was prosecuted for accusing the Prince of Wales and the Duke of York of so demeaning themselves as to incur the King's disapproval and for stating that the Duke of Clarence had left his naval station without leave. In addition to being fined £100 on each count he was sentenced to a further year's imprisonment on the first charge. His health suffered from the imprisonment, and after serving sixteen months he was released at the instance of the Prince of Wales.

John Walter's enterprise as a journalist was displayed in 1788 when *The Times* appeared promptly with a four-column report of an important Parliamentary debate which had lasted until seven o'clock in the morning. It was to be more conspicuously shown during the French Revolution, when the correspondent he dispatched to Paris sent special reports of the massacres of 1792 and the executions of Louis XVI and Marie Antoinette. Within seven years the circulation of the paper had grown to 3,000, a considerable figure for those days; in the next twelve months the circulation at times rose, but only for a time, to nearly 4,000 (the price was then fourpence)—"never before attained by any

Morning Paper under any circumstances." The traditional importance of foreign news in *The Times* dates back to its early years, for on its fifteenth anniversary it published a long list of important events on the Continent which it had been the first to announce in this country. John Walter created *The Times*, but it was not until his son, John Walter II, took over control that the paper came into the front rank and snapped its link with the Government. The first Walter not only took subsidies but also derived revenue from a form of journalistic blackmail that was not uncommon in the eighteenth century. The official history of *The Times*, with its characteristic objectivity, frankly reveals that Walter accepted fees for the suppression of paragraphs that were likely to embarrass the subjects of them.

From the beginning readers of daily newspapers had enjoyed scandalous paragraphs. Topham and Bell in the *World* set a new standard in personal detraction which *The Times* exerted itself to surpass. There was money as well as entertainment in the system of paragraphing practised at this time. The subject was often informed previously by the journal's agent that a paragraph was in type, and it was hinted to him that the paragraph need not appear if a sum, known as the suppression fee, were paid. If the subject of the paragraph had not been reached before publication, a cutting was sent to him with a hint that room could be found for any "statement." Inclusion of the second paragraph was delayed until a payment, known as the "contradiction fee," was forthcoming.

Four years after the founding of *The Times* a new man came to the head of the rival *Morning Chronicle* and made it for a generation the outstanding daily paper. James Perry (1756–1821), the first of the great editors, was a Scotsman who had arrived in London at the age of 21 and become a regular contributor to the *General Advertiser* at a salary of a guinea a week, receiving an additional half-guinea for helping to bring out the *London Evening Post*. He acted also as a special reporter, and his energy in that capacity is shown by the fact that during the trial of Admirals Keppel and Palliser by court-martial he sent up eight columns of evidence a day to the *General Advertiser*, whose circulation rose to several thousands for each issue. In 1782 he planned the *European Magazine*, which he edited for a year, and was then invited to become editor of the *Gazetteer*, on which paper he introduced a new method of reporting the proceedings of Parliament. He organized a team of reporters, with the result that the public were able to read a full account of the debates next morning. The success of this idea, then revolutionary, was a serious blow to the *Morning Chronicle*, since "Memory" Woodfall, working single-handed, could not get out his reports with the same promptness despite his remarkable energy. A few years later, alarmed by the decline of the paper, the partners wanted to follow Perry's lead by having their own corps of Parliamentary reporters, and Woodfall broke with them and left to start a daily which had only a brief life—the *Diary*.

The *Morning Chronicle* came into the market in 1789 and was bought by Perry, with a loan of £500 from a firm of bankers and additional money provided by Bellamy, a well-known wine merchant who was also the doorkeeper of the House of Commons (a personal association that proved useful when the new method of Parliamentary reporting was adopted and improved), and with him as joint owner he had James Gray, a Charterhouse schoolmaster, who put in £500. Gray, who did much of the original writing on the paper under the new ownership, died a few years later. Perry was 33 when he gained control of the *Morning Chronicle*, and the new importance of the editor may be said to date from his accession. The paper soon made headway under his direction and became the principal organ of the Whigs. Perry was in touch with life at many points and knew personally some of the most influential men of the day, and his paper gradually acquired a reputation for being well-informed. He was for a time his own special correspondent, spending a year in France at the time of the French Revolution in order to get a proper understanding of what was happening and provide his readers with clear, first-hand accounts. He was able to persuade many leading writers to contribute to his columns—among them Sir James Mackintosh, Sheridan, Ricardo, Coleridge, Charles Lamb,

Thomas Moore and William Hazlitt, the last-named writing theatrical criticisms for the paper.

Perry had to face several prosecutions during his career and like John Walter he suffered a term of imprisonment. The first brush with authority occurred when, in December 1792, the *Morning Chronicle* published an advertisement of the address passed at the meeting of the Society for Political Information at Derby held the previous July. He was charged with printing a seditious libel, and the special jury, after five hours' deliberation, returned a verdict of "Guilty of publishing, but not with malicious intent." The judge would not accept this, and the jury went back to their room and at five o'clock in the morning reached a verdict of "Not guilty." In 1798 Lord Minto called attention to a sarcastic reference by the *Morning Chronicle* to the House of Lords, and another peer described it as a scandalous paper which he would not admit into his home. The paragraph complained of suggested that in order to vindicate the importance of that House "the dresses of the opera-dancers are regulated there." In defence of Perry, Lord Derby said that the *Morning Chronicle* was distinguished for its "disdain of all scandal of individuals and all those licentious personalities by which the peace of families is destroyed." Other peers also spoke in his favour, but the House adopted, by sixty-nine votes to eleven, Lord Minto's motion that Perry and the printer of the paper should be imprisoned for three months and fined £50. The period of imprisonment was lightened for Perry by the visits of his friends, and on his release an entertainment in his honour was given at the London Tavern. He was again prosecuted in 1810—this time for publishing a paragraph extracted from the *Examiner* which suggested that the successor of George the Third would have "the finest opportunity of becoming nobly popular." He defended himself and was acquitted. Perry died in 1821. He had given up the editorship four years before, owing to failing health, but had kept the general control in his hands. After his death the *Morning Chronicle* was sold for £42,000.

John Black, son of a Scottish pedlar and born in a humble

cottage in 1783, succeeded to the editorial chair of the *Morning Chronicle* in 1817. He ranks as one of the outstanding journalists of his time, but lacked the touch of genius that enabled Perry to make the *Morning Chronicle* the greatest paper in England. From the age of 13 to 27 Black held various clerical posts but found time to attend classes at Edinburgh University. As a boy he had gained a knowledge of Greek and Latin at a parish school, and Greek was to be his favourite study throughout his life. He did translations from the German for the *Edinburgh Encyclopaedia* and contributed articles to the *European Magazine*. In 1811 he came to London and worked as a reporter under Perry and translated the foreign correspondence; he also published various translations from the German and Italian. As an editor he was courageous and outspoken, and he was a virile champion of reform. He did not hesitate when necessary to take an unpopular line, as when he was critical of Queen Caroline—and this candour about the idol of the hour injured the circulation of the paper. In the early days of his editorship he owed much to the counsel of James Mill, whose son John Stuart Mill long afterwards summed up Black's achievement in these words:

I have always considered Black as the first journalist who carried criticism and the spirit of reform into the details of English institutions. Those who are not old enough to remember those times can hardly believe what the sta.e of public discussion then was. People now and then attacked the constitution and the borough-mongers, but no one thought of censuring the law or the courts of justice, and to say a word against the unpaid magistracy was a sort of blasphemy. Black was the writer who carried the warfare into these subjects, and by doing so he broke the spell. Very early in his editorship he fought a great battle for the freedom of reporting preliminary investigations in the police courts. He carried his point, and the victory was permanent. Another subject on which his writings were of the greatest service was the freedom of the Press on matters of religion. All these subjects were Black's own.

After Perry's death the *Morning Chronicle* came into the

ownership of William Clement, proprietor of the *Observer*[1] and *Bell's Life in London*. He was handicapped by shortage of capital, and the *Morning Chronicle* lost ground under his management. When it changed hands again in 1834 its value as a property, measured by the price for which it was sold, had fallen from £42,000 to £16,500. Black was editor until 1843, when the continued decline of the paper led to his enforced resignation. He had been handicapped by not having the free hand enjoyed by Perry, but he lacked also the balance and shrewdness of his predecessor, and the *Morning Chronicle* under his editorship was outstripped by *The Times* under Thomas Barnes. He was a quick-tempered man, over-fond of issuing challenges, and engaged in at least one duel; but he was also a man of many friends, and when he resigned they raised a fund to buy him an annuity. Charles Dickens, who worked as a reporter on the *Morning Chronicle*, was one of these friends. "Dear old Black!" he wrote. "My first hearty out-and-out appreciator." Lord Melbourne, one of the public men he knew intimately, once said to him: "Mr. Black, you never ask for anything, and I wish you would. I should be most happy to do anything in my power to serve you." Black thanked him but said that he did not want anything. "I am editor of the *Morning Chronicle*. I like my business, and I live happily on my income." The Prime Minister acknowledged this reply with a comment that has become famous: "Then, by God, I envy you, and you are the only man I ever did."

James Perry's success in reviving the *Morning Chronicle* by able editing has a parallel in the career of Daniel Stuart, who in 1795 bought the *Morning Post* for £600 when it was on the point of extinction. What he got for his outlay was a house in Catherine Street, all the plant, and the copyright of a paper that was morally discredited. Not long before it had been ordered to

---

[1] The Sunday papers of that period were week-end journals published on Saturday. Clement made the *Observer* a "seventh day paper"—in his own phrase—by printing it in the early hours of Sunday morning and giving the public later news.

pay £4,000 damages for a shocking libel on "a lady of quality." The circulation had sunk to 350 a day.

Stuart was born in Edinburgh in 1766. He was sent to London at the age of 12 to join his older brothers, who had a printing business. One of these brothers, Peter, founded the *Star* in 1788, and in the same year Daniel took over from him the printing of the *Morning Post*. Their sister Catherine married James (later Sir James) Mackintosh in 1789, and it was about this time that Daniel began to reveal his liberal sympathies by helping Mackintosh, then secretary to the Society of the Friends of the People, whose aim was to promote Parliamentary reform. Sheridan and other leading Whigs were among the members of the Society. Peter was associated with the purchase of the *Morning Post*, but before long Daniel came into sole control, his brother's time being fully engaged by his other interests. Like Perry he knew how to attract brilliant recruits to the editorial columns. Coleridge was the most distinguished—and the most valued—of these contributors, and Daniel Stuart used to lament that he could not persuade him to devote more time to writing for the paper. The poet had no love of money. He could have had a partnership and an income of £2,000 a year, but preferred to live in the country and enjoy "the lazy reading of old folios," content to earn a salary of about one-tenth of that sum.

Stuart aimed to reflect the many-sidedness of life in the columns of the *Morning Post*. A man of radical views (though these became more conservative in the light of later developments in France), he was as interested as anyone in the drama of political events ushered in by the French Revolution, but would not allow politics to have a disproportionate share of his editorial space. What especially distinguished the *Morning Post* during his editorship was its literary quality and its agreeable diversity. He liked to have poetry and light paragraphs "making the Paper cheerfully entertaining, not entirely filled with ferocious politics." About the turn of the century Charles Lamb was one of those who helped to give light relief to the paper—though Stuart did not care much for his brand of humour—and he served also for a time as dramatic critic. Few things are more quickly perishable than topical humour, with its glancing allusions, so that a reader a century and a half later is not qualified to assess the appeal of jests that were strictly contemporary; but one type of humour much favoured in Stuart's day can be judged without much hesitation. Puns such as the following, which were numerous in the *Morning Post*, are as unsubtle as a sledge-hammer:

Mr. MONK LEWIS was so much hurt by his fall, that, we are told, he continued for some months *senseless. Very probable.*

General *Vial* is said to be an excellent *bottle companion.*

Other famous writers who contributed to the *Morning Post* included Wordsworth and Southey. Its reputation for sturdy independence was much to the liking of the leading authors who wrote for the paper. "The rapid and unusual increase in the sale of the *Morning Post* is a sufficient pledge," wrote Coleridge, "that genuine impartiality with a respectable portion of literary talent will secure the success of a newspaper without the aid of party or ministerial patronage." An ugly episode marred the record of the journal under Stuart. In 1796 the *Telegraph*, a rival morning journal, brought an action against the *Morning Post* for planting on it a forged French newspaper which contained details of "the preliminaries for peace between the Emperor and the French Republic." The *Telegraph* accepted the paper as authentic and claimed that it had suffered serious injury by publishing this faked news as true. The *Morning Post* had to pay £1,000 damages for misleading its rival. Two years later Stuart bought the *Telegraph* and incorporated it in the *Morning Post*; about 140 years later (in 1937) another paper of almost identical name—the *Daily Telegraph*—absorbed the *Morning Post.*

There was a steady growth in the circulation of the *Morning Post* from the time that Stuart became editor. It rose from 350 to 2,000 within three years. In addition to gaining new readers by improving the quality of the paper, he increased the circulation by acquiring first the *Gazetteer* and then, as already mentioned, the *Telegraph*. In 1803, when Stuart sold for £25,000 the paper which he had picked up for a few hundred pounds, the circulation had risen to 4,500—a considerable sale in those days of dear newspapers. When Pitt raised the stamp duty to threepence in 1800 Stuart daily reminded his readers of the cause of the high price of their paper by printing this notice: "Price—6d. Price in 1783—3d. Taxed by Mr. Pitt—3d."

Within eight years Stuart had transformed the almost moribund *Morning Post* into a newspaper nearly equal in influence to the *Morning Chronicle* and with a circulation of 1,500 in excess of that journal's sale in 1803. He had a shrewd perception of a fact that is familiar to the conductors of a modern newspaper—the dual importance of small advertisements in increasing both revenue and circulation. "Advertisements act and react," he said. "They attract readers, promote circulation, and circulation attracts advertisements." For this reason he encouraged the small and miscellaneous advertisements on the front page, "preferring them to any others, upon the rule that the more numerous the customers, the more permanent and independent the custom."

Stuart's name is so much associated with the *Morning Post* that another journalistic achievement in which he was concerned tends to be overshadowed. In 1796 he bought the *Courier*, a sevenpenny evening paper started years earlier, and after selling the *Morning Post* he concentrated on building up this second acquisition—in which Peter Street, first manager and later editor, had a half-interest—and again had Coleridge and Wordsworth among his contributors. The results were striking, the circulation being increased from 1,500 to 7,000. The *Courier* has a special place in the history of journalism as the first evening paper to issue second editions.[1] It broke into thrilling headlines to announce the victory at Waterloo:

[1] "Men with horns ran down the streets making the 'most hideous music,' and shouting between each blast, 'News, News, great News—Courier, Courier—great News, great News—second edition, second edition.' Two or three strong-lunged fellows would at times be within hearing at the same moment, and no one could avoid noticing the fact."—*The Fourth Estate* (F. Knight Hunt).

GREAT AND GLORIOUS NEWS
COMPLETE OVERTHROW OF BONAPARTE'S ARMY
OFFICIAL BULLETIN

A thirteen-line bulletin from Downing Street appeared below. A whole page was devoted to news of the fighting, including a "Letter from an Officer of High Rank."

Stuart again showed his independence when he refused any reward for his support of Addington against Bonaparte during the Peace of Amiens. Estcourt brought him a message of thanks from the Prime Minister, "offering me anything I could wish. I declined the offer." He retired from journalism in 1822, when he sold his interest in the *Courier*, and lived in the country until his death in 1846.

CHAPTER SEVEN

The Rebels

THE emergence of the independent daily newspaper was made possible by a change in the economic basis of the Press; but the right to print—the fundamental freedom without which *The Times*, for instance, could not have achieved the powerful influence on public affairs which it began to exercise under the editorship of Thomas Barnes—had to be wrested from authority step by step. A long and tenacious battle was necessary before the idea of free expression triumphed. The late eighteenth century and the early nineteenth saw a mounting challenge to official control that neither fine nor imprisonment could restrain, until finally government was compelled to abandon its repeated and at times panicky attempts to keep the Press in chains.

John Milton in his *Areopagitica* (1644) had put the case for unlicensed printing in stately prose, but the men who were responsible for securing the freedom of the Press used gustier language and a more audacious approach. Liberty has had many strange champions, but surely none more curious than John Wilkes (1727–1797)—a wit and a libertine whose courage and calculated insolence made him for some years the idol of the mob. Wilkes had a gift for putting authority in the wrong that almost amounted to genius, and to George the Third and his ministers this gay, cynical agitator with his adroit tactics became a nightmare figure. His main service to journalism was that he secured the tacit removal of the ban on the reporting of Parliamentary debates and that he fiercely asserted the right to criticize the Government; his public services included the vindication of the freedom of the electorate and the abolition of the general warrant. He made his stand aggressively clear in the first issue of his paper, the *North Briton* (June 5, 1762):

The liberty of the Press is the birthright of a Briton, and is justly esteemed the firmest bulwark of the liberties of this country. It has been the terror of all bad ministers; for their dark and dangerous designs, or their weakness, inability, and duplicity, have thus been detected, and shown the public generally in too strong colours for them long to bear up against the odium of mankind.

In his political articles Wilkes abandoned the method then current of indicating the politicians criticized by the consonants of their names only, e.g., "L–rd B–t–"; he did away with this disguise that was no disguise and boldly named them in full. But it was not this innovation that brought the *North Briton* under official displeasure. In No. 45—a number that was to haunt the ministerial mind for many years and to become to the mob a symbol of the stand against oppression—John Wilkes had a long and damaging article on the King's Speech, and his attack was directed principally to the peace treaty concluded by his *bête noire*—Bute. This is a sample:

The *King's Speech* has always been considered by the legislature, and by the public at large, as the *Speech of the Minister*. . . . This week has given the public the most abandoned instance of ministerial effrontery ever attempted to be imposed on mankind. The *minister's speech* of last Tuesday is not to be paralleled in the annals of this country. I am in doubt whether the imposition is greater on the sovereign or on the nation. Every friend of his country must lament that a prince of so many great and amiable qualities, whom England truly reveres, can be brought to give the sanction of his sacred name to the most odious measures, and to the most unjustifiable public declarations, from a throne ever renowned for truth, honour, and unsullied virtue. . . .

A nation as sensible as the *English*, will see that a *spirit of concord*, when they are oppressed, means a tame submission to injury, and that a *spirit of liberty* ought then to arise, and I am sure ever will, in proportion to the weight of the grievance they feel. *Every* legal *attempt of a contrary tendency* to the *spirit of concord* will be deemed a justifiable resistance, warranted by the *spirit of the English constitution*. . . . I wish as much as any man in the kingdom to see the *honour of the crown* maintained in a manner truly becoming *Royalty*. I lament to see it sunk even to prostitution.

George the Third was not appeased by the careful placing of the responsibility for the speech on the shoulders of the minister, and the action subsequently taken by the Government against John Wilkes apparently had his eager approval. The Attorney-General and the Solicitor-General held that the article was "an infamous and seditious libel, tending to inflame the minds and alienate the affections of the people from his Majesty, and to excite them to traitorous insurrections against his Government, and therefore punishable as a misdemeanour of the highest nature." The Government issued a general warrant, authorizing the arrest of the writers, printers and publishers of the offending issue of the *North Briton*. Wilkes instantly saw a way of turning against the Government the weapon they had chosen for his discomfiture. A general warrant, which specified the offence but not the persons by whom it was committed (in this case only the printer was named), would be impossible to justify and could be exposed as a direct blow at the liberty of the subject. In the developments that followed Wilkes was always master of the situation—a coolly alert picador provoking a not very intelligent bull. He spent a few days in the Tower and then appeared before a judge, who discharged him on the ground that as a member of Parliament Wilkes was immune from arrest. From this moment Wilkes became a popular hero. He was borne in triumph back to Westminster, and amid the cheers of the crowd could be heard the cry that was to become uncomfortably familiar to the administration—"Wilkes and Liberty!" He followed up this victory by taking legal action for wrongful arrest against Government agents, and the other forty-eight persons who had been arrested and detained under general warrant took similar proceedings. All the plaintiffs were eventually awarded heavy damages, and Lord Chief Justice Pratt ruled that the issue of a general warrant was illegal. Altogether the Government had to pay £100,000 in damages and costs.

A twofold blunder by Wilkes enabled the Government to take their revenge some months later. He reprinted in book form the back numbers of the *North Briton*, including No. 45, and on the motion of Lord North the House of Commons decided, by a large majority, that this issue was a "false, scandalous and seditious libel" and ordered that the *North Briton* should be burnt in public; and the House of Lords passed a resolution declaring that the *Essay on Woman*, an obscene parody on Pope's *Essay on Man* which Wilkes printed about the same time, was "a most scandalous, obscene and impious libel." It was thought to be somewhat odd that the peer chosen to move the resolution should be Lord Sandwich, a notorious rake who was known to have been the victim of one of the most devastating retorts on record. "Wilkes, you will die of a pox or on the gallows," he said on one occasion. "That depends, my Lord," came the swift reply, "whether I embrace your principles or your mistress." An attempt to burn the *North Briton* in front of the Royal Exchange led to a riot, in which officers of the law were roughly handled. Wilkes was ordered to appear before the House of Commons but pleaded illness—he had recently been wounded in a duel—and when two physicians were sent to examine him he declined to receive them. He went over to France, and in his absence the Commons passed a resolution expelling him from the House (January 19, 1764). He was prosecuted for the printing of No. 45 and the *Essay on Woman* and found guilty. A writ for his arrest was issued, and afterwards he was declared an outlaw.

This was apparently the end of John Wilkes, but a few years later—in March 1768—he returned to England, apparently tiring of a leisurely existence on the Continent in which amatory delights played as always the most important part in his life. He came back with the intention, announced through a London newspaper some months earlier, of standing as a Parliamentary candidate. He put up for the City of London but was rejected; better inspired, he stood for Middlesex, where the electors included tradesmen and artisans, and his reputation as a champion of liberty combined with his ready wit gave him the victory by more than 400 votes. The Wilkites chose 45 as their symbol and householders, anxious not to have their windows broken, saw the prudence of adopting the suggestion that they should display the significant number. The law now belatedly claimed its victim. Wilkes had persuaded the Court of King's Bench to reverse his outlawry, but subsequently he was tried and sentenced to twenty-two months' imprisonment for the reprinting of No. 45 and the publishing of the *Essay on Woman* and fined £1,000. We are not concerned here with his long struggle with the Commons over the right of the Middlesex electors to return him as their member, which they voted to do several times in succession: the House eventually had to own defeat on this constitutional issue. William Beckford, the Lord Mayor, and other supporters of Wilkes started in April 1769 the *Middlesex Journal, or Chronicle of Liberty*, a thrice-weekly paper, "to vindicate the cause of depressed liberty by exhibiting in full view to the people every measure that has already been taken, and every attempt that may further be made, upon that great charter of our laws, that palladium of English liberty, which, purchased by the best blood, has been maintained by the warmest zeal of the wisest and best men this nation has ever produced." Among its contributors was the precocious Thomas Chatterton, who wrote letters for the paper modelled on "Junius" and who shortly afterwards committed suicide at the age of 17.

Wilkes showed a return to his old adroitness in the way in which he foiled an attempt by the Commons in 1771 to enforce the ban on the publication of reports of their debates. R. Thompson, the printer of the *Gazetteer*, and John Wheble, the printer of the *Middlesex Journal*, had been summoned to appear before the House to answer to the charge of "misrepresenting the speeches and reflecting on several members." They ignored the order and a Royal proclamation was issued for their arrest. But they had powerful friends: Wilkes and the London democrats took up their case. The two printers were apprehended in circumstances that showed evidence of careful design. Wheble was arrested by E. T. Carpenter, a journeyman printer, and appeared at the

Guildhall before Wilkes, now a City alderman and acting as magistrate. The prisoner was discharged and bound over to prosecute Carpenter for assault and false imprisonment, and Wilkes addressed a formal complaint to Lord Halifax, the Secretary of State, pointing out that Wheble had been arrested by a person who was not an officer of the law and that he had been apprehended not for any legal offence but under a proclamation that directly violated the rights of an Englishman. On the same day Thompson was arrested by another printer, brought before Alderman Oliver at the Mansion House and discharged on the ground that he had not been accused of having committed any crime. John Miller, of the *London Evening Post*, was apprehended the next day, under a warrant from the Speaker, by a House of Commons messenger named Whittam, and not only protested but sent for a constable and gave the messenger into custody on a charge of assault and false imprisonment. The sequel was still more interesting. Both men were taken to the Mansion House and brought before Brass Crosby, the Lord Mayor, Wilkes and Oliver, who dismissed the charge against Miller and committed Whittam for trial. Wilkes sent another remonstrance to Lord Halifax concerning these illegal proceedings against the printers.

The House of Commons read between the lines and did not like what it read. The Lord Mayor and Oliver, who were both members, were ordered to appear at the House and answer for their conduct. Wilkes, having been expelled—his long constitutional battle was not yet decided—was ordered to appear at the Bar of the House and sent the characteristic reply that as he had not been addressed as a member of Parliament the summons was informal and he would not obey it. Twice the Commons repeated its command, and on the third occasion the day specified for his appearance was one on which the House was not sitting—and that was the end of the matter as far as he was concerned. The Lord Mayor and Alderman Oliver made two appearances at the House of Commons, accompanied by a crowd of supporters, who on the second occasion noisily demonstrated outside. The House resolved that there had been a violation of its privileges. Crosby, who was suffering from gout, was permitted to go home for the evening, and his supporters made the return to the Mansion House a triumphal journey. Oliver justified what he had done and defied the Commons, who sent him to the Tower. When Crosby next went to the House he was again accompanied by a crowd, who smashed Lord North's carriage and threw stones and mud at ministerialists. The Commons sought to conciliate the Lord Mayor because of the state of his health, proposing that he be placed in the custody of the Sergeant-at-Arms, but he declined to accept any favour. "I have no apology to make for having acted uprightly," he declared, "and I fear not any resentment in consequence of such conduct." He was therefore sent to the Tower.

A few weeks later, on the prorogation of Parliament, the Lord Mayor and the alderman were released from the Tower. The Government, alarmed by the strength of public opinion, made no further attempt to prevent the publication of reports of Parliamentary proceedings in the newspapers. Wilkes had won the greatest of all his victories.

It was not until thirty-two years later—in 1803—that the House of Commons assigned special seats in the public gallery for the use of reporters. In 1907 the House appointed its own reporting staff for the production of Hansard, as the official report of its proceedings is still called from its association with the family of that name as far back as the late eighteenth century.

In 1763, the year after the first issue of the *North Briton* appeared, a journalist was born who like Wilkes can be classified as a natural rebel and who was to be an immensely disturbing figure in British political life for over thirty years. No writer in the history of journalism has equalled the blunt simplicity of appeal to the masses that was the essential characteristic of William Cobbett's work. "Junius" was a master of invective in the superior eighteenth-century manner and addressed himself to a limited upper-class public; Cobbett, a man of the people, was a master of plain language and was inevitably likened to the traditional figure of John Bull because of his constitutional pugnacity and his sturdy Englishness.

Son of a small farmer, Cobbett joined the Army as a young man, serving in Canada, and within a few years attained the rank of regimental sergeant-major. He was shocked by the frauds that he observed in his regiment and got some figures together and after his discharge persuaded the authorities to court-martial the officers whom he accused; but an essential witness was held in the Army and the regimental books were not secured. Cobbett felt that in these circumstances he would not be able to make good his allegations, and he did not appear at the court-martial. He fled to France in 1792 and a few months later went to the United States, where he was to remain for nearly eight years. At first he earned a living by teaching English to French *émigrés* at Philadelphia and wrote an English grammar in French under the title *Le Tuteur Anglais*. In 1794 he read by chance a newspaper containing the text of addresses of welcome, by American Radical societies, to Dr. Joseph Priestley, the English scientist, who had recently settled in the country. Cobbett was infuriated by the attacks on England which he found in the addresses and the reply, and he wrote a blistering commentary in pamphlet form entitled *Observations on the Emigration of Dr. Priestley*. The pamphlet sold well and was reprinted in England. That was the beginning of his career as a writer. Stimulated by the hostile comment provoked by his pamphlet Cobbett followed with others, in which he vigorously defended his country. One reviewer told him that he was like a porcupine, and taking this as a compliment Cobbett wrote his next pamphlet, *A Kick for a Bite*, under the name of Peter Porcupine, a name which was to become well known in the United States.

He opened a bookshop in Philadelphia, then the most anti-British of cities, and provocatively dressed the window with a large portrait of George the Third, anti-democratic cartoons and other unpopular pictures. Soon the whole country was talking about this lively and aggressive Englishman. His other writings during the American period included the still very readable *Life and*

Adventures of Peter Porcupine, an account of his career. In 1797 he started a daily paper, *Porcupine's Gazette and Daily Advertiser*, which had a good circulation but according to Cobbett never made any money; and after two years he had to suspend publication because of financial difficulties resulting from a libel action in which a verdict for $5,000 was given against him. All his property was seized and sold. In 1800 he decided to return to England, and in an open letter addressed to American papers he delivered himself of these (and other equally blunt) parting words: "I depart for my native land, where neither the moth of *Democracy* nor the rust of *Federalism* doth corrupt and where thieves do not, with impunity, break through and steal five thousand dollars at a time."

Cobbett had left England surreptitiously; he returned to find himself famous. The greatest men in the land hastened to do honour to this 37-year-old journalist whose slashing controversial pamphlets, which had been reprinted here as they came out, made him the chief hope of the anti-Jacobins. William Windham, the Secretary at War, gave a dinner at which Cobbett met Pitt—who was most friendly—and Canning. Not long after George Hammond, the Under-Secretary for Foreign Affairs, offered him control of one of two daily papers, the *True Briton* (morning) and the *Sun* (evening), which had been started in 1792, with the help of Government money, to combat Jacobinical propaganda. But Cobbett did not relish the idea of losing his independence. Later, in the *Political Register*, he was to recall in explanation of his decision the fable of the hungry wolf which had been invited by a sleek mastiff to join him in his comfortable home and which was puzzled by the crease round the neck of its kind friend.

"What's your fancy," said he, "for making that mark round your neck?" "Oh," said the other, "it is only the mark of my *collar* that my master ties me up with." "*Ties you up!*" exclaimed the wolf, stopping short at the same time; "give me my ragged hair, my gaunt belly, and my freedom!" and so saying he trotted back to the wood.

There spoke the genuine Cobbett: he was by instinct a rebel, a nonconformer. He started a daily paper of his own, the *Porcupine*, which he said would give independent support to the Government and which would take no advertisements of patent medicines. The paper was not successful, one reason being that his hopes of building up a large sale in the United States were thwarted by the secretary of the Post Office, who had the monopoly of the right of sending periodicals to America by the only safe mode of conveyance in war-time—the King's packet boat—and demanded five guineas a year (afterwards offering to accept three guineas) for each copy that he forwarded. Cobbett would not do business on these terms, and in consequence met with much obstruction in his postal deliveries and lost the advertisements of the Post Office. The most characteristic episode in the short history of the *Porcupine* was the stand that Cobbett took on the proposal to make peace with France. He attacked the unwisdom of a policy that as he saw it would facilitate French supremacy and be disadvantageous to Britain; and when London was illuminated in honour of the peace in 1801 he deliberately left unlighted the windows of his house in Pall Mall, where he had a bookshop. The crowd broke his windows and forced the door, and Cobbett then prudently illuminated his house. Next year the Treaty of Amiens was formally ratified and Cobbett again refused to join in the celebrations. The mob attacked his unlighted house and a troop of Horse Guards had to be sent to disperse them. After little more than a year Cobbett sold the *Porcupine* to John Gifford, and two months later it was absorbed by the *True Briton*. This Gifford was not related to William Gifford, the editor of the *Quarterly Review*, having assumed the name to avoid his creditors, but he had one link with him in that he imitated the *Anti-Jacobin* when he produced the *Anti-Jacobin Review and Magazine* (1798), which he edited until 1821.

Windham, and others who shared his detestation of the Peace of Amiens, raised funds to enable Cobbett to start another paper —"with the express and written conditions," he stated some years later, that he was not to be regarded as under any sort of obligation. "And never did any one of the persons who advanced the money attempt in the slightest degree to influence my opinions, which were frequently opposed to their own." Undoubtedly some of those who made possible the starting of the *Political Register* in 1802 must often have been in the sharpest disagreement with its editorial policy, especially when Cobbett moved away from his old political alignment and developed into a Radical journalist. But there was no sign of this Cobbett in the early issues of the paper. Resolute to secure his own liberty of expression, he nevertheless denounced the freedom of the Press as a mere cloak for treason. He told his readers in 1803 that the newspapers were corrupt and degraded and would always be, as they had always been, the curse of the country: we owed to the Press the American Revolution, the Irish Rebellion and the Bonapartist usurpation. He conceded that if the Press were in the hands of free and independent men, instead of slaves and hirelings, it would be one of the greatest national blessings. But there was another form of slavery that had his approval, for he defended the slave trade as being necessary to British commerce.

The *Political Register* was a success from the first number, despite the high price of tenpence—after two issues had appeared it was converted from a fortnightly into a weekly to meet the public demand—and throughout the years that Cobbett edited it, up to his death in 1835, it was a paper that could not be ignored. He made it something more than a political review; he made it a great personal force, reflecting the views and prejudices of a journalist who had an incomparable gift for graphic and forthright expression. He wrote a great part of it himself, and every line that he wrote bore the stamp of his unmistakable style. The *Political Register* was Cobbett and Cobbett was the *Political Register*, and it survived his death only two years.

With his paper firmly established, Cobbett was able to realize his dream of living again in the country. The Cobbett who viewed London with loathing as "the Great Wen," the Cobbett of *Rural Rides* who described with such affection and vivid particularity the loveliness of the English scene and wrote so passionately about the economic ills of the countryside—this was the essential Cobbett, deeply-rooted and unchanging amid all the storms and trials, the recklessness and the inconsistencies of his vehement career. When in 1805 he returned to the country to live with his family on a farm that he had bought at Botley in Hampshire, it must have been one of the best moments in his life. It was no longer necessary for him to be in constant attendance at the office; it was his writing that gave the *Political Register* its power and prosperity and this he could do most happily in the country, where his family could grow up amid natural surroundings.

The Radical Cobbett soon emerged and made the *Political Register* the most vigorous, and often the most strident, organ of reform. He had lost his old admiration of Pitt, and now attacked him as the creator of paper money—to Cobbett the prime cause of the many evils that afflicted the country—and after Pitt's death he wrote the first of many bitter post-mortems of public men, arguing that historical truth would go at one sweep if we did not tell the truth about men when they were dead. Thus he harshly dissented from the prevailing sentiment that the loss of Pitt was a subject of regret to the people, and suggested that his death was regretted only by those who looked to him for emoluments—"the numerous swarm of blood-suckers and muckworms" (a phrase borrowed from Lord Chatham). Far from regarding his death as an irreparable loss, the people "express satisfaction at it. . . . They look upon his death as the first dawn of their deliverance from an accumulation of danger and disgrace." Was Cobbett sincere in urging that he wrote this and similar posthumous attacks in the interests of "historical truth," or was he merely employing the familiar technique of shocking the public mind in order to get talked about?

When he was in America he angrily retorted to those who criticized England; now he was beginning to realize that all was not well with his native land, that it was not quite the demi-Eden he had pictured, and he assumed the role of attacker himself. He assailed with especial venom what he called The Thing—the mass of borough-mongers, placemen, sinecurists, pensioners and contractors. What a prosperous country England could be if it rid itself of these tax-eaters! The *Political Register* became the favourite organ of those who wanted to root out political corruption and they kept Cobbett supplied with stories of patronage, jobbery and the like. At one time he was inclined to see in paper money the source of all evils; at another time he asserted that borough-mongering was "the cause of all our calamities and dangers" and exposed the traffic in pocket boroughs as revealed in the "agony columns" of the Press.

When a retired officer, Major Hogan, wrote a pamphlet in 1808 in which he stated that promotion in the Army could be bought and that a certain Mrs. Clarke, the Duke of York's mistress, was getting money by this means, Cobbett at first believed that the charges had no real foundation; but presently, having satisfied himself that the major would be able to make good his case against Mrs. Clarke, he gave much publicity to the scandal, demanding a full investigation. The committee of the House of Commons found the charges proved, and the Duke of York, whom they acquitted by only a small majority of personal corruption, resigned his post as Commander-in-Chief. The Government was gravely embarrassed by the whole affair and showed its displeasure at the freedom with which the Press had commented on it. Shortly afterwards Cobbett gave the offended Government a chance to strike at one of the most troublesome of its critics. Appalled by a report published in the *Courier* in June 1809 that a mutiny at Ely had been suppressed by calling in four squadrons of German Legion Cavalry, that five of the ringleaders had been sentenced to receive five hundred lashes each and that part of the sentence had been carried out, Cobbett wrote an article flaming with wrath and savage irony.

... *Five hundred lashes each!* Aye, that is right! Flog them! flog them! flog them! They deserve a flogging at every meal-time. "Lash them daily! lash them daily!" What! shall the rascals dare to *mutiny?* and that, too, when the German Legion is so near at hand? Lash them! lash them! lash them! They deserve it. Oh, yes! they merit a double-tailed cat! Base dogs! What! mutiny for the *price of a knapsack*? Lash them! flog them! Base rascals! Mutiny for the price of a goat's skin; and then, upon the appearance of the German soldiers, they take the flogging as quietly as so many trunks of trees!

That was strong enough, but Cobbett did not stop there. He reminded his readers that they had been told that Napoleon's lashing and chaining of his soldiers were necessary because the people of France hated him and would willingly arise against him. What, then, would British "loyalists" say now they saw that "our 'gallant defenders' not only require physical restraint, in certain cases, but even a little blood drawn from their backs, and that, too, with the aid and assistance of German troops"? An information was promptly taken out against Cobbett on a charge of sedition. There was, however, a noticeable delay in bringing him up for trial, and a hint was supposed to have been conveyed to him that on giving a promise of good behaviour he would be able to escape the consequences of his offence. It would not have been the first time a Government had adopted this method of persuading a critic to silence himself. Nearly a year later he appeared before Lord Ellenborough and defended himself so maladroitly as to prejudice his case, the jury reaching a verdict of "Guilty" within five minutes. Sentence was postponed and he was out on bail for some days, and this time there were undoubtedly negotiations between him and the Government. For once Cobbett seemed to have completely lost his courage. An unpublished "Farewell Article"—the full text is given in Melville's life of Cobbett—contained the promise, "I never will again, upon any account, indite, publish, write, or contribute towards, any newspaper, or other publication of that nature, so long as I live," and vindicated himself against any charge of desertion. Whose cause had he deserted? he demanded. Not the country's, because the country, by the voice of a jury, had condemned him; not the cause of the Press, for a large part of the Press had fiercely demanded his prosecution. It seems inconceivable that Cobbett should have consented to gag himself, but that he wrote this article is well substantiated. Whether he changed his mind and withdrew his promise or whether the Government decided that in the nature of things such a promise could not stand, it would be fruitless to speculate. The one certainty is that he was called up for judgment and sentenced to two years' imprisonment in Newgate and a fine of £1,000 and ordered to give bail of £3,000 at the end of his term, and also to find two sureties in £1,000 each that he would keep the peace for a further seven years. The printer was sent to prison for three months and the publishers for two months. The Government had gained their revenge, though the sentence was less harsh in its consequences than it would be today, for at that time a prisoner of means could make a convenient arrangement with the head gaoler—at a price—to take apartments in the prison and have his meals brought in; and Cobbett was able to entertain his friends while he was in prison and to conduct his newspaper. During those two years he wrote articles that were as vigorous as ever and did not hesitate to attack the Government. When at the time of the Luddite Riots powers were given to magistrates to search everywhere for arms and to "disarm the people," he made this forthright comment:

DISARM THE PEOPLE! Disarm the people of England! And for WHAT? No matter what. The fact is quite enough. The simple sentence stating this one fact will save foreign statesmen the trouble of making any inquiries relative to the internal state of England. It speaks whole volumes.

The final article he wrote from Newgate was followed by this footnote: "State Prison, Newgate, where I have just paid a thousand pounds fine TO THE KING; and much good may it do his Majesty." The morning after his release *The Times*, one of his favourite targets—his many epithets for that journal included "the bloody old Times" and "That cunning old trout The Times"—greeted him with an attack in which he was described as a double-dealer and quoting, most damagingly, the opening paragraphs of his farewell address. A reproduction of the article in leaflet form was handed to each of the 600 guests at a dinner, presided over by Sir Francis Burdett, given the same evening to celebrate his release.

Britain after Waterloo was beset with financial and economic problems. There had been a huge increase in the National Debt, and Cobbett naïvely urged that it was possible to write down the moral liability of the nation to a fraction of the nominal amount of the debt. Repudiation always has a more engaging form—except to the creditors—when it is called idealism. Cobbett had his own economic troubles, too, for the circulation of the *Political Register*—now 1s. 1½d. a copy because of the stamp duty—was falling off. Somehow the appeal of the paper must be broadened. Acting on a suggestion that he should put the case for reform in a plain statement addressed to the workers, Cobbett wrote an *Address to the Journeymen and Labourers of England, as well as Scotland and Ireland*, which appeared on November 3, 1816. He also issued a cheap edition, from which all the news was omitted; and at the then low price of twopence, with reduced terms for those who wished to buy it in quantities for popular distribution, it had a big sale. Cobbett thus discovered by chance a method of reaching the masses, and thereafter the *Political Register* was issued in two editions. His enemies promptly dubbed the cheap edition "Cobbett's twopenny trash." The circulation rose rapidly and reached over 40,000 a week.

Cobbett now became more than ever a popular leader, and his writings were eagerly read throughout the country. He vigorously advocated reform as the real cure for the evils from which the country was suffering, and by demolishing the arguments of the machine-breakers in *A Letter to the Luddites* he provided a healthy corrective at a time of dangerous popular emotionalism. The authorities immediately took alarm when they saw his cheap paper being widely bought all over the country, and their first reaction—a parallel with Cromwell's time—was to hound down the hawkers who offered it for sale, heavy fines being imposed on them for peddling the paper without a licence. Next the law officers ruled that a justice of the peace might issue a warrant for the arrest of any person found selling Radical literature. *The Times* protested that if the law was as defined it would be impossible to conduct a newspaper except on sufferance, for there was not a single journal that was not obliged, as part of its duty to the public, to publish matter which some aggrieved person would be ready to swear was libellous and upon which he might find magistrates who were willing to commit to prison. The Government soon produced an even more drastic weapon for repressing agitation. The Habeas Corpus Act was suspended in 1817, and henceforth any person who proved troublesome to authority could be imprisoned without trial. Cobbett at once took fright. He believed that the new measure was directly aimed at him and that the Government would find a pretext in his writings to send him to prison. On March 27th, three weeks after the suspension of the Habeas Corpus Act, he left for the United States. He took great precautions to keep his decision to leave the country secret, because he was afraid that his creditors would have him detained; he feared still more that the Government, who had offered to give him compensation if he would cease writing, would arrest him if he refused their offer. In a farewell message to his readers, "Mr. Cobbett's Taking Leave of His Countrymen," he announced that the *Register* would be suspended until he could send copy from America. Publication was resumed within three months, and in some of the earliest contributions written from his place of refuge he exposed the folly of gagging measures adopted by the Government.

Meanwhile the authorities continued their policy of intimidating booksellers and hawkers who offered political pamphlets for sale, but though fines and sentences of imprisonment were imposed here and there magistrates did not make as much use as had been feared of the special powers that had been given to them. Five measures designed to combat the unrest in the country had been passed; now the Government sought for a more effective means of suppressing cheap publications and found it in the Newspaper Stamp Duties Act of 1819, whose avowed purpose was "to restrain the abuses arising from the publication of blasphemous and seditious libels." The Act made more flexible the definition of a newspaper in order to prevent evasion of the fourpenny stamp duty, and provided that all pamphlets or papers issued more than once a month and costing less than sixpence were liable to duty. In justification of this new policy Lord Ellenborough told the House of Lords that it was not against the respectable Press that the Bill was directed but against the pauper Press, which, administering to the passions of the mob, sent forth a continual stream of falsehood and malignity. The last of the "Six Acts" was a death-blow to the cheap Radical papers. Cobbett, who had returned from America after two years' absence, decided to meet the new conditions by publishing an unstamped edition of the *Register* at sixpence, and in 1821 he printed in addition a shilling stamped edition designed to be sent through the post. His mass circulation shrank overnight. Most of the new readers he had attracted were unable to pay sixpence a week and had to club together to buy a copy. In 1820 he started *Cobbett's Evening Post*, but heavy losses forced him to stop publication after three months. An unsuccessful attempt to get into Parliament as the representative of Coventry added to his financial troubles in the same year. He was declared bankrupt, and though his creditors treated him well—to quote his own words—he had to give up his farm. In 1830 he made another bid to secure a wide audience for his political writing by publishing a twopenny monthly, which he entitled *Cobbett's Two-Penny Trash, or, Politics for the Poor*. The introduction is a good specimen of his ability to make direct appeal to the heart and mind of the reader.

1. The object of this publication is, to explain to the people of this kingdom *what it is* that, in spite of all the industry and frugality that they can practise, *keeps them poor.* . . . This *was* the happiest country in the world; it was the country of roast-beef; it *was* distinguished above *all* other nations for the good food, good raiment, and good morals, of its people; and it is now as much distinguished for the contrary of all of them.

2. It is, therefore, to explain to the suffering people at large, the

causes of this lamentable change, that this little cheap work is intended. . . .

In 1831 Cobbett was accused of being an instigator of a rural revolt that led to the burning of ricks and barns in many parts of England. An 18-year-old labourer who was under sentence of death for firing a barn near Battle made a "confession," of which there were several versions, in which he stated that he "never should of thought of douing aney sutch thing if Mr. Cobet had never given aney lectures." Cobbett was actually charged with publishing a libel to incite labourers to acts of violence, and the indictment was based on this extract from an article in the *Political Register* of December 11th concerning the riots:

> Out of evil comes good. We are not, indeed, upon that mere maxim, "to do evil that good may come from it." . . . They have been always told . . . that their acts of violence, and particularly the burnings, can *do them no good*, but *add to their wants*, by destroying the food that *they would have to eat*. Alas! they know better: they know that one thrashing-machine takes wages from ten men; and they know also that *they* should have none of this food; and that *potatoes* and *salt* do not burn! Therefore, this argument is not worth a straw. Besides, they see and feel *that the good comes*, and comes *instantly* too. They see that they *do* get *some* bread, in consequence of the destruction of part of the corn; and while they see this, you attempt in vain to persuade them, that that which they have done is *wrong*.

There was more to the same effect. The Government felt that the language used was sufficiently violent and tendentious to secure a conviction, and Cobbett was tried at the Guildhall in July. But this was a very different Cobbett from the one who had made such an unfavourable impression on the occasion of his first trial. He defended himself with immense effectiveness in a speech that constituted a powerful indictment of the Government.

> What are the heinous sins I have committed? Calling upon the Government to repeal the hard-hearted laws—the hard-hearted laws

that drive the labourers of the country to desperation. Let them do away with the old Game Laws and with the new Game Laws. Can you conceive of anything more horrible? ... They are now reforming the Parliament. Many writers have been urging the necessity of Parliamentary reform. I am one. They have lately found out, for it is a late discovery, what sort of reform they must have, and it is very like that I have for twenty years recommended. They are compelled to adopt it, though they do not like it. They are going to be married to this reform. They are going to be married in a halter. I furnished that halter, and for that they would cut me in pieces. ... If I am compelled to meet death in some stinking dungeon into which they have the means of cramming me, my last breath shall be employed in praying to God to bless my country, and to curse the Whigs to everlasting; and revenge I bequeath to my children and to the labourers of England.

Melodramatic stuff, but the age itself was raw and melodramatic. Cobbett had a useful witness in Lord Brougham, one of the Whig ministers, who agreed that, as president of the Society for the Diffusion of Useful Knowledge, he had written to Cobbett during the disturbances to ask for permission to reprint and distribute his *Letter to the Luddites*, which expressly condemned machine-breaking. The jury, after deliberating all night, failed to reach agreement, six being for acquittal and six against, and the proceedings were allowed to lapse. Cobbett died in 1835.

A less virile personality, but one who was nevertheless courageously outspoken at times, was Leigh Hunt (1784–1859)— poet, essayist, critic and journalist. In 1808 he became editor of his brother John's *Examiner*, a quarto-size Sunday paper of "Politics, Domestic Economy, and Theatricals." It was an interestingly written paper, challenging in tone, and its scope was wider than the sub-title suggests. The issue for March 22, 1812, in which appeared an article that cost the brothers two years' imprisonment, consisted of sixteen pages, and the contents included a five-page report of Parliament, extracts from the *London Gazette*, editorial articles, many news paragraphs, comments on the opera and on pictures exhibited at the London Institution, a letter from "A Constant Reader" (already embarked on his ubiquitous activities), a report of a speech on the East India Charter and a half-page report—with editorial comment—on two executions. The first article was headed "The Prince on St. Patrick's Day," and it was stated that at the annual St. Patrick's Day the toast of "The Health of the Prince Regent" was "drunk with partial applause, and *loud and reiterated hisses*" and that Sheridan's championship of the Prince as "unchangeably true" to his principles was received with loudly expressed disapproval. The article, after contemptuous reference to the "sickening adulation" of the Prince Regent in the *Morning Post*, went on:

What person, unacquainted with the true state of the case, would imagine, in reading these astounding eulogies, that this *"Glory of the People"* was the subject of millions of shrugs and reproaches!—that this *"Protector of the Arts"* had named a wretched foreigner his historical painter, in disparagement or in ignorance of the merits of his own countrymen!—that this *"Mecœnas of the Age"* patronized not a single deserving writer!—that this *"Breather of eloquence"* could not say a few decent extempore words—if we are to judge, at least, from what he said to his regiment on its departure for Portugal!—that this *"Conqueror of hearts"* was the disappointer of hopes!—that this *"Exciter of desire"* (bravo! Messieurs of the *Post*!)—this *"Adonis in loveliness"* was a corpulent man of fifty!—in short, that this *delightful, blissful, wise, pleasurable, honourable, virtuous, true*, and *immortal* prince, was a violator of his word, a libertine over head and ears in disgrace, a despiser of domestic ties, the companion of gamblers and demireps, a man who has just closed half a century without one single claim on the gratitude of his country, or the respect of posterity!

Four years earlier the Hunts had been threatened with an action for libel in respect of a long article on "Military Depravity" which charged that the Army had been grossly mismanaged under the Duke of York, but the case never came into court; in 1809, in an article entitled "Change of Ministry," Leigh Hunt had caustically observed, "Of all monarchs since the Revolution the successor of George III will have the finest opportunity of becoming nobly popular," and with his brother was proceeded against for seditious libel and found not guilty; and in 1811 the brothers, more fortunate than Cobbett, were acquitted on an indictment for reprinting from the *Stamford News* an article condemning flogging in the Army. The attack on the Prince Regent was so offensive that the result of the subsequent proceedings in 1813 could never have been in doubt. The brothers were fined £500 each and sent to prison for two years—Leigh to Horsemonger Lane and John to Coldbath Fields. It was a mild sort of imprisonment; they continued to edit and manage their paper and Leigh Hunt regularly entertained his friends, among his visitors being Lord Byron, the Lambs, Thomas Moore and Jeremy Bentham. At the doctor's suggestion he was removed to the infirmary, where (as he tells us in his autobiography) he had a private apartment which he "turned into a noble room."

I papered the walls with a trellis of roses; I had the ceiling coloured with clouds and sky; the barred windows I covered with Venetian blinds; and when my bookcases were set up with their busts, and flowers and a pianoforte made their appearance, perhaps there was not a handsomer room on that side of the water. . . . Charles Lamb declared there was no other such room, except in a fairy tale. But I possessed another surprise; which was a garden. . . . Here I wrote and read in fine weather, sometimes under an awning. In autumn, my trellises were hung with scarlet runners, which added to the flowery investment. I used to shut my eyes in my armchair, and affect to think myself hundreds of miles off.

Three years after starting the *Examiner* the brothers Hunt founded the *Reflector*, a quarterly which made only four appearances. In later life Leigh Hunt conducted single-handed the *Tatler* (1830–1832), a four-page folio daily periodical dealing with literature and the theatre—"the work, slight as it looked, nearly killed me; for it never prospered beyond the coterie of playgoing readers"—and adopted the title of *London Journal* for a miscellany of essays, criticisms and passages from books which ceased publication "after attaining the size of a goodly folio double volume."

The figures of Wilkes and Cobbett, both larger than life, stand out boldly in the struggle for the freedom of expression, but lesser men played the decisive part in the final battle. In the years of civil disturbance that followed Waterloo authority sought to curb sedition by placing new restrictions on the Press, as already described. Scores of prosecutions were instituted for libel, blasphemy, and defamation of the King and his ministers, and many offenders were severely punished. Some of the Radical publications were viciously irresponsible and made attempts to promote sedition that could not have escaped prosecution at any period of our history; but the Government was badly frightened and struck without discrimination at its enemies in the Press, and this violently oppressive policy had the effect of provoking obstinate and even heroic resistance. The story is told fully in Mr. William H. Wickwar's *The Struggle for the Freedom of the Press 1819–1832*: here only the main events can be given.

What impresses one most in studying this stormy period of journalistic history is that so many obscure men, mostly without means and without influence, should have faced so stout-heartedly the prospect of almost certain punishment. Not more than a small proportion of them can be honestly called little Hampdens; some of them were coarse and venomous, men without a shred of principle, reckless inciters of murder and rebellion; a few were mere pedlars of vulgar blasphemies and coarse libels; but when every discount has been made the fact remains that a large number of persons—journalists, publishers, printers, booksellers, assistants and volunteers—resisted persecution with a courage and tenacity that wore down and ultimately discredited the policy of repression. Consider the punishment inflicted on some of the more obscure offenders. Joseph Swann, a hat-maker, was sentenced at Chester to a total of four and a half years' imprisonment for seditious conspiracy, blasphemous libel and seditious libel; Gilbert Macleod, editor and publisher of the *Spirit of the Union*, a Glasgow Radical paper, was sentenced to transportation for five years for seditious propaganda; two successive publishers of the *Manchester Observer* were sent to prison for twelve months. In the five years from 1819 to 1824 scores of men and women were sentenced to imprisonment or fines, or both, for printing, publishing or distributing publications that were held to be libellous or seditious.

The men whom successive Governments feared most of all were Cobbett, Thomas Jonathan Wooler (a printer by trade, whose *Black Dwarf*, which had titular imitators in the *Yellow Dwarf* and the *White Dwarf*, was a vigorously conducted Radical weekly that for a time vied with Cobbett's *Political Register* for popularity), William Hone and Richard Carlile. Wooler did not write his articles but set them up in type. When he was prosecuted on two charges of libel arising out of an article in the tenth number of the *Black Dwarf* (1817), he was convicted on one count, but a new trial was ordered because there was a question about the unanimity of the verdict. At the second trial he made the novel plea that he could not be said to have written articles that he set up in type without a manuscript. The jury worried over this interesting point and were unable to agree upon a verdict.

Hone, an antiquarian bookseller who issued a twopenny weekly called the *Reformist's Register* that did not last long, had a gift for parody that got him into trouble but at the same time made authority look ridiculous. When he produced a parody of the Anglican Catechism, Litany and Creed as a humorous attack on three Cabinet ministers (Lord Chancellor Eldon and Lords Castlereagh and Sidmouth), informations were filed for blasphemous libel. Unable to give the required bail he was imprisoned and his trial did not come on until several months later —in December 1817. Hone effectively defended himself and lightened the proceedings by quoting parodies by George Canning, Church dignitaries and others which had escaped punishment. He was acquitted three times, to the complete discomfiture of the Attorney-General who had imprudently laid the informations. Hone received a magnificent advertisement. He published reports of his trials, which ran into numerous editions, and he sold nearly 100,000 copies of his parodies; a dinner was given in his honour, and he was presented with £3,000 raised by public subscription.

The most resolute, the most fanatical, of all the champions of free expression was Richard Carlile (1790–1843), who with his family and his staff suffered constant and savage persecution. He was born at Ashburton in Devon, worked in a druggist's shop as a boy of 12 and then took up tinplate working, at which he was employed—latterly in London—until the age of 27. There is a flavour of Cobbett in his reminiscences of his early struggles:

> I was a regular, active, and industrious man, working early and late. . . . Many a day I have breakfasted early, gone to the shop with a sixpence in my pocket for a dinner, worked hard all day, eaten nothing, and carried home a sixpenny publication to read at night.

Short time made him look round for some other employment, and he began selling Wooler's *Black Dwarf*. He met W. T. Sherwin, a young man who had recently started a weekly that he first called the *Republican* and then *Sherwin's Weekly Political Register*. Sherwin planned to limit his liability. He wanted someone to take the risk of publishing and Carlile, whose subsequent career suggested that he was almost without fear, agreed to do the publishing and to pay a rent of £3 a month for the shop. He got into trouble almost at once. Hone had recently suppressed his parodies on receiving complaint about them, not having any blasphemous intentions; and Carlile, apparently without Hone's authority, defied the Attorney-General by republishing them. He was arrested and committed to King's Bench Prison, not being able to furnish bail, and remained there for ten weeks awaiting his trial, being released when Hone was acquitted. Unsubdued by his first taste of imprisonment, Carlile willingly co-operated in making *Sherwin's Weekly Political Register* a determinedly Radical paper and in challenging the law by publishing extracts from Thomas Paine's *The Rights of Man*, for disseminating which the author, now in France, had been found guilty by a jury. Carlile next produced a half-crown edition of

The Rights of Man, as well as a two-volume reprint of Paine's political works which he sold for a pound. Still the Government refrained from taking action, probably because their humiliating failure in the Hone trials had made them wary. The Press was left almost entirely alone in 1818, despite instigations to rebellion in the more irresponsible Radical journals. But this was only a pause, for in 1819 there were to be more prosecutions than in any other year.

January 1819 saw the opening by Carlile of a dilapidated shop at No. 55, Fleet Street—an address which he was to make notorious in the coming years. Encouraged by the immunity from prosecution which he had enjoyed for a time, he planned to push the sales of Paine's writings—for Paine to him was the greatest moral and political teacher who had ever lived. "My whole and sole object, from first to last . . . has been a Free Press and Free Discussion," Carlile wrote later. "When I first started as a hawker of pamphlets I knew nothing of political principles, I had never read a page of Paine's writings; but I had a complete conviction that there was something wrong somewhere, and that the right application of the printing-press was the remedy."

When he published Paine's *Age of Reason* his watchful enemies were quick to strike. In January 1819 two prosecutions were started against him and then the Society for the Suppression of Vice obtained a warrant against him for having sold Paine's *Theological Works*. He was imprisoned in Newgate, whence he was released on bail a few days later. Months passed before he came up for trial, and in the meantime the number of indictments against him had grown and included one for seditious libel in respect of a report of the "Manchester Massacre" published in *Sherwin's Register*. Subsequently he took over the editorship of this paper and gave it back its original name—the *Republican*.

Carlile came up for trial in October and after three days was found guilty on the first indictment, which charged him with republishing the *Age of Reason*, and the following day another verdict of "Guilty" was returned against him, this time for publishing Palmer's *Principles of Nature*. The trials aroused immense popular interest and were reported at length in the newspapers. Ten thousand copies were sold of *The First Day's Proceedings of the Mock Trial*. The circulation of the *Republican* rose sharply, and there was a rush to buy the publications offered for sale at 55, Fleet Street. Carlile was unable to provide the heavy bail demanded—£4,000—and remained in prison until judgment was pronounced a month later. The sentence was cruelly severe—two years' imprisonment and a fine of £1,000 for publishing the *Age of Reason*; one year's imprisonment and a £500 fine for publishing the *Principles of Nature*; and in addition he was ordered to provide security, £1,000 and two others in £100 each, that he would be on good behaviour for the term of his natural life. Such was the punishment for something that would not even constitute an offence today. His shop was closed and the stock of 70,000 publications seized. Carlile saw what lay behind this seizure. The Government had rendered it impossible for him to pay the fines and could thus keep him in prison indefinitely. On their part the authorities no doubt thought that no penalties could be too harsh against a man who had published such comments as these on the "Battle of Peterloo" in the *Republican*:

Let every man be prepared to sell his life as dearly as possible, and I'll pledge mine that we can beat off all the combined yeomanry cavalry of the whole country. In this country under the present state of things, I will never attend a public meeting on any political question of Reform without arms.

One month has now elapsed since the peaceable inhabitants were indiscriminately massacred and murdered by the drunken and furious Yeomanry Cavalry, set on by the Magistrates of that town to perform the horrid deed.

Strangely enough, Carlile was never tried for his inflammatory writings in the *Republican*. It was the men and women who sold the paper who were prosecuted, and it was for this offence that Jane Carlile, who had reopened her husband's shop, was indicted in 1820. On a charge of selling a number of the *Republican* which held that it was legal to destroy tyrants, described the majority of the present ministers as tyrants and recommended assassination, she was sent to join her husband in prison at Dorchester and remained there until 1823. Carlile's sister Mary Ann took over the management of the shop and the publications, and about a year later she was prosecuted in her turn, the indictment being for selling *An Appendix to Paine's Theological Works*. The punishment was out of all proportion to the offence—a year's imprisonment, a fine of £500 and sureties for good behaviour (£1,000 and two others in £100 each), with an order that imprisonment was to continue until payment of the fine and provision of the sureties.

Three members of the Carlile family were now lodged in Dorchester gaol, but though the *Republican* suspended publication for a time the shop continued to remain open, and the authorities—abetted by prosecuting societies which were then active—were goaded into vindictive fury against the obstinate rebels, mostly volunteers, who carried on. When several assistants had been sentenced to terms of imprisonment ranging from six weeks to two years, books that had been made the subject of prosecution were sold from behind a screen on which was a dial giving the titles of the publications. The purchaser turned the hand of the dial to the title of the book that he required and deposited his money on receiving his purchase through a hole in the screen. The purpose of this device was to conceal the identity of the person who sold the book. More salesmen were sent to prison, but still volunteers came forward. Eventually, in 1824, nine assistants were brought up for trial at once and the sentences ranged up to three years' imprisonment. The *Morning Chronicle*, commenting on the trial, concluded by looking forward "to the closing of the shop in Fleet Street as a matter of course." In the next issue of the *Republican* Carlile retorted: "THE SHOP IN FLEET STREET WILL NOT BE CLOSED AS A MATTER OF COURSE, nor closed at all." Not long afterwards there was a fire at the shop, which was demolished to give a view of St. Bride's Church: St. Bride's Avenue now stands on the site. When asked to dispose of the house Carlile insisted on his release as one of the conditions, and Sir Robert Peel was approached in the matter. In 1825, after six years' imprisonment, Carlile was once more a free man, the fines and the securities for good behaviour having been remitted.

In January 1831, as the result of an article in the *Prompter*, a weekly which he had recently started, Carlile again stood trial. The subject of the article was the rural disorders, and Carlile was indicted for incitement to acts of violence. In his defence he argued that the whole of his crime was sympathy for suffering humanity. "If there has been an absence of laws for protection with regard to one part of the people, you cannot justify putting the laws in force on the other side, even supposing illegalities committed." He was sentenced to two years' imprisonment, to pay a fine of £200 and to provide security, but he was let out unconditionally after serving eight months of his sentence. Carlile got into trouble again in 1834 as a result of a provocative exhibition at a new shop he had opened at 62, Fleet Street. He refused to pay Church rates and his goods were seized. His resentment at this action was expressed by removing the two first-floor windows and exhibiting in one effigies of a bishop and the devil arm in arm ("Spiritual Brokers") and in the other an effigy of a distraining officer ("Temporal Broker"), another bold placard proclaiming that they were "Props of the Church." Crowds flocked to Fleet Street and obstructed the traffic. He was again prosecuted and sentenced to pay a fine of 40s. and provide sureties of £200 for good behaviour; but rather than find sureties he elected to go to prison for three years.

Richard Carlile is no subject for blind hero-worship, but his place in the history of British journalism is secure. It was his unbreakable spirit that discredited the policy of savage and indiscriminate persecution. Altogether he served over nine years' imprisonment. No one else made comparable sacrifices for the cause of free discussion—except those who, having nothing to gain in any form, suffered vindictive punishment for supporting him. No ordinary man and no ordinary cause could have commanded the loyalty of so many brave people.

The passing of the Reform Bill produced a change of political atmosphere in the country. Advocacy of violent measures began to ebb when it was realized that a more liberal spirit was emerging in public life and that progress could be achieved by constitutional means. Prosecutions of the Press almost ceased. Ministers began to see the folly of making martyrs and, in the words of one Attorney-General, providing political libellers with "the valuable advertisement of a public trial." Wiser leaders saw that toleration, however irksome, was essential to promote the return of sanity in national life.

The authorities had one very troublesome rebel to deal with in the 'thirties who refused to stamp the various papers that he produced—Henry Hetherington (1792–1849), a printer and bookseller. Best known of his journals was the *Poor Man's Guardian*, a weekly edited and printed by him and (as boldly stated in the heading) "Established, contrary to 'Law,' to try the power of 'Might' against 'Right.' " A pictorial device at the right of the title embodied a printing press and the motto "Liberty of the Press." The first number devoted nearly three pages to a report of an appeal by Hetherington "against a conviction obtained by the Commissioners of Stamps before the PAID Magistrates at Bow-street Police Office." The appeal, which he lost, was in respect of a paper called the *Republican*. No. 82 of the *Poor Man's Guardian* (December 29, 1832) contained an article headed "Persecution of H. Hetherington," and this extract is typical of his disrespect for authority:

You will see by our Bow Street news, that two informations were heard *exparte*, last week, (Friday the 21st) against Mr. Hetherington, "for printing and publishing an unstamped paper called the *Poor Man's Guardian*." Mr. H. having the fear of God, but not of Sir F. Roe, before his eyes, and thinking his time better employed in diffusing cheap knowledge among the people, than in pleading guilty to such diffusion, before a set of grovelling fellows in Bow Street, *did not obey the summons*. The result is, that two convictions were obtained in his absence, and he has now the choice either to pay the penalty of £20 each, *which he never will,* or going to gaol for twelve months, to live with thieves and vagabonds, which, in like manner, he will decline *if he can.*

The report of the proceedings in the same issue included this: "Mr. Thomas James, of 16, Gloucester Street, Hoxton, proved the purchase of two copies. (This fellow looked quite ashamed of his job.)" Hetherington was sent to Clerkenwell gaol for six months, followed by another six months' imprisonment when he defied the law by continuing to issue his paper unstamped. He was a bravely obstinate man: his press and type were smashed with hammers, his property was seized and his shop assistants were imprisoned, but he continued to publish the *Poor Man's Guardian* and had the enthusiastic—and ingenious—aid of many volunteers in distributing it.

Hetherington was again prosecuted in 1834—this time in respect of a new paper, the *Destructive and Poor Man's Conservative*, as well as the *Guardian*. He was fined £120 for publishing the former journal but acquitted on the other charge, thus scoring a victory that freed political sheets from the stamp duty. He proudly announced in No. 159 of the *Poor Man's Guardian*: "This paper, after sustaining a persecution of three years and a half duration, in which upwards of five hundred persons were imprisoned for vending it, was declared in the Court of Exchequer to be a strictly legal publication."

CHAPTER EIGHT

The Independent Newspaper Emerges

IN the early years of the nineteenth century newspapers were beginning to free themselves from financial dependence on the Government. The great expansion of industry and commerce brought about an increase in the volume of advertising, and once they had built up a good revenue from this source newspapers no longer required subsidies, either direct or indirect, and could break free from official influence.

The development of *The Times* under John Walter II and Thomas Barnes illustrates how this important transition came about. Ten years after the founding of the paper the first John Walter handed over the direction to his son William, who revealed talent neither for editing nor for management. Some years later John Walter thought of stopping the paper, seeing no prospect of getting it on to a prosperous footing. His son John, who had come into the office in 1797 at the age of 21, persuaded him to give the paper another chance. He took over control in 1803 and within ten years, by skilful editing and shrewd management, he had turned it into a sound journalistic property. But his father was not primarily interested in the paper, and he showed displeasure at the way in which this transformation in its fortunes had been achieved. He had two grievances—he did not like the fact that his son had put *The Times* first and neglected the printing and bookselling side, which in the view of John Walter I was a safer business than a daily newspaper could possibly be; and he disapproved of his son's independent attitude to the Government. Three years after gaining control John Walter II had signalized the new policy of independence by breaking away from the influence of the Addingtons. *The Times* could no longer be bought. Thereafter he firmly pursued an independent line, and

THE INDEPENDENT NEWSPAPER EMERGES

the paper began to rise in public esteem. But what recommended *The Times* to more and more readers was not merely the new editorial freedom: it was now a better written and a more complete and enterprising paper. Walter engaged new men to strengthen the editorial staff, and one of them was Henry Crabb Robinson, who also acted in 1807 as a foreign correspondent on the Continent.

About this time Walter was engaged in a strenuous battle with the vested interests at the General Post Office which claimed and profitably enforced a monopoly right in foreign news. Newspaper proprietors were required to pay one hundred guineas a year for summary translations from the Continental journals that arrived twice a week, and it was notorious that certain papers bribed officials to secure priority in the receipt of important news. Walter, aiming to be first with the news, had his own correspondents abroad and used the summaries only for checking purposes. Post Office clerks sought to foil his enterprise by delaying and sometimes opening letters addressed to *The Times*, and Walter countered this by having the correspondence addressed to merchants' offices. At one time (1805) officials boarded the ships arriving at Gravesend with papers and seized packets addressed to *The Times*, and when it was pointed out that other papers had been allowed to pass without interference the Secretary to the Postmaster-General replied that this was a favour limited to those who supported the Government. In July 1807 *The Times* had to pay £200 and make an apology for publishing an article exposing "the unwarrantable proceedings" of the Post Office and suggesting that the Secretary and the Comptroller of the Foreign Department were participating in the profits. Three weeks later *The Times* devoted a whole page to a plain account of Post Office practices, and the Attorney-General, to whose notice the article was brought, decided that no proceedings should be taken against the paper.

When the first John Walter died in 1812 he left only a three-sixteenths interest in *The Times* to the son who had been responsible for the great change in the prosperity of the journal; on the other hand, he made him sole owner of the printing business. One result was that John Walter II in future gave more attention to the development of the latter, and his enterprise in conducting it founded the reputation of *The Times* as a pioneer in printing methods. In 1814 the paper installed the first steam-driven press, built by Frederic Koenig and Andrew Bauer; in 1827, under William Cowper and Ambrose Applegarth, it installed a new machine with four cylinders that printed 4,000 sheets an hour from flat formes; and in 1847 (the year that John Walter II died) the first rotary press was invented in its office by Applegarth. The change-over in 1814 took place secretly because of the fear of machine-breaking. There had been a demonstration by compositors who realized that there would be less demand for their labour when it was no longer necessary to set the pages in duplicate. On the first night Walter personally organized the printing on the steam presses; meanwhile the men who had threatened mischief had been told to wait to deal with expected news from the Continent. Just before 6 a.m. Walter came in and announced to the waiting men, "*The Times* is already printed—by steam." He promised to continue the payment of wages to every compositor until suitable employment was found. In the issue for November 29th *The Times* published an article describing the new method as "the greatest improvement connected with printing since the discovery of the art itself." The new system of machinery was "almost organic" and performed its complicated acts "with such a velocity and simultaneousness of movement that no less than eleven hundred sheets are impressed in one hour."

John Walter II's biggest problem was to find an editor. To edit and manage *The Times* single-handed was a heavy task even for a man of his energy. In 1808 he appointed Crabb Robinson, who had to interrupt his duties to go to Corunna to do special correspondence; but Robinson had no gift for editing and gave up the position in the following year, when Walter again became the editor. Among those he engaged as special contributors was Edward Sterling, who wrote for *The Times* from 1812 to 1840.

It was his use on one occasion of the Olympian phrase "We thundered forth the other day" that earned the nickname of "The Thunderer" for *The Times*. In 1814 Walter found an editor and principal leader-writer in John Stoddart, D.C.L.—but an editor who was to give him many uncomfortable moments. Stoddart had a violent, abusive style of leader-writing that irritated many of his readers: someone said of the paper that it had become a magazine of curses. Walter was continually appealing to him to write with more moderation, but Stoddart could not be persuaded to be reasonable.

A few years earlier Thomas Barnes, just down from Cambridge, had begun to work for *The Times*. In 1810 he served as dramatic critic and in the following year he joined the Parliamentary staff, and he also worked in the editorial department. He was a friend of Leigh Hunt and Charles Lamb and contributed to the former's *Examiner*. Walter decided in 1815 that he must have a new editor, for in that year—Crabb Robinson's *Diary* tells us—he authorized Barnes to revise and correct the manuscript of Dr. Stoddart's leading articles. Barnes left out so many of his articles in 1816 that the doctor complained to Walter that his influence in *The Times* was declining almost to nothing. In December he was informed that the paper would have no further use for his services after the end of the year. Walter was in no great hurry to make another appointment, experience having shown the wisdom of extreme caution. It was not until the Autumn of 1817 that he decided to promote Barnes, who became editor at the age of 32, having been born in the same year as *The Times*. The paper was still publishing only four-page issues, as in 1785, but the sale had now reached 7,000 (at sevenpence a copy), or about four times the sale at the time that the second John Walter assumed control.

The new editor, in contrast to the old, was a man who shared the more liberal ideas that were beginning to gain ground in the country. After two years Walter was satisfied that he had at last found a man of character and balanced judgment to conduct *The Times* sanely and responsibly, and felt himself free to take up the life of a country gentleman and leave Barnes in charge of the paper; and he formally transferred to him his salary of £1,000 a year. Barnes, with more freedom than was enjoyed by most editors in those days, rose to the height of his opportunity. He occupied the editorial chair for nearly a quarter of a century, and during that period he developed *The Times* into a powerful independent journal, far ahead of its contemporaries in circulation and influence.

The new liberal attitude of *The Times* was evident in the comments which it made on the "Battle of Peterloo." The incident which has gone into the history books under this name occurred at a meeting held at St. Peter's Field, Manchester, on August 16, 1819. *The Times*, anticipating disturbances, had urged that the meeting should not be held. However, 30,000 people collected to listen to a speech by Henry Hunt, a Radical reformer (no relation of the Hunt brothers who conducted the *Examiner*). The magistrates, foiled in their attempt to arrest Hunt, ordered a regiment of cavalry to take action against the crowd. The consequences were tragic: eleven persons were killed and sixty or more injured. A seven-column account of the affair appeared in *The Times*, which commented on "the dreadful fact, that nearly a hundred of the King's unarmed subjects have been sabred by a body of cavalry in the streets of a town in which most of them were inhabitants, and in the presence of those Magistrates whose sworn duty it is to protect and preserve the life of the meanest Englishman." The inquests on the victims were reported at length.

In the same year *The Times* argued firmly against the restrictions on the Press that formed part of the repressive legislation known as the "Six Acts." It took the popular side when it gave support to Queen Caroline, and the circulation soared during her trial. Crabb Robinson cautiously notes in his diary: "I have no doubt W. [Walter] really thinks he is doing right . . . but he is not aware perhaps how much he is influenced in the line he is pursuing by finding that since the trial the sale of the paper has risen from 7 to more than 15,000." The office of the *Morning*

Post, which opposed the Queen, "became the object of a furious attack by the mob, who collected in front of it, yelling like savages; they drew up before the façade a huge cart filled with stones and brickbats with which they smashed all the windows they could reach and battered the walls."[1] The *Morning Post*, regarded by the Anti-Jacobins as a subversive journal, had changed sides under the editorship of Nicholas Byrne, who bought the paper from Stuart in 1803. The centenary number (November 2, 1872) records that Byrne aroused much political hostility and that his life "was twice attempted, and on the second occasion with lamentable success. One winter's night, or rather morning, nearly forty years ago, when Mr. Byrne was sitting alone in his office, a man entered unchallenged from the street, and made his way to his room. He wore a crape mask, and rushing upon his victim stabbed him twice with a dagger. Mr. Byrne, though mortally wounded, gave the alarm, and managed to follow his assailant to the street, but he escaped in the darkness of the night, and was never brought to justice." Byrne did not die shortly afterwards, as this account suggests, but some months later. The only reference made to his death in the *Morning Post* was this simple announcement in the issue for June 28, 1833: "DIED—Yesterday, June 27, after an illness of many months, in his 72nd year, N. Byrne, Esq., of Lancaster-place."

Barnes made *The Times* the interpreter of public opinion. He was probably one of the first editors to organize the collection of information on what various classes of people were thinking about. He appointed correspondents throughout the country, and their reports enabled him to detect any changes in public sentiment. Always shrewdly informed about the real opinion in the country on particular measures and policies, Barnes made *The Times* increasingly the voice of the nation. He developed the leading article into a powerful instrument for guiding as well as expressing public opinion, and he encouraged readers to contribute their personal views in the form of letters, thus establishing what has since become one of the most inter-

[1] *Gossip of the Century* (Julia C. Byrne).

esting and valuable departments of the paper. Under Barnes *The Times* assumed the distinctive character which it has ever since jealously guarded—that of an independent, responsible, impersonal national institution. No mention of the editor's name ever appeared in its columns, for Barnes recognized the power of dignified anonymity, but everyone who mattered in public life knew him: "Why, Barnes is the most powerful man in the country," declared the Lord Chancellor (Lord Lyndhurst) on one occasion. His achievement lay in the fact that he moulded the paper into a forceful organ that spoke for the nation, and it became a matter of course for people interested in public affairs to turn to its leading article each day to see what *The Times* had to say on the subject of the hour.

The liberal outlook of Barnes led him to support Catholic emancipation. He was also a strong advocate of reform, which he supported with such urgency that many people found *The Times* dangerously Radical on this subject. In the issue for January 29, 1831, the paper said that "unless the people—the people everywhere—come forward and petition, ay, thunder for reform, it is they who abandon an honest Minister—it is *not* the Minister who betrays the people. But in that case, reform, and Minister, and people too, are lost." Henry Brougham (later Lord Brougham), long a friend of Barnes, was said to have inspired this particular line of argument.

The growing independence of the Press was resented by the Government, which in 1834 sought to manage the newspapers. Thomas Drummond, secretary to Lord Althorp, the Whig leader of the House of Commons, was the selected instrument for the purpose. In its issue of December 22, 1834, *The Times* frankly exposed this latest attempt to make the Press subservient to the Government:

> For some time before the dissolution of the Ministry a kind of inquisition was instituted to take secret cognizance of the political heresies of the newspaper press, and to persecute the authors by damaging their publications by various contrivances. Our power enabled us to defy such arts, but we fear that a portion of the inde-

pendent press must have felt the workings of an untraced and unseen enmity.

A few months earlier Lord Althorp had written a note to Brougham, then Lord Chancellor, asking him to call on him at Downing Street. When Brougham, who was heavily pressed at the time, sent back to inquire whether the matter was urgent, the messenger was dispatched with a second note. This was passed up to Brougham while he was sitting on the Bench in the Court of Chancery. This was what Althorp wrote:

Private
My dear Brougham,
    The subject I want to talk to you about is the State of the Press, & whether we should declare open war with The Times or attempt to make peace.
Yours most truly,
ALTHORP.

Brougham rather casually tore up the note and dropped the pieces into a wastepaper basket, and after he had left the court some curious person extracted the pieces, stuck them on a sheet of paper and addressed them to the editor of *The Times*, with this marginal note on the sheet: "Picked up by a Friend and sent thinking it may be of service as a private principle of action." Barnes acted at once by writing this letter to Le Marchant, Brougham's secretary (with a note at the head, "Show this to the Lord Chancellor"):

June 11th, 1834.

My dear Sir,
    I told you I would always treat you frankly: and in that spirit I think it right to say that I am aware of Lord Althorp's application to the Chancellor for his opinion whether "the Govt. should declare war with The Times or attempt to make peace." What does the Gaby mean?
Yours ever,
T. BARNES.

Writing to him again two days later, Barnes added this postscript: "I ought to mention that your friends should be cautious about their letters. Fragments are picked up by a set of hangers-on of the Press. Luckily they have fallen into safe hands: but they might have been taken to some of the slanderous Sunday Papers."

An attempt was now being made to revive the influence of the *Morning Chronicle*, which had been outstripped by *The Times*. A few weeks after the incident of the Althorp letter the *Morning Chronicle* published a series of letters signed "Vindex," obviously written or inspired by Brougham, which Barnes interpreted as the opening of an attack upon him. Not many days before he had assured Le Marchant that "the greatest pain which I can contemplate would be that which I should suffer if I were ever called upon to admit one word in the Paper which . . . could occasion him [the Lord Chancellor] a moment's personal annoyance," and he had been loth to criticize the Poor Law Bill, which he much disliked, for the reason that Brougham was the main instigator of it. Now he turned round suddenly, and there was a harsh rasp in the comments made by *The Times* (July 19, 1834) on Brougham's handling of the Coercion Bill:

> We will venture to say that an inconsistency so palpable—that a levity of political principle so all but preternatural—that a forgetfulness of everything like public decency so wonderful, has never before been exhibited by any man conscious of being exposed to the observation of his fellows, and to the moral and social consequences of his own actions.

This was very much in the emphatic manner of the eighteen-thirties, but as Barnes pursued the attack in subsequent issues he made use of other and coarser controversial weapons that were also very much in the mode then. Brougham was a brilliant, energetic but vain man whom few men in public life trusted and who was generally disliked, but that did not justify the description of him by *The Times* as a mountebank and miserable trickster and the accusation of drunkenness and conspiracy and the sug-

THE INDEPENDENT NEWSPAPER EMERGES

gestion that he was going out of his mind. A few years later the *Morning Chronicle*—once elegantly described by *The Times* as "that squirt of filthy water"—accused its contemporary not very convincingly of falsifying a report of a dinner at which Brougham gave a toast. The editorial exchange over this incident was only too typical of the journalistic manners of the age:

We have looked in vain to *The Times* for some apology for the flagrant misrepresentation of the toast given at the dinner to the London Reform Almshouses—namely, the substitution of "The health of Daniel O'Connell, Esq. *redresser* of the grievances of Ireland," for "Daniel O'Connell, Esq.; and redress of the wrongs of Ireland and happiness to her people." This misrepresentation could not be accidental, and it argues consummate depravity in that perpetrator. The man who would be guilty of it, only does not pick pockets because it is less safe.—*Morning Chronicle*, June 10, 1835.

THE "LIBERAL" LIARS. A disgraceful morning print, which, made up of such contributions as the licentiousness and the leisure of stock-jobbers may furnish, actually feeds on falsehoods and lies so largely day by day that one might think in its case "increase of appetite had grown by what it fed on," has in its impression of yesterday the following:—"*The Times* and Lord Brougham.—*The Times* makes a very lame excuse for its conduct in falsifying the toast given by Lord Brougham at the Almshouses dinner on Saturday last." Our readers know well enough that *The Times* made no excuse in the matter, and that *The Times* merely demonstrated the malignity of the lie about "falsifying," &c. by stating that the report of the dinner was copied from the "Observer." . . . Surely the people who have been picked up to do this sort of dirty work, which no newspapers, not even the most infamous, ever did before, will see upon reflection that even sweeping crossings is a cleaner, and likely to be a more lasting, occupation, than the filthy trade they have embarked in. . . . For the future, we shall not condescend to notice these persons; because we cannot help feeling that the respectable part of the community must be shocked to know that there are such beings as these scribblers *out of the tread-mill*, and because every exposure of the ragamuffins gives foreigners the additional proof that there has crept into the press of this country a number of scoundrels, who are not only unfit for the society of gentlemen, but who would be a disgrace to the vilest *coteries* in Europe.—*The Times*, June 13, 1835.

The new and decisive influence of *The Times* was dramatically recognized when the new administration was in process of formation in 1834. Charles Greville, Clerk to the Privy Council, suggested to the Duke of Wellington and to Lord Lyndhurst (the new Lord Chancellor) that it would be very advisable to obtain the support of *The Times* if that could be done. Wellington seemed favourably disposed and Lyndhurst said that he desired nothing so much as an understanding with *The Times* but did not like to "place himself in its power." Barnes was sounded through an intermediary and laid down the terms on which he would support the Duke. According to Greville, these were no interference with the Reform Bill, and the adoption of those measures of reform already sanctioned by the votes of the House of Commons—the Tithe Measure and the Corporations Act—and no change in foreign policy. Barnes expressed himself "quite satisfied" with the reply, and to celebrate the agreement a dinner was given in his honour by the Lord Chancellor. "The dinner has made a great uproar," commented Greville. Unfriendly journals suggested, precisely or broadly according to taste, that Barnes had sold himself to the Duke of Wellington. Barnes, who was more in sympathy with the new Prime Minister, the liberal-minded Sir Robert Peel, than with the Duke, urged that the former should make a popular declaration of his adherence to reform principles, and suggested alterations to a draft address. Peel issued a statement of his views in a manifesto to his constituents—the famous Tamworth Manifesto—which was in accord with the conditions that Barnes had specified. The Government lasted only six months, and when he had given up the seals of office Peel wrote to Barnes expressing at length his appreciation of "a support the more valuable because it was an impartial and discriminating support." In the course of a graceful reply Barnes said:

Such an acknowledgment is the only one which an Independent

Journalist should expect from any Minister. Such reciprocities are, in my humble opinion, creditable alike to the Govt. and to the Press of this Country: because they demonstrate that each is actuated by motives which, whether of good or evil tendency, are at least personally pure.

When Barnes died in 1841 *The Times* lost, in the opinion of Lord Northcliffe, its greatest editor. Delane is the better-known figure, but he had the advantage of building on the foundations solidly laid by John Walter II and Barnes. These two men were essentially the moulders of *The Times* as we know it. They had made it a great name in the land. It was now an altogether more prosperous journal, with eight large pages instead of the four small ones of 1817 and frequent eight-page supplements to accommodate the increasing flow of advertisements.[1] But it was above all else a newspaper that prized its anonymity, and the issue of May 8, 1841, made no reference to the passing of its editor but printed only this simple announcement in the Births, Marriages and Deaths column:

On the 7th inst., at his house in Soho-square, Thomas Barnes, Esq., in the 56th year of his age.

Some months later, however, *The Times* had occasion to comment on a case in which the name of Thomas Barnes was mentioned as having responded with characteristic good nature to a tale of distress, and without going so far as to disclose that he had been editor described him with some warmth as "a gentleman connected with us who died last year and whose valuable services we must ever most highly appreciate."

The most delightful, and the least characteristic, of the stories of John Thadeus Delane (1817–1879) tells how he announced to a friend the news of his appointment to the editorship of *The*

[1] As recorded in the 150th anniversary number, the first whole-page advertisement in *The Times* appeared in January 1829; a four-page advertisement —a loyal address to King William the Fourth subscribed by merchants, bankers and others—was published in December 1834; and the largest advertisement ever to be printed in the paper—an announcement of Mexican bonds that occupied nearly nine pages—appeared in December 1910.

Times. He burst into his room, radiantly enthusiastic, and called out: "By Jove, John, what do you think has happened? I am editor of *The Times!*" Despite the romantic fact that he became editor at the age of 23, it is now almost impossible to picture Delane as a young man. One thinks of him always in his formidable maturity, when he wielded an influence that shook Governments: a supremely confident man who judged great issues swiftly and boldly. As Mowbray Morris, manager of *The Times*, once explained: "It is those flashes of sure intuition that save him; if he were in the habit of hesitating he would often be blundering."

Once again John Walter II made a shrewd choice, but as in the case of Barnes, he prudently avoided committing himself until the soundness of his judgment was confirmed by experience. The event proved him to have been brilliantly right in his selection. Delane was the second son of W. F. A. Delane, a barrister who held the post of treasurer to *The Times*, and Walter had known him as a boy and been impressed by his character and suggested to his father that in planning his education he should have in view employment on the editorial staff. He came to Printing House Square in July 1840, and did Parliamentary reporting and other journalistic work. On the death of Barnes ten months later Walter resumed active direction of the paper and made Delane his chief editorial assistant. He was editor in name, but he did not acquire the full authority of his predecessor, who had been in sole control for twenty-two years, until Walter died in 1847. An upheaval at Printing House Square in 1846, which must be briefly described, almost led to the severance of his connection with the paper. Walter had discovered that W. F. A. Delane and T. M. Alsager (the assistant manager) were responsible for the omission from the accounts of a charge for paper, the effect being to conceal the true position by showing a credit balance that did not exist. Alsager, who had done valuable work for *The Times* as a writer on City matters for thirty years,[1]

---

[1] During the railway mania of 1845 newspapers gained enormous revenue from railway advertisements. *The Times*, which received up to £6,000 a week

left the paper and a month later committed suicide. Walter sought to dismiss W. F. A. Delane, but it was not until his son intervened that he could be persuaded to resign from the printing partnership. A few weeks later Walter died, and just before his death he had apparently given J. T. Delane a firm assurance that he had not lost his confidence, as this letter of acknowledgment (quoted in the official history) reveals: "I am sure I need not express the gratification your very kind reply to my note has afforded me. I take it as evidence that in the very embarrassing circumstances of the past six months I have not lost the good opinion it has been the object of seven years of my life to deserve. . . ." Read in this context an entry which Delane made in his diary on the day of Walter's death (July 28, 1847) appears stiffly grudging: "He was a strange man, & in many respects a hard one, but still by no means destitute of good. Towards myself his kindness was undeviating and extreme until these late unhappy troubles; but even then he appeared to experience a true pleasure in making up with me." The obituary notice of Walter in *The Times* occupied three and a half columns. Its verdict was that the monument of his merits and his powers was to be found in the columns of the paper and that "Mr. Walter was the prime author and the chief upholder of that celebrity and influence which *The Times* journal possesses." That judgment stands undisturbed a century later. When he assumed control of *The Times* its circulation was low and its influence negligible; he transformed a subsidized journal into the most independent and powerful newspaper in the country, with a sale greater than that of all the other dailies combined; and his bold initiative in the organization of news services and the revolutionizing of the printing department made *The Times* a synonym for enterprise.

Delane now took over the direction of *The Times*, and John

from this source at the height of the boom, steadily warned the country against the dangers inherent in this craze and prophesied—correctly as events showed—that the concentration of capital upon one set of schemes was bound to bring disaster. In November 1845 a supplement was published which gave figures demonstrating that more money was being invested, on paper, than there was in the country.

Walter III (then 29 years of age) became manager and succeeded to the ownership of the printing business. From 1847 until he retired in 1877 broken in health, Delane exercised an editorial influence greater even than that of Thomas Barnes. He was not a writing editor in the real sense of that term, for he rarely wrote a leader; he was the conductor of a brilliant editorial team and controlled by suggestion, discussion and revision; he was, in short, the directing and co-ordinating mind of *The Times*. Probably no editor has ever been better informed, more closely and constantly in touch with the influential people of his time. He dined out regularly during the season, stayed in the great country houses, met everyone who mattered—Royalty, Cabinet Ministers, ambassadors, men of letters, leaders of society. Lord Morley, in his life of Richard Cobden, tells of the latter's scornful comments on the deference paid to the editor of the paper he so much disliked: Delane was to be seen dining at tables, he said, "where every other guest but himself was an Ambassador, a Cabinet Minister, or a bishop." Lord John Russell wrote to Queen Victoria in 1854: "The degree of information possessed by *The Times* with regard to the most secret affairs of State is mortifying, humiliating, and incomprehensible." There is a more genial sidelight on this aspect of Delane's life in the story that one day a member of *The Times* staff proudly reported that he had seen the editor riding down Whitehall with a duke walking on each side.

John Walter II and Thomas Barnes transformed *The Times* into a fearlessly independent journal; Delane brilliantly continued and reinforced the tradition. In March 1854 Lord Derby attacked the paper for publishing the ultimatum to Russia before that country had received it and demanded to know how the editor reconciled to his conscience the act of having made public that which he must have known was intended to be kept secret. This was the reply of *The Times*:

To accuse this or any other journal of publishing early and correct intelligence, when there is no possibility of proving that such intelligence has been obtained by unfair or improper means, is to pay us one of the highest compliments we can hope to deserve. . . . We hold ourselves responsible, not to Lord Derby or the House of Lords, but to the people of England, for the accuracy and fitness of that which we think proper to publish. Whatever we conceive to be injurious to the public interests, it is our duty to withhold; but we ourselves are quite as good judges on that point as the Leader of the Opposition.

Two years earlier Louis Napoleon, stung by criticisms of his regime, had tried to bribe *The Times* into silence and finding that this was impossible he sought to bring pressure to bear upon the paper through the British Government. In debates held in both Houses of Parliament the Press—no journal was named—came under heavy criticism and Lord Derby put forward this view of the responsibility of newspapers:

If, as in these days, the Press aspires to exercise the influence of statesmen, the Press should remember that they are not free from the corresponding responsibility of statesmen, and that it is incumbent on them, as a sacred duty, to maintain that tone of moderation and respect even in expressing frankly their opinions on foreign affairs which would be required of every man who pretends to guide public opinion.

In two leading articles published on successive days (February 6 and 7, 1852) *The Times* gave a reasoned answer to Lord Derby. The distinction between the responsibility of statesmen and the Press was defined in these words, which are as fresh and vigorous and cogent today as when they were written a century ago:

The press lives by disclosures; whatever passes into its keeping becomes a part of the knowledge and the history of our times; it is daily and for ever appealing to the enlightened force of public opinion—anticipating, if possible, the march of events—standing upon the breach between the present and the future, and extending its survey to the horizon of the world. The statesman's duty is precisely the reverse. He cautiously guards from the public eye the information by which his actions and opinions are regulated; he reserves his judgment on passing events till the latest moment, and then he records it in obscure or conventional language; he strictly confines himself, if he be wise, to the practical interests of his own country, or to those bearing immediately upon it; he hazards no rash surmises as to the future; and he concentrates in his own transactions all that power which the press seeks to diffuse over the world. The duty of the one is to speak; of the other to be silent.

Delane's greatest hour was during the Crimean War, when he published William Howard Russell's dispatches containing ruthless exposures of the sufferings of the troops and when in leading articles he mercilessly criticized official neglect and ineptitude—a neglect that was early made clear when *The Times* organized a fund to relieve the sick and wounded and thus make good the gross deficiencies of the medical service.[1] Delane visited the Crimea and remained there several weeks studying the situation. Exercising boldly the right of criticism as well as the right of disclosure, *The Times* overturned one administration, brought about changes in another and secured the removal of the Commander-in-Chief (Lord Raglan).[2] The public gained an impression of editorial courage and journalistic enterprise that outweighed the legitimate criticism that Russell had sometimes been indiscreetly specific about military operations. There was no censorship, and headquarters showed no interest in Russell's proposal to submit his letters for examination before posting them to *The Times*.

Sir William Howard Russell (1820–1907) was the first of the great war correspondents. It was a new thing to be able to read long and vivid accounts of great battles not many days after they had taken place—to see them through the eyes of a professional observer with a graphic style. It was a new thing, too, to have a man on the spot who reported with startling candour the evidence of mismanagement in the conduct of the war—a man with a conscience who sent messages to his paper that could not be ignored by the home authorities because they were painfully

[1] This was one of the earliest of the many large funds raised by *The Times* and other newspapers in aid of national causes. The most notable was the contribution of £16,510,023 through *The Times* fund to the British Red Cross in 1914–1919.
[2] See Chapter XII, in which a comparison is made between *The Times* attacks on Lord Raglan in 1854 and the *Daily Mail* attack on Lord Kitchener in 1915.

true. Sidney Herbert, the Secretary for War, expressed the hope that the Army would lynch Russell. Lord Clarendon, the Foreign Secretary, said that three pitched battles gained "would not repair the mischief done by Mr. Russell and the articles upon his letters," but many weeks later admitted to Greville that it was by "the power and enterprise of the Press that the deplorable state of the Army was brought to the knowledge of the public and even of Ministers themselves." Russell was to report several more wars—the American Civil War, the German-Austrian War of 1866 and the Franco-German War of 1870–1871—but though he did notable work in these campaigns none of them brought him opportunities comparable to the Crimea, where a tragic occasion inspired him to render brilliant and courageous service to the Army and the nation and to his paper.

Not long after the Crimean War *The Times* published a leading article (December 6, 1858) which contained an eloquent statement of its conception of a free Press that showed how completely Delane interpreted the tradition of independence created by John Walter II and Barnes.

> Liberty of thought and speech is the very air which an Englishman breathes from his birth; he could not understand living in another atmosphere. Nor when you once allow this liberty can you restrict the range of its subjects. The principle must have free exercise, or it dies. There is no medium. It would be fatal to say, "Discuss home matters, but not foreign ones." A press so confined would lack the inspiration of that universal sympathy which is necessary to sustain its spirit. Every issue of an English journal speaks to the whole world; that is its strength; it lives by its universality; that idea imparts conscious power, elevates the tone and braces the will of this great impersonality, invigorates the statement, points the epithet, and nails the argument. It could not speak with half the power it does on domestic subjects if it could not speak of foreign; it could not fly with its wings clipped; it would not be the whole which it is and it would cease to be an epitome of the world.

When Delane retired, at the age of 59, he was prematurely aged and his handwriting was reduced to a tremulous scrawl: he was "thin, old, bowed, speaking slowly," William Howard Russell sadly reported to a friend. "I may or may not live a few months, but my real life ends here," Delane wrote to John Walter III, admitting that he could not dispute that the time had come to take a rest. He died a little over two years later. He had worn himself out by the incessant labour of watching closely every department of the paper. As the Rev. Henry Wace, one of his leader-writers, said: "He maintained an absolute mastery of the whole of the paper in all its details. He 'read,' in the Press sense of the word, everything which was to appear in the paper next morning, and edited it so as to ensure that the whole was in harmony and was fitted to produce one clear impression on the public mind.... In short, the paper every morning was not a mere collection of pieces of news from all parts of the world, of various opinions, and of more or less valuable essays. It was Mr. Delane's report to the public of the news of the day, interpreted by Mr. Delane's opinions, and directed throughout by Mr. Delane's principles and purposes."

CHAPTER NINE

End of the "Taxes on Knowledge"

THE development of the spirit of liberalism in this country after the passing of the Reform Bill had as one of its consequences a new attitude to the Press. In retrospect, over a century and a quarter after the events that provoked them, it is easy to understand the alarm and disgust aroused by some of the reckless publications that sprang up in the post-Waterloo period of unrest. Ministers in their angry bewilderment at the stubborn and even heroic resistance they encountered increased restrictions and penalties, but all the time they were handicapped by the fact that public opinion was largely against them. Only a few wise statesmen appreciated that the remedy was to be found in pushing through long-overdue constitutional reform that would purge the political life of the country of its grosser anomalies and provide a broader basis for government that would command general respect; and when this policy eventually triumphed in 1832 the way was cleared for new and liberating influences.

Among the chief beneficiaries of this changed attitude to national problems was the Press. For two centuries journalism had been either the tool or the butt of Governments; now it was beginning to show a healthy independence, and the reformers, the most active force in public life, saw that if the Press were freed from the stamp duty and other fiscal burdens its economic position would be strengthened, cheaper newspapers would become possible and public opinion would have many more channels of expression. Bulwer-Lytton, one of the foremost champions of the Press on this issue, made a striking comparison between journalism in this country and the United States when on June 14, 1832, he moved resolutions in the

House of Commons for the repeal of the principal taxes on knowledge.[1]

In America the newspaper sells for 1½d. There is not a town in America with 10,000 inhabitants that has not its daily paper. . . . In 1829 the number of newspapers published in the British Isles was 33,050,000 or 630,000 weekly, which is one copy for every thirty-sixth inhabitant. In Pennsylvania, which had only in that year 1,200,000 inhabitants, the newspapers amounted to 300,000 copies weekly, or a newspaper to every fourth inhabitant. What was the cause of this mighty difference? The newspaper in one country sells for one-fourth of what it sells for in the other. . . . We have heard enough in this House of the necessity of legislating for property and intelligence, but we now feel the necessity of legislating for poverty and intelligence. At present we are acquainted with the poorer part of our fellow-countrymen only by their wrongs and murmurs, their misfortunes and their crimes. But let us at last open happier and wiser channels of communication between them and us. . . . Is it not time to consider whether the printer and his types may not provide better for the peace and honour of a free state than the gaoler and the hangman—whether, in one word, cheap knowledge may not be a better political agent than costly punishment?

The resolutions were seconded by Daniel O'Connell, but they were withdrawn when it was seen that the House would not accept them. The first step in the economic liberation of the

[1] Some months before Bulwer-Lytton made his speech the first number was published of *Berthold's Political Handkerchief*, a news-sheet printed on cotton fabric instead of paper in order to evade the paper duty. Reporting that a copy of the first issue would shortly come up for sale in a London auction-room, the *Westminster Gazette* of November 29, 1898, gave these details: "It is dated London, September 3, 1831, price fourpence, and the letterpress, which is fairly legible, is as remarkable as the material on which it is printed. The tone of this news rag is intensely Radical, but it reproduces the order of ceremonial to be observed at the Coronation of King William IV and Queen Adelaide on the following Thursday, and it is announced that a proclamation to the people of Europe will appear in 'our next cotton.' It is embellished with a medallion woodcut of Napoleon crossing the Alps, but the ink in this pictorial effect is too much for the cotton, and the Alps are in a fog and the Emperor on horseback very indistinct."

END OF THE "TAXES ON KNOWLEDGE"

Press was taken in the following year, the tax on advertisements being lowered from 3s. 6d. to 1s. 6d. in 1833. Three years later—on September 15, 1836—the stamp duty on newspapers was reduced from fourpence to a penny a copy, and a reduction in the duty on paper was also made.[1]

The Times and other journals lowered their price from sevenpence to fivepence. It was customary in those days of dear newspapers for many readers to borrow the paper from subscribers or from newsvendors at a penny an hour, the stupid legislation forbidding this practice having become a dead letter; but then as now a souvenir issue could powerfully stimulate actual sales. The *Observer*, normally a sevenpenny four-page Sunday journal with a second edition on Monday giving later news, added an eight-page supplement (sevenpence extra) on July 22, 1821, containing a detailed report of the coronation of George the Fourth and four large engravings representing scenes at the ceremony: of this enlarged issue 61,500 copies were sold. Even more striking was the enterprise of the daily *Sun*, which on June 28, 1838, included in a four-page coronation supplement a large portrait of Queen Victoria which they had specially commissioned. This was admirably reproduced in black, and the remainder of the page was printed in gold ink. The remarkable demand fot the "Golden *Sun*," as it was called, is indicated by the fact that the Newspaper Library file contains a copy of the twentieth reprint, the special number having been kept on sale for several weeks. This appears to have been the first commemorative issue of a newspaper printed in colour and thus anticipated by sixty years the special "silver" and "golden" numbers which

[1] The first issue of the *Northern Star: or Leeds General Advertiser* (1837), the principal organ of the Chartist movement, contained this note by Feargus O'Connor: "Reader, behold that little red spot in the corner of my newspaper. That is the stamp; the Whig *beauty* spot; your *plague* spot." Notwithstanding the handicap of the newspaper stamp, the Chartist leader was able to claim at the end of the first year of publication that the *Northern Star*, sold at fourpence-halfpenny, had an average weekly circulation of "nearly 2,000 copies more than any other provincial paper in the three Kingdoms." The weekly averages for Leeds, as shown by the stamp returns, were: *Northern Star*, 10,450; *Leeds Mercury*, 8,599; *Leeds Intelligencer*, 3,461; *Leeds Times*, 2,769.

the *Daily Mail* has issued from time to time since Queen Victoria's Diamond Jubilee in 1897.

The concessions to the Press made in 1833 and 1836 typified the growth of a more tolerant and understanding attitude on the part of government, but years were to elapse before the removal of the remaining shackles on the Press and a major political struggle was necessary to secure this final victory. The main driving force behind the campaign was Thomas Milner-Gibson, a former vice-president of the Board of Trade, who served as president of the Association for Promoting the Repeal of the Taxes on Knowledge. He had some valuable allies, the most powerful of whom was Richard Cobden, who in 1850 argued the case for the removal of the stamp duty with his usual robust effectiveness.

So long as the penny lasts there can be no daily press for the middle or working class. Who below the rank of a merchant or wholesale dealer can afford to take in a daily paper at fivepence? Clearly it is beyond the reach of the mechanic and the shopkeeper. The result is that the daily press is written for its customers—the aristocracy, the millionaires, and the clubs and news-rooms. . . . The governing classes will resist the removal of the penny stamp, not on account of the loss of revenue—*that* is no obstacle with a surplus of two or three millions—but because they know that the stamp makes the daily press the instrument and servant of the oligarchy.

Another organization, founded in 1849, was the London Committee for Obtaining the Repeal of the Duty on Advertisements, and when it had achieved its object it changed its name to the Newspaper Press Association for Obtaining the Repeal of the Paper Duty. Active propaganda by means of pamphlet, petition and deputation was carried on by both societies. On April 16, 1850, Milner-Gibson introduced resolutions in the House of Commons calling for the repeal of the newspaper stamp duty, the advertisement tax and the duties on paper and imported books. Sir Charles Wood, the Chancellor of the Exchequer, opposed the resolution on the ground that it would be an act of political suicide to give up the income of £1,329,000 that was

END OF THE "TAXES ON KNOWLEDGE"

obtained from these duties in the previous year.[1] The speech in which Lord John Russell, the Prime Minister, opposed the resolutions makes curious reading at the present day; he could give no countenance, he said, to any plans for encouraging such abominations as popular newspapers or popular education in England. The resolutions were defeated. In 1851 Milner-Gibson secured the appointment of a Select Committee to inquire into the working of the Newspaper Stamp Act. Reporting the same year, the committee directed attention to

> the objections and abuses incident to the present system of newspaper stamps, arising from the difficulty of defining and determining the meaning of the term "news"; to the inequalities and evasions that it occasions in postal arrangements . . . to the limitation imposed by the stamp upon the circulation of the best newspapers; and to the impediments which it throws in the way of the diffusion of useful knowledge regarding current events among the poorer classes, and which species of knowledge, relating to subjects which must obviously interest them, calls out the intelligence by awakening the curiosity of those classes.

Milner-Gibson returned to the attack in 1852, moving resolutions in favour of the repeal of the stamp duty, the advertisement tax and the paper duty—all of which were defeated by substantial majorities. Disraeli, now Chancellor of the Exchequer, defended the taxes as necessary evils. Gladstone was in favour of the abolition of the paper duty when the proper time arrived, but thought that dear newspapers and books were the consequence not so much of taxation as of trade unionism that raised the wages of compositors and others to a level far above their deserts. The reformers persisted in their campaign for the removal of the objectionable duties and concentrated especially on the advertisement tax, which had received the least support in the latest debate. In the following year Milner-Gibson again brought

[1] Ninety years later a Chancellor of the Exchequer also called Wood sought to reimpose taxation on the Press. On August 13, 1940, Sir Kingsley Wood withdrew after strong representations his proposal in the Purchase Tax Bill to impose a tax of $16\frac{2}{3}\%$ on newspapers, periodicals and books.

forward his resolutions and on this occasion Gladstone, who had become Chancellor of the Exchequer, said the Government had no wish to retain any restraint whatever upon the Press for the sake of restraint, and he would be delighted to see the day when the duty on newspapers might be removed—but he could not dispense with the £180,000 a year yielded by the advertisement tax. The House was won over to the policy of cheaper advertisements and would not accept Gladstone's compromise plan to make the tax 6d. instead of 1s. 6d., and on August 4, 1853, the advertisement tax came to an end.

Milner-Gibson's next move was shrewdly thought out. He brought forward a non-contentious resolution declaring that in the opinion of the House "the laws in reference to the periodical press and newspaper stamp are ill defined and unequally enforced, and it appears to this House that the subject demands the early attention of Parliament," and the House of Commons accepted this motion without a division. In a leading article the next day *The Times* made these comments:

> With all our talk about knowledge, about the achievements of science, about education, schools, churches, enlightenment, and Heaven knows what not, there is something positively ridiculous in taxing that intelligence which really constitutes the great medium of a civilised country. We make a great stir about teaching everybody to read, and the state—that is, the nation—pays a quarter of a million a year in teaching children to do little more than read. Then we proceed to tax the very first thing that everybody reads. . . . But we have several times enlarged on the absurdity of a tax which, as it is a tax on news, is a tax on knowledge, and is thus a tax on light, a tax on education, a tax on truth, a tax on public opinion, a tax on good order and good government, a tax on society, a tax on the progress of human affairs, and on the working of human institutions.

Yet *The Times* had nothing to gain from the removal of the newspaper tax. On the one hand it would be able to reduce its price to London customers by one penny, but on the other hand it would lose the privilege of free postage conferred by the stamp duty and would have to make a charge to country

END OF THE "TAXES ON KNOWLEDGE"

customers to cover this expense. Moreover, it was common knowledge that one aim of the reformers was to weaken what was regarded as the monopoly enjoyed by *The Times*—which with its circulation of 60,000 had a sale that was nearly three times that of all the other morning papers put together[1]—and it was equally well known that this attitude had considerable backing in the House of Commons. The circumstances attending the removal of the stamp duty confirmed this belief. A change of administration brought Lord Palmerston to power, and on March 19, 1855, the new Chancellor of the Exchequer (Sir George Cornewall Lewis) introduced the Newspaper Duties Bill, which made it optional for every newspaper to issue all or any of its copies stamped or unstamped, the stamped copies having the privilege of transmission through the post; and it was estimated that the gross loss of £400,000 to the revenue would be reduced by £200,000 received for the copies sent through the post. Gladstone and Milner-Gibson suggested that it was unfair that *The Times*, with an average weight of six ounces, should pay only a penny postage while the charge for printed matter was twopence if the weight exceeded half an ounce. Bulwer-Lytton spoke in defence of *The Times* and criticized the proposal for differential taxation. "If I desired to leave to remote posterity some memorial of existing British civilization," he said, "I would prefer, not our docks, not our railways, not our public buildings, not even the palace in which we now hold our sittings; I would prefer a file of *The Times* newspaper." John Bright, who declared that there was no journal to which the country was more indebted than to *The Times*, made this prophecy about the results that would follow the freeing of the Press:

I am willing to rest on the verdict of the future, and I am quite convinced that five or six years will show that all the votes of Parliament for educational purposes have been as mere trifles compared with the results which will flow from this measure, because, while the existing papers retain all their usefulness, it will call to their aid

[1] The *Morning Advertiser*, which was bought by all licensed victuallers, had the second largest sale (6,600).

numbers of others not less useful, and, while we enjoy the advantage of having laid before us each morning a map of the events of the world, the same advantage will be extended to classes of society at present shut out from it.[1]

In a long and angry article *The Times* (May 14, 1855) denounced what it called the hypocrisy that treated the proposal for a differential rate as a postal question, and demanded equality of treatment.

We well know, and everybody knows, that our just claim to pass as a newspaper at the same charge as other newspapers would never have been disregarded but for our honest exposures of favouritism, incapacity, and inertness in the conduct of the war, and our evident determination to be bound to no party. We know, too, that there are men in the House of Commons who are opposed not only to us, but to any independent and respectable press.

The Newspaper Duties Bill passed the second reading in the House of Commons by 215 to 161 and was eventually approved by both parties, coming into force at the end of June. Some days before this the Treasury gave effect to the suggestion made by Gladstone and Milner-Gibson by issuing an order that in future the postal charge for printed matter would be one penny for four ounces. *The Times* adjusted its price at the beginning of July to 4d. unstamped and 5½d. stamped, other papers charging 4d. and 5d. respectively. Country readers were urged to take advantage of the lower rate of a halfpenny charged by the railways for the transmission of a paper of any weight. Three years later *The Times* and the *Illustrated London News* asked the Post Office to reduce the postal charge to the railway rate but the request was denied, though as a concession the limit of weight was raised to six ounces—a belated acceptance of the proposal originally put

[1] Already there had been a great increase in newspaper sales as a result of the reduction of the stamp duty from fourpence to one penny, though part of the gain must be ascribed to the growth of population. The circulation of all newspapers, as shown by the stamp duty returns, was 39,423,200 in 1836, the last year of the fourpenny tax, and 122,178,507 in 1854, the year preceding the removal of the penny tax.

END OF THE "TAXES ON KNOWLEDGE"

forward by *The Times*. In 1870 Parliament conceded the other point by establishing a newspaper rate of a halfpenny irrespective of weight. The First World War brought about an increase to a penny and the Second World War to 1½d., which is now the rate for four ounces only, additional weight being charged at a halfpenny for four ounces.

The last of the taxes on knowledge was removed in 1861, when Gladstone, again Chancellor of the Exchequer, proposed the repeal of the paper duty of 1½d. per lb., and Milner-Gibson and his allies thus gained the crowning triumph of their long agitation. Lord Robert Cecil, one of the opponents of the measure, declared that it was a prostitution of real education to talk of this tax upon a penny paper as a tax on knowledge. "Could it be maintained that a person of any education could learn anything from a penny paper?" Not long afterwards Lord Robert himself became a regular contributor to the *Standard*, a penny paper.

The final battle for the economic freeing of the Press was, in Gladstone's words, "the severest Parliamentary struggle in which I have ever been engaged." The House of Lords threw out the Bill by 193 votes to 104, but eventually a way was found of giving effect to the proposal without interference by the Upper House, and paper was freed from duty on October 1, 1861.

The removal of the "taxes on knowledge" gave a fresh impetus to journalistic enterprise. Despite the crippling handicap of this taxation there had been a number of attempts in the first half of the nineteenth century to establish new daily papers. A few survived—the *Globe* (1803) and the *Standard* (1827), both evening journals, the latter becoming a morning paper in 1857; and the *Daily News* (1846)—the present *News Chronicle*—which had a companion evening paper, the *Express*, from 1846 to 1869. The *Globe* absorbed no fewer than five papers and survived until the twentieth century, when it was itself absorbed by the *Pall Mall Gazette*. It was originally started, with an associated morning paper (the *British Press*), by the booksellers in opposition to the *Courier* and the *Morning Post*, which did not give as much space to their advertisements as they required. The *Globe* incorporated the *Traveller* in 1823 and was renamed the *Globe and Traveller*; the *British Press* was discontinued.

The *New Times*, a paper that sought to rival *The Times* with the transparent aid of an imitated title, ran for eleven years. It was launched in 1817 by Dr. John Stoddart (later Sir John Stoddart), whose contract of service with *The Times* had been curtly terminated the previous year by John Walter II; and its original name was the *Day and New Times*, incorporating a paper called the *Day* which had been started in 1798 and which made a specialized appeal to auctioneers. In his prospectus of the new journal Stoddart referred to his former connection with *The Times* and implied that he was largely responsible for its success; and he concluded by saying that the proprietor of that paper having thought fit to recede from his contract, "the Writer, with regret, perceived himself under the necessity of transferring the *spirit* of the Times to a new undertaking." Tartly commenting on Stoddart's claims, *The Times* declared that his "articles were rejected from our columns on account of the virulence and indiscretion with which they were written. . . . There are in the office sacks full of his rejected writings. . . ." Imitation became more blatant when Stoddart presently shortened the title of his journal to the *New Times*. He continued to edit the paper until 1826, when he was appointed chief justice and justice of the vice-admiralty court in Malta. Two years later it ceased publication.

John Murray the publisher, whose *Quarterly Review* had quickly established itself as one of the two most influential periodicals of the time—the other being the *Edinburgh Review*—was not able to repeat his success in daily journalism. At the suggestion of Benjamin Disraeli he started the *Representative* in 1826 as a Tory morning paper. He engaged an able staff, but despite generous expenditure his journal lasted only six months and he lost £26,000 on the venture.

END OF THE "TAXES ON KNOWLEDGE"

A bold attempt to establish a Radical daily was seen when the *Constitutional*—a forbidding title—made its appearance in 1836, immediately after the reduction of the stamp tax to one penny. The new venture, which incorporated the *Public Ledger*, had substantial capital backing for those days: in all £42,000 out of the nominal capital of £60,000 was called up. The promoters declared that they were reformers "in the fullest meaning of the term," and that they would "advocate the shortening of the duration of parliaments, an extension of the suffrage, and the vote by ballot." Although it had a first-class staff, under the editorship of Samuel Laman Blanchard—and had the then little-known Thackeray as a contributor and subsequently as foreign editor—the paper failed to establish itself. It was too Radical for its Whig-and-Tory generation, and neither at its original price of fourpence halfpenny nor at the later figure of fivepence could it be made a success, lasting only nine months. The *Public Ledger* was revived by its former owner to provide commercial intelligence and is still published daily.

The *Daily News*, started in 1846 with Charles Dickens as editor and Joseph Paxton (who was to design the Crystal Palace for the Great Exhibition of 1851) and Bradbury and Evans (the owners of *Punch*) as proprietors, was strongly imbued with the spirit of reform. In his introductory leading article Dickens wrote that the principles to be advocated by the *Daily News* would be "principles of progress and improvement; of education, civil and religious liberty and equal legislation. . . . Very much has to be done, and must be done, towards the bodily comfort, mental elevation and general contentment of the British people." The new paper was sold at fivepence, which was twopence less than *The Times* but the usual price for a morning paper in those days. Dickens resigned his £2,000 a year post within three weeks: "tired to death and quite worn out." He was not fitted for the exacting work of an editor, and he unwisely appointed several of his relatives to key positions, the strangest choice of all being that of his father (the model for Wilkins Micawber) as chief reporter. The *Daily News* was to pass through many vicissitudes before it was firmly established, and the original capital of £50,000 was found to be inadequate, substantial additional sums being put into the undertaking. A few months after Dickens left the price of the paper was reduced to twopence halfpenny and the circulation rose from 4,000 to 22,000, but this bold policy proved unprofitable and the price was put up to threepence and later went back to the original fivepence. Another literary figure associated with the early history of the *Daily News* was Harriet Martineau, who in 1852, at the age of 50, was invited to become a leader-writer and is said to have been the first woman writer on the staff of a newspaper, though her writing was not done at the office but in her home at Ambleside.

Herbert Ingram, who had achieved a striking triumph with the *Illustrated London News*, came forward as a pioneer of cheap daily journalism in February 1848, when he started the *London Telegraph* at threepence, which was twopence lower than the prevailing price. Other original ideas were publication at noon—in order to provide later news than the morning papers—and the inclusion of a serial, this feature having already become an established part of French newspapers. The venture could not be made to pay and came to an end after five months. Another paper of similar name—the *Daily Telegraph*—but under different ownership was to succeed a few years later where Ingram had failed.

Short-lived dailies in the first half of the nineteenth century included two that have had no parallel since—the *Iron Times* (morning) and the *Railway Director* (afternoon), which appeared during the railway mania of 1845 and soon expired. A host of specialized weeklies also sprang up during a boom which saw the expenditure of thousands of pounds a week on railway advertisements—and mostly vanished when the boom collapsed. The *London Gazette* was one of the papers that benefited handsomely. Announcements of the railway schemes for which Parliamentary sanction was required during the forthcoming session had to be published by December 1st, and there were so many of these advertisements during November 1845 that the *London Gazette* had to appear daily for a short time and rapidly to increase the number of pages until each issue was as thick as a city telephone directory. The peak was attained with an issue containing nearly 600 pages. At 2s. 8d. a copy these were the highest-priced dailies ever issued.

CHAPTER TEN

The Age of Expansion

COBDEN and Bright, who had been among the most vigorous champions of the Press during the "taxes on knowledge" agitation and had foreseen the upspringing of many new daily journals, had a special interest in two penny papers that started publication on March 17, 1856—the *Morning Star* and the *Evening Star*. These newspapers were founded to support the Radical views of the "Manchester School," but promised their readers that they would report occurrences "without lengthened observations." Part of the £80,000 capital was subscribed by Cobden and his friends, and Samuel Lucas, John Bright's brother-in-law, was appointed editor.

But these papers were not the first in the field. On June 29, 1855—one day before the removal of the stamp duty—Colonel Sleigh started the *Daily Telegraph and Courier*, and in the same month several provincial weeklies became dailies. The first number of the *Daily Telegraph* (to use the shortened form adopted later) consisted of four pages of six columns each and carried four columns of advertising. The leaders occupied three and a half columns on page 3, and the first article introduced the paper in a heavily sententious manner. After urging that the Press had revealed itself, under a constitutional monarchy, as the safeguard of the Throne, the improver of morality and the guardian of the subject, the leader continued:

Let not, then, the new era of journalism, which we this day inaugurate in the Metropolis of the world, be viewed in any other light than as an additional monitor of the people, and a loyal champion of the Sovereign and the Constitution. . . . Our mission is to extend to this country the benefit of a cheap and good Daily Press, and now that Parliament has wisely knocked off the last shackle which fettered the progress of the Press, in this great metropolis, we take our stand, availing ourselves, the first possible moment the law permitted, of the Repeal of the Stamp Duty, to issue our Journal at the price of TWO-PENCE, as a candidate for popular favour.

There was nothing revolutionary about the paper except its price—twopence instead of the fourpence which became the standard charge immediately after the stamp duty was removed. No item had more than a single headline, and in some instances this was merely the name of the country of origin. However, something approaching modern display was to be found in the paper on September 12th, when the fall of Sebastopol was announced with three single-column captions extending to nine lines.

Advertisement revenue declined sharply after the first issue, and soon the *Daily Telegraph* was in financial difficulties. Its principal creditor was Joseph Moses Levy, editor and proprietor of the *Sunday Times*, who had taken over the printing of the paper a month after it was started. Levy bought the new journal to protect his financial stake in it, and then took the bold decision to reduce the price to one penny; but it was not the first penny daily in the country, having been preceded by the *Sheffield Daily Telegraph* (June 8, 1855), the *Liverpool Daily Post* (June 11, 1855) and the *London Evening News* (August 14, 1855). The last-named paper, which had no connection with the present *Evening News* (founded in 1881), gave a poor news service and had only a short life. The *Edinburgh War Telegraph* (October 1854), the *Manchester Examiner and Times* (December 12, 1854) and the *Northern Express* (April 25, 1855), first published at Darlington and afterwards at Newcastle, are stated to have been penny dailies—although the penny stamp was then in force—but this cannot be verified, for in consequence of war-time damage at the Newspaper Library these and most other provincial journals are temporarily not available for inspection.

The first issue of the *Daily Telegraph* at the new price appeared on September 17, 1855, and in a leading article the case for cheap journalism was thus stated:

There is no reason why a daily newspaper, conducted with a high tone, should not be produced at a price which would place it within the means of every class of the community. . . . The future stability of the revered institutions of this country must depend more upon the enlightenment of the million, than all the bayonets and legions the enormous wealth of the nation would enable it to collect upon its shores.

Otherwise there was no change in the paper. The editorial policy was obviously that of producing a paper which was as dignified-looking as its contemporaries selling at four times its price. Despite its small size, the *Daily Telegraph* continued to devote several columns to leading articles. Letters to the editor were a regular feature. The halving of the price led to a quick rise in the sale of the paper. Within a few months the circulation had grown to 27,000, about half the sale of *The Times*.

Levy's 22-year-old son Edward joined the staff and shortly afterwards took over the editorship. J. M. Levy had a quarter interest in the paper; his brother, who had adopted the name of Lionel Lawson for professional reasons, owned a half interest; and Edward Levy (who later added Lawson to his name when he inherited under the will of his uncle Lionel) and another had one-eighth each. Edward Levy Lawson was the real maker of the *Daily Telegraph*. He partly anticipated the new journalism of W. T. Stead, T. P. O'Connor and Alfred Harmsworth by widening the range of interest and producing a newspaper that was more human in its appeal. As time went on he borrowed cautiously from American journalistic practice, especially in the use of numerous headlines to introduce a big news story. The French collapse in the Battle of Sedan was announced on September 5, 1870, in ten headlines that occupied a quarter of a column. But this generous use of headlines was a recent innovation. A few years earlier the *Daily Telegraph* had been as conservative as its contemporaries. A comparison of the headline treatment of outstanding home and foreign events in the London Press in one month of 1865 shows no important difference. *The Times*, the *Morning Post*, the *Standard*, the *Daily Telegraph* and the *Daily*

THE AGE OF EXPANSION

News all published long obituaries of Richard Cobden in their issue for April 3rd, in each case with only a single headline in 10 or 12 point capitals. There was some display when the news of the assassination of President Lincoln (April 14th) was belatedly published in the issues dated April 27th. The cable service was not yet established, and "Reuter's Telegrams" from the United States had to travel by ship to Ireland, whence they were wired to London. The *Times* gave the news three headlines, the *Morning Post* two, the *Daily News* three, the *Standard* three and the *Daily Telegraph* four; in each "America" or "Latest from America" was the first heading. A study of the contemporary issues of James Gordon Bennett's *New York Herald* and Horace Greeley's *New York Daily Tribune* reveals that the American Press was already using heavy and numerous headings (all single column) and that when important news was printed these headings were carried to a depth never matched by any popular British newspaper even in the twentieth century. The *New York Herald* of April 15th gave a column of headlines to the report of the assassination of Lincoln, and in the next day's issue a fuller account of the tragedy was preceded by headings extending nearly to the foot of the column. The *New York Daily Tribune* for April 15th had only three headlines for the first news of the assassination: "HIGHLY IMPORTANT! THE PRESIDENT SHOT! SECRETARY SEWARD ATTACKED!" In the next day's issue the front-page news of the assassination was headed with seven captions, of which the first was "THE GREAT CALAMITY!" which was also the first of the seventeen headlines given to a detailed account of the tragedy on page 2.

Three years after its foundation the *Daily Telegraph* claimed that its circulation was greater than that of all the other morning papers put together. In 1862 it absorbed the *Morning Chronicle*,[1]

---

[1] The *Morning Herald*, another eighteenth-century newspaper, was discontinued in 1869 after close upon ninety years of publication. It had apparently gained a new lease of life in the 'forties, under the ownership of Edward Baldwin, who made a bold attempt to transform it into a rival of *The Times*; but this Indian summer of enterprise did not last and the paper failed to prosper in the era of intense competition after 1855.

once the premier daily journal, which had long lost its old vitality. Lawson early adopted the policy of enlisting brilliant men to serve on the staff of the *Daily Telegraph*. Among them were Thornton Hunt, son of Leigh Hunt, who was one of the chief writers on the *Daily Telegraph* in the early years; Sir Edwin Arnold, a distinguished member of the leader-writing staff; Clement Scott, the leading dramatic critic of the day; Bennet Burleigh, who did notable work as war correspondent; and John (later Sir John) Merry Le Sage, who joined the staff in the early 'sixties and served the paper as special correspondent and later, for many years, as editor, retiring at the age of 86 after sixty years' service. Le Sage scored a famous "beat" during the Franco-German War by getting through, hours ahead of other correspondents, an account of the entry of the German army into Paris. The *Daily Telegraph* was associated with the *New York Herald* in sending H. M. Stanley to Africa in 1871 to find Livingstone. The dispatches received from Stanley created extraordinary interest and gave the *Daily Telegraph* an impressive reputation for enterprise.

G. A. Sala, who was to become the best-known of *Daily Telegraph* men and to undertake special commissions the world over on its behalf, first became connected with the paper as early as 1857, when he was an occasional contributor. George Augustus Sala (1828–1895) wrote for many other journals besides the *Daily Telegraph*, and edited several periodicals and wrote many books. He contributed to Charles Dickens's *Household Words* and *All the Year Round*, and in 1856 Dickens "warmly and gladly" accepted his proposal to visit Russia and write a series of descriptive essays. Later they quarrelled because Sala was unpunctual with the delivery of his essays; he had many quarrels with editors and others, and was constantly in financial difficulties; but the picturesqueness and gusto of his writing—too elaborate for modern tastes, Sala being the chief among the practitioners of the now vanished style of writing which his contemporaries called "Telegraphese"—made him the most successful popular journalist of his time. For over a quarter of a century he contributed a gossipy feature headed "Echoes of the Week" to the *Illustrated London News*. The best account of his career is to be found in Ralph Straus's *Sala: The Portrait of an Eminent Victorian*, from which this description of his remarkable personal appearance is quoted: "He was a heavy man, short and stoutish, and his face was blotched and coarse-featured: distinctly a florid person. . . . [He had] a feature which, alike for its size, its peculiar contours, and its fiery hues, was destined to become, as another journalist once facetiously observed, 'Fleet Street's most prominent landmark.' Sala's nose, indeed, was like nothing else in the civilized world. It was a potato of a nose, a very gargoyle of a nose. . . ." Three years before his death he launched *Sala's Weekly Journal*—"A Weekly Magazine for All" —but the paper failed to maintain the interest aroused by the first number, of which 200,000 copies were sold, and did not live long.

Of all the men of talent who joined the *Daily Telegraph* in the last quarter of the nineteenth century, probably one of the most gifted was the versatile, mysterious Dr. Emile Joseph Dillon (1854–1933), who served the paper as correspondent in Russia from 1887 to 1914, and undertook special assignments in other countries from time to time. One of the greatest philologists of the age—he had studied at several Continental universities, acquiring Oriental and medieval as well as European languages, and wrote leading articles in five languages—and a friend and confidant of statesmen and diplomats, he had a genius for gaining authoritative information about contemporary affairs. His reputation as a man of mystery grew out of his secrecy about how he got this information. W. T. Stead said of him: "He is far and away the ablest, must cultured and most adventurous newspaperman I have ever met, with an extraordinary combination of varied faculties, an artist in temperament, a journalist by instinct, a scholar and philosopher by choice, a statesman in ambition." This quiet-voiced, scholarly-looking man, who seemed to know everyone of importance and to have been everywhere, was also, as Stead declared, a courageously enterprising journalist ready for any adventure to get important news. Forbidden by the Sultan to visit Armenia after the manœuvres in 1894, he disguised himself as a Russian officer and sent striking dispatches to his paper; three years later, when reporting the Cretan insurrection against Turkey, he assumed the disguise of an insurgent monk—originally intended for the priesthood, he had lived for a time in Pantasaph Monastery as a young man—and accompanied the Greek statesman Venizelos on board the flagship of the Allied Fleet; and in 1900 he was with the international forces during the "Boxer" outbreak in China. Before joining the *Daily Telegraph* he had edited a newspaper in Odessa and lectured in Russian, as professor of comparative philology, at Kharkov University. Sir Cecil Spring-Rice, for some years British Ambassador at Washington, paid the most remarkable of many tributes to Dr. Dillon when he said that he had learned more from him than from anyone else about foreign politics.

At the time of the Franco-German War the *Daily Telegraph* sale reached 200,000; in the 'eighties, and until the *Daily Mail* appeared in 1896, it claimed "The Largest Circulation in the World." It had become a highly prosperous newspaper and carried an immense number of classified advertisements; the box number device was originated by the *Daily Telegraph*. Lawson was made a baronet in 1892 and given a peerage in 1903, becoming the first Lord Burnham. In 1914, two years before his death, he was publicly honoured as Father of the Press, Lord Northcliffe presenting to him an address signed by over 250 representative British and overseas journalists.

Printing House Square, where John Walter III now reigned, did not view with alarm the success of the *Daily Telegraph*. A four-page paper could not hope to equal the comprehensive service provided by the eight-page *Times* with its occasional supplements.[1] But presently competition came from an unex-

[1] As an example: The twelve-page issue of December 13, 1854, gave six and a half pages to reporting the speeches delivered in Parliament on the opening day of a critical session. Incidentally, there was not a single cross-heading of any kind in five pages of the report—not even a heading at the top of turnover pages to indicate what the report was about.

pected quarter. In June 1857 the *Standard*, the old-established evening paper sold at fourpence, changed to a morning journal at twopence, with "Eight Full-sized pages, the same size as *The Times*." This was a direct challenge and caused an immediate fall of 2,000 in the circulation of *The Times*. On February 4, 1858, the *Standard* gave a violent shock to its contemporaries by bringing down its price to one penny without any reduction in size. After a few months' hesitation the *Daily Telegraph* enlarged its size to eight pages. It claimed at this time a circulation of 30,000, and the *Standard* was not far behind. *The Times* suffered a severe loss in circulation, the figure dropping from 55,000 to 50,000 in 1858. The effect of the new competition would probably have been more pronounced but for the immense prestige gained by *The Times* during the Crimean War.

The *Standard*, a soundly edited paper supporting the Conservative Party, continued to be an embarrassing competitor of *The Times*, and the decline in sales was not arrested until the removal of the paper duty in 1861 enabled John Walter to reduce the price to threepence. From this time there was a steady revival in the circulation, which reached 65,000 at the end of the year. The sale fluctuated for some years within a range of a few thousand copies, and when Delane resigned (1877) the figure had fallen to 61,000 despite the introduction of the "sale or return" policy six years earlier.

The old supremacy of *The Times* had gone. Before 1855 its sale had exceeded that of all the other morning papers combined; now the *Daily Telegraph* had by far the largest sale and several other dailies had substantial circulations.[1] The *Daily News*, which had reduced its price from threepence to a penny in 1868 and absorbed the *Morning Star*[2] in 1869, increased its sale from

[1] A single circulation figure strikingly illustrates the growth of the Press outside London during this period. In 1877 the daily sale of the *Scotsman* was 50,000—nearly equal to that of *The Times* in the same year.

[2] The *Morning Star* had several prominent journalists on its staff, and one of its editors was John Morley, but the prevailing climate of opinion was not favourable to its determinedly Radical views and the reduction in the price of the Liberal *Daily News* struck it a mortal blow. The *Evening Star* ceased

50,000 to 150,000 during the Franco-German War as a result of its brilliant special correspondence. Archibald Forbes of the *Daily News* proved a more resourceful correspondent than William Howard Russell during this war, constantly being first with the news, and Henry Labouchere sent vivid dispatches by balloon post from besieged Paris. Russell was asked to secure the services of this energetic rival for *The Times*, but Forbes preferred to stay with the *Daily News*. The paper was then under the management of Sir John Robinson, who ably directed it from 1868 to 1901. Forbes was only one of several correspondents whom he engaged to report the Franco-German War, and he encouraged them to use the telegraph freely. News by post, he urged, was out of date.

Reviewing the dangerous competition that had sprung up since the removal of the stamp duty,[1] John Walter could feel that *The Times* had satisfactorily overcome its problems by holding its circulation at a figure slightly higher than it had enjoyed in the 'fifties. "As Walter saw it"—to quote the official history—"*The Times* could make no sort of compromise with the new journalism or the new price. Although the newspapers published in London at the price of one penny were daily delivered to Bear Wood [Walter's country house], they were never read by the Chief Proprietor, and not always by his family. It is

publication at the same time as its morning partner. At one time the morning edition was known as the *Morning Star and Dial*. Through the reforming zeal of the Rev. David Thomas, a Nonconformist minister, a large sum had been raised years earlier with the idea of starting a righteous daily newspaper, but it was decided to begin by publishing a weekly. This paper, called the *Dial*, was a costly failure, and it was amalgamated with the *Star* company in the hope that journalism could be reformed through the medium of that paper; but the *Morning Star* disappointingly continued to publish sporting news and other worldly matter and the *Dial* ceased to exist as a separate journal.

[1] Three of the new dailies started during this period of expansion had only a short life—the *Day* (1867), which lasted only seven weeks; the *Hour* (1873) which was discontinued, after heavy losses, in 1876; and the *Daily Express* (1877), which ceased publication within a few months. The first two were Conservative journals; the *Daily Express* was described as an experiment to determine "whether there was a demand for a Church paper, conducted on Church principles, and designed for the perusal of Churchmen."

believed in Printing House Square that at no time during his life did the Chief Proprietor of *The Times* ever open a copy of the *Daily Telegraph* or the *Daily News*. . . . But to sell *The Times* at threepence was a problem that taxed all the resources of newspaper management."

John Walter III (1818–1894)—known to Delane and G. W. Dasent,[1] who disliked his interference, as "The Griff" (short for "griffin")—was an austere man with a high sense of responsibility who was guided in his control of the paper by his conception of *The Times* as a great national institution. The official history records that he reigned over the paper with a conscious despotism. "After his father's death he initiated articles and leaders only occasionally. But although Walter's leading articles were rare, his influence over the leader page was marked and constant." Like his father he made two appointments to the editorship during his lifetime—Thomas Chenery (who succeeded Delane in 1877) and George Earle Buckle (editor from 1884—on the death of Chenery—to 1912). Both were gifted men and were called to the editorial chair in a more strenuous competitive era than Barnes or the young Delane had known, but while they maintained the best traditions of *The Times* they left no particular impress on the paper. Buckle had the special handicap of being editor during the most difficult period of its history.

During the 'seventies and 'eighties the picturesque and brilliantly resourceful Henri de Blowitz (1825–1903) was at the height of his fame as foreign correspondent of *The Times*. He joined the paper in 1871 as assistant and four years later became chief Paris correspondent, but his wide sources of information enabled him to embrace the whole field of Continental politics. No journal had ever had a more enterprising and a more consistently successful foreign correspondent than Blowitz in the years of his greatest influence. His first important and exclusive news story came through his acquaintance with the duc de Decazes, the

---

[1] George Webbe (afterwards Sir George) Dasent, brother-in-law of Delane, was assistant editor of *The Times* from 1845 to 1870, when he resigned to take up a post as Civil Service Commissioner.

French foreign minister, who in 1875 showed him a confidential dispatch from the French ambassador in Berlin giving warning that Germany was contemplating an attack on France and asked him to expose the German plan in *The Times*; his most remarkable achievement, the reward of thorough advance preparation, was to secure the complete text of the treaty signed after the Congress of Berlin in 1878, which appeared in *The Times* ahead of any other journal. The influence of Blowitz declined when Donald Mackenzie Wallace, who had worked as his assistant and who disliked his sensationalism, became head of the foreign department of *The Times* in 1891. "The two men were absolutely dissimilar writers," says the official history. "Accuracy and impartiality were Wallace's idols, while Blowitz respected neither. Colour fascinated him. . . . He was unrivalled in his day for appreciation of speed and journalistic tactics. Blowitz never wasted discretion upon news that could be obtained without it."

Walter's last years were shadowed by the consequences of the ill-fated decision, for which he accepted full responsibility, to buy and publish certain letters alleged to have been written by Charles Stewart Parnell, the Irish leader, but which in fact had been forged by one Richard Pigott. Parliament appointed a special commission, consisting of three judges, to inquire into the charges made by *The Times* in a series of articles entitled "Parnellism and Crime," published in 1887. Pigott broke down under cross-examination about a letter in which Parnell was shown as condoning the Phœnix Park murders (the assassination of the Chief Secretary for Ireland and the Under-Secretary). Afterwards he went to the flat of Henry Labouchere, the editor of *Truth*, to make a confession and Labouchere called in as witness G. A. Sala, who later recorded that "he minutely described how he, and he alone, had executed the forgeries in question." Pigott fled to Madrid and shot himself in an hotel when he was on the point of being arrested. The findings of the Parnell Commission, issued in 1890, were—briefly stated—that some of the charges were true, some false and some unproved: the public verdict, much influenced by the affair of the forged letters, was largely unfavourable to *The Times*. The financial loss to the paper was staggering. The proceedings before the Commission cost *The Times* over £200,000. Walter rejected offers of financial aid and suggestions for raising a public subscription, holding that the paper should bear its own burden —and a heavy burden it was to prove to be.

Not generally known is the fact that *The Times* under John Walter III produced for nearly a year a halfpenny morning newspaper—an experiment that might have succeeded if the management had publicized it adequately, and that would have had a better chance of success if the make-up had been less conservative. The first number of the *Summary*, an eight-page newspaper half the size of the parent journal, appeared on July 26, 1883. It contained a summary of the principal news and features of *The Times*, mostly classified under such headings as "Foreign and Colonial Intelligence," "General News," "*The Times* Leaders," "Letters to *The Times*," "Sporting Intelligence" and "Finance," and nearly a column was given to an account of the drowning of Captain Webb. The paper offered excellent value for money and had a clear field, no other London morning journal then being sold at less than a penny. No reference was made in *The Times* to this enterprising venture and—even more strangely—the paper was not included in the list of associated journals issued from Printing House Square. The *Summary* languished under this half-hearted exploitation, its average daily sale being only 2,500, and on October 11, 1884, it was discontinued. There had been several earlier attempts to establish a halfpenny morning paper:

(1) The *London Morning Mail* (April 1864), published by David Faulkner of 5, Whitefriars Street. No. 17, dated April 28, 1864 (Press Club Collection), had four medium-size pages —five columns to the page. It was a clean-looking and not uninteresting paper, with advertisements on the front page. In the tradition of the period it had two columns of leading articles, but otherwise the contents aimed at lightness by

including a gossipy "On Dits" feature and extracts from *Punch*, and there was a good variety of home and foreign news. This is the only issue which has been traced, and it is not known how long the *London Morning Mail* continued. (A halfpenny paper with a similar title—the *Morning Mail*—was started on April 20, 1885, and apparently ceased publication on July 9th of the same year. It had four large pages, with advertisements on page 1. The paper had no special feature, apart from the substitution of four columns of paragraphs—news, comment and gossip—for leading articles; No. 1 lacked even the traditional address "To the Reader." The paper was printed and published by John Smith, 12, Whitefriars Street.)

(2) The *Morning Latest News* (May 30, 1870), printed and published by George Maddick, Shoe Lane. This paper, which had four large pages, proclaimed in its first issue (Press Club Collection) that it would give "Home and Foreign, Political and Social" news, but devoted an undue proportion of its space to police-court reports. The front page, entirely occupied by news, led off with a four-column report—with a pointedly unambiguous heading—of an unsavoury case. There were two columns of short leaders and notes, preceded by an announcement that two large engravings ("Goin' to the Derby" and "The Return") would be given away with the Wednesday and Thursday issues. The paper had all the usual news features and was not unattractive in general appearance, judged by contemporary standards. No other issue has been traced.

(3) The *Echo*, started as a halfpenny evening paper by Cassell, Petter and Galpin on December 8, 1868, was sold for £20,000 in 1875 to Albert Grant (better known as Baron Grant, the barony being conferred by Victor Emmanuel II of Italy), a notorious company promoter, who on October 4, 1875, began issuing the paper as a halfpenny morning journal —with evening editions as before—and changed the size from eight small to four large pages. The morning edition was not a success and the last issue was published on May 31, 1876;

thereafter the *Echo* was solely an evening journal and continued to appear in the new large-page form.

A new proprietor took over the *Echo* in 1876—John Passmore Edwards (1823–1911), who had previously bought the *Mechanics' Magazine* and the *Building News* and developed them into profitable properties. Edwards edited the *Echo* himself and under his direction the paper made rapid progress. Eight years later he sold a two-thirds interest to Andrew Carnegie and Samuel Storey for £50,000, but repurchased it (at a cost stated to have been double that sum) when the partners failed to agree on management. In 1896 he sold the *Echo* to a syndicate; nine years later it was discontinued. In the meantime other halfpenny evening newspapers—notably the *Evening News* and the *Star*—had invaded the field once monopolized by the *Echo*. Passmore Edwards was a combination of the shrewd business man and the idealist. His beginnings were modest and unpromising. At the age of 27 he started his first paper, the *Public Good*, which he wrote and published himself from a small room in Paternoster Row rented from "Isaac Pitman Brothers, Phonographers," for four shillings a week, and to save expense he slept there at night "on a mattress spread out on the little counter." This and other early journalistic ventures—the *Biographical Magazine*, the *Peace Advocate* and the *Poetic Magazine*—came to grief and he was made bankrupt; some years later he paid off the debts in full and received a presentation of a watch and chain from his appreciative creditors. He recovered from this setback, as already seen, and his subsequent success brought him great wealth. To the general public he was chiefly known as a philanthropist who made gifts of public libraries and hospitals and as an ardent propagandist for peace and other idealistic causes.

Most curious of all experiments in cheap journalism was the *Penny-a-Week Country Daily Newspaper* ("Price if delivered by Newsmen, One Farthing each"). The Newspaper Library has no record of it, but the Press Club Collection contains a "Specimen Copy" (without serial number) dated Wednesday, June 25,

1873. This is a four-page paper of an odd size—11¾ in. by 6 in.—with two columns to the page, printed and published for the proprietors by the Central Press Company, Ltd., 112, Strand. An announcement at the head of the first column states: "The Penny-a-Week Country Daily Newspaper, established to supply every Rural Parish with a Daily Newspaper friendly to Christianity and Good Government. . . . A sufficient antidote must be supplied to the spread of unsound and revolutionary opinion amongst the masses. . . . The Country Daily Newspaper will contain the latest telegrams up to the hour of posting (6 p.m.). . . . Country shopkeepers may give invaluable aid to the Country Daily Newspaper, and clear 50 per cent as their profit, by delivering it at ONE FARTHING per copy, or 1½d. per week." It also stated that six issues would "contain equal to any 30 news columns of *The Times*," and that "Twelve persons subscribing ONE PENNY each per week, may have 12 Copies every morning, post free." In addition to numerous brief items of news, this specimen issue contains a leading article nearly a column in length, "Condensed Extracts" from current periodicals and quotations from humorous and other journals under the heading "The Breakfast Table—Fun and Fact." Later the title was changed to *Six-a-Penny, or Country Daily Newspaper*, but "after a very brief and greatly harassed existence" this farthing daily was incorporated in the *Sun*.[1]

John Bright's prediction that numbers of new papers would appear within five or six years after the repeal of the stamp duty was amply fulfilled. The era of expansion that began in 1855 was further stimulated by the cheapening of paper in 1861. The *Newspaper Press Directory* (founded 1846) stated in its 1851 edition that at that time there were 563 journals in existence. The year after the removal of the paper duty the directory gave the total as 1,165 newspapers plus 213 magazines; in 1870 there were 1,390 newspapers (including 99 dailies against 14 in 1846) and 626 magazines; in 1880, 1,986 and 1,097; in 1890, 2,234 and

[1] *The Press* (Sir Alfred Robbins).

THE AGE OF EXPANSION

1,778; and in 1900, 2,488 and 2,446. In 1836, the year when the Provincial Newspaper Society (now the Newspaper Society) was founded to provide country journals with representation in London, there were only 221 newspapers in Great Britain.

Morning newspapers were established in all the big provincial centres, in Edinburgh and Glasgow and in Irish and Welsh cities, either by conversion from weekly to daily publication (the *Manchester Guardian, Leeds Mercury, Bradford*—now *Yorkshire —Observer, Yorkshire Post, Nottingham Journal, Scotsman, Glasgow Herald, Aberdeen Journal, Belfast News-Letter, Northern Whig* and others) or by the founding of new journals (the *Sheffield Daily Telegraph, Liverpool Daily Post, Western Morning News, East Anglian Daily Times, Birmingham Daily Post, Northern Echo,*[1] *Nottingham Guardian,* etc.). But these were not the first daily papers outside London. Several had previously appeared, including the *North British Mail,* Glasgow (April 14, 1847), a threepenny paper; the *Liverpool and Northern Daily Times* (September 24, 1853), which reduced its price from threepence to three halfpence when the stamp duty was removed and continued publication until 1861; the *Daily War Telegraph* (October 1, 1854), afterwards the *Manchester Daily Telegraph,* which reversed the usual order of things in the 'fifties by afterwards becoming a weekly and had an advertisement under its new title—the *Manchester Weekly Telegraph*—in the 1857 edition of the *Newspaper Press Directory;* and the *Birmingham Daily Press* (May 7, 1855), published at three halfpence. According to Axon's *Annals of Manchester* (1886) there was an even earlier daily paper in the north—the *Northern Express and Lancashire Daily Post,* printed at Stockport and published in Manchester from December 1, 1821. The same writer's account of a "newspaper war" at Manchester later in the century may conveniently be quoted here: "Some remarkable incidents in the history of local journalism occurred during the year [1882]. The *North Times* began July 25, as a penny evening paper, in the interests of the

---

[1] Founded in 1870, the *Northern Echo* was the first halfpenny morning paper outside London.

Conservative Party. The *Latest News* was started from the same office, September 11, as a halfpenny morning paper. The proprietors of the *Evening News* started the *Morning News*, September 14, and the proprietors of the *Evening Mail* started the *Morning Mail* on the same date. This batch of daily papers did not prove long-lived, for the *North Times* and the *Latest News* came to an end December 15, and were followed on December 30 by the *Morning Mail* and *Morning News*—as soon as it was clear that the new rivals had been disposed of."

Most of the provincial evening papers now in existence were founded in the 'sixties, 'seventies and 'eighties. A number of evening papers that were boldly started in comparatively small towns within the area of big-city competition failed to establish themselves permanently—among them the *Royal Press* (Windsor), *Southport Daily News* (afterwards the *Liverpool and Southport Daily News*), the *East Lancashire Echo* (Bury), the *Dewsbury Daily Reporter* and the *Wakefield Daily Free Press*.

Several London evenings were established during the same period—the *Pall Mall Gazette* (1865), a twopenny "Evening Newspaper and Review" (later one penny), which in 1870 had a brief interlude as a morning paper; the *London Daily Mercury*[1] (1862), the *Evening Mercury*[2] and the *Echo* (1868), the *Evening News*[3] (1881) and the *Star* (1888), all halfpenny papers;

---

[1] There is a copy of No. 7 (May 30, 1862) of the *London Daily Mercury* in the Press Club Collection. It was a four-page paper, half size, and was published by Evelyn Nugent at Red Lion Court, Fleet Street. The advertisement revenue must have been negligible: a four-line "miscellaneous" cost only sixpence. The front page was filled with this type of advertisement. A curiously humble editorial note announced: "Cricket Clubs are respectfully informed that reports of matches will be inserted gratis, if duly authenticated by the name of one of the players, Secretary, or Umpire."

[2] The *Evening Mercury*, a four-page "Newspaper and Literary Journal," had as one of its features a serial story. Started two months before the *Echo* and produced by James Henderson, a well-known periodical publisher, it lived only from October 1 to 13, 1868, an editorial note in the last issue stating that the experiment was premature.

[3] Originally the *Evening News* was printed on light blue paper. At one time many London and provincial evenings were printed on papers of various tints: the pleasantest was the green of the *Westminster Gazette*.

MID-VICTORIAN HEADLINES

The headline treatment of these main news pages of the *Daily Telegraph* is typical of mid-Victorian practice in the daily press

THE AGE OF EXPANSION

the *Evening Illustrated Paper* (1881) and the *St. James's Gazette* (1880), the latter started by Frederick Greenwood one month after giving up the editorship of the *Pall Mall Gazette* when the new proprietor announced a change of policy. The first financial daily—the *Financial News* (now incorporated in the *Financial Times*)—appeared in 1884; of the four financial dailies once published only one remains. The *Evening Illustrated Paper* (Press Club Collection) published its first issue on October 25, 1881, and appears to have had only a brief existence. There are no copies in the Newspaper Library. A folio paper, eight pages for a penny, it was printed and published by Lewis Grose, of 174, Fleet Street. The front page was entirely occupied by a block depicting "The Trial of Mabel Wilberforce—Mr. Justice Hawkins Passing Sentence"; another whole-page block (page 3) gave impressions of an Irish demonstration in Hyde Park; there were also half-page blocks. The leading article stated: "Of late years the preparation of drawings for printing purposes has undergone a great revolution: wood engraving, except for such purposes as those in which time is of no consequence, has lapsed into dessuetude [*sic*] and a process, commonly known as zincotypography, has assumed a supremacy it appears likely to maintain." The paper was not interestingly planned and had no novelty apart from the lavish use of illustration.

The founding of the pioneer evening papers outside London was a particularly interesting chapter of journalistic enterprise. Apparently the first provincial journal to issue an evening edition was the *Liverpool Daily Post*, which began publication as a penny daily on June 11, 1855, and published the morning edition at 3.0 a.m., the second edition at 9.0 a.m., and the evening edition at 3.0 p.m. Honours were divided between the *North and South Shields Gazette* (now the *Shields Gazette*) and the *Greenock Telegraph* for the production of the first halfpenny evening paper. The former, which had been established as a weekly in 1849, began issuing a daily telegraphic edition (at first only a quarto sheet printed on one side) on July 2, 1855—only two days after the removal of the stamp duty—and this appeared every evening except Friday, when the weekly edition was published. Single copies were sold at a penny, but the charge for the weekly and the telegraphic editions was only threepence halfpenny, so it is calculated that the evening issues cost subscribers only a halfpenny each. The telegraphic edition was gradually enlarged, and in January 1864 it was converted into a four-page daily, price one halfpenny (with a weekly edition sold at three halfpence). The first six-day halfpenny evening paper established outside London, however, was the *Greenock Telegraph*. Started as a weekly in 1857, it became a halfpenny daily in 1863. The first halfpenny evening journal in the United Kingdom was, as already stated, the *London Daily Mercury* (1862).

Local weeklies sprang up everywhere, in the London suburbs and in the provinces, many of them being started on small capital as an offshoot of a general printing business. In a decade or so there was hardly a town which did not possess at least one weekly; the larger towns had two, one being Conservative and the other Liberal and neither (as a rule) giving much space to speeches made by political opponents. Many of these papers supplemented a meagre local news service with a general news summary and literary features furnished in proof or stereo by agencies that were set up to meet the needs of the provincial press; later such agencies were to specialize in the provision of serial stories and other features designed to gain and hold circulation. An earlier service was the one offered by *Charles Knight's Weekly Newspaper* (1851), which by the removal of the outer sheet and the substitution of another could be "transformed from a London to a country paper. The internal sheets were to contain all the general news, so arranged that the country printer need only add a sheet outside with his local title, news and advertisements, to produce a first-class paper."[1] The experiment proved a failure; it was probably too early. Partly printed sheets came into existence in the United States in 1861 and were known as "ready-print" or "patent insides." Others were to adapt Knight's idea successfully—among them John Cassell, who founded the

[1] *The History of British Journalism* (Alexander Andrews).

firm of Cassell, Petter and Galpin (later Cassell & Co.). In a short biography of Cassell published in 1894, G. Holden Pike stated: "If John Cassell did not actually originate partly printed news sheets for country or local editors to complete, he was one of the first in the field with that enterprise; probably he did more than anyone else to develop it, and until this day this represents one of the great departments at Belle Sauvage Yard." According to the author of an article on "The Newspaper Press" which appeared in the *Quarterly Review* in October 1880, the inventor of partly printed newspapers was William Eglington. Describing the work of the National Press Agency, the writer said:

Its managers announced their readiness to supply partially printed sheets for the benefit of newspaper proprietors in small towns. These sheets are printed on one, two, or three pages, and on receipt of them the local editor, who has ready the local matter and advertisements, can at once go to press with his paper. Mr. William Eglington, of Bartholomew Close, the originator of the partially printed sheets, and Messrs. Cassell, Petter and Galpin, it may be added, undertake this last kind of business and now supply the inside pages of not a few local sheets.

A similar scheme for reducing the costs of production was devised for daily papers by William Saunders and his brother-in-law Edward Spender, proprietors of the *Western Morning News*, who in 1863 established the Central Press for the purpose of supplying general news and features in stereo form to provincial daily papers—everything that the editor required, even leading articles. Among the papers which subscribed to this service were the *Western Morning News* (Plymouth), the *Eastern Morning News* (Hull), the *Northern Daily Express* (Newcastle) and the *Caledonian Mercury* (Edinburgh). The idea did not secure general acceptance, most provincial newspapers deciding that the economy and convenience would not compensate for the sacrifice of individuality, and eventually the scheme faded out. Meanwhile the Central Press had changed hands and become a general news agency. Earlier in the century some provincial weeklies were edited by London journalists—from London. William Jerdan, editor of the *Literary Gazette*, says in his autobiography that he edited several country journals, i.e. provided the non-local editorial features: probably the earliest recorded example of what is now known as syndication.

The daily papers established outside London from 1855 onwards were not able immediately to give their readers a comprehensive news coverage, the expense being at first too heavy. The electric telegraph had ended the news monopoly enjoyed by the capital for over two centuries. Formerly provincial readers had to await the arrival of the London papers before they could get the general news; now this news came by telegraph and was printed in the local dailies hours ahead of the arrival of the London journals. But it was not until they established a co-operative news-gathering organization—the Press Association (1868)—that the provincial dailies could begin to provide a general and Parliamentary news service at all comparable with that of London journals; and with the institution of cheap rates for Press messages in 1870 and the previous establishment of London offices equipped with private wires a tremendous stimulus was given to the use of the telegraph.[1] The improvement of telegraphic facilities also speeded up the development of Reuters Agency, recently started by Julius de Reuter in Paris. He opened an office in London in 1851 to provide a service of commercial intelligence and in 1858 began supplying London newspapers with digests of foreign news (the first subscriber was the *Morning Advertiser*). The agency later became a world-wide organization; it is now wholly owned and controlled by the Press. The Central News was founded in 1870 and the Exchange

[1] Transmission of news over private wires began in March 1866. Writing thirty years later, Charles A. Cooper, editor of the *Scotsman*, said: "Since March 1866 there has been a continuous growth of telegraphic and telegraphed news in the papers.... One special wire, in the case of the *Scotsman*, speedily became two; and these two now carry scarcely more than half of the news telegraphed from London during the year. In the old days there might be a column of telegraphed news in the paper in one day. Now it is not uncommon to find forty columns, and the daily average must be thirty."—*An Editor's Retrospect: Fifty Years of Newspaper Work* (1896).

THE AGE OF EXPANSION

Telegraph Company in 1872.[1] The service provided by the various agencies enabled London and provincial dailies alike to expand their news considerably, at a moderate cost; and as the agency idea developed—in particular, as Reuters extended its operations and raised the general level of foreign correspondence—the few leading journals ceased to enjoy the overwhelming superiority as newspapers which their greater financial resources had long maintained.[2] The telegraph soon established itself as the normal mode of transmission of news, and papers such as *The Times* which predominantly used the work of their own correspondents found their expenditure on foreign intelligence heavily increased.

The reduction in the price of newspapers, combined with the development of quick and cheap transport by the construction of a countrywide network of railways, led to a remarkable increase in the reading of daily newspapers. Simultaneously with the rapid growth in circulation of London rivals of *The Times*, some of the new provincial newspapers built up considerable sales and by sound and responsible editing became institutions within their own circulation area comparable in standing and character with the principal metropolitan journals. It was the age of great editors. Delane of *The Times*, the most influential of them all, had no outstanding successor until the twentieth century; but such men as Algernon Borthwick (later Lord Glenesk) of the *Morning Post* and W. H. Mudford of the *Standard* gave their journals a fresh lease of power by vital leadership. Algernon Borthwick became managing editor of the *Morning Post* in 1852, at the age of 22, on the death of his father (Peter Borthwick). In 1876 he bought the paper and in 1881 he reduced the price from threepence to a penny, which brought new

[1] Over thirty years later came the London News Agency, whose service of metropolitan news gradually restricted and finally killed the scope for penny-a-liners, who lived precariously on the fringe of journalism in the nineteenth century, doing "chance" reporting of police courts and miscellaneous news and being notorious for their elaborate wordiness and their frequent inventiveness.

[2] See Appendix A for a survey of the news agencies and their work at the present day.

prosperity to the *Morning Post* but did not, as he lamented, get rid of the prejudice that it was "a mere fashionable paper." Typical of this attitude was *Punch's* amusing comment through the mouth of "Jeames" on the decision to cut the price:

> "Sir Halgernon! Sir Halgernon! I can't believe it true,
> They say the Post's a penny now, and all along of you;
> The paper that was once the pride of all the swells in town,
> Now like a common print is sold for just a vulgar brown."

Outside London several notable journalists put their impress on the new papers—among them C. P. Scott (who edited the *Manchester Guardian* from 1872—he was then 25 years old—to 1929); Sir Edward Russell, later Lord Russell of Liverpool (editor of the *Liverpool Daily Post* for over half a century), and Alexander Russel (editor of the *Scotsman* for twenty-eight years). The *Glasgow Herald* had several editors of mark, including George Outram, Dr. James Pagan and Dr. J. H. Stoddart.

Scott made the *Manchester Guardian* the greatest Liberal journal in the country, with a national as well as a local influence and with an international reputation for sane and distinguished journalism. The conduct of a newspaper, as he once said, demands a sense of duty to the reader and to the community. "The newspaper is of necessity something of a monopoly, and its first duty is to shun the temptations of a monopoly," declared Scott. "Its primary office is the gathering of News. At the peril of its soul it must see that the supply is not tainted. Neither in what it gives, nor in what it does not give, nor in the mode of presentation, must the unclouded face of Truth suffer wrong. Comment is free, but facts are sacred. . . . Comment is also justly subject to a self-imposed restraint. It is well to be frank: it is even better to be fair." He surrounded himself with a brilliant staff, some of whom were to achieve fame as editors, writers and critics. Of one of them—C. E. Montague, leader-writer, critic, novelist and essayist—H. W. Nevinson said that he was "the only man I know whose white hair in a single night turned dark through courage," an allusion to the fact that Montague, at the age of

47, dyed his hair and, "with a splendid lie," enlisted in the "Sportsman's Battalion" in 1914. The *Manchester Guardian* under Scott developed into a paper that admirably reflected all the interests of civilized men and women, a paper in which good writing could be found in every department: in the splendid words of Lord Cecil, "He made righteousness readable." W. P. Crozier, one of his successors in the editorial chair, recalling his memories of Scott at work in a chapter contributed to J. L. Hammond's biography,[1] gave this picture of how he approached his major responsibilities as editor:

> No interruption, no visitor, no office conference was allowed to delay the sacred task of fixing for the night the subject of "the Long." This was the Long Leader, prime instrument of policy, the voice, persuasive or protestant, for whose utterance, more than for any other single purpose, he believed the newspaper to exist. . . . When a discussion raged about a fundamental question, when he thought that anyone was proposing to palter with principle, then the eyes flashed and the beard shook and the Commandments came down again in thunder and lightning. He was a poor speaker, but in writing he had a voice whose sound was like the sea.

Thus an era of newspaper expansion that began with the removal of the taxes on knowledge produced results far transcending the modest hopes of John Bright, who lived to see the tradition of honest and responsible journalism firmly stamped on many new daily journals that were established outside London and to see the complete justification of the belief he expressed in 1855 that "never was so large a measure involved in so small a measure, so to speak, as is the case with regard to this proposition of making the Press free."

Daily journalism was no longer a London monopoly, no longer reflected merely the views of metropolitan writers. It had become widely diffused and healthily varied. The significance of this change was noted in the *Yorkshire Post* (formerly the *Leeds Intelligencer*, a weekly dating back to 1754) when it started daily publication in 1866: "When we consider that the population of

[1] *C. P. Scott* (J. L. Hammond).

two such counties as Lancashire and Yorkshire, to say nothing of the North of England in general, now draws its political opinions quite as much from the Press of Manchester, Liverpool and Leeds as from the Press of London, we shall understand at once the whole extent of the power which for good or for evil may be wielded by provincial journalism."

The removal of the taxes on newspapers, advertisements and paper brought new prosperity to the Sunday journals. Their costs were reduced, and by lowering their prices they were able to secure a great accession of new readers. The two papers that achieved highest sales about the middle of the century were *Lloyd's Weekly Newspaper* (1842) and the *News of the World* (1843).

Edward Lloyd (1815–1890), the founder of the weekly that bore his name, was a man of remarkable enterprise. His first venture was the publication, at the age of 18, of *Lloyd's Stenography*: he printed this volume himself from type set up for him, inserting the symbols in written form, and then carried the book round for sale. He next published a number of songbooks and issued *The Penny Pickwick* (edited by "Bos" and illustrated by "Phis"), with transparent variations of the characters' names, e.g. Snodgreen for Snodgrass. Dickens brought proceedings against him, without success, but afterwards he and Lloyd reached a friendly reconciliation. Imitative, too, was the title of his first newspaper, the *Penny Sunday Times and People's Police Gazette* (1840)—later *Lloyd's Penny Sunday Times*.[1] In 1842 he started he started *Lloyd's Illustrated Sunday Newspaper*, price twopence, and after publishing eight issues abandoned the use of illustration and renamed the paper *Lloyd's Weekly London Newspaper* (later shortened to *Lloyd's Weekly News*). In 1843 the paper was increased from eight to twelve pages and the price raised to threepence. The abolition of the newspaper stamp enabled Lloyd to revert to the price of twopence. The sale rose to 170,000 by 1861, when the removal of the paper duty

[1] The *Sunday Times* began life as the *New Observer* (later the *Independent Observer*), changing to its present title in 1822.

THE AGE OF EXPANSION

encouraged him to make a further reduction to one penny, which had the effect of doubling the circulation within two years. Meanwhile he had prepared to cope with the big increase in sales that he foresaw by introducing, in 1856, the Hoe rotary printing press—the first to be installed in England. This machine printed the newspaper from type; each page was locked into a "turtle," as the segments of the impression cylinder were called. A few years later this ingenious device was superseded by curved stereotyped plates, which made possible the simultaneous use of a number of presses and the vast output per hour which is now a commonplace of newspaper production. *Lloyd's Weekly News* became the most successful of Victorian week-end journals, reaching a sale of over a million copies. In 1876 Lloyd bought the *Daily Chronicle* for £30,000 and spent £150,000 on its development. It had become a daily in 1866, when it was called the *London Daily Chronicle and Clerkenwell News*; formerly it was a halfpenny local weekly, the *Clerkenwell News*, started in 1856 in succession to a free advertisement sheet, the *Business and Agency News*, established a year earlier. Lloyd also became a leading figure in the paper-making industry, building a large factory at Sittingbourne.

One of the early editors of *Lloyd's Weekly Newspaper* was Douglas Jerrold (1803–1857), a well-known figure in Early Victorian journalism. Son of an actor, he was apprenticed to the printing trade at the age of 13, and three years later he began to write for the *Sunday Monitor* while working for its printers. He became a successful playwright and was a contributor to *Punch*, and some of his contributions—including *Mrs. Caudle's Curtain Lectures*—were reprinted in book form. He edited the *Illuminated Magazine* (1843) until it ceased publication two years later, and then founded *Douglas Jerrold's Shilling Magazine* (1845–1848). In 1846 he started *Douglas Jerrold's Weekly Newspaper* and edited it for eighteen months, but was unable to make the paper pay and had to dispose of it. Edward Lloyd invited him to edit *Lloyd's Weekly Newspaper*, at a salary of £1,000 a year, and he held this post from 1852 until he died.

The success of *Lloyd's Weekly Newspaper* and the *News of the World* stimulated fresh competition in week-end journalism. The *Weekly Times* (1847), a threepenny, attained a sale of 75,000; many years later—in the 'eighties—it was acquired by Passmore Edwards, who amalgamated it with his *Weekly Echo*, and under the title of *Weekly Times and Echo* it survived until 1912. In 1850 George William Reynolds started *Reynolds's Weekly Newspaper* (now *Reynolds News and Sunday Citizen*) as a Radical journal, at the price of fourpence—subsequently reduced—and within a few years its circulation was nearing 50,000. A short-lived attempt to establish a halfpenny Sunday journal (the only one ever published at this price) was made in 1861, when the four-page *London Halfpenny Newspaper* issued only four numbers. Headlines on the front page of No. 1 included "Dreadful Death of Female Through Intoxication" and "Horrible Murder in Glasgow." The *Weekly Dispatch* (now the *Sunday Dispatch*) was sold at fivepence until 1869, when the price came down to twopence; about eighteen months later it became a penny paper. Ashton Wentworth Dilke bought the *Weekly Dispatch* in 1875, gave it a Radical policy and introduced literary features, and the circulation increased considerably. Over a quarter of a century later, after a period of ownership by Sir George Newnes, the paper was bought by Lord Northcliffe.

Most of the popular Sunday journals of the nineteenth century addressed their appeal to the working classes and were Radical in tone. It was not considered respectable to read a Sunday journal, since these weeklies gave so much of their space to crime and scandal; and not until the *Observer* and the *Sunday Times*—neither of which enjoyed more than brief intervals of real prosperity in Victorian days—were remodelled in this century as well-informed, well-written and responsible journals catering for all the interests of serious-minded readers did the reading of Sunday newspapers spread to all classes of the community. A parallel development was the introduction of magazine and "personality" features into several of the popular Sunday journals, and among the pioneers of this change was the *Sunday Chronicle*

THE AGE OF EXPANSION

(1885), which about forty years ago had among its regular contributors Robert Blatchford ("Nunquam") and Hubert Bland, both writers of exceptional lucidity, and Sir John Foster Fraser, one of the first journalists to gain a wide public with signed popular-style "feature" articles in the Sunday press.

Among other Sunday journals started in Victorian days were the *Weekly Budget* (1861–1912), the *Referee* (1877) and the *People* (1881). The last-named now has a sale of over 5,000,000, its present prosperity dating from its acquisition by Odhams Press over a quarter of a century ago. The *Referee* was a unique paper: there has never been anything like it before or since (it was discontinued in 1939). It made its appeal to readers interested in literature, the drama and sport, and its most popular contributor was George R. Sims, whose entertaining "Mustard and Cress" page was the main feature for many years. In the nature of things the *Referee* could not achieve a big sale, and this limited appeal was to prove its economic undoing in the era of mass circulation and higher costs of production that began after the First World War.

CHAPTER ELEVEN

Nineteenth-Century Periodicals

FOUR men who met in Edinburgh at the beginning of the nineteenth century adopted "with acclamation" a proposal by one of their number to start a review. The place of their meeting was the flat of Francis Jeffrey, a barrister who later became a successful advocate and was made a peer on his appointment as judge; and his guests were Sydney Smith, then working as a private tutor in Edinburgh, whose idea it was to establish a review; Henry (afterwards Lord) Brougham, who was to become Lord Chancellor; and another friend who later became Lord Murray and Lord Advocate for Scotland.

There have been many such meetings in the history of periodical journalism and many promising literary barques that have been launched with equally generous enthusiasm; but this occasion was destined to be as significant as the fortunate partnership of Steele and Addison ninety years before. The quarterly that sprang from this meeting was to bring the review to full and splendid maturity and to give it a form that has substantially endured to this day. This achievement was mainly the work of three of these young men—Francis Jeffrey, Sydney Smith and Henry Brougham. Their aim was "to erect a standard of merit, and secure a bolder and purer taste in literature, and to apply philosophical principles and the maxims of truth and humanity to politics," and in the application of this policy they were to arouse vigorous controversy and at times the most bitter strife. We have a first-hand account of the beginning of the *Edinburgh Review* in Sydney Smith's preface to his collected works.

I was appointed Editor, and remained long enough in Edinburgh to edit the first number of the Edinburgh Review. The motto I proposed for the Review was,

"*Tenui musam meditamur avena.*"
"We cultivate literature upon a little oatmeal."

But this was too near the truth to be admitted, and so we took our present grave motto from *Publius Syrus*, of whom none of us had, I am sure, ever read a single line, and so began what has turned out to be a very important and able journal. When I left Edinburgh it fell into the stronger hands of Lord Jeffrey and Lord Brougham, and reached the highest point of popularity and success. . . .

To appreciate the value of the Edinburgh Review, the state of England when that journal began should be had in remembrance. The Catholics were not emancipated—the Corporation and Test Acts were unrepealed—the Game Laws were horribly oppressive—Steel Traps and Spring Guns were set all over the country—Prisoners tried for their lives could have no Counsel—Lord Eldon and the Court of Chancery pressed heavily upon mankind—Libel was punished by the most cruel and vindictive imprisonments—the principles of Political Economy were little understood—the Law of Debt and of Conspiracy were upon the worst possible footing—the enormous wickedness of the Slave Trade was tolerated—a thousand evils were in existence, which the talents of good and able men have since lessened or removed; and these effects have been not a little assisted by the honest boldness of the Edinburgh Review.

Steele and Addison's periodical had been a mere sheet; the first number of the *Edinburgh Review*, published by Constable, was a substantial octavo book of 252 pages, price five shillings. The editorial "Advertisement" in No. 1 was brief and austere: "In committing this work to the judgement of the Public, the Editors have but little to observe. It will be easily perceived, that it forms no part of their object, to take notice of every production that issues from the Press; and that they wish their Journal to be distinguished, rather for the selection, than for the number, of its articles." Of the twenty-nine articles nine were written by Sydney Smith, six by Jeffrey, four by Francis Horner and three by Brougham; and other contributors within the next few years included Sir Walter Scott and Henry Hallam. The reception was favourable, and as time went on the review gained a high reputation. Beginning with a circulation of 800, it attained a sale of 9,000 within six years and by 1818 had reached the peak figure of 14,000; in addition, sales in book form (two numbers to a volume) ran into many editions. Neither editor nor contributors received any payment for their work for the first three numbers, but Sydney Smith urged on Constable that a payment of £200 a year to the editor and ten guineas a sheet for contributions would make him the owner of "the best review in Europe." Jeffrey sounded his contributors and found that they would not be averse to receiving payment for their work, and therefore concluded that he might accept a salary without suffering "any degradation."

"The *Edinburgh* has but two legs to stand on," Jeffrey once told Scott, who complained of the strongly partisan note of the review. "Literature is one of them, but its right leg is politics." But what most impressed readers of the early numbers and was the main reason for the success of the review was the independence of its literary judgments. Nothing like the quality of its critical work had been known before; previously criticism had mostly been indistinguishable from puffery. In their attitude to politics and literature the conductors of the new review revealed a striking contradiction. They were all fervent reformers, but in their approach to literature they were firmly traditional. Any hint of innovation in contemporary writing was sharply rebuked and authors were didactically reminded of "the loftiness of Milton" and "the pointed and fine propriety of Pope." The Lake poets especially came under the lash, and Jeffrey's notorious article on Wordsworth's *Excursion*, opening with the brusque sentence "This will never do," illustrates this dislike of literary experimentalism. Byron's *Hours of Idleness* was roughly handled in a review written by Brougham but generally thought to be the work of Jeffrey, and Byron retorted with his famous poem *English Bards and Scotch Reviewers*. One of the allusions in this satire was to a duel arranged between Jeffrey and Thomas Moore. The latter was angry at the criticism of his *Odes and Epistles* in the *Edinburgh Review* and challenged Jeffrey. The duel had been much talked about in advance, and when the two men arrived at Chalk Farm, Hampstead, they found police on the scene. They and their seconds were taken into custody and, as Moore wrote, "replaced in our respective carriages and conveyed crestfallen to Bow Street." There was no bullet in Jeffrey's pistol, and he and Moore afterwards became friends.

But if they were prejudiced, and sometimes arrogant and ill-mannered, the *Edinburgh* reviewers at least took literature seriously: "no genteel family *can* pretend to be without it, because, independent of its politics, it gives the only valuable literary criticism which can be met with," Sir Walter Scott wrote to George Ellis (November 2, 1808). Jeffrey became the chief literary critic of his day, though most of his verdicts have been reversed by posterity; and his public reputation as a writer who dipped his pen in gall contrasts with the picture of the man as he was known to his intimates—a man who never lost a friend, who was sensitive and apprehensive and who gave liberal aid to impecunious writers. It was during his editorship, which lasted just over a quarter of a century, that Macaulay began writing for the *Edinburgh*. The first of his essays, the one on Byron, brought him instant fame at the age of 25.

In later years the *Edinburgh Review* became more conservative, and Walter Bagehot, writing in 1855, professed that there was a general belief that at that time it was written by privy councillors. "It is odd to hear that the *Edinburgh Review* was once thought an incendiary publication." It continued to appear until 1929, and its last editor was Harold Cox, a well-known Liberal economist.

The letter to George Ellis from Scott which has already been mentioned quoted a remark made by the *Edinburgh Review*, "We foresee a speedy revolution in this country as well as Mr. Cobbett," and made this comment: "I think, that for the last two years past, they have done their utmost to hasten the accomplishment of this prophecy." The remedy was to establish a review "on a plan as liberal as that of the Edinburgh, its literature as well supported, and its principles English and constitutional." As he revealed in another letter—to Charles

Kirkpatrick Sharpe—"it had long been the decided resolution of Mr. Canning and some of his literary friends, particularly Geo. Ellis, Malthus, Frere, W. Rose, &c., that something of an independent Review ought to be started in London. This plan is now on the point of being executed, after much consultation. I have strongly advised that politics be avoided, unless in cases of great national import, and that their tone be then moderate and manly; but the general tone of the publication is to be literary." William Gifford was chosen as editor of the new review—to be called the *Quarterly Review*—and John Murray, then "a young bookseller of capital and enterprise," agreed to publish it. Writing at great length to Gifford, Scott outlined his ideas on the scope and policy of the new review and suggested that "if it can burst among them like a bomb, without previous notice, the effect will be more striking." Every projector of a new periodical hopes that it will immediately become the subject of eager discussion; the actual genesis of the *Quarterly Review* was to be a much quieter affair than Scott proposed. The first number appeared in February 1809, contained eighteen articles —four written by Scott—and had no editorial foreword. Not until several numbers had appeared did it begin to be talked about, an article on the character of Charles James Fox in No. 4 stimulating the demand for the review. From this point the circulation rose until by 1818 it equalled that of the *Edinburgh Review*. Scott gave his active support to the review, and other regular contributors included Southey, Samuel Rogers, Moore and John Wilson Croker. The editor wrote chiefly on literary subjects and showed as much dislike for the new writers as did Jeffrey, though he made an exception for Byron, who responded to his friendliness by submitting to him his later poems. Gifford is thought to have been the author of the savage assault on Keats's *Endymion* that appeared in the *Quarterly Review* in 1818. Southey declared that Gifford looked upon authors as Izaak Walton looked upon worms—as creatures beyond the pale of human sympathy. Gifford's compression of his articles to fit the available space so angered Southey that he said that he would have broken off the connection if he could have afforded to do so. Among the writers of whom Gifford fell foul was Hazlitt, who took his revenge by writing a pamphlet, *A Letter to William Gifford, Esq.*, which was a bitter indictment of the *Quarterly* editor, whom he described as "by appointment, literary toad-eater to greatness, and taster to the court."

William Hazlitt (1778–1830), now remembered mainly as an essayist, did much writing for newspapers and reviews and was the outstanding literary journalist of the time. He worked on the *Morning Chronicle*, first as Parliamentary reporter and later as dramatic critic and writer on art, and he contributed to Leigh Hunt's *Examiner* and to John Scott's *Champion*. At the suggestion of Thomas Barnes, John Walter II engaged him as theatrical critic in 1817—not long after Dr. Stoddart, Hazlitt's brother-in-law, had been dismissed from *The Times*. He stayed only a few months and it is not known why he left; but in a preface to *A View of the English Stage* (1818) he advised anyone who had "an ambition to write and write his best, in the periodical press, to get, if possible, 'a situation' in *The Times* newspaper. . . . He may write there as long and as good articles as he can, without being turned out for it." Nevertheless, *The Times* was not to his taste, "either in matter or manner," he later wrote in the *Edinburgh Review* (May 1823). "It might be imagined to be composed as well as printed with a steam engine. . . . Its style is magniloquent; its spirit is not magnanimous. It is valiant, swaggering, insolent. . . ." Hazlitt's finest journalistic work was probably in the field of theatrical criticism, and it is chiefly his vivid impressions of their performances that have immortalized Sarah Siddons, Edmund Kean, the Kembles and other contemporary actors. He wrote lucidly and vigorously on a wide range of subjects; the vigour was often edged with bitterness when he touched on politics or one of his antipathies—he was a moody, quarrelsome and unhappy man—and he was searingly effective in attack.

Gifford continued to edit the *Quarterly Review* until shortly before his death in 1826. He was succeeded for a short period by John Taylor Coleridge, and from 1825 to 1853 John Gibson

Lockhart held the editorship. Like the *Edinburgh* the review mellowed with time, becoming less extreme in its views. It has outlived its senior, is still published by the house of Murray and is edited by Sir John Murray.

A third important literary periodical was born in April 1817, when the *Edinburgh Monthly Magazine*—renamed *Blackwood's Edinburgh Magazine* after several issues—was established by William Blackwood, who also founded the publishing house which, like the magazine, still bears his name. The new monthly made a dull start. The two editors he had appointed were unable to give it the "more nimble" touch that its founder wanted, and he took over the editorship himself at the time that he changed the title. He looked round for talented writers and found two able recruits in John Wilson (Christopher North) and Lockhart, who became regular contributors, the latter continuing to write for *Blackwood's* after he became editor of the *Quarterly*. William Blackwood's aim was to startle the public into the realization that they had a new magazine of character in their midst and he embarrassingly succeeded. He published what purported to be a translation from an ancient Chaldee manuscript, which in Old Testament style satirized the *Edinburgh Review* and Edinburgh Whigs and enthusiastically described the new magazine. The article caused a great deal of commotion, and its imitation of scriptural language gave offence to religious readers; and when the number was reprinted in response to public demand Blackwood cautiously omitted it. The magazine published also the first of a series of articles, signed "Z," on "The Cockney School of Poetry," believed from internal evidence to have been the joint work of Lockhart and Christopher North. The assault on the new poets which found contemptuous expression in the *Edinburgh* and the *Quarterly* was pursued with cold malice in *Blackwood's*. The first article deplored the "extreme moral depravity" of the Cockney School and said of Leigh Hunt's *Hippocrene:*

His poetry is that of a man who has kept company with kept-mistresses. He talks indelicately like a tea-sipping milliner girl. Some excuse for him there might have been, had he been hurried away by imagination or passion. But with him indecency is a disease, as he speaks unclean things from perfect inanition. The very concubine of so impure a wretch as Leigh Hunt would be to be pitied, but alas! for the wife of such a husband! For him there is no charm in simple seduction; and he gloats over it only when accompanied with adultery and incest.

When this number was reprinted the attack on Leigh Hunt was toned down, but later articles in the series showed that the "Mother of Mischief" (as Scott called *Blackwood's*) had not yet repented. The fourth article, which attacked Keats, was brutal as well as mischievous. There were shrewd criticisms of the weaknesses in the poetry of Keats, who was described as a still smaller poet than Hunt—"only a boy of pretty abilities which he has done everything in his power to spoil." The article ended in cruelly patronizing style:

We venture to make one small prophecy, that his bookseller will not a second time venture £50 upon any thing he can write. It is a better and a wiser thing to be a starved apothecary than a starved poet; so back to the shop Mr. John, back to "plasters, pills, and ointment boxes," etc. But, for Heaven's sake, young Sangrado, be a little more sparing of extenuatives and soporifics in your practice than you have been in your poetry.

Macaulay's criticism of Southey's *Colloquies of Society* brought down upon him the wrath of Christopher North. His essay was described as "malignant trash" and Macaulay himself as "an ugly, cross-made, splay-footed shapeless little dumpling of a fellow." This attack appeared in a feature called "Noctes Ambrosianæ," which ran for many years. Mainly written by North, it treated literary and topical subjects in the form of imaginary dialogues. William Maginn, another notable contributor, was credited with the invention of this feature. In 1830, with Hugh Fraser, he founded *Fraser's Magazine*, a literary monthly which obviously owed its inspiration to *Blackwood's* but developed into a journal of original quality that attracted contributions from Carlyle, Thackeray and others; in 1882 it became *Longman's Magazine*, and in 1905 it ceased publication. Maginn was for a time joint editor of the *Standard*. Thackeray took him as the model for the character of Captain Shandon in *Pendennis*. Maginn was a gifted journalist who would have made a greater mark but for his drunkenness.

The early "Maga"—to use the diminutive by which *Blackwood's* soon came to be known—would be misjudged if it were regarded simply as the medium for a cruel vendetta against the poets of its generation. It was much more than that. As a magazine it owed its considerable success to its skilful catering for the intelligent reader who wanted sound and varied literary fare, and this fare—especially in the "Noctes Ambrosianæ" department—was salted with wit and humour. Coleridge wrote for it occasionally, and De Quincey was another contributor in the early years; but the men whose contributions gave *Blackwood's* its distinctive character were North and Lockhart. It was they who "made" the magazine.

The literary violence that marked the early history of these reviews was perhaps less shocking to contemporaries than to us. It was an age of gross abuse in newspapers as well as in periodicals: *The Times*, for instance, once referred to Macaulay as "Mr. Babbletongue Macaulay," suggesting that he was "hardly fit to fill up one of the vacancies that have occurred by the lamentable death of one of her Majesty's two favourite monkeys." Journalistic manners grew more civilized as the century advanced, and reviews especially came to symbolize an attitude to life distinguished by sobriety and balance. *Blackwood's*, like the *Edinburgh* and the *Quarterly*, gained mellowness with age; later it evolved into a purely literary magazine. Today, with a century and a third of life completed, it is still edited by a member of the Blackwood family.

An interesting new monthly which, like the later *Fraser's Magazine*, showed the influence of *Blackwood's*, came into existence with the founding of the *London Magazine* in 1820. The prospectus stated that the magazine was designed "to combine the Principles of sound Philosophy in Questions of Taste,

Morals, and Politics, with the Entertainment and Miscellaneous Information expected from a Public Journal" (the "Miscellaneous Information" being a register of colonial intelligence, public documents, foreign and domestic news, works preparing for publication, foreign books imported, markets, etc.). The magazine ran for nine years and is now chiefly remembered as the monthly in which first appeared Charles Lamb's *Essays of Elia* and De Quincey's *Confessions of an Opium Eater*. Lamb received twenty guineas a sheet (16 pages) for contributions; the usual rate was £1 a page. The editor, John Scott, had the temerity to criticize *Blackwood's* and especially Lockhart, and this attack was to cost him his life. Lockhart asked for an apology or satisfaction in the usual way. Negotiations took place and the quarrel having apparently been settled Lockhart returned to Scotland; but the dispute would not die down, both sides continuing to add to the bitterness. At last Lockhart's second, Jonathan Henry Christie, personally challenged Scott to a duel,[1] and the two men met by moonlight at Chalk Farm on February 16, 1821. Christie did not fire until the second time. His bullet hit Scott above the hip and inflicted what proved to be a mortal injury. Scott was removed to Chalk Farm Tavern, where he died eleven days later. The inquest verdict was "Wilful murder," but Christie and his second were found not guilty when tried at the Old Bailey.

No survey of the periodical journalism of this time is complete without some reference to the career of Theodore Hook (1788–1841), editor and novelist, who impressed many famous contemporaries by his gifts, but who was regarded by his enemies either as a reckless journalistic wit or as an impudent mountebank with a dubious past. Son of a well-known musical composer, he collaborated with his father at an early age by supplying the words for the songs in his comic operas and before he was

[1] This is the usually accepted story of what happened, but Christie, in a letter to Lockhart (reproduced in Andrew Lang's *Life*), said that Scott sent an intermediary (Patmore) demanding an "explanation" that he (Christie) meant nothing disrespectful to him in a certain written statement, and when Christie declined to do anything of the sort Patmore produced a challenge from Scott which had to be delivered in the event of refusal.

twenty-one had produced, in partnership or independently, several farces and melodramas. His charm and his talent were such that, in the words of Lockhart, it was "hard to be often in his society without regarding him with as much of fondness as of admiration." He was a brilliant conversationalist and had remarkable gifts as a literary and musical improvisator and parodist—Leigh Hunt tells of one sparkling performance that led Thomas Campbell, the poet, to hurl his wig at him with the remark, "You dog! I'll throw my laurels at you"—and he was perhaps the greatest practical joker of all time.[1] At the age of 21 he was responsible for the notorious Berners Street hoax, sending out an enormous number of letters and orders for goods in the name of a Mrs. Tottenham (who had offended him) and causing her house to be besieged by visitors—among them the Duke of Gloucester, the Lord Mayor, the Archbishop of Canterbury, the Governor of the Bank of England, the Lord Chief Justice—and by a mass of vanmen and others seeking to deliver the goods, from books to loads of coal, which had been ordered for a particular hour. The secret of the author of this impudent hoax was well kept at the time and Hook escaped punishment.[2]

The Prince Regent was one of those who fell under the enchantment of his amazing powers of improvisation and commented that "something must be done for Hook." Something was done for him; in 1813 he went out to Mauritius to fill the

---

[1] Lockhart, writing in the *Quarterly Review* (May 1843) after the death of Hook, said that no mirth in the world ever surpassed the fascination of those "early mountebankeries" as they were described by Hook to his friends. "They are nothing without the commentary of that bright eye—the deep gurgling glee of his voice—the electrical felicity of his pantomime—for in truth he was as great an actor as could have been produced by rolling up Liston and Terry and Mathews into one."

[2] Lockhart gave a different version of the origin of the hoax. "It is recorded that in walking down that street one day his companion called his attention to the particularly neat and modest appearance of a house, the residence, as appeared from the door-plate, of some decent shopkeeper's widow. 'I'll lay you a guinea,' said Theodore, 'that in one week that nice modest dwelling shall be the most famous in London.' The bet was taken. . . ."

post of accountant-general and treasurer at a salary of £2,000 a year. A few years later a deficiency of 62,000 dollars in the treasury—said to have been stolen by one of his subordinates, though Hook could give no explanation of how it had happened—brought his delightful stay on the island to an ignominious end. His property there was confiscated and he was arrested and sent back to England. An investigation revealed no foundation for a criminal charge, but Hook was held to be personally responsible for the loss and his property in this country was seized; later he spent two years in prison, from 1823 to 1825, having made no effort to pay off his debt. Three years after his return —in the meantime he had engaged in literary work and written, among other things, a satire on Queen Caroline—he was selected, on the recommendation of Sir Walter Scott, to edit *John Bull*, which made its first appearance in November 1820. This new Sunday journal, half political weekly and half newspaper—with the motto, "For God, The King, and the People!"—was primarily designed as a counterblast to the popular agitation in favour of Caroline. It offered Hook the fullest possible scope for the exercise of his extraordinary gifts, and he mercilessly and persistently ridiculed the Queen. As the practical joke in Berners Street had revealed, Hook was not held back by normal scruples, and he now revelled in the chance to use all his talents of sarcasm, parody, invective and ingenious malice. The first shot in the campaign, a long article in No. 1, was diabolically clever and mischievous. Within a few weeks everybody in London was reading and talking about this witty and scandalous new journal, and the circulation reached 10,000. Hook carefully disclaimed in its columns any connection with the paper: this may have been partly due to caution, for when later the authorities realized that he was now in receipt of a good income they secured his imprisonment, as already mentioned, for not attempting to defray his liability to the Treasury. The editorial comment was highly plausible:

Mr. Theodore Hook

The conceit of some people is amusing: and it has been not

infrequently remarked, that conceit is in abundance, when talent is most scarce. Our readers will see that we have received a letter from Mr. Hook, disowning and disavowing all connexion with the Paper. Partly out of good nature, and partly from anxiety to shew the gentleman how little desirous we are to be associated with him, we have made a declaration which will doubtless be quite satisfactory to his marked sensibility, and affected squeamishness. We are free to confess that two things surprise us in this business; first, that any thing which we have thought worthy of giving to the public, should have been mistaken for Mr. Hook's; and secondly, that *such a person* as Mr. Hook should think himself disgraced by a connexion with *John Bull*.

Even more plausible was an editorial note in the next issue:

We have received Mr. Hook's second letter. We are ready to confess that we may have appeared to treat him too unceremoniously; but we will put it to his own feelings whether the terms of his denial were not in some degree calculated to produce a little asperity on our part. We shall never be ashamed, however, to do justice, and we readily declare that we meant no kind of imputation on Mr. Hook's personal character.

Not everyone was taken in by this elaborate piece of deceit. Within two months Queen Caroline's supporters produced a rival journal, *The Real Old John Bull*, and an attack on Hook in No. 1 accused him of being editor of what was described as the "*Scurrilous Impostor.*" The precaution had been taken of appointing a nominal editor of *John Bull*, one Shackell, to act as "a legal lightning conductor"—or, in the phrase used in other countries, as the prison editor—who received a salary and a share of the profits. There were several libel actions and one charge of breach of Parliamentary privilege within two years, resulting in heavy fines and two spells of imprisonment for the useful deputy. Hook's active connection with *John Bull* was limited to the first few years of its existence, but he continued to write for the paper occasionally up to his death. He was also for a time editor of the *New Monthly Magazine* and he wrote numerous novels, some of which achieved considerable success. He never paid off his debt to the Treasury and he died—in his own words—"Done up in purse, in mind and in body."

Two quarterlies and one monthly had brilliantly succeeded, and it occurred to a Scots journalist, Robert Stephen Rintoul, who had made contact with *Blackwood's* staff while he was working in Edinburgh, that there were undeveloped possibilities in weekly journalism. He edited for a time a new London weekly called the *Atlas*—"A General Newspaper and Journal of Literature"—and when (according to a letter he wrote to William Blackwood) he was asked to vulgarize the paper he decided to withdraw from it. Friends subscribed capital that enabled him to start a new weekly in 1828 for which he revived the name of the *Spectator*, and the contributors to the *Atlas* came over to his side. Advertisements of the new paper stressed that "the tone and character of the *Spectator*, the variety of its contents, and even its external form, peculiarly fit it for the use of respectable families."

Its plan is entirely new, comprising (1) the whole news of the week; (2) a full and impartial exhibition of all the leading politics of the day; (3) a separate discussion of interesting topics of a general nature, with a view to instruction and entertainment at the same time; (4) a department devoted to literature, consisting of independent criticisms of the new books, with specimens of the best passages; (5) dramatic and musical criticism; (6) scientific and miscellaneous information.

The price was at first ninepence (which included fourpence tax) and in 1831, when the number of pages was increased from sixteen to twenty-four, it was raised to a shilling. The *Spectator* made headway slowly: ten years passed before its circulation climbed to 3,000. Rintoul showed character as an editor and was enlightened in his policy, but it was tenacity rather than brilliance that pulled the paper through the difficulties of its early days and gave it modest success during the thirty years that he edited it. The intelligent reader could find more forceful journalism in the *Examiner*, which during the editorship (1830–1847) of Albany

Fonblanque,[1] one of the ablest journalistic writers of the time, enjoyed a striking revival. In order to finance the installation of new machinery to lower the cost of production, admirers of Fonblanque paid their subscriptions to the paper for ten years in advance. After he gave up the editorship the *Examiner* began to decline, and in 1880 this once-famous weekly ceased publication. In 1861, three years after the death of Rintoul, the *Spectator* began a new and more prosperous chapter when it came under the joint editorial direction of Richard Holt Hutton and Meredith Townsend, who gave the paper the alert, well-balanced outlook on life characteristic of the review at its best and made it a pulpit for thoughtful liberalism; and this tradition was continued, with the addition of a practical crusading zeal, by J. St. Loe Strachey, who edited the paper from 1898 to 1925.

Other literary and political weeklies established in the nineteenth century included the *Literary Gazette* (1817), a pioneer in this field, started by Henry Colburn and edited for over thirty years by William Jerdan, who had many noted writers among his contributors; the *Athenaeum*[2] (1828), for long the most influential of critical journals, which continued independent existence for nearly a century before incorporation in the *Nation*, which in turn was absorbed by the *New Statesman*; the *Economist* (1843), which was edited by Walter Bagehot from 1860 until his death in 1877; the *Leader* (1850), started by George Henry Lewes, assisted by Thornton Hunt; the *Saturday Review* (1855), which quickly gained a reputation for editorial liveliness and was to have some famous editors and contributors; the *Academy* (1869), a literary and critical journal of quality that passed through many

[1] Leigh Hunt, in his *Autobiography*, says of his successor in the editorship of the *Examiner*: "Mr. Fonblanque ... had all the wit for which I toiled, without making any pretensions to it. He was, indeed, the genuine successor, not of me, but of the Swifts and Addisons themselves; profuse of wit even beyond them, and superior in political knowledge."

[2] Austere in tone and appearance, the *Athenaeum* provoked the famous irreverent comment by a character in R. L. Stevenson and Lloyd Osbourne's *The Wrong Box*: "Golly, what a paper!" In its great days, when it had established a new standard of coolly impartial literary criticism, the very name of the *Athenaeum* had the deep, booming sound of authority itself.

changes of ownership and had a last flicker of brilliance in the twentieth century under the editorship of Lord Alfred Douglas; the *Statist* (878); the *Scots Observer* (1888), afterwards the *National Observer*, which had an editor of remarkable talents in W. E. Henley[1] but failed to establish itself permanently; *Literature* (1897), edited by H. D. Traill, which was amalgamated with the *Academy* in 1902; the *Speaker* (1898), which was incorporated some years later in H. W. Massingham's *Nation*; and the *Outlook* (1898), which had several well-known editors—among them J. L. Garvin—and enjoyed a brilliant revival in the nineteen-twenties but failed to achieve prosperity and had to be discontinued.

The *Saturday Review*, edited by John Douglas Cook, formerly editor of the *Morning Chronicle*, struck a fresh and vigorous note. Its articles ranged over a wide field, and they were written in such clear, incisive English that a century later many of them read as if they had been written last week. The *Saturday* made a profound impression from the start. It was a potent influence on the development of the weekly review and partly inspired the publication of the *Pall Mall Gazette* (which proclaimed itself "An Evening Newspaper and Review"). At first the organ of the Peelites, the *Saturday Review* was particularly opposed to *The Times*, of which it was said in an article published in No. 1 on "Our Newspaper Institutions":

> No apology is necessary for assuming that this country is ruled by *The Times*. We all know it, or, if we do not know it, we ought to know it. It is high time we began to realize the magnificent spectacle afforded by British freedom—thirty millions of *cives Romani* governed despotically by a newspaper. . . . We suggest that the existing despotism may be mitigated by the exercise of common sense and ordinary perspicacity. We say to a confiding public, Do your best to resolve the "we" into "I." Because William Jones addresses you on

[1] Henley built up a notable list of contributors and had the valuable assistance of Charles Whibley, who later contributed a monthly causerie, "Musings Without Method," to *Blackwood's Magazine* for many years and also wrote "The Letters of an Englishman," a weekly feature, for the *Daily Mail*.

Monday with vigorous logic and persuasive rhetoric, do not take the conclusions of John Smith for granted because they happen to be printed on Tuesday in the same place. Reflect that both William Jones and John Smith are gentlemen working three times a week, be there matter or no matter, be there straw for the bricks or none.

Another journalistic subject in No. 1 was a review, extending to nearly two pages, of *Memoirs of James Gordon Bennett and His Times*. It began: "This is the biography of a scoundrel, written not in the simple phrase of the *Newgate Calender*, nor with the humorous irony of *Jonathan Wild*, but in very much the sort of language which was employed towards Louis the Fourteenth by his literary courtiers." Here is another sample at least equally blunt: "We are told that Bennett is, 'as it is vulgarly called, squint-eyed.' This peculiarity is admirably brought out in the lithograph at the beginning of the volume. A countenance more eloquent of evil we do not remember to have seen." Strong language—but the creator of the *New York Herald* was accustomed to receiving hard words.

The *Spectator* in its early years was rather fond of discussing journalism and its problems and responsibilities. On April 2, 1831, it made these observations on the prospects for the magazine form:

We are afraid the day for Magazines is gone by; it is a form of publication which does not suit the wants of the reading world, in the present state of literature. The Newspapers and the Weekly Reviews, in their improved and extended form, have taken the ground formerly occupied by the Magazines, with the great advantage of more frequent publication. . . . Magazines formerly occupied the precise position of some of the present Weekly Papers; witness the list of bankrupts, the obituary, the prices of stocks, etc., which formerly adorned them, and which are now omitted simply because they are forestalled by the Newspaper.

Actually "the day for Magazines" had only just dawned and many fresh inventions would delight readers in the years to come.

In 1832 the brothers Chambers launched a bold innovation in popular journalism with the publication of the first weekly number of *Chambers's Edinburgh Journal* (renamed *Chambers's Journal of Literature, Science and Arts* in 1854), which was the third significant periodical venture born at Edinburgh since the beginning of the century. The two brothers who founded this new magazine, which was to lead to the building up of an important publishing house that rendered valuable service to the cause of popular education, were William Chambers (1800–1883) and Robert Chambers (1802–1871). Robert is best remembered as the author of *Vestiges of Creation*. As a boy he made the discovery that his father had a copy of the fourth edition of the *Encyclopaedia Britannica*, which was (he said) like a gift of a whole toyshop to other boys: "I plunged into it and roamed through it like a bee." Many years later he and his brother produced *Chambers's Encyclopaedia*, the serial publication of which was spread over ten years, the work being issued in 520 weekly parts at three-halfpence each. A low unit price, as will be seen, was the essence of their policy.

William Chambers was apprenticed at the age of 14 to an Edinburgh bookseller for four years at a wage of 4s. a week, and as his father lived some distance away he had to support himself. His budget was heroically simple—1s. 6d. for lodging, 1s. 9d. for food and 9d. to cover sundry expenses. Every morning he read to a baker and his men, and for this he received "a penny roll newly drawn from the oven." His apprenticeship over, he started in business for himself as a bookseller in Leith, and by the age of 23 he was successfully established. On February 4, 1832, with his brother as joint editor, he began the publication of *Chambers's Edinburgh Journal*, a four-page weekly of foolscap folio size issued at three-halfpence, a low price for those days. The copy of the first number in the British Museum is the seventh edition and of the second number the eighth edition: sufficient proof of the immediate welcome given to the new magazine. The editor's address to the readers in No. 1 occupied four columns.

The grand leading principle by which I have been actuated is to take advantage of the universal appetite for instruction which at present exists. . . . Every Saturday, when the poorest labourer in the country draws his humble earnings, he shall have it in his power to purchase, with an insignificant portion of even that humble sum, a meal of healthful, useful, and agreeable mental instruction: nay, every school boy shall be able to purchase with his pocket money, something permanently useful—something calculated to influence his fate through life—instead of the trash upon which the grown children of the present day are wont to spend it.

Chambers's Journal quickly attained a sale of 30,000. A remarkable achievement for those times was the publication, a week after the death of Sir Walter Scott, of a twelve-page supplement (threepence extra) containing a detailed account of the novelist's career. Of this 180,000 copies were sold. Characteristically enterprising, too, were the steps taken to increase the sale of the magazine. At first it circulated only in Scotland, but after some weeks it was decided to print an English edition from stereotyped plates, which were dispatched weekly from Edinburgh. By the autumn the two editions had a combined sale of 50,000. With the starting of an Irish edition in the second year the magazine was being printed simultaneously in three capitals—"a circumstance with no parallel in the history of letters," as the brothers justly claimed. Reprints of the principal articles were regularly produced in New York. Requests came from the colonies for the printing of separate editions to meet the local demand, but this was found to be impracticable. In January 1844 *Chambers's Journal*—now sixteen pages in size—was sold also in monthly parts, "neatly done up in a printed wrapper." Later it became essentially a monthly, but the weekly parts continued to be obtainable until the end of 1931, when the magazine completed a century of publication.

Another pioneer of the cheap periodical was Charles Knight (1791–1873), who in 1827 became superintendent of the publications of the Society for the Diffusion of Useful Knowledge, one of the founders of which was Lord Brougham. In 1832

Knight started the *Penny Magazine*,[1] which attained a sale of 200,000, and in the following year the *Penny Cyclopaedia*: the latter, completed in eleven years, imposed such a financial strain on the society that it was driven into bankruptcy. He was connected at various times with other periodicals, including the *Plain Englishman* (1820), a literary journal which he founded that ceased publication within three years; and his general publishing activities included a popular history of England in twelve volumes. An earlier and lesser-known pioneer was John Limbird, who published the *Mirror* (1823–1841), a sixteen-page octavo weekly, price twopence. Each issue contained a diversity of short articles and one or more engravings, and the paper was designed to enable "readers in the humblest circumstances" to become acquainted with the literature of the day.

The names of Charles Knight and John Limbird are now known only to those who are interested in the history of journalism; the surname of John Cassell, another Victorian pioneer, is still borne by a great publishing house and within the memory of middle-aged readers of today was part of the titles of two popular periodicals. Born in 1817, the son of a Manchester innkeeper, Cassell was apprenticed to a joiner as a boy. He had little education in the formal sense, but his hunger for knowledge stimulated him to read widely and to study the French language. At the age of 16 he became interested in the temperance movement and while still in his teens undertook a lecturing tour on behalf of that cause. In 1836, soon after his arrival in London in search of employment, a speech that he made at a temperance meeting led to his engagement as a temperance agent. In the late 'forties he gained considerable success as a tea and coffee dealer in the City and made the widely advertised command "Buy Cassell's Shilling Coffee" (the sale of coffee in packet form was then a new idea) familiar to everyone who could read. He was now able to take the first step towards the achievement of his

[1] "The excellent Dr. Arnold . . . described it as 'all ramble-scramble.' It was meant to be so—to touch rapidly and lightly on many subjects."—*Passages of a Working Life* (Charles Knight).

main ambition, which was to assist the development of popular education. Cassell's *Popular Educator*, published from 1852 to 1855, provided an economical means of self-education for artisans and others. *Cassell's Magazine*, which also first appeared in 1852, continued in various forms until 1933. *Cassell's Illustrated Family Paper* (1853) was a popular weekly that achieved a large sale, especially during the Crimean War; its pictures included many that were printed from electrotypes supplied by *L'Illustration* of Paris. Cassell's sanguine temperament led him to undertake more publishing ventures than he could properly finance. The position was strengthened when he became associated with two printers, Thomas Dixon Galpin and George William Petter, and under the style of Cassell, Petter and Galpin (later Cassell & Co.) the firm issued a large number of popular illustrated and educational works and various periodicals, among the latter being the *Quiver* (1861). At the time of his death, at the early age of 48, the firm which John Cassell had started fifteen years earlier employed nearly five hundred workers.

Among other popular periodicals started in the first half of the century was Charles Dickens's *Household Words* (1850), which continued until 1859, when *All the Year Round* took its place. Well known to his contemporaries, but almost forgotten until he figured in two recent biographies, was Samuel Orchart Beeton (1838–1877), who started at the age of 21 the *Englishwoman's Domestic Magazine*, a twopenny monthly that originated the idea of selling paper patterns to readers and of giving advice to younger readers about their problems of the heart (the feature was called "Cupid's Letter Bag"). Later the magazine was increased in price to sixpence and included fashion plates in colour, and it attained a sale of 60,000. Among other periodicals started by Beeton was the *Queen* (1861), and he appointed his old friend Frederick Greenwood as editor. In the same year he issued his wife's *Book of Household Management*, better known as "Mrs. Beeton's Cookery Book."

The eighteen-forties saw the establishment of two weeklies

that have become part of the national scene—*Punch* (1841) and the *Illustrated London News* (1842). M. H. Spielmann, in his *History of Punch* (1895), says that G. F. Watts once told him that the new paper was regarded with but little encouragement by the occupants of a bus in which he was riding, one gentleman, after looking gravely through its pages, tossing it aside with the remark, "One of those ephemeral things they bring out; won't last a fortnight."[1] The *Somerset County Gazette*, however, was kindly and encouraging: "It is the first comic paper we ever saw which was not vulgar. It will provoke many a hearty laugh, but never call a blush to the most delicate cheek." The first number appeared on July 17, 1841, at the price of threepence—a figure that was maintained until the First World War, when the rise in the costs of production necessitated an increase to sixpence. A circulation of 10,000 was required to make the paper a financial success, but the actual sale in the early days was from 5,000 to 6,000 and the slender capital of the founders was quickly exhausted. Bradbury and Evans, the printers, agreed to undertake the risk of carrying on the journal and assumed control, which their successors retain to this day. The first *Punch Almanac* had a sensational success, the sale leaping from 6,000 to 80,000. New features were introduced into the weekly issue and the average sale reached 30,000 (now it is about five times that figure). Mr. Punch in the early years was not the genial sage that he has now become: he was an ardent reformer and at times fiercely political. "Fougasse" (Cyril Kenneth Bird), who has edited *Punch* since 1949, is the seventh to occupy the editorial chair. His predecessors were: Mark Lemon, 1841–1870; Shirley Brooks, 1870–1874; Tom Taylor, 1874–1880; Sir Francis Burnand, 1880–1906; Sir Owen Seaman, 1906–1932; E. V. Knox, 1932–1949. Scores of famous authors and artists have helped to make *Punch* a national institution. Apart from the editors, who have included several

---

[1] *Punch* had had several forerunners within the previous ten years which failed to gain a public—among them *Punch in London*, *Punchinello* and *The Devil in London*. The penny *Figaro in London*, started in 1831 by Gilbert Abbot à Beckett and Henry Mayhew, lived for nearly eight years.

notable writing men, the list of contributors contains the names of Thackeray, Henry Mayhew, Douglas Jerrold, Thomas Hood, Artemus Ward and Sir H. W. Lucy (whose Parliamentary sketches, signed "Toby, M.P." were a brilliant feature)—to mention but a few nineteenth-century names; and the best-known modern contributors are Sir Alan Herbert, the late E. V. Lucas, A. A. Milne, Anthony Armstrong and the late E. M. Delafield. The roll of artists is a long and distinguished one. Richard Doyle, John Leech, Charles Keene, John Tenniel, George du Maurier, Phil May and Harry Furniss are among the great names of the past; Sir Bernard Partridge (who probably drew more cartoons for its pages than any other artist), "Fougasse," George Morrow, George Belcher, Frank Reynolds, Charles Grave, Ernest Shepard, G. L. Stampa, L. G. Illingworth and Graham Laidler ("Pont") are among the chief names in this century.

The *Illustrated London News* was more fortunate than *Punch* at the outset, for it was a success from the start. The first number appeared in May 1842, and was a sixteen-page paper, price sixpence. Several reprints were called for, and within a year it was selling 60,000 copies a week; fourteen years later the circulation was nearing the 200,000 mark. The idea of starting the journal was suggested to its founder by his observation of the great interest shown by the public in the news illustrations appearing in the *Observer*, the *Weekly Chronicle* and other contemporary weeklies. Three generations of Ingrams spanned the first hundred years of its history—Herbert Ingram (1811–60), the former printer's apprentice who founded the paper and who was drowned with his eldest son, when the steamer on which he was making an excursion from Lake Michigan to Lake Superior was sunk in a collision; his son, Sir William Ingram, who directed it (in association with his brother Charles) for thirty years; and his grandson, Sir Bruce Ingram, who has been editor since 1900. The range of illustrated journalism has, of course, been greatly extended by new pictorial methods since the days when the founder had to rely on wood engravings. The invention of the half-tone process towards the end of the century opened up new possibilities for illustrated papers, and the development of the rotary photogravure process and of natural colour photography has further widened the scope and improved the quality of pictorial journalism. Many well-known artists contributed to the paper—Sir William Ingram paid Millais £3,000 for his picture *Cinderella*, specially painted for a Christmas number, and a similar sum for *Bubbles*—and its war artists drew pictures of the Crimean War and the later wars of the century. Its special Coronation, Jubilee and other commemorative issues provide a fascinating record of great occasions.

Other pictorial weeklies included the *Illustrated Times* (1855), which was issued at twopence, and the *Penny Illustrated Paper* (1861)—both ultimately acquired by the *Illustrated London News*; the *Graphic* (1869), attractively produced and the first real rival to the *Illustrated London News*; and *Black and White* (1891), which was absorbed by the *Sphere* (1900) early in this century. The *Illustrated Times* was started by Henry Vizetelly (1820–1894)—with David Brogue as partner—who had printer's ink in his veins, being the son and grandson of printers. He had previously, in partnership with his elder brother, James Thomas Vizetelly, founded the *Pictorial Times* (1843), which continued for several years. The *Illustrated Times* had among its contributors G. A. Sala, Edmund Yates and Frederick Greenwood, and when the paper was sold to Herbert Ingram in 1859 Vizetelly received £4,000 for his share in it. He joined Ingram's staff and in 1865 was appointed Paris correspondent of the *Illustrated London News*. Later Vizetelly took up publishing and got into trouble with the law when he issued translations of Zola's works, being sentenced at the Old Bailey in 1889 to three months' imprisonment, as a first-class misdemeanant, for publishing obscene libels. The *Graphic*, founded by William Luson Thomas (1830–1900), was highly popular for several decades, and like its senior it commissioned famous artists to record important events. The Franco-German War, which broke out shortly afterwards, provided obvious scope for pictorial enterprise and helped to establish the *Graphic* in public favour. Thomas had started his career as an engraver in wood with his elder brother, George Housman Thomas, in Paris, and he accompanied his brother and his partner to America in 1846 to help in the production of two illustrated journals: both failed and they returned to Europe, working together in Rome for a time. Later William Luson Thomas started an engraving business in London and did considerable work for the *Illustrated London News*. In 1890 he launched the first morning pictorial journal—the *Daily Graphic*.

The *Cornhill Magazine*, an illustrated literary monthly which made its appearance in January 1860, was one of three distinguished publishing ventures sponsored by George Smith, son of the founder of Smith, Elder & Co. The other two were the *Pall Mall Gazette* (1865) and the *Dictionary of National Biography* (original sixty-six volumes completed in 1901, the year of his death). The new magazine derived its name from the street in which the firm had its offices. A generous-spirited man of large and splendid ideas, George Smith threw his whole energy into making the *Cornhill* a great success, and with Thackeray as editor he produced a magazine that stands out as a landmark in periodical journalism. The sale of the first number was 110,000: "without precedent in English periodical literature." Smith was so delighted at this achievement—the most sanguine estimate had been 80,000—that he doubled Thackeray's salary. The policy was to attract the best writers and artists by liberal payment, and Anthony Trollope in his autobiography pleasurably recalls the offer of £1,000 for the serial rights of a new novel. Later he received nearly three times as much for a serial, and George Eliot was paid an even higher figure—£7,500. Writing to G. A. Sala, Thackeray announced: "About to start a new magazine. First-rate bill of fare. Want rich collops from you. Come and see me." The outcome of this interview was a series of articles on William Hogarth, for which the payment was from £50 to £60 a month, and George Smith showed his appreciation by presenting Sala with a magnificent elephant folio of the complete works of Hogarth. Every quarter the proprietor gave a banquet to which he invited the writers and artists who contributed to the *Cornhill*. Thackeray found the cares of editing irksome and resigned in 1862, but continued to write for the magazine until his death in the following year. Later editors included Frederick Greenwood, Leslie Stephen, St. Loe Strachey and Leonard Huxley. Peter Quennell took over the direction when the magazine resumed publication in 1944 after a few years' war-time suspension, and was succeeded by John Grey Murray in 1951.

Two months before the publication of the *Cornhill* the first number of *Macmillan's Magazine* had appeared. During its life of nearly half a century (it was discontinued in 1907) *Macmillan's* had among its contributors many great names—among them Tennyson, Matthew Arnold, Huxley, Meredith, Pater, Thomas Hardy, Kipling and Henry James. It is interesting to recall that Mr. Winston Churchill was among its serialists, for it was in this magazine that his novel, *Savrola: A Military and Political Romance*, first appeared. Other periodicals of note were *Murray's Magazine*, which ran from 1887 to 1891, and the *English Illustrated Magazine* (1884), which was a favourite monthly of late Victorian days and survived until 1913.

The success of the *Cornhill* suggested to John Maxwell, the publisher, the starting of a similar magazine, but without illustrations, and Sala, whom he appointed editor, chose the name *Temple Bar*. A drawing of the Bar served as frontispiece, and in a moment of irresponsibility Sala attached to it a purely imaginary quotation from Boswell: "And now, Sir," said Dr. Johnson, "we will take a walk down Fleet Street." This invention has been frequently quoted in the innocent belief that Dr. Johnson really did say it. *Temple Bar*, beginning with a circulation of 30,000, established itself warmly in the favour of the Victorian reading public and continued for several decades. It absorbed the once popular *Bentley's Miscellany* (founded 1837), which had Charles Dickens as editor for the first three years of its existence. Another monthly, started a few years after *Temple Bar*, was *St. Paul's Magazine*, which James Virtue, a well-known printer, paid Anthony Trollope £1,000 a year to edit. The novelist had to be persuaded to accept the post, strongly advising Virtue to abandon the project; and he firmly declined to have the magazine named *Anthony Trollope's*. "Money was spent very freely," he says in his autobiography. "On my own part, I may declare that I omitted nothing which I thought might tend to success. . . . I was too anxious to be good, and did not enough think of what might be lucrative. It did fail, for it never paid its way. It reached, if I remember right, a circulation of nearly 10,000."

The 'sixties and 'seventies witnessed important fresh developments in the review form; since the early years of the century there had been only one major new publication in this field—Jeremy Bentham's *Westminster Review* (1823). Two new reviews, one a fortnightly and the other a monthly, were established in successive years—the *Fortnightly Review* (1865) and the *Contemporary Review* (1866)—and a third appeared in the next decade with the founding of the *Nineteenth Century* as a monthly in 1877. The *Fortnightly*, with George Henry Lewes as editor, had a remarkable list of contributors in No. 1—among them Walter Bagehot, Sir John Herschel, George Eliot, Trollope, F. T. Palgrave and Frederic Harrison. "It has often been regretted that England has no journal similar to the *Revue des Deux Mondes*, treating of subjects which interest cultivated and thoughtful readers, and published at intervals which are neither too distant for influence on the passing questions, nor too brief for deliberation," stated an editorial foreword. The trade did not take kindly to the innovation of fortnightly publication, and the review became a monthly but retained its title—as it does to this day. The *Nineteenth Century* solved its titular problem at the beginning of the new century by adding the words "And After." The obvious name had then been pre-empted, but in 1951, at mid-century, the review at last became the *Twentieth Century*. The *Contemporary Review* was fortunate in the choice of a name which is ever new and which clearly defines its editorial programme.

Trollope, one of a number who helped to found the *Fortnightly Review*, says in his autobiography that they subscribed £1,250 each and that the board determined that all contributions must be paid for liberally and promptly. "We carried out our principles until our money was all gone, and then we sold the copyright to Messrs. Chapman and Hall for a trifle." The amount lost by the original projectors was about £9,000. From 1867 to 1883 the *Fortnightly* was edited by John (afterwards Lord) Morley and acquired a considerable reputation as a forum of liberal ideas; from 1886 to 1894 it had an audacious phase under the editorship of Frank Harris (1856–1931), who made the circulation soar but occasionally horrified readers by publishing disturbingly unorthodox articles, including a eulogy of two Anarchists. His list of contributors included most of the famous writers of the day. A series of frank articles on Russia, signed "E. B. Lanin" (Dr. E. J. Dillon), included revelations about prison conditions in that country which deeply stirred public opinion and provoked Swinburne to contribute an ode that caused the number containing it to run to several editions. No other editor would have printed lines so inflammatory as these about Czar Alexander the Third (whose father had been assassinated in 1881):

> "Night hath but one red star—Tyrannicide.
> God or man be swift—hope sickens with delay.
> Smite and send him howling down his father's way."

After eight years of Frank Harris's turbulent editorship—ended by his discharge—the publishers, Chapman and Hall, were understandably cautious when they appointed his successor, inserting a clause in his contract that the contents bill of each issue must be submitted in advance for their approval; but W. L. Courtney, who conducted the *Fortnightly* for over thirty years, soon restored the traditional sobriety to the review. Harris bought the *Saturday Review*, which he edited until 1898 and then sold; and during those four years he made it the most discussed of the weekly reviews because of the quality of its writing —Bernard Shaw, H. G. Wells, Max Beerbohm and Cunninghame Graham were among the contributors—though he was not able to turn it into a financial success. Parallel with his dramatic editorial career from 1886 to 1898 he sought to establish himself in society—he married a wealthy widow who had a charming little house in Park Lane—and let it be known that his political ambitions were to become the English Bismarck, but though he was a brilliant conversationalist and a fluent public speaker (in his early days in London he addressed open-air meetings for the Social Democratic Federation) the grand design came to nothing; and his marriage, too, failed after a few years. To this period belongs Oscar Wilde's biting retort to Harris's boast that he had dined at every great house in London—"Yes, Frank, but only once." During the next fifteen years he edited several periodicals (mostly of a minor type) without success, and gradually the editorial genius deteriorated into a shabby adventurer who derived part of his income from journalistic blackmail. This phase of his life culminated in 1914 in a prison sentence for contempt of court in respect of paragraphs that appeared in *Modern Society*, which he then edited, reflecting on the private character of the defendant in a divorce case while the hearing was taking place. The defendant happened to be the proprietor of a weekly who had terminated Harris's connection with his paper a year or two before. Harris wrote a number of good short stories and a few books that were much discussed. His scandalous autobiography, like the contradictory oral accounts of his early career that he gave from time to time, is untrustworthy. No one knows with certainty the facts about his life before he took up his first journalistic appointment in London as editor of the *Evening News*, but he appears to have lived in Ireland as a boy and to have run away at the age of 14 to the United States, where he worked as bootblack, labourer, hotel clerk, cowboy and reporter, and attended the State university in Kansas; and later, after serving as correspondent in the Russo-Turkish War, he claimed to have studied at two German universities. Bernard Shaw's summing-up of the strange personality of Frank Harris, as quoted by Hugh Kingsmill in *Frank Harris*, is bitingly expressive: "He is neither first-rate, nor second-rate, nor tenth-rate. He is just his horrible unique self."

In the 'sixties and 'seventies a number of publications of a lighter type came into existence—all weeklies. The first of these was *Vanity Fair* (1868) a sixpenny weekly founded by Thomas Gibson Bowles,[1] which is now chiefly remembered as the paper in which appeared the cartoons of well-known people by "Ape" (Carlo Pellegrini) and "Spy" (Sir Leslie Ward). Lithographed in colour and inserted loose, these prints were collected and framed and a great number of them have survived. It was a frivolous, gossipy "Society journal" which had a long run of varying success. (The title has recently been revived as the name of a monthly magazine for "the younger, smarter woman.") Among the contributors to *Vanity Fair* was a brilliant, reckless man who was regarded as one of the ablest journalists of his time—E. C. Grenville Murray (1824–1881), natural son of Richard Grenville, second Duke of Chandos. His abilities made a favourable impression on Lord Palmerston, who was responsible for his entry into the diplomatic service. While serving as attaché to the British Embassy at Vienna, Murray arranged to act as *Morning Post* correspondent in that city, contrary to all the principles of the diplomatic service, and by accident this fact came to the notice of the Foreign Office. He was not dismissed—Palmerston's protection saved him from that—but after thirteen years as Consul-General at Odessa he began to notice that the Foreign Office, now under Lord Stanley (later Lord Derby), was changing in its attitude towards him and resigned his appointment. He took

---

[1] Thomas Gibson Bowles was associated with Algernon Borthwick (of the *Morning Post*) and several friends in the production of the *Owl*, described as "A Wednesday Journal of Politics and Society"—a witty, high-spirited little paper which appeared at irregular intervals from 1864 to 1868. The first issue (four large quarto pages, price sixpence) was numbered 1001. In the second issue (No. 1002) were several spoof news items, including this one: "Turin, April 25. The Bey of Turin has telegraphed to the French Emperor for troops to assist him in taking a popular vote by universal suffrage." Borthwick was the moving spirit behind the paper, which was published by the Owls—as the little group running it called themselves—mainly for their own amusement. It was very well informed, especially on Society news, and *The Times* quoted from it occasionally. The *Owl* is thought to have given Bowles the germ of the idea which he evolved into *Vanity Fair*.

up journalism as a career and was partly responsible for the creation of the light, impertinently outspoken type of writing represented by *Vanity Fair*. Murray felt that he could improve on the first model and started in 1869 the *Queen's Messenger*, in which he gave his talent for caustic writing freer scope and soon got himself into trouble. One of his articles reflected adversely on the first Lord Carrington, whose son, the second Lord Carrington, retaliated by horsewhipping Murray at the entrance of a club in St. James's Street. He was summoned for assault, and when the case was heard Murray denied that he had written the article but refused to answer questions about his connection with the *Queen's Messenger* or to say whether certain letters and manuscripts and a corrected proof of an article shown to him were in his handwriting. Lord Carrington was bound over on one summons and committed for trial on the charge of assault. Ten days later Murray was charged at Bow Street with having committed perjury by denying that he was the author of the article. The case was remanded and he was allowed bail. When it came up for hearing again he failed to appear, having fled to France, and a warrant was issued for his arrest. He never returned to England. Settling in Paris, he wrote for the *Daily News*, the *Pall Mall Gazette* and other papers.

Grenville Murray was a partner with Edmund Yates—who had edited the *Temple Bar* and other periodicals and made a hit with a gossip feature, "The Lounger at the Clubs," in the *Illustrated Times*—in the establishment of *The World: A Journal for Men and Women*, a sixpenny weekly, in 1874. It was Murray who wrote the prospectus, which stated that the *World* would be an amusing chronicle of current history, that it would recognize women as a reasonable class of the community and that it would be "fair in its criticism, plain in its language, honourable in its intentions, written throughout by gentlemen and scholars." The partnership did not last more than a few months: Murray, despite an explicit promise, could not keep Lord Derby, his special enemy, out of his articles. Though it had some gifted contributors the *World* made no impression at the beginning and might not have survived but for the publicity given to legal proceedings arising out of articles which it published. Henry Labouchere wrote a series of City articles, and a stockbroker who had reason to believe that he would be criticized said that he would horsewhip him if he published his observations. He was summoned for threatening to commit a breach of the peace, and bound over in sureties for his good behaviour. The case was widely reported because both sides had engaged famous lawyers. Another series of articles, written to expose West End usurers, provoked an action for libel by two moneylenders; the case was dismissed after a two-days' hearing. All this publicity had a tonic effect on the circulation of the *World*, and within six months it was a firmly established success. A libellous paragraph referring, though not by name, to the Earl of Lonsdale led to a sentence of four months' imprisonment for Yates on April 2, 1884, the court deciding that a fine would be a matter of indifference to a successful paper. Lord Coleridge, in passing sentence, made these comments:

It appears that a "lady of title" is paid at the rate of two guineas for such paragraphs. . . . To open a sort of "lion's mouth" into which all the personal gossip of what is pleased to call itself Society is to be shot anonymously, at the rate of two guineas a personality, and to take no trouble to inquire into the truth of what is published—one cannot suppose a system more certain to lead, as it led in this case, to the publication of cruel slander and stories tending to the discomfort and unhappiness of those who are the subjects of them.

Yates was released after serving seven weeks of his sentence. The *World* continued until early in the present century, passing through various ownerships, including Lord Northcliffe's. In 1879 Yates founded *Time*, an octavo-size "Miscellany of Interesting and Amusing Literature," which ceased publication five years later.

Labouchere felt that there was an opening for a weekly journal with a more vigorous character and in 1877 he founded *Truth*: it would be "another and a better *World*," he promised. He was at that time a well-known member of Parliament and a part proprietor of the *Daily News*. The new paper quickly gained success. Labouchere was a trenchant writer with a considerable knowledge of the City and exposed many financial scandals. The paper was Radical in tone and wittily written, and the contents were shrewdly planned. One feature, "Queer Stories"—mostly written by Grenville Murray in the early years—has continued to this day.

The eighteen-nineties produced many novelties in periodical journalism. There was the much-discussed *Yellow Book*, which was a literary quarterly in book form; there were also the *Savoy*, the *Dome*, the *Hobby Horse*, the *Pageant* and other original periodicals that had a brief hour of fame in that decade of exciting, and sometimes feverish, literary and artistic activity. There was the *Idler*, a distinctive magazine of general appeal— edited by Robert Barr and Jerome K. Jerome—which had a run of some years. And there were *Today*, the *Butterfly*, *Pick-me-up*, the *Poster* and the *Studio*. The last-named is still admirably discharging its stimulating and constructive purpose; the others are now only memories.

A Newnes creation that made journalistic history in the 'nineties was the *Wide World Magazine*, founded in 1898, which is in a class by itself and has a large sale at home and overseas. In its early days it serialized the remarkable adventure story of Louis de Rougemont, who read a paper at a British Association meeting and twice appeared before the Royal Geographical Society by invitation; but certain statements he made in the exciting account of his adventures in Northern Australia aroused scepticism and then inquiry, and he was finally discredited, the kindliest verdict being that he had described over-imaginatively a life of unusual experiences. A description of other developments in popular periodical journalism in the 'eighties and 'nineties originated by Sir George Newnes and the Harmsworths is included in the story of the New Journalism in the next chapter.

A complete list of nineteenth-century periodicals (most of them started in the remarkable era of creative enterprise that began with the removal of the taxes on knowledge) would be monotonous to read, but a few more titles must be mentioned to make this picture of Victorian inventiveness fully representative—the *Field* (1853), *Public Opinion* (1861), *Nature* (1869), the *Illustrated Sporting and Dramatic News*[1] (1874), the *Boy's Own Paper* (1879), the *National Review* (1883), the *English Historical Review* (1886), the *Classical Review* (1887) and *Country Life* (1897). No mention has been made of the immense number of religious,[2] professional, technical and other periodicals devoted to special interests that appeared within that period, but enough names have been cited to show what an intricate pattern of enterprise developed during the century and how the periodical, first conceived as a simple sheet of polite reading for the leisured class of Steele and Addison's days, had become a rich and flexible medium of information, criticism and entertainment adaptable to all the interests and activities of mankind.

[1] Now *Sport and Country*.

[2] The oldest religious periodical is the *Methodist Magazine*, which dates back to 1778. Some other dates: The *Record* (now incorporated in the *Church of England Newspaper*), 1828; *Tablet*, 1840; *Jewish Chronicle*, 1841; *Guardian*, 1846; *Baptist Times*, 1855; *Christian World*, 1857; *Catholic Times*, 1859; *Christian*, 1859; *Universe*, 1860; *Church Times*, 1863; *Methodist Recorder*, 1863; *Christian Herald*, 1866; *Church Quarterly Review*, 1875; *War Cry*, 1879; *British Weekly*, 1886; *Religious Review of Reviews* (1890–1896). The *British Weekly* was started by Sir William Robertson Nicoll, whose regular contributions to its columns included a literary article signed "Claudius Clear." He also founded the *Bookman* (1891) and *Woman at Home* (1893).

CHAPTER TWELVE

The New Journalism

THE end of the nineteenth century found some of the leading British newspapers in a precarious condition. The official history of *The Times*, recording the decline in the fortunes of that journal, states that the paper was paying diminishing dividends and that the *Standard*, long its chief competitor, was paying none and was rapidly losing its position. "The situation at Printing House Square was obviously not satisfactory, but the fact was that with the exception of the *Daily Telegraph* and the *Daily Mail* the London newspaper trade as a whole was not flourishing."

The old-established newspapers, with their solidly composed pages and their small uninformative headlines, had a grey and static look about them, and for many decades now one issue had not appreciably differed from another in outward appearance. Much ingenuity and large sums of money had been expended on improving the mechanical equipment of the newspaper; great enterprise had been shown in speeding up the collection of news and the distribution of the paper; but not since the days of John Bell and other designers of elegantly composed eighteenth-century journals had anyone been interested in making the newspaper agreeable to look at and pleasant to read. The Press had lived through several generations of social and economic change without making any concessions to the new age either in the scope of its contents or in the technique of presentation. The pattern of journalism was frozen almost throughout the nineteenth century.

With rigid conscientiousness newspapers continued to give the public a heavy overdose of politics every day and to neglect almost entirely the lighter interests of life. Typical would be a page report of a speech headed simply with the name of the politician making it and the place at which it was delivered—"Mr. Gladstone at. . . ." was one of the most familiar of nineteenth-century headlines—and set in long paragraphs without a single crosshead to give relief. It was the age of the verbatim report, of carefully organized teams of expert reporters doing five-minute "takes" and rapidly transcribing their notes, so that the task was completed almost as soon as the speech ended. "Did any reader of the last twenty years ever read the speeches that were reported?" Lord Rosebery once asked.[1] "I have no doubt that those whose duty it is to criticize, laud them, or rebuke them in the public Press felt it their painful duty to read the speeches. But did anyone else? . . . I can conscientiously say, having been a speaker myself, that I never could find anybody who read any speeches." The newspaper reader was flatteringly pictured as a serious-minded person whose interests were confined to politics, the law courts and the Stock Exchange and who did not need any help in absorbing the news beyond good eyesight and abundant leisure: the latter was obviously essential. It was not even thought necessary to attract his attention to the three column-length leaders by putting titles on them.

When innovators came along in the 'eighties and 'nineties who strongly urged that the primary task of a newspaper was to get itself read, and that there was a whole range of human interests that found no reflection in the columns of existing journals, the reaction of the majority of journalists was violently unfavourable. Why this should have been so is not so apparent today, when our most responsible newspapers are distinguished by clear, attractive and orderly arrangement and by their comprehensive coverage of the many activities of modern life, and achieve this readableness and variety without any loss of dignity.

If the old guard of journalism was wrong—as the course of events proved it to be—it was wrong mostly for righteous reasons. What more than anything else characterized end-of-the-

[1] In a speech at the Press Club in 1913.

century journalism was its dignity, its high sense of public responsibility, its tradition of giving its readers good substantial fare in the sure confidence that as intelligent men (few women read newspapers then) they required no aids to digestion, for as a matter of interest and duty they would want to read the whole paper to keep themselves well informed. This had been the tradition for many decades and most editors saw no reason to change it, though in the meantime papers had grown in size and become correspondingly more difficult to read without the help of sensible arrangement and the proper signposting of the contents. Tradition ran right through the organization. Editors were superior creatures who kept themselves aloof and were not receptive to fresh ideas. Lord Northcliffe, who as a young journalist noted this Olympian detachment when he was free-lancing in the 'eighties, and who was later to revolutionize the technique of journalism and considerably disturb these remote figures, thus recalled his experiences: "As I went in and out of these newspaper offices I found that their organizations were so constructed that one could never convey an idea to the man at the top. Contact with the staff was, as a rule, by postcard."

The distaste felt by most journalists for the new methods of appeal—the New Journalism, as Matthew Arnold christened it—is more understandable when the events that preceded the transformation of our newspapers are seen in the context of the times. The fact that the first of these innovators, William Thomas Stead (1849–1912)—better known as W. T. Stead—was a deeply religious man, for whom journalism was primarily a means of doing good in the world, did nothing to lessen the enormity of his offence. Few journalists were convinced at that time that he had any objective but the increasing of circulation, and they regarded as at the best undignified and at the worst abominable the devices to which he resorted for arresting public attention.

When in 1871, at the age of 22, Stead was appointed editor of the *Northern Echo* (Darlington), the proprietor sug-

THE PALL MALL GAZETTE

An Evening Newspaper and Review.

No. 1.—Vol. I. TUESDAY, FEBRUARY 7, 1865. Price Twopence.

THE QUEEN'S SECLUSION.

A LITTLE paragraph appeared in the newspapers lately, to revive a hope which was to have been fulfilled to-day, and has not. "We are informed that Her MAJESTY the QUEEN will open Parliament in person next session:" this was the little paragraph—printed, too, in that authoritative large type which carries conviction straight into the minds of most newspaper readers. But somehow the herald who brought such good tidings from Court was little credited. The trumpet sounded—that we all heard; but no confirming echo answered it—not even in those hollow places in our own hearts where dwells the hope of what we much desire. The most timid inquirer hesitated to believe; and he whose faith in editorial announcements had hitherto been complete, found himself disturbed by a strangely courageous scepticism. Was the announcement authorized at all by any one? Had we not been told of journalists and politicians who endeavoured to achieve what they wished by declaring it already certain? These questions were asked by many people. The answer to the first one is that the QUEEN never at any moment intended to open Parliament this session—(there is our own authoritative large type to prove it)—and to the other, that if the trick was played, it was a trick which only a very few philosophers can muster morality enough to condemn. There may be some politicians of the fermentative platform kind who secretly rejoice that (if tried) it did not succeed, but they are not philosophers.

It is when we consider what these gentlemen are that we most regret the QUEEN'S long absence from what is called public life. If it were not for them, and if Her MAJESTY'S retirement were not brought home to us strongly *now*, when a Parliament is about to end and agitation to begin, we should say nothing about it. There are, indeed, other reasons for regret, but none that we can think of which justifies the remonstrant tone in which some journalists have lately discussed the subject. What *would* justify such a tone is a state of things which does not exist. The Sovereign of England is not an autocrat, sold to cares and committed to responsibilities which must necessarily be neglected in the indulgence of personal sorrow. Her Ministers are able and honest; and, what is more—what is conclusive, in fact—the QUEEN is known never to neglect the real duties of her sovereignty. Their faithful performance goes on, and has always gone on; and while that is so, our concern that her grief should cease with the sympathy of a loyal and home-loving people. Of such sympathy there cannot be too much. Taking it for a moment out of the region of mere human kindness where it were better left, we may go so far as to say there are sound political reasons why it should be encouraged; unless, indeed, the country has had enough of the great blessing which the QUEEN'S reign is said to have brought upon it ever since her rule began. We have all been lying under a mistake for twenty years if the nation has not been purified by an example of homely affection and of household faith in that place where example is so potent for good or evil—the palace. Some observers are of opinion, indeed, that a certain reaction against this beneficent influence has set in: be that as it may, we cannot think the reaction likely to be forwarded by the sincere and lasting sorrow of a wife for the loss of her husband; or by our respect for it.

There are some other considerations which have been almost as much forgotten as these. There is the fact that a monarch is still a human being; and that a people has no right to ask him to smile when his heart is ill at ease, or violate the most natural, most pious, most imperative instincts of his human nature in order to make a pageant. Again, our affection for the QUEEN, our deepest reverence for her, has grown out of the knowledge that she is not only a queen, but a good and most womanly woman; and yet how many people have considered that the very qualities they reverence in the woman have embittered the grief of the queen? We all understand what is meant by the "sacredness" of sorrow, and know that to turn our eyes upon one whose heart is deeply smitten, is to add to the pain a new and intolerable distress. This is so if you are happily unknown to all but a dozen people, whose gaze you easily can and do escape. But if you are a queen, then you cannot escape; your grief, which should be secret to be endurable, is known to all the world—talked of by all the world—gazed upon wherever you turn. And the more womanly you are, the more you are conscious of an observation which is scarcely the less painful for being sympathetic. Therefore we say Her MAJESTY'S seclusion is exactly what might have been expected of her position and her virtues; and inasmuch as we respect them we must respect their natural consequences, nor forget that her retirement is the most natural one of all.

But this is not saying we wish the seclusion to continue. What we do say is, that with the fullest sense of what is due to Her MAJESTY, with the strongest inclination to take no part in the discussion of this subject, we cannot resist the suggestions of the ceremony of to-day. In brief, we cannot help speculating, not upon the regret or the disappointment of the nation at large on seeing another fair occasion for the QUEEN'S re-appearance amongst us pass by, but upon the satisfaction it may give that small, determined coterie of Americanized politicians who are so particularly active just now, and whom we shall behold still more active before another Parliament can be assembled. Who can doubt that they *do* find satisfaction in the QUEEN'S absence, once more, from the most important and significant of all State ceremonials? To be sure, they are not likely to acknowledge such sentiments. There are many bold speakers amongst them, and a carnival of declamation is fast approaching; but we do not suppose any demagogue so rash as to suggest the question yet awhile, that as the country gets on very well with a monarch in retirement (the Board of Trade returns will sufficiently prove it), why not abolish the monarchy altogether? We do not expect *him* to point out so soon that people may become so accustomed to the absence of a Sovereign from public business as to make them ready converts to Americanism and the democratic idea. But it is just because he is not likely to speak that we feel bound to speak for him—now, while the people are *not* quite accustomed to the QUEEN'S seclusion, and earnestly desire her back again. Perhaps the event of to-day was not the most fitting occasion for her return to public life; perhaps we may hope that when the new Parliament is called together, Her MAJESTY will come once more face to face with her people. If so, we shall all rejoice—all but those who are speculating hopefully now upon the probability that her seclusion may be confirmed by habit, and who are perfectly prepared to turn it into a political argument.

Private letters from St. Petersburg and Moscow say that the example of the Moscow assembly, which has adopted by a very large majority an address in favour of a constitution, will be followed by the nobles of the other provinces of the empire. The proceedings at the Moscow assembly were published without being submitted to the censorship, and the printer of the journal in which they appeared is being prosecuted criminally.

The *Standard* published a letter yesterday from St. Petersburg, in which the writer, apparently an official, sets before the English public, with great complacency, the reasons current among Russian functionaries, of all classes for discountenancing the courageous endeavours of the nobility to obtain the establishment of a representative assembly. Such an assembly would, of course, be a terror to the members of the public service, whose acts it could criticise, if it could not legally control them. This is just the good—perhaps the only good—that the Reichsrath has done in Austria. "But," say the functionaries and the democrats of the baser kind, "if a legislative body were to be formed by election "in the present day, only members of the aristocracy would be chosen, "for it is well known that they alone are capable of discussing political "questions. The merchants are careless about such matters, and the "peasants are steeped in the greatest ignorance." The functionaries, then, from fear of exposure, and the democrats from mere envy, would postpone the formation of political assemblies indefinitely, or what comes to the same thing, until the spread of education throughout the empire should raise the other classes to the level of the nobles! These views, in default of more plausible ones, have been adopted by the Russian Government, and we find them expressed with great earnestness in a paragraph which bears the following curious heading:—"The Moscow Nobility demanding a Constitution!"

How perverse on the part of the Russian nobility! So in ancient times the discontented Hebrews, in the sinfulness of their hearts, called out for a King! But the Hebrews *had* their King; whereas the Russian landed proprietors, with an autocrat, supported by a mass of bribe-taking officials on one side, and with hordes of newly-liberated serfs on the other, have no chance whatever of getting a constitution. A few of the leaders may have the privilege accorded to them of going to the East of Russia in their own carriages, and remaining there until further notice. The others will have to be silent; or they may have the same measure meted out to them which they were so glad to see meted out last year and the year before to the Poles.

[1]

THE FIRST OF THE LITERARY EVENINGS

gested that before taking up his duties he should have a talk with T. W. Reid (later Sir Wemyss Reid), editor of the *Leeds Mercury*, then a great name in the provinces. It was a remarkable interview. "For hour after hour he talked with an ardour that delighted me," said Reid many years later, telling how Stead declared to him that the Press was the greatest agency for influencing public opinion in the world—the true and only lever by which throne and Governments could be shaken and the mass of the people raised. "I see you think I am crazy," remarked Stead. "Well, not crazy perhaps, but distinctly eccentric," was the reply. "Many a time since I have recalled that long night's talk," Reid added, "when I have recognized in some daring development of modern journalism one of the many schemes which Stead flashed before my eyes." Other people soon became aware that the *Northern Echo* had secured an unusual personality as editor. The fourth Earl Grey discovered, as he subsequently related, that this editor of a provincial morning paper was "corresponding with kings and emperors all over the world and receiving long letters from statesmen of every nation. This struck me as odd and interesting. Later on I discovered that the man was a sincere patriot, with a fervent desire to make things better and with a keen sense, too, of the value of the Empire. I used to go long walks with him, talking about the state of the people in England and discussing the best ways of improving their condition."

In 1880 Stead was invited to become assistant editor of the *Pall Mall Gazette* under John (later Lord) Morley. The *P.M.G.* as it was often called, had been founded in 1865, with George Smith as proprietor and Frederick Greenwood (1830–1909) as editor. The title was taken from Thackeray's *Pendennis*, but whereas the journal in the novel was "written by gentlemen for gentlemen" the real *Pall Mall Gazette* was planned as an independent evening newspaper and review for a cultivated, well-to-do public interested in politics, social questions and the arts. An eight-page paper, large folio in size, it was published at twopence. As Greenwood wrote later, the purpose was "to bring into daily journalism . . . the full measure of thought and culture which was then found only in the reviews." The reception of the new paper was disappointing: only 3,897 copies were sold of No. 1 and within six weeks the circulation had fallen to 613. The advertisement revenue in the second month averaged little over £3 a day; ten years earlier another new daily paper which made a faltering start—the *Daily Telegraph*—had an even more disastrous day, when the advertisement receipts totalled only 7s. 6d. However, George Smith's diary shows that there was presently a recovery in the sale, for eight months after the start it was "2,000 and increasing regularly." J. A. Spender[1] gives 9,000 as the highest circulation attained under Frederick Greenwood's editorship. Greenwood brought lightness, polish and intellectual alertness into daily journalism at a time when the morning papers had become heavy and tradition-bound; he created the model on which the *St. James's Gazette* (which he started in 1880 when he left the *P.M.G.* because the new proprietor, George Smith's son-in-law, decided to change the political policy) and the *Westminster Gazette* were founded and which influenced the restyling of the venerable *Globe*. His sole attempt at sensationalism was a commission to his brother, James Greenwood, to spend a night in the casual ward of Lambeth workhouse and frankly record his experiences. The outcome was a series of three articles, entitled "The Amateur Casual," which led to an extra sale of 1,500 of the issues in which they appeared and a permanent increase of 1,200 in the circulation. *The Times* republished the articles in full.

Frederick Greenwood based his editorial policy on good writing. He had a clear and vigorous style himself—not the product of a classical education, for he had started life as a printer's apprentice and supported himself by journalism from the age of 16, ultimately editing first the *Queen* and then the *Cornhill Magazine*—and he had a flair for picking contributors of quality. One of the most prolific of these was the brilliant Fitzjames Stephen, who on his way out to India to become legal member of council wrote twenty articles: "If I were in solitary

[1] *Life, Journalism and Politics* (J. A. Spender).

confinement I should have to scratch newspaper articles on the wall with a nail," he said. G. H. Lewes, Leslie Stephen, R. H. Hutton, Meredith Townsend, Matthew Arnold, Trollope, Laurence Oliphant, Sir Henry Maine, Matthew J. Higgins ("Jacob Omnium")—these names are representative of the contributors. The most important service rendered by Greenwood during his editorship was the information he secretly gave to the Government in 1875 that the Khedive of Egypt was on the point of transferring his Suez Canal shares to French hands. Disraeli, the Prime Minister at that time, got Cabinet approval to the purchase of the shares, and four million pounds secured a holding which, apart from its political importance, proved to be an excellent investment for this country, yielding a million and a half a year to the Exchequer. Not a word of public acknowledgment of this great service did Greenwood receive from Disraeli, who in a letter to Queen Victoria dramatized himself as the sole hero of the occasion; after Greenwood's death a belated—and beggarly —acknowledgment was made by the grant of a pension of £100 a year to his two daughters. Perhaps the strangest feature of the whole affair is that Greenwood did not even score any journalistic advantage. He could easily have been the first to announce the news—but he refrained.[1]

Such was the background of the paper which now sought the services of W. T. Stead. He was not certain that he was qualified for the post, and as a "barbarian of the North" he regarded London as "destructive to vigour and earnestness." But the thought that the paper would provide him with a more important platform, even though he had to share it with another, decided him to accept the offer. Never, surely, has there been a more oddly assorted pair in editorial partnership—Morley, the scholarly, austere rationalist, and Stead, the vehement Christian journalist with a mission to reform the world. "His extraordinary vigour and spirit made other people seem like wet blankets, creatures of moral défaillance," says Morley in his *Recollections*. Stead

---

[1] A full account of this extraordinary affair, as well as of Greenwood's editorship, is given in *The Story of the Pall Mall Gazette* (J. W. Robertson Scott).

summed up their relationship in a characteristically vivid way: "Morley and I approached almost everything from a different standpoint. We disagreed, as I often said, on everything from the existence of God to the make-up of a newspaper." In 1883 Stead became sole editor and there followed two years of remarkable achievement that made him, in Morley's words, "the most powerful journalist in the island." The chief technical innovations during his editorship were the use of illustrations, the introduction of crossheads and the development of the interview, and he showed great enterprise in securing scoops. The commonsense case for the insertion of crossheads was stated by Stead in a note (March 27, 1888) on the conversion of the *Morning Post* to the use of this device. "Wonders will never cease," he commented:

> The new departure is wonderful indeed—wonderful in that it should have been adopted at last and by so conservative a journal as the *Morning Post*; wonderful in that it should not have been adopted before. What would have been thought of a publisher who should bring out a book, not only with no division into chapters, but even without the relief of so much as a single fresh paragraph from the first word to the last? Yet Mr. Goschen's Budget Speech last night, covering, as it does, eight columns of *The Times*, has as much in it in mere matter of words as many books, and a great deal more in it in matter of sense than most books. ... Nothing can be less intelligent than the way in which English journals as a rule present their parliamentary reports; nothing more enterprising than the amount of them they amass.

The main change in the *Pall Mall Gazette* was in the tone of the paper. When Stead saw that a thing required to be done he campaigned for it with a vigour and urgency that no one has ever excelled. He had a gift of the flashing, picturesque phrase, and he had the compelling ardour that springs from absolute conviction in the rightness of a cause. Among other things, he urged that prompt measures should be taken to improve the conditions of the London poor; that General Gordon (whom he interviewed) should be sent to the Sudan; that the Navy should be strengthened (his "Truth about the Navy" crusade brought about a renaissance of sea-power, J. L. Garvin later declared); and that the Penjdeh dispute be arbitrated.

"A compound of Don Quixote and Phineas T. Barnum," Lord Milner (then Alfred Milner), his assistant editor, called him. "It was such fun to work with him." Certainly he had a talent for what we now call showmanship, and this was never more dramatically displayed than in the most successful—and the most bitterly condemned—of all his campaigns. When the conservative-minded readers of the *Pall Mall Gazette* opened their paper on July 6, 1885, they were appalled to read the first of a series of articles, sensationally headed "The Maiden Tribute of Modern Babylon," exposing the white slave traffic. Learning that the Criminal Law Amendment Bill for the raising of the age of consent (then only 13) was unlikely to get through, Stead had decided to shock the public conscience by revealing the shameful facts about the child victims of white slavery. (As a child he had wished that "God would give me a big whip that I could go round the world and whip the wicked out of it," and throughout his career he was always ready to do battle with evil.) It was a courageous thing to do in an age when the subject was unmentionable in print outside the Parliamentary reports. His articles published the results of an investigation of vice in London, and he had previously disclosed to the Archbishop of Canterbury, the Bishop of London and Cardinal Manning his scheme for impersonating one of the men engaged in the traffic in order to demonstrate how easy it was in the existing state of the law to procure a young girl—without, of course, going so far as to commit the actual offence. The Archbishop, though sympathetic, thought the idea horrible; the others approved, believing that only in such a way could public opinion be mobilized to compel the passing of the Bill.

The opening sentence of the first article read: "The report of our secret commission will be read today with a shuddering horror that will thrill throughout the world." Neither public nor Press took kindly to Stead's dreadful revelations. He was strongly attacked by other newspapers; letters of abuse poured into the *P.M.G.* office; a firm of bookstall proprietors cancelled its order for the paper. But Stead, prepared for a violent reaction, was undismayed and followed up his articles by addressing meetings throughout the country. Four days after the first article appeared the House of Commons speeded the Criminal Law Amendment Bill through its second reading; on August 10th the measure, strengthened by amendments, was passed by the House of Lords. Stead's case had triumphed, but he had to pay the penalty of his audacity. In planning his campaign he omitted one precaution and thus made himself technically guilty of abduction. He was arrested and tried at Bow Street and sentenced to three months' imprisonment, despite the efforts of famous counsel on his behalf. Sympathizers who were convinced of the honesty of his intentions subscribed £6,000 for his defence. He served the sentence in Holloway Gaol—the first genuine rest from his editorial labours that he had been able to enjoy, as he cheerfully informed his friends. According to J. A. Spender the circulation of the *Pall Mall Gazette*, which had risen from 10,000 to 13,000 under Stead's editorship, had a sudden increase during the "Maiden Tribute" agitation but there was a sharp reaction afterwards.

Five years later Stead devised a new type of sixpenny magazine, the *Review of Reviews*, which was to summarize the events of the month, give a digest of the chief reviews and magazines (because of this feature someone promptly christened it "The Magazine Rifle") and print articles on subjects of current interest. The new monthly made instant appeal, and American and Australian editions were started in 1891 and 1892 respectively. His partner for a time in this new enterprise was George (afterwards Sir George) Newnes, who had achieved phenomenal success with *Tit-Bits*, and the business manager was an energetic man of 24 named Cyril Arthur Pearson, who had joined Newnes's staff at the age of 18 as the result of winning a competition for a £100 a year clerkship and was later to establish a number of weekly and monthly periodicals (among them

Pearson's Weekly,[1] Home Notes, Pearson's Magazine[2] and the Royal Magazine) and to start the Daily Express.

Stead had to give up the editorship of the Pall Mall Gazette, the proprietor not being sympathetic to the idea that he could divide his time between the two journals. This was probably fortunate for Stead, who was thus compelled to concentrate his amazing energy on the Review of Reviews. Since he was always erupting fresh ideas and frequently clashed with popular sentiment—especially when he championed the Boers at the time of the South African War and when he wrote about Spiritualism—his magazine was being constantly discussed. His original and vigorously written "lead" articles and his enterprising exploitation of the interview form—among those he interviewed were famous statesmen and two successive Czars of Russia—kept the magazine excitingly alive and controversial. When he perished in the Titanic disaster in 1912 there were many who felt that they had lost a brave and warm-hearted friend.

Greenwood left the Pall Mall Gazette because Henry Yates Thompson, who had received the paper as a gift from his father-in-law, decided to support the Liberal Party; in 1892 the staff of the same journal—which included E. T. Cook[3] (editor) and J. A. Spender (assistant editor)—departed when Thompson sold it to Conservative interests. George Newnes provided the capital

[1] Pearson's Weekly owed much of its success to "Missing Words" competitions, which were eventually (1892) pronounced illegal. The number of entries for the final competition was 473,574, representing £23,678 in shilling postal orders. Competitors were required to supply the missing word in verses printed in the paper, and the whole sum received in entrance fees was divided among those who sent correct guesses. The most novel of Pearson's many "stunts" was the spraying of copies of the paper with eucalyptus during an influenza epidemic, a doctor having told him that this was the best preventative.

[2] An American edition of Pearson's Magazine was started in 1899. After two years it was sold to an American publisher and during the First World War it was edited for a time by Frank Harris, who turned it into an anti-British periodical and was eventually deported from the United States as an undesirable alien. Pearson, like Lord Northcliffe, found America stimulating and both had the experience of editing the New York World for a day.

[3] Sir Edward Tyas Cook (1857–1919) joined the staff of the Pall Mall Gazette in 1883 and succeeded W. T. Stead as editor in 1890. He twice resigned editor-

to start the *Westminster Gazette* as a Liberal organ to fill the gap made by the defection of the *Pall Mall Gazette*, and it was at his suggestion that the new paper (which appeared in January 1893) was printed on green paper to make it distinctive from the two rival gazettes. Cartoons by "F. C. G." (Francis Carruthers Gould), who had a good-humoured and quietly effective style, were one of the most appreciated features. With Cook again in the editorial chair, and Spender as his chief lieutenant (he succeeded to the editorship when Cook left in 1896 to direct the *Daily News*), the journalistic quality of the new paper was assured. The *Pall Mall* under the new regime was edited from 1892 to 1896 by H. J. C. Cust, a lively, unconventional journalist who kept the paper in high spirits. Later editors included J. L. Garvin (who was simultaneously editing the *Observer*). In 1921 the *Globe* was amalgamated with the *Pall Mall Gazette*, which in 1923 was absorbed in its turn by the *Evening Standard*; the last-named had in 1905 incorporated the *St. James's Gazette*. Thus the *Evening Standard* of today is a combination of what were once four independent journals. In 1928 the *Westminster Gazette*, after an unsuccessful attempt for several years to establish it as a morning paper, was merged with the *Daily News*.

The *Pall Mall Gazette*, the *St. James's Gazette*, the *Globe* and the *Westminster Gazette* appealed to a limited cultivated class and were subsidized by a succession of wealthy proprietors. A blend of newspaper and review, these literary evenings long provided congenial employment for some of the finest journalists of the time, but economic conditions were against their survival. Something very pleasant and distinguished was lost to journalism when this group of London evenings disappeared.

The next chapter in the remaking of journalism opened on

ships for political reasons, the second occasion being when he left the *Daily News* because his views on the Boer War did not agree with those held by the proprietors. From 1901 to 1911 he worked as a leader-writer on the *Daily Chronicle*, and from 1915 to 1919 he was joint director of the Press Bureau. He was author of *Delane of The Times*, a life of Ruskin and other works. Garvin described Cook as "the statesman among journalists."

January 17, 1888, when T. P. O'Connor (1848–1929), a journalist M.P., founded the *Star*, a halfpenny evening paper—one hundred years after the first London evening, also called the *Star*, made its appearance. The new journal, launched with a capital of £48,000, was journalistically as well as politically Radical. Its editor boldly declared that the *Star* would "do away with the hackneyed style of obsolete journalism" and that there would be no place in the paper for the "verbose and prolix articles" to which most of its contemporaries still adhered. The public liked the new paper. Next day the *Star* proudly announced:

> OUR FIRST DAY
> AN EPOCH IN JOURNALISM
> THE WORLD'S RECORD BEATEN
> 142,600 COPIES SOLD

"T. P.," as he was generally called, held that there was not enough human interest in existing papers; he believed also in the value of the personal note, which he was to exploit agreeably—though sometimes repetitively—in most of the periodicals he founded and the features that he contributed to other journals in the later years of his long career. No evening paper of the times had a more brilliant staff than the *Star* in its early days. It included H. W. Massingham (its second editor, who later edited the *Daily Chronicle* and founded the *Nation*); Ernest Parke (who took over the management when "T. P." left and started a companion paper, the halfpenny *Morning Leader*, in 1892); Wilson Pope (editor of the *Star* from 1920 to 1930); Sir Robert Donald (for many years editor of the *Daily Chronicle*); Thomas Marlowe (editor of the *Daily Mail* from 1899 to 1926); W. J. Evans (later editor of the London *Evening News*); Gordon Hewart, afterwards Lord Hewart (a leader-writer, who later became Lord Chief Justice); Sir George Sutton (later chairman of the Amalgamated Press, Ltd., and Associated Newspapers, Ltd.); A. B. Walkley (later dramatic critic of *The Times*); George Bernard Shaw (who was the music critic); Lincoln Springfield (first news editor of the *Daily Mail*); Richard Le Gallienne (who reviewed books); James Douglas (the first editor of the *Sunday Express*); Charles E. Hands (who was to become one of the best known of *Daily Mail* reporters); and Clement K. Shorter (creator of the *Sphere* and other illustrated weeklies). O'Connor left the *Star* presently, selling his interest for £17,000—"the greatest mistake I ever made"—and later founded and edited the *Sun* (1893) but was unable to repeat his success despite a brave start. He also originated the *Sunday Sun* (1891), later the *Weekly Sun*.

The popularization of the newspaper entered a new stage when in 1894 Alfred Charles William Harmsworth (later Lord Northcliffe) and his brother Harold (later the first Lord Rothermere) bought the London *Evening News* and successfully modernized it. There is an interesting prologue to this story that goes back thirteen years. In 1881 George Newnes (1851–1910)—a fellow-student with Stead at Silcoates, a school for the sons of Congregational ministers, in the 'sixties—started *Tit-Bits*, a penny weekly that opened a new era in popular periodical journalism. He was then 30 years of age. His career had so far been a modestly successful one in business, and at the time his journalistic adventure began he was working in Manchester as representative of a London fancy goods firm. While reading a newspaper one evening he called his wife's attention to a paragraph that struck him as unusually interesting and remarked, "Now, this is what I call a tit-bit. Why doesn't somebody bring out a paper containing nothing but tit-bits like this?" Why should he not make the attempt himself? . . . Soon he had gathered enough items from books, newspapers and periodicals to fill several issues, and he looked round for a capitalist to back his venture or a printer with sufficient confidence in it to extend credit, but without success. A way to raise the necessary capital occurred to him. Vegetarian restaurants were popular in Manchester at that time, and he believed that one which offered pleasant surroundings could not fail to succeed. Renting a disused basement he transformed it into an attractive restaurant, and on the first day he was "eaten up in half an hour." He sold the business shortly afterwards for a sum that he felt was adequate to launch his publishing venture. On October 30, 1881, the first number appeared of a sixteen-page weekly called *Tit-Bits from all the Most Interesting Books, Periodicals and Newspapers of the World*. It contained no advertisements, but later Newnes was persuaded to accept them and added a green cover for the purpose. Within a very short time *Tit-Bits* was an established success: six weeks after its appearance Newnes refused an offer of £16,000 for it from the printers who had previously declined to allow him credit. Three years later he transferred the publishing office to London. At first the paper contained only extracts from other publications, but after a time original matter was introduced. Under the stimulus of ingenious advertising ideas the circulation reached figures that had never previously been approached by a popular periodical: one idea, an offer of £100 free insurance against railway accidents, pushed the sale up to 700,000. A scheme with an irresistible appeal to human nature was based on the age-old lure of hidden treasure. Tubes containing five hundred sovereigns each were buried in the earth and readers, informed that whoever found the money could have it, eagerly searched for clues given in a *Tit-Bits* story. Newnes's next publishing venture was the *Strand Magazine* (1891), which he started to employ the additional staff he had engaged for the *Review of Reviews*, Stead having bought his interest in this monthly after a few issues, when they both came to the conclusion that, though good friends, they were not intended to work together. Lavish illustrations, constant ingenuity in the devising of attractive features, and the early publication of the Sherlock Holmes stories by Conan Doyle soon made the sixpenny *Strand* the most successful of the monthlies. Once more Newnes had pioneered a fresh development in popular periodical journalism, and several rivals entered the field before the end of the century. Afterwards came the *Wide World Magazine* and various other periodicals, and Newnes also started (in addition to the *Westminster Gazette*) the *Daily Courier* (1896)—a small-page "magazine-y" penny newspaper with a Society flavour that had only a brief life.

Among the free-lances who contributed to *Tit-Bits* in its early days was Alfred Harmsworth (1865–1922), one of the six sons of a barrister. He had already been assistant editor of *Youth*—owned by Sir William Ingram—at the age of 17; later, in consequence of an attack of pneumonia, he was medically advised to live outside London. Iliffe and Sons, to whose *Bicycling News* he had contributed, invited him to join their staff at Coventry. He spent eighteen months there, and as the firm also published a daily journal he gained a useful insight into newspaper production. Both Sir William Hardman, editor of the *Morning Post*, and G. A. Sala had earlier advised him not to take up journalism as a profession; but William Iliffe was so impressed by his ability that he was willing to pay £1,000 a year to retain his services. Harmsworth, however, decided that his future lay in London and, at the age of 22, he returned there and joined a friend, W. Dargarville Carr, in publishing cheap books: one of those he wrote himself was *A Thousand Ways of Earning a Living*. But Carr & Co., as they styled themselves, soon realized that there was no money to be made out of this kind of publishing.

Harmsworth began to think more deeply about the reasons for the success of *Tit-Bits* and to consider whether it did not point the way to other opportunities in the periodical field. The basic explanation was clear—George Newnes had found a way of catering for the huge new reading public created by the Education Act of 1870. It was a public with simple tastes, a keen hunger for information predominating. While working temporarily on the staff of the *Lady's Pictorial* Harmsworth had been impressed by the popularity of the "Answers to Correspondents" column. Could this idea be profitably developed? He eventually decided to start a weekly of which the entire contents would be "Answers to Correspondents"—and with that title. "The public will call it *Answers*," he was told by James Henderson, a friendly periodical publisher who was one of the first to recognize his journalistic promise; and the title was, in fact, thus shortened after eighteen months. On June 2, 1888, the first number was published from a tiny first-floor office at 26, Paternoster Square. It was a twelve-page paper, sold at a penny, and after five months it was given a more attractive dress by the addition of what was to become the familiar orange cover. The sale of No. 1 was disappointing—less than 12,000 copies—but the circulation steadily improved until at the end of twelve months it had reached 48,000. The business side was now in the capable hands of his brother Harold, whose remarkable financial ability was later to play such an important part in the building up of the Harmsworth enterprises. Then came a simple fertilizing idea that caused the circulation to leap in the second year—the offer of a prize of £1 a week for life to the reader who submitted the nearest calculation of the total of gold and silver in the Bank of England on December 4, 1889, with the shrewd condition that every person who entered the competition must get five others to witness his signature. One pound a week for life meant vastly more in those days of low prices, low wages and no old-age pensions: it was a sum on which a man could then live modestly. The appeal of the offer was instant and tremendous, 700,000 people sending in entries; and the average sale of the paper for the second year was 352,000. Success was now taken at the flood. Plans to improve *Answers* and to make it even more widely known were followed by ideas for new publications—women's papers, boys' weeklies and comic journals—and before long the Harmsworth brothers (other members of the family had now joined the staff) were publishing a group of periodicals earning £100,000 profit a year. But there were still journalistic worlds left to conquer....

Kennedy Jones, then news editor of the *Sun*, came to see Alfred Harmsworth one day in 1894 with an interesting proposal. Louis Tracy, a journalist who afterwards became a popular novelist, held an option to buy the London *Evening News* for £25,000, and Kennedy Jones suggested that Harmsworth should provide the money and give them an interest in the property. It was not an obvious bargain, for the *Evening News* was then in a bankrupt condition. Alfred and his brother Harold studied the books and decided that the *Evening News* could be made to pay:

the latter noticed especially that by proper buying there would be a considerable saving in the cost of newsprint. The investment turned out well—the profit on the first year's working was £14,000—because the paper now had clever editing and good management. Kennedy Jones was a shrewd and hard-working partner on the journalistic side. "K.J.," as he came to be known in Fleet Street, understood the tastes and the limitations of the new reading public, and he saw that the news was presented in the simplest and most readable form and made clear by the use of maps, illustrations and explanatory footnotes. His favourite dictum (as recorded in his book *Fleet Street and Downing Street*) was, "Don't forget that you are writing for the meanest intelligence." In the *Evening News* Alfred Harmsworth had a useful testing-ground for the new journalism, but it was to be a prodigious success on its own. For very many years it has had the largest sale of any evening newspaper in the world—now about 1,750,000.

Harmsworth saw that an even greater success was to be achieved by a national morning paper, and his ideas eventually took shape in the founding of the *Daily Mail*.[1] None of the existing journals was effectively catering for the new reading public of clerks and artisans and others with small incomes. They could be most surely reached by bringing out a new type of paper, to be sold at a halfpenny, compact in size, easy to read; but not, the partners decided, a paper that was radically different in appearance. The English were a conservative people and would take more kindly to the new journal if it looked respec-

[1] According to Kennedy Jones, the original scheme was to found a circle of morning papers, "centring on London and looking to London for their news and opinions." A test was made with the starting of the *Glasgow Daily Record* in October 1895. It made a dull beginning and looked more like an evening paper than a morning journal: the *Daily Mail*, on the other hand, was to have a reassuringly conventional form. The *Daily Record* (now a successful newspaper with a big sale) had a poor first year and was saved by giving racing tips and selections from the London morning journals, which were not to be found in rival Scottish papers. "It saved the position so far as the *Record* was concerned, but the experience caused us to abandon the projected ring of provincial dailies edited from a common centre in London," commented Kennedy Jones.

table and unsensational. Very well then—make it resemble the existing papers, with advertisements on the front page and containing the main features that the reader would expect to find in, say, the *Daily Telegraph*. But with an important difference. There were to be no long articles, and the keynote of the contents would be variety and universality of appeal. Women would be specially catered for in the "Daily Magazine" feature, and it was confidently expected that they would like the concise, attractive way in which the news was written. At the beginning of May 1896 advertisements proclaimed "A Surprise. Daily Mail"—this line being repeated many times in the newspaper announcements in the manner of those days—and on May 4th the *Daily Mail* appeared. It was an eight-page paper which claimed to be "A Penny Newspaper for a Halfpenny" and "The Busy Man's Daily Journal." In the first of four short leaders it was asserted that the *Daily Mail* represented the first endeavour to give all the news of the morning press for one halfpenny.

But the note of the *Daily Mail* is not so much economy of price as conciseness and compactness. It is essentially the busy man's paper. . . . It is no secret that remarkable new inventions have just come to the help of the Press.[1] Our type is set by machinery, we can produce 200,000 papers per hour, cut, folded and, if necessary, with the pages pasted together! Our stereotyping arrangements, engines, and machines are of the latest English and American construction, and it is the use of these inventions on a scale unprecedented in any English newspaper office that enables the *Daily Mail* to effect a saving of from 30 to 50 per cent., and be sold for half the price of its contemporaries.

The general plan of the paper was conservatively attractive. There was no column without its interesting captions, but none of them ran to more than a few lines and they were modestly set.

[1] The Linotype, which can set type—in solid lines—ten times as fast as a hand compositor and does not require stocks of type, came into use in the 'nineties. Faster rotary presses had made possible the rapid printing of large-circulation dailies. Later came the Monotype (which, as its name suggests, sets letters singly instead of in solid lines) and the Intertype composing machines.

The leader page had no signed articles—these were shortly to become an important feature—the page being devoted to "Political Gossip," "In Society" and "The World's Press" (brief extracts from the leading papers of this and other countries). Pages 1 and 8 contained advertisements; page 2 Stock Exchange news and reports from the law and police courts and page 3 home news; page 5 was the main news page; page 6 was chiefly devoted to sport, and on page 7 was "The Daily Magazine" ("an entirely new feature in morning journalism"), consisting of articles and paragraphs of general appeal, contributions of interest to women and the first instalment of a serial. Alfred Harmsworth had great faith in the circulation-building value of a well-designed serial, and this was to be a feature of the paper for many years to come.[1]

The *Daily Mail* was planned as a newspaper for everyone, with particular appeal to the middle-class, the working-class and the woman reader. The response was encouraging: 397,215 copies were sold on the first day, which is not an impressive figure by present-day standards but then represented the highest sale ever achieved by a morning newspaper. What people liked about the new journal was that everything in it was simply arranged, with bright captions that told at a glance what each article or paragraph was about. Inevitably there were to be many sneers at this new halfpenny paper—one of the most quoted was Lord Salisbury's gibe about "A newspaper for office boys written by office boys"—just as there had been contemptuous references by Lord Salisbury (then Lord Robert Cecil) and others to penny papers forty years earlier. Most journalists disliked the new methods; they disliked especially what they considered to be the "bittiness" and triviality of the *Daily Mail*; few as yet recognized that a revolution in journalism had begun which, in addition to making almost everyone a newspaper reader, would

---

[1] Since the paper shortage set in serials have been only an occasional feature in daily newspapers. Once—and once only—*The Times* published a serial, this being an unfinished novel (no title given) by Disraeli. The first instalment, three columns in length, appeared in the issue for January 20, 1905.

ultimately revitalize the technique and widen the scope of all the leading journals. Most of the things that interested the "new sort of newspaper reader"—Harmsworth recalled many years later—were things which the pre-*Mail* newspapers never used to mention.

You could search the Victorian newspapers in vain for any reference to changing fashions, for instance. You could not find in them anything that would help you to understand the personalities of public men. We cannot get from them a clear and complete picture of the times in which they were published, as one could from the *Daily Mail*. Before that was published, journalism dealt with only a few aspects of life. What we did was to extend its purview to life as a whole. This was difficult. It involved the training of a new type of journalist. The old type was convinced that anything which would be a subject of conversation ought to be kept out of the papers. . . . The only thing that will sell a newspaper in large numbers is news, and news is anything out of the ordinary.

Harmsworth had learnt from his experience on *Answers* that no popular journal can succeed and maintain its position without getting itself talked about and without constantly changing and improving its contents. He was not seriously concerned when the circulation fell off—after all, first numbers notoriously sold well if they were widely advertised—and the average sale of 200,000 to which the paper settled down was double the original estimate. He would make the new paper a synonym for enterprise, and he would send correspondents to all parts of the world to provide *Daily Mail* readers with first-hand accounts of great events. He engaged brilliant recruits and paid them well. Among them was G. W. Steevens, a quiet, scholarly man who was to reveal unique gifts as a descriptive writer. Steevens travelled through the United States and told readers of the *Daily Mail* about the "Cross of Gold" presidential election of 1896; he reported the Turco-Greek War of 1897, the installation of Lord Curzon as Viceroy of India, the Sudan campaign and the trial of Dreyfus, and he described the first months of the South African War—and then, early in 1900, came the tragic news that he had died of enteric fever at Ladysmith. He was only 30: "this is a sideways ending to it all," he said when he knew there was no hope of recovery. Harmsworth edited the paper himself during the first three years, with S. J. Pryor as his assistant. When Pryor was sent out to South Africa to organize the Boer War news service his place was taken by Thomas Marlowe, who presently became editor, a post that he filled with great ability and with cool judgment for twenty-seven years.

Within three years the circulation of the *Daily Mail* had reached half a million a day. The third anniversary number had as the main news story a two-column report of a speech by Lord Rosebery in which he appealed to the *Daily Telegraph* and the *Daily Mail* to discontinue the Sunday editions which they were then running. In an editorial on the subject the *Daily Mail* reminded readers that they had followed the lead of the *Daily Telegraph* in starting a Sunday edition because they did not propose to allow any paper to secure a twenty-four hours' start in the publication of news—and concluded with a friendly suggestion to the *Daily Telegraph* to give Lord Rosebery's remarks their earnest attention. The Sunday editions, which had appeared for only a few weeks, were almost immediately stopped. A bold headline in the *Daily Mail* of May 17, 1899, announced: "Death of the Sunday Daily Mail. Frank Concession to the Religious Feeling of the Public." Following straight on after a statement of the reasons for the stoppage of the Sunday issue was an announcement of the early publication of the *Illustrated Mail*, "a complete, artistic, illustrated weekly newspaper," timed to appear early on Saturday morning so that it could be bought with that day's issue of the *Daily Mail*. This now almost forgotten offshoot of the *Daily Mail* ran for only a few years. There is a postscript to the story of the *Sunday Daily Mail*: when a few years later Alfred Harmsworth bought the *Weekly Dispatch*, which Sir George Newnes had been unable to turn into a successful journal, the inevitable comment was made that the *Daily Mail* had its Sunday edition after all.[1]

[1] London and provincial dailies issued Sunday editions in the early months of the First World War.

By the end of the fourth year the circulation of the *Daily Mail* had grown to 700,000 and the exceptional coverage of war news gave a further stimulus to sales. In addition to G. W. Steevens, the correspondents sent out to South Africa[1] included Julian Ralph, a brilliant American journalist, and Charles E. Hands, a very likeable man with a delightfully human style of reporting, whom *The Times*, after his death, described as "The Laughing Cavalier of the New Journalism." Perhaps a more important factor in the growth of the circulation at this period was the improvement of distribution, first by the chartering of special trains[2] to the West and North of England and later by the starting of simultaneous publication at Manchester, which for the first time enabled a morning paper to reach quickly every part of the kingdom.[3] Subsequent developments included the founding of the *Continental Daily Mail*, the weekly edition (the *Overseas Daily Mail*), the Braille edition for the blind, the *Atlantic Daily Mail* (started in 1923 and printed for some years on the principal Atlantic liners), and the *Weekly Transatlantic Edition* ("the world's first transoceanic newspaper"), large quarto in size, which was experimentally produced in 1944, being set up in London and photographed on microfilm, this being flown to New York, where it was re-enlarged and printed. The story of Harmsworth's acquisition of *The Times* will be told in a later chapter.

It was in middle life that Lord Northcliffe (as Alfred Harmsworth had become in 1905) launched the first of many campaigns that startled the country. He was one of the few people who early

---

[1] Rudyard Kipling was invited to act as war correspondent for the *Daily Mail* at a fee of £10,000, but declined the offer.

[2] This was not a new idea. The *Scotsman* speeded up distribution by this means as far back as 1872, having special trains from Edinburgh to Glasgow and to Perth.

[3] Simultaneous printing was carried a stage further in 1928, when the *Daily Express*, which already had a Northern edition in Manchester, started the *Scottish Daily Express* in Glasgow; and in 1940, when the *Sunday Express* and *Sunday Chronicle* began triplicate publication on the same date in London, Manchester and Glasgow. The *Daily Mail* prints its Scottish edition in Edinburgh.

in this century foresaw that there would be immense development in aviation, and it is now curious to recall that when in 1906 the *Daily Mail* offered £10,000 to the first person who flew in one day from London to Manchester there was considerable ridicule: one contemporary countered with a jesting offer of £10,000,000 for a flying machine of any description that flew five miles from London and back to the point of departure. The £10,000 prize was won by Paulhan in 1910; another Frenchman, Blériot, had received the previous year a *Daily Mail* prize of £1,000 for the first cross-Channel flight. In 1913 another £10,000 prize was offered, this time for a Transatlantic flight; six years later it was won by Sir John Alcock and Sir A. Whitten Brown.

A new Northcliffe emerged during the First World War, a man who was sternly concentrated on doing all that lay in his power to speed the victory of the Allied cause and who spoke out frankly without fear of consequences. Rarely does a leading article provoke any popular reaction, but Northcliffe wrote one a column and a half long on "The Tragedy of the Shells: Lord Kitchener's Grave Error" (*Daily Mail*, May 21, 1915) which stirred the greater part of the nation to fury by its blunt assertion that Lord Kitchener had starved the British Army in France of high-explosive shells.

> ... The admitted fact is that Lord Kitchener *ordered the wrong kind of shell*—the same kind of shell which he used largely against the Boers in 1900. He persisted in sending shrapnel—a useless weapon in trench warfare. He was warned repeatedly that the kind of shell required was a violently explosive bomb which would dynamite its way through German trenches and entanglements, and enable our brave men to advance in safety. The kind of shell our poor soldiers have had has caused the death of thousands of them. Incidentally, it has brought about a Cabinet crisis, and the formation of what we hope is going to be a National Government.

No one had written like this since the days of Delane.[1] The

---

[1] The attacks made by *The Times* on the conduct of the Crimean War were more bitterly phrased than Northcliffe's indictment of Kitchener. Delane was determined to rouse the national conscience about the sufferings of the British

reaction to Northcliffe's article was violent and overwhelming. Lord Kitchener was then the most popular man in the country, and ironically it was the *Daily Mail* that had done as much as any journal in the past to create the dazzling Kitchener legend. The paper was burnt on the Stock Exchange and the Baltic Exchange; many public libraries and clubs banned it from their reading-rooms; hundreds of letters and telegrams poured in from readers angrily protesting at the attack on Kitchener; local authorities passed resolutions of condemnation; the circulation of the *Daily Mail* declined and many advertisers ceased to use its columns. Northcliffe was severely condemned in comment on his article by other newspapers—for instance, by A. G. Gardiner in the *Daily News*:

The most serious problem at this moment is not who is going to form the new government, but what that government is going to do with Lord Northcliffe. For this thing is clear, either that frenzied office boy must be suppressed or no government can live. . . . We have to choose, in fact, between responsible government and a Press

forces who had not been properly equipped for the severe Crimean winter. "The noblest army ever sent from these shores has been sacrificed to the grossest mismanagement. Incompetency, lethargy, aristocratic hauteur, official indifference, favour, routine, perverseness, and stupidity reign, revel and riot in the camp before Sebastopol, in the harbour of Balaklava, in the hospital of Scutari, and how much nearer home we do not venture to say." (*The Times*, December 23, 1854.)

Lord Raglan, the Commander-in-Chief, was strongly criticized—unfairly so in the opinion of some well-informed people. In its December 30th issue *The Times* harshly declared: "There are people who would think it is a less unhappy consummation of affairs that the Commander-in-Chief and his staff should survive alone on the heights of Sebastopol, decorated, ennobled, duly named in despatch after despatch, and ready to return home to enjoy pensions and honours amid the bones of fifty thousand British soldiers, than that the equanimity of office and the good-humour of society should be disturbed by a single recall, or a new appointment over the heads of those now in command." It was a leading article that could not be ignored. Opening with the question, "Are we, or are we not, to publish the letters that pour in from the Crimea?" it went on to tell of the hundreds of letters received from the Army and to describe the sufferings of the underfed, ill-equipped British troops. A month later Lord Aberdeen's Government resigned when a motion for an inquiry into the conduct of the war was passed by a large majority.

dictatorship. . . . The freedom of the Press is a great thing, but that freedom involves responsibility, and there comes a time when even the freedom of the Press must give place to the safety of the State. That time has come with us. . . . He [Northcliffe] is no longer a jest: he is the most deadly enemy this country or this Empire has to face. He is ready to set either in a blaze to light a placard.

The *Daily Chronicle*, in a leading article headed "Journalism and Public Safety," thus reflected the public indignation at the attack on the nation's idol:

> If this country were Russia, Germany, or Austria, the scurrilous and mendacious attack on Lord Kitchener which was made yesterday in *The Times* and the *Daily Mail* would have a swift sequel. Lord Northcliffe would have been taken out into a courtyard and shot within 48 hours. That is not a conjecture, but a statement of fact. If it were France or Italy, he would probably have been lynched within a shorter interval, and his premises at Carmelite-street and Printing House-square would certainly have been gutted. These are not examples for our countrymen to follow, but they are illustrations to ponder. . . . We have suggested before, and repeat, that the mistake of the censorship has been to restrict news too much, and not to restrict criticism sufficiently. Of course, the restriction of criticism is a very difficult and delicate thing. We fully appreciate its danger. But a nation must live; and at least the obvious offence against public safety ought to be checked.

Northcliffe was fully aware of the risks he took when he printed the article, but he knew that nothing short of a brutal shock would awaken the nation to the true position of affairs and provide the necessary backing for the few men in power who saw that only by drastic reorganization could the war be won. "I did not care whether the circulation of *The Times* dropped to one copy and that of the *Daily Mail* to two," he told Wickham Steed[1] (as quoted in his reminiscences, *Through Thirty Years*).

[1] Henry Wickham Steed (born 1871) edited *The Times* from 1919 to 1922 and previously served the paper as correspondent at Berlin, Rome and Vienna and as foreign editor from 1914 to 1919. He took part in the big propaganda campaign in enemy countries in 1918 and headed a special mission to Italy in the same year.

"I consulted no one about it except my mother, and she agreed with it. I felt that the war was becoming too big for Kitchener, and that public belief in him, which was indispensable at the outset, was becoming an obstacle to military progress. Therefore I did my best to shake things up."

Northcliffe followed up with other articles, undeterred by the abuse that he received. The storm died down presently; more and more people realized that something was radically wrong with the conduct of the war, and when the Ministry of Munitions began the full mobilization of the manufacturing resources of the country it was increasingly felt that Northcliffe had been right in his assessment of the situation. Thereafter he campaigned with a new vigour and confidence for a more complete and efficient war effort. The nation began to listen to him, to admire his courage and to note that he had correctly anticipated various steps that were taken to enable the country to throw its whole strength into the waging of war. Public opinion swung to the other extreme. Formerly he had been derided as irresponsible and as a scaremonger; now it was being said of him—with the exaggeration that thrives so readily in war-time—that he was the most powerful man in the country. The Government enlisted his services: he was sent out to the United States as chief of the British War Mission there, and in the opinion of those who knew him well he laboured so strenuously that he never recovered from the strain that he imposed on his constitution. He was put in charge of the war propaganda which played such an important part in the ultimate downfall of Germany, and he declined invitations to become Air Minister and War Secretary.

The aftermath was tragic. He parted company with Geoffrey Dawson, editor of *The Times*, who resigned because he disagreed with Northcliffe's ideas on the kind of peace that should be made; he broke with Lloyd George, whose war leadership he had so firmly supported, because of his disappointment that he was given no part in the making of the peace. Early in 1921 he returned from a world tour a tired and shrunken man, and during a visit to Germany in 1922 he sent home articles which revealed that his mind was beginning to fail. There were other distressing signs, including an attack on two of the ablest men on the *Daily Mail* staff (Sir Andrew Caird and W. G. Fish) that led to the issue of writs for libel. Finally came his collapse at Evian-les-Bains, in June, his journey across France to Calais in the Presidential train (sent by the French Government) and his death in London on August 14, 1922, in a temporary wooden shelter erected on the roof of his Carlton Gardens home, from infective endocarditis. Crowds lined the streets on the occasion of his funeral, and a memorial service was held at Westminster Abbey.

In *My Northcliffe Diary*, an intimate account of Northcliffe at work in his later years, Tom Clarke—then news editor of the *Daily Mail*—disposes of the widely held belief that his chief died mad. "It is true there was a period during his illness when the Chief's pitiable physical collapse reacted on his mental condition and his mind rambled. . . . Yet even when he was suffering from the passing delirium his mind was on the passion of his life —reporting; so that he sent that dramatic message in a ghostly whisper across the telephone: 'I hear they are saying I am mad. . . . Send down the best reporter for the story.' Northcliffe recovered from this phase. He became normal again. Once or twice there was a ray of hope. . . . He had begun to discuss things again; had talked quietly of various affairs and people—of his mother, of the chimes of Big Ben, whose tower he could just see from his roof retreat. But he was much too weakened to pull through."

Northcliffe was 57 when he died. No man in the history of the British newspaper has left a more decisive impress on the journalism of his generation. He gave the newspaper a fresh and creative impulse at a time when several famous journals were staggering towards bankruptcy through blind loyalty to an outmoded technique; he restored the prosperity of *The Times* and made the great days live again; and at a critical hour in the history of the country he showed vision and courage. No one more clearly summed up the significance of Northcliffe than J. A. Spender when he wrote:

He was immensely important, however much solemn people might try to blink or evade the fact. He and his imitators influenced the common mind more than all the Education Ministers put together; of all the influences that destroyed the old politics and put the three-decker journalist out of action, his was by far the most powerful. In a sense he was the only completely convinced democrat I ever knew. He did really believe that things ought to be decided by the mass opinion about them, and to find out what that was or what it was going to be, and to express it powerfully, seemed to him not only profitable but right and wise.[1]

Northcliffe had travelled far since that unspectacular beginning on a June day in 1888. From *Answers* had sprung the largest periodical publishing house in the world; newspapers that had transformed the methods of every daily journal and multiplied the reading public; a vast paper-making industry in Newfoundland and a host of subsidiary enterprises. "For me he was always a cataract of human energy sending currents of electric energy far and wide," said J. L. Garvin in a tribute after his death. "I feel as one might if Niagara itself were to cease and vanish. There will not be another Lord Northcliffe. To that Alexander's Empire of journalism, however it may be divided, no one man can succeed."

As Garvin had predicted, the Northcliffe empire was broken up after his death. His brother Harold, Lord Rothermere—he had been made a peer in 1914—bought control of Associated Newspapers, Ltd. (*Daily Mail, Evening News, Weekly*—now *Sunday—Dispatch* and *Overseas Daily Mail*) and made an unsuccessful bid for Northcliffe's shares in *The Times*, which were acquired by the Hon. J. J. Astor; the Amalgamated Press, Ltd., was sold to the Berry brothers—now Lord Camrose and Lord Kemsley.

Rothermere already had newspaper interests of his own, having acquired years earlier the *Glasgow Daily Record* and the *Leeds Mercury* (the latter was later sold to the proprietors of the *Yorkshire Post* and eventually amalgamated with that paper). In

[1] *Life, Journalism and Politics.*

1915 he started the *Sunday Pictorial*, which immediately gained a large sale. During the First World War he was made Director-General of the Royal Army Clothing Department and subsequently became the first Air Minister. In 1928 he founded Northcliffe Newspapers, Ltd., with the object of establishing a chain of new provincial evening journals. After his brother's death Rothermere played a more active role in journalism and frequently contributed signed articles to the *Daily Mail*. He was jointly associated with Lord Beaverbrook in a short-lived attempt to establish a new political party—the United Empire Party. His championship of Hungary, which he urged had been unfairly treated under the Treaty of Trianon, evoked striking expressions of gratitude from that country. He campaigned steadily for British rearmament for some years before the Second World War, beginning in 1933 with an article headed "We Need 5,000 War-Planes." He ordered from the Bristol Aeroplane Co., Ltd., a plane to which he gave the name "Britain First"—which became the prototype of the Blenheim medium bomber—and in 1935 presented it to the Royal Air Force.

Primarily a business genius, Rothermere lacked his brother's passionate and continuous interest in the technique of journalism. He was constantly travelling and in later years was rarely seen in Fleet Street, preferring to delegate the day-by-day conduct of the undertakings in which he was interested. In a memoir written for the *Daily Mail* on his death (at the age of 72) in 1940, Mr. G. Ward Price said: "Lord Rothermere might have seemed to an onlooker strangely casual in his habits of life. During the period of ten years after the death of his brother in which the *Daily Mail* was under his direction, he came to Northcliffe House on one occasion only, which was when it was inaugurated by the present Duke of Windsor, then Prince of Wales, as the new editorial headquarters of this paper and the *Sunday Dispatch*. Private telephone lines kept him in touch with the editors and managerial departments, and his extraordinarily unfailing memory enabled him to carry in his head all the intricate details not only of his own affairs but of the manifold outside interests with which he was connected." Lord Rothermere's two elder sons were killed in the First World War. He was succeeded by his only surviving son, Esmond, who has been chairman of Associated Newspapers since 1932.

CHAPTER THIRTEEN

Newspaper Developments in the Twentieth Century

THE British Press has been revolutionized since the twentieth century began, and the most significant change is the growth of mass circulations far beyond the imaginings of the man who was chiefly responsible for the popularization of the Press—a growth that has taken place since Northcliffe died. Parallel with this development there has been a shrinkage in the number of daily journals, competition and rising costs having forced the suspension of many newspapers. When the twentieth century dawned the New Journalism had not made much headway in the Press generally; in the fifty years that have ensued it has transformed the face of our newspapers—both serious and popular.

No attempt to compete with the *Daily Mail* on its own ground was made until in 1900 Cyril Arthur (later Sir Arthur) Pearson started the halfpenny *Daily Express*, which from its first issue adopted the American policy of printing news on the front page. Some years passed before any other London morning paper followed its example; not until the outbreak of war in 1939 did the *Daily Mail* decide that, valuable though the front page was to advertisers, who then readily paid £1,400 for a single insertion, the news must have priority. The *Daily Express* was edited from 1902 to 1932 by R. D. Blumenfeld (1864-1948), an accomplished American journalist who spent the greater part of his career in London and worked as news editor on the *Daily Mail* before going to the *Express*. Before settling in London he was associated for some years with James Gordon Bennett II as editor of the *New York Evening Telegram* and as superintendent of the head office of the *New York Herald*, which he also served for a time as London correspondent. One day in 1890 his eccentric chief sent him to England to close down the London edition of the *New York Herald* (started in 1889), which was losing money heavily, but gave him discretion to continue the Sunday edition, which was costing the proprietor about £200 a week. When Blumenfeld reported a few months later that he had made a profit of £9 on the Sunday edition Bennett immediately wired from Paris: "Congratulate you on having made a profit at last. Stop the paper at once. Close the office. Dismiss everybody." It then had a circulation of about 60,000—more than the combined sales of several Sunday journals (among them the *Observer* and the *Sunday Times*) which have since become prosperous undertakings. Though Blumenfeld was prominent in British journalism for several decades, he will probably be best remembered by his diary (*R.D.B.'s Diary*), which presents an intimate picture of the London scene from 1887 to 1914. Mr. Arthur Christiansen, who has edited the *Daily Express* since 1933—a period during which it has more than doubled its circulation—introduced the "dynamic" make-up which broke away from the old symmetrical formula in the 'thirties and gave a new liveliness to the newspaper.

The publishing of a "Daily Magazine" feature in the *Daily Mail* of 1896 and the special appeal made to women—this at a time when newspapers were chiefly read by men—began the trend that has culminated in the popular magazine newspaper of today, with its multiplicity of features designed to gain and hold millions of readers. In more than one journal the features now constitute the main content—this despite the fact that important news stories are far more frequent today. It is hardly an exaggeration to say that before 1914 there would be only one or two big news stories a year—leaving out of account the Russo-Japanese War and the Balkan and Italo-Turkish wars—and this thinness in the news columns partly explains Northcliffe's policy of periodically running campaigns (standard bread, sweet-pea competitions and other subjects that got people talking) as it also explains the one-time vogue of silly-season topics in the *Daily Telegraph* and other papers. Because important news was rare, the impression made on the public mind by such events was more vivid than today, when a generation sated with war, horror and crises almost immediately dismisses the most disturbing news from its mind.

The printing of duplicate editions of London journals in provincial centres, which started with the Manchester edition of the *Daily Mail* in 1900, brought new competition to local dailies, the numbers of which have shrunk since the beginning of the century. Several famous London papers have also succumbed or been amalgamated during the period, for various reasons—chiefly competition and rising costs of production. Foreign news services, with the heavy expenditure they entail, are among the costs that have grown tremendously in this century. The scope of the editorial side has been constantly expanding. Specialist staff writers have multiplied. Once they were almost confined to sport and finance; now their number includes experts on international affairs, military and naval problems, aeronautics, the drama, music, the cinema, radio, television, motoring, farming, gardening, psychology, women's interests and other subjects—not to mention political commentators, industrial and labour correspondents, gossip writers and other columnists.

The greatest loss was that of the *Morning Post*, which was incorporated in the *Daily Telegraph* in 1937 after an independent existence of 165 years. Its sale was 100,000 at the time of the amalgamation, and it was one of the best written and best produced newspapers in the country; but, it was stated, "The high costs of production . . . and the ever-increasing service which is demanded from a modern newspaper militate heavily against an organ whose appeal is necessarily a limited one. In the light of these facts, the continued publication of the *Morning Post* as a separate newspaper presented difficulties which it has been found impossible to overcome." The *Morning Post*, founded in 1772, was the oldest daily newspaper. *Lloyd's List and Shipping Gazette* (1734) and the *Public Ledger* (1760), both dailies, are not newspapers but commercial organs, though in its early life the latter paper gave part of its space to news. *The Times* (1785) is now our senior daily newspaper. Only a few years its junior is the *Morning Advertiser* (1794), founded and still owned by the Society of Licensed Victuallers as the organ of the trade, which in recent years has expanded its general news service.

The *News Chronicle* (formerly the *Daily News*) has absorbed no fewer than three dailies—the *Morning Leader*, the *Westminster Gazette* and the *Daily Chronicle*. The *Morning Leader*, a halfpenny paper started four years before the *Daily Mail*,[1] was acquired in 1912. The *Westminster Gazette*, which J. A. Spender made into an influential organ of opinion despite its small circulation (about 20,000), showed a profit only once during its nearly thirty years as an evening paper and lost about £500,000 altogether, and there were further considerable losses when the first Lord Cowdray changed it into a morning journal. As an evening paper it was pleasant to look at with its green dress and its wide columns, and it was urbanely written for an exclusive public of politically-minded readers; as a newspaper, before it became a morning journal, its inefficiency was unkindly typified by the Fleet Street legend that on one occasion some news got into its pages but the editor saw that this did not happen again. In his autobiography Spender denied the suggestion that the *Westminster Gazette* was bought for its articles and not for its news. "The *Westminster* did its news, as it did other things, for its own particular readers, and there were other readers to whom all its ways seemed flat and heavy. These others wanted the splash and the headline and the goods in the shop-window." Spender was the most prolific of the great writing editors. "I have written, I suppose, about 11,000 leading articles, and, including special articles and book-reviews, I had a weekly output of from twelve to fifteen thousand words for many years of my life. . . . I have been surprised in later years to hear myself described as among

[1] Two days before the *Morning Leader* appeared Chester Ives, an American journalist, published the first number of *Morning*, also a halfpenny daily. It was not a success, either under that title or under its later names of *London Morning* and *Morning Herald*, and Pearson bought the paper and incorporated it in the *Daily Express* in 1900. The *Morning*, like the *Morning Latest News* (1870), anticipated the *Daily Express* by printing news on the front page.

the quickest writers in Fleet Street, for I have seldom or never felt that sense of rapid movement which sends the pen flying over the paper. By long practice and with the aid of a relay of very soft pencils and rough-faced paper, I did generally manage to get the 1,200-word leading article of the old *Westminster Gazette* finished within the allotted time of an hour and a quarter. But only the inexorable clock and knowledge of the disaster which would follow, if I failed, made this possible, and I still remember the dreadful occasions when the manager brought me lists of trains lost through my hesitation over a phrase."[1]

John Alfred Spender (1862–1942), who was made a Companion of Honour in 1937, edited the *Westminster Gazette* from 1896 to 1922. He was formerly assistant editor under E. T. Cook, and from 1886 to 1891 he edited the *Eastern Morning News* (Hull). The *Westminster's* period of greatest influence was during the reign of Liberal governments from 1905 to 1915. Spender twice declined a knighthood and once a baronetcy; the single honour he accepted, long after his retirement from editorship, carried no title and was conferred at the suggestion of a Prime Minister to whom he was politically opposed. His biographer, Mr. Wilson Harris, records that when a dinner was given in honour of Spender at the Reform Club in 1938, on the occasion of the presentation of a portrait of him painted by Clive Gardiner, two of the speakers—Lord Simon and A. G. Gardiner—had independently chosen to build their speeches round these lines from Pope's *Epistle to Mr. Addison*:

> "Who broke no promise, served no private end,
> Who gained no title and who lost no friend."

The *Daily Chronicle*, which had several distinguished editors and was at one time famous for its literary page, went through various changes of ownership and was finally amalgamated with the *Daily News* in 1930. The news of the passing of the *Daily Chronicle* stunned Fleet Street. It seemed incredible that an old-established newspaper with a sale approaching a million could be

[1] *Life, Journalism and Politics.*

eliminated almost at a moment's notice. Political entanglements and over-capitalization had undermined the stability of the paper; a slump in advertising (for which the Great Depression of 1929 was responsible) coincided with the enormous cost of re-equipment, and new competition from the remodelled *Daily Herald* magnified the difficulties; but it was the conviction of many who were associated with the paper that given time it could have been restored to financial health. The *Daily Chronicle* had its most prosperous and influential period from 1904 to 1918, under the editorship of Robert Donald (1860–1933), who had previously worked on the *Pall Mall Gazette* and the *Star* and founded and edited *London* (1893)—now the *Municipal Journal*—a weekly devoted to civic affairs. From 1895 to 1899 he was news editor of the *Daily Chronicle*, after which he did publicity work for several years before returning to edit the *Chronicle*. In 1919 he bought the *Globe* for £40,000 but resold it the following year. When the *Daily Chronicle* ceased its separate existence Donald told a *Daily Mail* interviewer: "The first blow to its prestige was when it became the organ of Mr. Lloyd George. This meant that its political news had to be shaped to suit his policy—in other words, that its political reports lacked the true perspective—and that its independence in opinion was sacrificed." Lloyd George bought the paper for £1,600,000 from Frank Lloyd in 1918, and Donald resigned the editorship. "It is at least a coincidence," commented the *Morning Post*, "that the journal was developing into an outspoken critic of Lloyd-Georgian policies." In 1926 the *Daily Chronicle* was sold to Sir David Yule and Sir Thomas Catto for £3,000,000; two years later it changed hands again—this time, it was stated, for £2,000,000—the purchaser being Mr. William Harrison, a solicitor who headed the Inveresk Paper Co., Ltd., and who for a time controlled Illustrated Newspapers, Ltd.

The *Daily News*, which thus outlived rival Liberal morning journals, had itself passed through a difficult period when it lost ground because of its attitude to the South African War. T. P. Ritzema, proprietor of the *Northern Daily Telegraph*, became manager of the *Daily News* after it was acquired by the Cadbury family and on his recommendation A. G. Gardiner (1865–1946), editor of his paper, was invited to come to London. His appointment as editor of the *Daily News* surprised Fleet Street, but Gardiner was to justify the selection. He looked round for fresh talent to strengthen an editorial staff that already included H. W. Massingham and Harold Spender, and among those he engaged were H. W. Nevinson, R. C. K. Ensor, J. L. Hammond and H. N. Brailsford as leader-writers and C. F. G. Masterman as literary page editor and later as leader-writer. G. K. Chesterton (who contributed a Saturday essay), E. C. Bentley, H. M. Tomlinson, R. A. Scott-James, William Archer, Wilson Harris, S. K. Ratcliffe and Stuart Hodgson (later editor) were other recruits to the distinguished staff of the Gardiner period. More attention was given to the arts—especially literature. For a considerable period Gardiner wrote weekly portrait sketches of prominent men of the day which attracted much attention and which were later published in book-form; and he also wrote essays for the *Star* under the signature of "Alpha of the Plough." He retired from the editorship of the *Daily News and Leader* (as it was then called) in 1919. The *Daily News*, like the *Daily Chronicle*, had reduced its price to a halfpenny early in the century. All halfpenny newspapers increased their price to a penny in the First World War.[1]

The *Standard*, one of the leading morning papers in the last

[1] Few daily papers raised their prices during the Second World War. *The Times* went up from 2d. to 3d. and the *Daily Telegraph* and a number of provincial evening papers from 1d. to 1½d. Not until 1951, six years after the war had ended, was there a general increase in prices. This was precipitated by a sudden jump in the price of newsprint from £47 to £60 a ton (six times the pre-war figure) which, combined with steep rises in other expenses, made dearer papers inevitable. The penny newspaper was no longer practicable, 1½d. becoming the new minimum for morning and evening journals (many of the provincials went up to 2d.). The *Manchester Guardian*, the *Glasgow Herald* and the *Scotsman* increased their price from 2d. to 3d. and the *Daily Telegraph* went up to 2d. The *Sunday Times* and the *Observer*, which had previously increased their price to 3d., went up to 4d. and 3½d. respectively and other Sunday newspapers from 2d. to 2½d.

quarter of the nineteenth century, was bought for £300,000 in 1904 by Sir Arthur Pearson. "The paper has, of course, gone down very much of late," he told Joseph Chamberlain, "but not too far to be saved from the total wreck which will befall it if it is left any longer under its present management." Chamberlain and Pearson were then energetically campaigning for Tariff Reform—"The greatest hustler I have ever known," Chamberlain said of his enterprising associate—and the change of proprietorship meant that the *Standard* ceased its championship of a Free Trade policy. Pearson's investment did not turn out well: he was later to lament that every time there was a fog or an east wind the *Standard* lost at least one of its elderly readers and that there were never any young readers to replace the veterans. In 1910 he sold the *Standard*, together with the *Evening Standard* (restarted in 1860), and seven years later the once-famous morning paper was discontinued. He disposed of his remaining newspaper interests when his sight began to fail. Early in the century he had started several provincial dailies, including the *North Mail* (1901). In 1913 Pearson began the work which earned for him the name of "The Blind Leader of the Blind." He was appointed treasurer of the National Institute for the Blind in 1914, and in the following year he opened a hostel for training blinded soldiers and sailors to become self-dependent, later moving it to a large house in Regent's Park called "St. Dunstan's." His other war-time work included the collection of over £1,000,000 for the Prince of Wales's Fund and the inauguration of the Blind Soldiers' Children's Fund. He died as the result of an accident in 1921—at the age of 55—and his funeral was attended by blind men from all over the country.

The heaviest casualties have been among London evening papers. In addition to the present *Evening News*, *Star* and *Evening Standard*, London had six other evening papers fifty years ago—the *Westminster Gazette*, the *Pall Mall Gazette*, the *St. James's Gazette*, the *Globe*, the *Sun* and the *Echo*. Two new evening papers—the *Evening Times* (1910) and the *Echo and Evening Chronicle* (1915)—had only a short life. The latter, an offshoot of the *Daily Chronicle*, never looked like becoming a success, but the *Evening Times* was a brightly produced journal which, given adequate capital, might have established itself firmly. It struggled on gallantly for over a year, and at the end the weekly loss had been reduced to £152. One of the experienced newspapermen associated with this venture was Edgar Wallace, a former editor of the *Rand Daily Mail* and previously war correspondent for Reuters and afterwards the *Daily Mail* in South Africa, where he gained a remarkable "scoop" by being first with the news of the signing of the peace treaty. He had known one of the sentries when he himself was serving in the Army, and he arranged with him a simple code of signals—the use of a red handkerchief indicated "No progress," of a blue one "Nearer to a settlement" and of a white one "Treaty about to be signed." Afterwards Wallace worked as a reporter on the *Daily Mail* and the *Evening News* but was careless about verification and one of his inaccurate reports—or rather inventions, as he had written an interview with a non-existent washerwoman who bitterly complained about the hardship of having to pay more for her soap—served as part of the case against his paper when in 1907 the record sum of £50,000 was awarded as libel damages against Associated Newspapers, Ltd., in an action brought by Lever Bros., Ltd. In another news story, through failure to check back, he made an untrue and libellous statement concerning a naval officer, and the *Daily Mail* had to pay £5,000 to settle the matter out of court. Northcliffe then discharged him. Wallace held other journalistic appointments and wrote many readable novels, but consistent success evaded him until he reached middle age, when he suddenly became a sensational best-seller as the most fertile and the most talked-about writer of "thrillers" and on top of this wrote several plays that were excellent "box-office." The best of these plays, *On the Spot*, was written by hand in a few days; for his novels he used a dictating machine, and once he completed a book in a week-end. He died in 1932 in Hollywood, whither he had gone to fulfil a script-writing contract. Towards the end of his life he was earning—and spending—

£50,000 a year; he died heavily in debt, but the royalties from his many novels paid off the liabilities in a little over two years.

The most ambitious attempt to found a daily paper was the starting of the *Tribune*, a penny Liberal morning which appeared at the moment when Liberal fortunes were at their peak—1906. It was a serious-minded journal, with some excellent men on its staff, but it never succeeded in gaining a large public, and when it died after just over two years of life its proprietors—of whom Franklin Thomasson, a cotton manufacturer, was the chief—had lost about £300,000. "The *Tribune* was too good, and there was too much of its goodness. That was due partly to the scarcity of advertisements," declares Sir Philip Gibbs, a member of its staff, in *The Pageant of the Years*. In his novel *The Street of Adventure*, written in a month after he left the *Tribune*, Sir Philip drew on his experiences and chose one of his former colleagues, Randall Charlton—a tall, elegant, dandyish reporter who was for long one of the most familiar figures in Fleet Street—as the hero under the name Christopher Codrington. Not liking the touches of caricature in the portrait of himself—though he had received advance proofs, with the promise that anything to which he objected would be altered—Charlton issued a writ for libel. On the day before the hearing they met in Fleet Street and shook hands and Sir Philip invited Charlton to have lunch with him. The lawyers, hearing of this, said that for the two principals to get together in this way made the whole case ridiculous, and that evening Charlton agreed to withdraw his action. Sir Philip Gibbs presently joined the *Daily Chronicle* as special correspondent. One of his assignments was to interview Dr. F. A. Cook at Copenhagen on his return from an expedition in the Arctic regions (1907–1909), during which he claimed to have reached the North Pole before Peary. Dr. Cook was angry when asked a few searching questions, and his interviewer decided that he was a liar and had the courage to imply this disbelief in the long story that he sent to his paper. The *Daily Chronicle* exposure was quoted all over the world, and later Cook's story was officially disproved.

A journalistic experiment that survived only a few weeks was Stead's *Daily Paper* (1904). "I doubt whether there will be a sufficient demand for a new paper issued between the morning and evening papers at a time when men are at work, children at school and women engaged in their domestic affairs," his friend, Sir John Leng, warned Stead. But what really doomed the *Daily Paper* was that it chiefly reflected the cranky ideas that had made him an arresting figure in Fleet Street for a generation. Other morning journals that failed were the *Majority, The Organ of All Who Work for Wages or Salary* (1906), a halfpenny morning paper that was doomed by its mainly propagandist purpose; the *Picture Paper* (1911)—later the *Daily Picture Paper*—a Sheffield halfpenny morning that lived for only a few months; the *Daily Citizen* (1912–1915), a halfpenny Labour newspaper that attained a fairly good sale but was unable to attract much advertising; and the *Daily Call* (1914–1915), a small-size paper started by Davison Dalziel, who was at that time owner of the *Standard*.

New dailies established during the half-century include the *Daily Mirror* (started in 1903 as a penny woman's newspaper by Lord Northcliffe, and after a loss of £100,000 turned into the first halfpenny illustrated daily,[1] achieving a big circulation in its new form); the *Daily Sketch* (founded in 1909, it later absorbed the *Daily Graphic*—the first pictorial morning paper, started in 1890 and sold at a penny—and eventually assumed its name); the *Bulletin*, a Scottish picture newspaper that began publication in 1915; the Labour *Daily Herald* ("the miracle of Fleet Street," it was started with a capital of £300 in 1912 and had a chequered career for many years until Odhams Press, Ltd.,[2] acquired a 51

---

[1] The turning-point was when Arkas Sapt, one of the Amalgamated Press editors, came forward with a "crazy notion" that he could show the *Daily Mirror* how to print news pictures on a rotary press. He succeeded after many experiments and thus made possible the substitution of photographs for drawings in the dailies and the supplementing of the letterpress with pictures that were as newsy as the reports.

[2] Odhams Press, Ltd., was mainly the creation of Julius Salter Elias, Viscount Southwood (1873–1946), who started life as an office boy and became one of the leaders of the newspaper industry. It was a small jobbing printing firm when he joined it; when he died Odhams had grown into a vast organization owning

per cent. interest in it in 1929 and quickly raised its sale from a few hundred thousands to over a million[1]); and the Communist *Daily Worker* (1930). Northcliffe subsequently sold the *Daily Mirror* to his brother Lord Rothermere. A few years before his death in 1940 Rothermere parted with control to the present owners, who remodelled the paper and widened its appeal. It has now the largest circulation (4,566,930)[2] of any daily newspaper in the world, having forged ahead of the *Daily Express* (4,222,787),[2] which until 1948 had held the lead since the early nineteen-thirties.

Though its most interesting phase was in the last decade of the nineteenth century, some mention should be made here of the special achievement of the *Daily Graphic*. Started by William Luson Thomas as an offshoot of the *Graphic*, it had many brilliant artists on its staff and regularly published fine drawings of the contemporary scene, among which Reginald Cleaver's Parliamentary sketches were especially admired. Phil May served as cartoonist for a time. Writing in *Alphabet and Image*, under the title "Some Draughtsmen of the Early 'Daily Graphic,'" James Thorpe summed up a delightfully illustrated appreciation in these words: "No daily paper has ever produced so regular a supply of drawings of such a high standard. . . . As the scope and power of the camera increased, and competition made economy of production more necessary, photographs were used more generally and almost entirely replaced the drawings. Finally, the *Daily Graphic*, which maintained its individuality and dignity to the end, lost its public."

New Sunday papers include the *Sunday Pictorial* (planned and produced in eight days in order to be first in the field) and the *Illustrated Sunday Herald* (now the *Sunday Graphic*), started in

---

numerous journals with a mass circulation and occupying many buildings, included a large modern printing works at Watford. Physically he was a small man—he was known affectionately to his staff as "The Little Man"—but he had an enormous capacity for work and a genius for business, and he allowed himself hardly any leisure.

[1] Now double that figure.   [2] 1950 circulation figures.

successive weeks in 1915 by Lord Rothermere and Sir Edward Hulton[1] respectively, and the *Sunday Express*, founded at the end of 1918 by Lord Beaverbrook,[2] who had recently bought an interest in the *Daily Express*. The *Sunday Illustrated*, started by Horatio Bottomley in 1921, was absorbed by the *Sunday Pictorial* after a comparatively short life. The *Sunday Evening Telegram*, which was started in 1917 and ran for several years, was never favoured by the trade because of its time of publication.

The most important event in the Sunday newspaper field was the remodelling by J. L. Garvin (1868–1947) of the *Observer*, which he edited from 1908 to 1942. He revitalized an almost moribund paper into a new type of Sunday journal for the serious reader. Lord Northcliffe bought the *Observer* for £5,000 and appointed Garvin editor with a third interest in the paper. They did not agree on policy, and though their friendship endured their partnership soon came to an end. Northcliffe suggested a choice—either that he should buy Garvin out or that Garvin should buy him out. The first Lord Astor bought the paper; Garvin continued in editorial control, but the new owner insisted on buying his one-third interest because the Astor tradi-

[1] Sir Edward Hulton (1869–1925) was the second son of Edward Hulton, a former *Manchester Guardian* compositor who founded the firm of E. Hulton & Co., Ltd., which grew into one of the biggest newspaper publishing organizations in the country. The first paper was the *Sporting Chronicle*, a daily sheet; next came the *Athletic News* (1875), a weekly, and the *Sunday Chronicle* (1885). It was the son who was responsible for the major development of the firm, starting —among other publications—the *Manchester Evening Chronicle* (1897), the *Daily Dispatch* (1900) and the *Daily Sketch* (1909) as well as the *Illustrated Sunday Herald*, and buying the *Evening Standard* in 1915.

[2] William Maxwell Aitken (born 1879), a Canadian by birth and son of a Presbyterian minister, became Lord Beaverbrook in 1917. A millionaire at 30, he retired from business and came to England, where he entered politics as Unionist M.P. for Ashton-under-Lyne (1910–1916). He was knighted in 1911. During the First World War he served as "Eye-Witness" with the Canadian Expeditionary Force (1915) and was Chancellor of the Duchy of Lancaster and Minister of Information in 1918. In the Second World War he was Minister of Aircraft Production (1940–1941) and concentrated his phenomenal driving power on speeding up the output of planes in the most critical period of the struggle with Germany. He was later Minister of Supply (1941–1942) and Lord Privy Seal (1943–1945).

tion was against having partners from outside the family. Within a few years Garvin raised the circulation of the *Observer*, which had dwindled to a few thousand copies a week, to 200,000 (it is now double that figure). He built up a fine team of special writers on the arts and other interests, but the main feature was a three-column article on the editorial page in which he wrote vigorously on some question of the day. In 1942 he resigned the editorship because of a difference of opinion on policy with the then chief proprietor, the second Lord Astor. Garvin was born at Birkenhead, of Irish parents, and began life in humble circumstances. His father was a labourer and was lost at sea when his son was only 10 years of age. Anxious to earn money to help his mother, young Garvin found work as a newsboy for the *Liverpool Daily Post*. "He loved the old office, and he told me that it was this, and not anything else, that turned his mind towards the romance of journalism," writes his daughter, Katharine Garvin, in *J. L. Garvin: A Memoir*. "For him, journalism was a grind, but it was nevertheless always an adventure." He had little formal education, but gave all his spare time to self-education, in which he was helped by his exceptional power of concentration. He read widely and deeply, and acquired a profound knowledge of English literature as well as a considerable acquaintance with French, German and Spanish literature in the original. After holding various clerical posts he became, at the age of twenty-three, a proof-reader on the *Newcastle Chronicle*, under Joseph Cowen. He stipulated that he should be allowed to write leaderettes, and the quality of his writing quickly brought him promotion. Eight years later he went to London to join the staff of the *Daily Telegraph*, which he served as leader-writer and special correspondent. About this time he started writing for the *Fortnightly Review* under the signature "Calchas," and his contributions attracted wide attention. For a short period he edited the *Outlook* and the *Pall Mall Gazette*.

In 1915 William Ewert Berry (now Lord Camrose) and James Gomer Berry (now Lord Kemsley) acquired the *Sunday Times* when its sale was only 50,000 and by alert editing provided the country with another Sunday newspaper of distinction. Like the *Observer*, it has a notable array of signed features. The first "Scrutator" was the brilliant Herbert Sidebotham (1872-1940), who was also the "Student of Politics" of the *Daily Telegraph* and "Candidus" of the *Daily Sketch* and formerly military critic of the *Manchester Guardian* and *The Times*. The *Sunday Times* has now a sale of over half a million. It was in 1901 that the Berry brothers, who within a quarter of a century were to gain control of more newspapers and periodicals than any other publishing house in the country, made their debut in Fleet Street with the founding by William (then only 22) of the *Advertising World*—assisted by Gomer (then 18). In 1923 the first Lord Rothermere, in conjunction with Lord Beaverbrook, bought the London and Manchester daily and Sunday newspapers owned by E. Hulton & Co. and sold most of them to William and Gomer Berry, who financed the purchase by forming a company called Allied (now Kemsley) Newspapers, Ltd. Later the group acquired many other London and provincial journals.[1] In 1926 the Berry brothers bought the Amalgamated Press, Ltd., the largest periodical publishing organization, and in the following year the *Daily Telegraph*. Associated with them in these publishing interests was Lord Iliffe, who is now chairman of Birmingham Post and Mail, Ltd. In 1937 the three partners rearranged their holdings. Lord Camrose took over his brother's interest in the *Daily Telegraph* and the major portion of Lord Iliffe's holding, as well as their shares in the Amalgamated Press, Ltd., and Financial Times, Ltd. Lord Kemsley bought his brother's holdings in Allied Newspapers, Ltd., and succeeded him as chairman, with Lord Iliffe as deputy chairman. Lord Iliffe acquired control of Kelly's Directories, Ltd., and succeeded Lord Camrose as chairman.

The *Sunday Referee*, founded in 1877 as the *Referee*, was merged with the *Sunday Chronicle* in 1939 after a costly attempt to turn it into a popular Sunday journal, during which phase it reached a circulation of 400,000. The *Sunday News*—edited by

[1] See Appendix B.

Edgar Wallace in its last days—which under its old name of *Lloyd's Weekly Newspaper* was for many decades one of the most prosperous journalistic properties in the country, was merged with the *Sunday Graphic* in 1931.

Critics of the British Press in recent years have dwelt almost exclusively on the developments that have taken place in popular journalism and have ignored the qualitative gains that have been scored in the last half-century. The examples of the *Observer* and the *Sunday Times* have just been quoted: two weeklies that have achieved an immense gain in circulation since early in the century by the process of giving the public (in the words of J. L. Garvin) what it ought to have in a form that it "will like when it gets it." In the daily press, too, we have solid evidence that there is a large and increasing public for serious journalism. The great increase in the sales of *The Times* and the *Manchester Guardian* since 1939 illustrates this heartening trend—as does the substantial circulation of the *Daily Telegraph*.

The renaissance of *The Times* is the outstanding journalistic event of the last half-century. Since the great days under Delane the paper had steadily declined in circulation; the disastrous blunder over the forged "Parnell" letters in 1887 had damaged its moral credit and caused heavy financial losses; and in the early days of this century the fortunes of *The Times* were at a dangerously low ebb. Sponsoring of a reprint of the *Encyclopaedia Britannica* and of other publishing ventures promoted by H. E. Hooper and W. M. Jackson, two enterprising Americans, brought substantial extra revenue that helped to postpone the final crisis. C. F. Moberly Bell, the general manager, toiled heroically for many years to restore the prosperity of the journal, but all the efforts of this devoted "servant of *The Times*" were in vain. New capital and a change in control had become imperative to ensure the continuance of the paper.

When it was announced in 1908 that Lord Northcliffe had acquired control (after an unsuccessful attempt by Sir Arthur Pearson to buy the paper) the public reaction was unfavourable and continued so for some years. Later it became obvious that with the change of ownership *The Times* had gained fresh vitality. Known only to a few behind the scenes was the fact that for some years the previous chief owner had watched the decline of *The Times*, whose traditions he deeply cherished and was so anxious to maintain, with the fatalistic attitude that nothing could be done about it. Geoffrey Dawson, who edited the paper from 1912 to 1919 (when he resigned because of a difference on policy with Northcliffe) and again from 1922 to 1941, was of all men the one best qualified to assess his old chief's contribution to the revival of *The Times*. He has this to say in the course of an outline of Northcliffe's career written for the *Dictionary of National Biography:* "The hasty verdict that 'Northcliffe ruined *The Times*' is manifestly grotesque. The truth is that at a critical moment he was wholly responsible for saving it from extinction; but it is also true that his association with it had lasted long enough when he died and that another change of proprietorship was needed to add steadiness to vitality." The circulation had sunk to its lowest point, 38,000, when Northcliffe assumed control, and the price was still threepence. "It rose very rapidly at 1d. to a high-water mark of 318,000 after the outbreak of war, which, like all great national events, brought a host of new readers. But the tale thenceforward was one of steady decline in numbers through all vicissitudes of price, and at Northcliffe's death both circulation and finance were once more seriously imperilled by the instability of later years."

George Geoffrey Dawson (1874–1944)—formerly Geoffrey Robinson, assuming the name of Dawson by deed poll in 1917 as a condition of his inheritance of the Langcliffe estate in Yorkshire—spent about seven years in public service before entering journalism, including a period as assistant private secretary to Lord Milner when he was Governor of the Transvaal and High Commissioner in South Africa. From this association with Milner, Dawson gained the inspiration to dedicate himself to the furtherance of the cause of the British Empire, and when he was offered the editorship of the *Johannesburg Star* in 1905, at a critical moment in the history of South Africa, he made the decision to give up his Civil Service career and to devote himself to journalism because he saw in the appointment an opportunity for personal service in the cause which he had so much at heart. In 1906 he established his first connection with *The Times* when he agreed to become South African correspondent. He resigned his editorship of the *Star* in 1910 and returned to England because of family affairs. Moberly Bell offered him a post on the editorial staff in December 1910, and in August 1912, after the death of George Earle Buckle (who had edited the paper since 1884), Dawson was appointed editor at the age of 37. For the next few years he was engaged, in association with Lord Northcliffe, the new chief proprietor, in modernizing *The Times*. The make-up was rationalized; the main news page facing the leading articles was evolved; a "light leader" was introduced; the headline practice was improved; and generally the paper was made more attractive to the eye and more convenient to read, without any loss of dignity. This association continued smoothly until Northcliffe began to press his judgment on an editor who preferred to exercise his own. When Dawson retired in 1941 he was succeeded by R. M. Barrington-Ward, who died in 1948 at Dar-es-Salaam while on his way back from a cruise round Africa taken on medical advice. The present editor is Mr. W. F. Casey.

Among the most absorbing chapters in the official history of the paper is the one on Northcliffe. There is a vivid portrait of the man: there is also a critical estimate of his attitude to *The Times*. "That he should wish to preside over the paper's fortunes was natural and also just. But he wished also to dominate and not merely to direct its policy; he would make it his personal organ; and this the old family, the Editor, the Manager and leading members of the editorial staff felt bound to prevent. It was a supreme test of the old traditions, deriving from John Walter II and III, from Barnes and Delane." Of Northcliffe's contribution to the technical improvement of *The Times* (and how necessary that had become is obvious to anyone who has had occasion to study the ill-arranged, uncompromisingly solid-looking issues that were being produced at the beginning of the century), and to the revival of its fortunes, the official history says:

> To the craft of journalism itself one of his indisputable gifts was a stable and orderly simplicity in arrangement—in the "make-up" of a page and of a paper. To remember his resolve to maintain that simplicity against the later fashion for patchy complexity is to do good service to his memory. It must be long before the profession of journalism forgets the advantages that Northcliffe conferred upon it. To him, *The Times* owes its transformation from a bankrupt nineteenth-century relic into a flourishing twentieth-century property. . . . *The Times* would have foundered without him. Northcliffe alone had the genius. It was he, his work, his inventions and his changes that alone re-established the property.

After Northcliffe's death *The Times* came under a new ownership in which the Hon. J. J. Astor has the predominant interest, a minor holding being the property of the Walter family. *The Times* was the first of several national journals—others include the *Manchester Guardian*, the *News Chronicle* and the *Observer*—to establish a trust in order to ensure that the ownership of the paper does not get into the wrong hands, transfers of shares being subject to approval by the trustees (among them the Lord Chief Justice of England, the President of the Royal Society and the Governor of the Bank of England).

Like *The Times*, the *Manchester Guardian* has successfully blended the best of the old and the new—the old tradition of editorial responsibility and balance, of serious writing and objective reporting, and the best of the modern ideas of well-ordered arrangement of the contents and attractive typographical treatment of the page. The changes have been carried out gradually over several decades, under the inspiration of C. P. Scott and his successors.

The revival of the *Daily Telegraph* under Lord Camrose, in addition to being of immense interest to students of the newspaper, surprised Fleet Street by its revelation that there is a much larger public for a serious journal than was generally believed.

When Lord Camrose and his associates bought the paper in 1927 its sale had dropped to 84,000; once it had been 300,000. Three years later, with the installation of a new printing plant, the cumbrous page that had long been the subject of criticism and jest was replaced by one of a more convenient size and the price reduced from twopence to a penny, and in one day the circulation rose by 100,000. New features were introduced and the circulation continued to grow at an encouraging rate; and in 1937 another overnight gain of 100,000 readers took place as the result of the incorporation of the *Morning Post*. By 1939 the sale had grown to 750,000; now it is about a million, despite the fact that its price has gone up to 2d. We shall never again see such amazing value as the *Daily Telegraph* was able to offer in pre-war days—thirty-two pages for a penny. Costs have risen so tremendously that such value for money is no longer possible, and for many years to come this country will not be able to import newsprint on the scale required for such large issues.

Many provincial morning papers that once were honoured names have been merged or discontinued since the beginning of the century—among them the *Manchester Courier*, the *Liverpool Mercury* and the *Leeds Mercury*. Founded over two centuries ago, the *Leeds Mercury* was a newspaper of considerable influence in the second half of the nineteenth century. About fifty years ago it was bought by Lord Rothermere, who reduced its price to a halfpenny and turned it into a popular journal. Subsequently the proprietors of the *Yorkshire Post* acquired it. In November 1939 they merged the *Yorkshire Post* (twopence) and the *Leeds Mercury* (then one penny) under the title of the *Yorkshire Post and Leeds Mercury*—price one penny. The new journal, under the editorship of Mr. W. L. Andrews, has preserved the best quality of the old *Yorkshire Post* and at the same time evolved a character of its own: it has been discreetly modernized, with news on the front page, and its sale exceeds the combined circulation of the two papers whose names it carries on. This achievement in the field of responsible journalism by no means stands alone. The remodelling of the *Birmingham Post* in recent years is another striking example. The immense gain in circulation by the *Manchester Guardian* has been noted. Altogether the provincial press has had a new vitality and a new importance since 1939.

The various reasons for the shrinkage in the number of provincial dailies in the last half-century were brought out in evidence before the Royal Commission on the Press (1947–1949). The competition of the nationals is one explanation; another is that the heavy rise in costs weakened the position of many journals that had never been really prosperous in the most favourable times. Fifty years ago, in the days of light taxation, there were still a number of wealthy men who were prepared to conduct a paper at a loss or at a bare profit either as a service to the party they supported or because they felt it was their duty to the community in which they lived to ensure the continuance of a long-established paper. That class has now disappeared, and the provincial morning paper must either pay its way or be swallowed up by a more efficient rival. Now it is clear that the casualties would have been more severe if the "chains" had not taken over certain papers that had not the resources (financial and journalistic) to carry on alone. The progressive rise in the costs of newspaper production has had the same effects in the United States, where the number of dailies has been declining for many years; in both countries, too, there has been a similar reduction in the number of local weeklies.

The provincial evening press, largely immune from outside competition because the circulation area of an evening journal is necessarily circumscribed by the time factor, has gained in prosperity in the last half-century. Some amalgamations there have been, chiefly in sparsely-populated areas where two evenings could survive only in the days when costs were low and when Conservatives and Liberals felt that they must have their separate organs; on the other hand, several new papers have gained a firm footing. Attempts to establish new evenings near London—the first at Croydon forty years ago and the second at Reading in the nineteen-thirties—were not successful.

The Times

"THE TIMES" THEN AND NOW

The page facing the leader page in 1907 and 1951

Some of the provincial evening papers are highly profitable, and this fact tempted the first Lord Rothermere into a disastrous adventure in 1928, when, at the age of 60, he boldly founded Northcliffe Newspapers, Ltd., with the intention of starting a chain of *Evening Worlds* in the provinces, each provided with its own Northcliffe House embodying the latest ideas in equipment. But two factors thwarted the realization of this ambitious dream —(*a*) the Great Depression, which sharply contracted the available volume of advertising; (*b*) the strength of local sentiment and the toughness of local competition. Within two or three years Northcliffe Newspapers signed a truce with Allied Newspapers (now Kemsley Newspapers) agreeing not to start newspapers in Cardiff, Sheffield and Aberdeen, one condition being that Allied Newspapers should refund expenditure on the buildings under construction in Cardiff and Sheffield for the *Evening Worlds* which had been planned for publication a few months ahead. A drastic stroke of rationalization ended the competition between the rival groups in 1932. Four provincial dailies ceased to exist as a result of the peace terms. The outstanding casualty was the *Newcastle Evening World*—the first journal started by Northcliffe Newspapers—which was incorporated in the *Newcastle Evening Chronicle*. Bristol lost two papers—the *Evening Times and Echo* (incorporated in the *Bristol Evening World*) and the *Times and Mirror* (incorporated in the *Western Daily Press*) —and local people promptly subscribed capital for the starting of a new independent journal, the *Bristol Evening Post*, which made its appearance within three months. The fourth casualty was the *Derby Daily Express*, which was taken over by Northcliffe Newspapers and incorporated in the *Derby Daily Telegraph*. After these mergers were carried through, the Rothermere group was left with one new journal—the *Bristol Evening World*— and a number of papers in various centres which had been taken over and remodelled. Lord Camrose in his book *British Newspapers and Their Controllers* reveals that an enormous sum was spent by Northcliffe Newspapers in the unsuccessful attempt to consolidate their position in Newcastle:

The Newcastle *World* lasted for just over three years, and in that time had more money spent on it than has ever been expended on any other journalistic venture in the provinces. I do not know the exact amount, but the late Lord Rothermere, at the time a truce was arranged, gave me to understand that his company had invested in the Newcastle venture much more than £1,000,000.

At first, as the result of buying readers on a wholesale scale with gifts of admission tickets and free meals at the Great Exhibition, then being held in that city, a considerable sale was achieved. But the exhibition came to an end, other schemes lost their novelty and the readers fell away.

It was the age of free gifts for readers, who were tempted by the ever-mounting bribes offered by hordes of canvassers. In the early nineteen-thirties popular national newspapers were offering their readers the complete works of Dickens, encyclopaedias, war histories, sets of children's classics and other attractive book bargains for a small payment plus coupons cut from a specified number of issues. The *Daily Express* was candour itself about the cost of the extra circulation gained by canvassing. An article published on November 10, 1933, explaining why the sale had not been held at the recent figure, stated that the system of door-to-door canvassing for new readers had been considerably curtailed since June, the peak expenditure of £24,000 on canvassing during one week of June having been brought down by progressive weekly reductions to £5,870 in the last week of October.

The beginning of this intensified competition for readers was about fifteen years earlier, when the *Daily Mail* stepped up its free insurance offer to readers, with a gratifying effect on circulation. In January 1914 the *Mail* offered accident insurance to every reader who registered for benefit, and up to 1921 £19,300 had been paid out in death benefits alone. In the latter year the payment for the death of an insured reader in a railway accident was raised to £3,500 or £7,000 should both husband and wife be killed. (When Sir George Newnes originated the idea of free railway insurance, long before this, readers of his *Tit-Bits* were much impressed by the undertaking to pay £100 and the circulation rose substantially.) The idea of free insurance on this scale was so attractive that hundreds of thousands of new readers registered during the 'twenties and every popular newspaper followed suit and had a similar experience. Competitive boosting of benefits made the cost of this free insurance a heavy drain on the resources of the papers engaged in this frenzied battle for circulation.

With the outbreak of the Second World War newspapers decided to suspend wasteful circulation-building practices. Under the powerful stimulus of the greatest war in history the appetite for news was so sharpened that newspaper circulations soared. As compared with 1938 the aggregate sales of dailies rose from 19,000,000 to 25,000,000 and of Sunday papers from 16,000,000 to 25,000,000 by the end of the war. There were further great increases when circulations were unpegged after the war. The biggest individual sale is that of the *News of the World*, with a circulation of 8,428,000.[1] Until about forty years ago the popular Sunday journals gave the news of the week—hence the old names *Lloyd's Weekly News* (which later became the *Sunday News*) and *Weekly Dispatch* (now the *Sunday Dispatch*)—and had a special appeal for readers who did not buy daily papers. When they changed to the present form, giving Saturday's news plus magazine features, they tapped a much larger public and

---

[1] Lord Riddell (1865–1934)—formerly George Riddell—who started his career as a solicitor, was mainly responsible for creating the organization that early in this century made the *News of the World* the most widely circulated Sunday journal. He acted for a time as legal adviser to Lascelles Carr—who bought the paper in 1891, when its circulation had fallen to 40,000, and made his nephew Emsley (later Sir Emsley) Carr editor—and became chairman of the company. In those days most newsagents' shops, especially in the provinces, were closed on the Sabbath, then much more strictly observed. Riddell gained a decisive lead over rival papers by building up a special network of agents to sell the *News of the World* in every town and village. Later he expanded his journalistic activities when he assumed the direction of George Newnes, Ltd. He was a close friend of Lloyd George and saw much of what was happening behind the scenes in the First World War, and his book *Lord Riddell's War Diary, 1914–1918*, makes informative reading.

since then have made extraordinary gains in circulation. Odhams Press took over the *People* in the 'twenties and increased its sale from 300,000 to 3,000,000 (5,089,500 in 1950). There are several other papers which by 1950 had attained a seven-figure circulation—the *Sunday Pictorial* (5,093,935), *Sunday Express* (3,454,117), *Sunday Dispatch* (2,650,616), the *Empire News* (2,085,107), *Sunday Chronicle* (1,118,348) and *Sunday Graphic* (1,168,915). *Reynolds News and Sunday Citizen*, which was acquired by the Co-operative movement about twenty years ago, has a circulation of 705,385. Add the sales of the *Sunday Times* and the *Observer* and of the Sunday papers published outside London—the *Sunday Mail* and the *Sunday Post* (Glasgow), the *Sunday Mercury* (Birmingham), the *Sunday Sun* (Newcastle) and the *Western Independent* (Plymouth)—and we get the astonishing grand total of about 32,000,000 Sunday newspapers sold every week. The *Western Independent*, founded in 1808, is the third oldest Sunday newspaper, being junior only to the *Observer* and the *Sunday Dispatch*.

These statistics reveal immense growth in this century. Almost everybody now reads at least one daily newspaper, and sales have been multiplied about tenfold since 1901. Advertisement revenues have also grown tremendously. Before 1914 people used to discuss with awe, and even with incredulity, the fact that the *Daily Mail* charged advertisers £350 for a whole front page; and that figure became £1,400 between the wars. A new record for the cost of daily newspaper space was created in 1950, when the *Daily Express* charge for a half-page solus became £2,200 (or £2,700 for an advertisement printed in two colours) and the single-column inch rate £25 (£50 an inch for a front-page solus announcement). The art of advertising in British newspapers fifty years ago consisted of little more than the repetition (sometimes to the extent of a column) of one or two phrases with no more display than the use of drop letters. It was not until well-equipped agency service departments and commercial art studios sprang up in the first decade of this century that advertisement design was taken seriously in this country. Department stores became great buyers of space, especially after Gordon Selfridge had heralded the opening of his new building with an impressive series of full-page announcements. After the First World War (during which paper rationing had reduced newspapers to four pages) advertising continued to gain in quality and volume, and popular dailies swelled in size from eight pages (pre-1914) to twenty-four, with occasional thirty-two-page issues.

These fifty years have seen a marked improvement in the status of the journalist. Credit for this must be given in the first place to Northcliffe, who offered more generous rewards to attract talented recruits to his staff and established new standards of pay, and in the second place—and mainly—to organized effort by journalists[1] to secure minimum salaries more consonant with the exacting and responsible nature of their work. Even when allowance is made for the low cost of living, salaries were for the most part wretchedly inadequate early in the century.

Two world wars, both of which had drastic effects on newspaper production, are obvious landmarks in the history of the Press in this century. Another is the nine-day General Strike of 1926—called in support of the miners—when printers in the offices of several London journals requested the omission of certain news items and the modifying of editorial comment to which they objected, and ceased work when editors refused to accede to their demand. (This was before the strike began—mainly on the previous day.) When the editor of the *Daily Mail* declined to alter a leading article, "For King and Country," which among other points urged that a general strike was a revolutionary movement which could succeed only by destroying the Government and subverting the rights and liberties of

[1] The Institute of Journalists was incorporated by Royal Charter in 1890, and the National Union of Journalists was founded in 1907.

Two journalists' organisations recently established are the Guild of British Newspaper Editors (1946) and the Young Newspapermen's Association (1948). The oldest journalistic institution is the Newspaper Press Fund, which has distributed over half a million pounds in grants and pensions since it was founded in 1864.

the people, and called upon all law-abiding men and women to hold themselves at the service of King and country, printers at the London office stopped work and there was no issue of the London edition on May 3rd.[1] The article was, however, printed in the Manchester and Paris editions.

The next day the General Strike began, but the Press was not silenced. Emergency measures promptly came into operation. *The Times*, after issuing 48,000 copies of a multigraphed sheet, was able to resume the production of four-page papers in the normal way; the *Daily Mail* printed a quarter of a million copies a day in Paris, restarted its Manchester edition with volunteer labour and got out strike issues of various sizes from a number of printing plants; some provincial dailies printed their issues in normal form throughout. But the main picture was the production of emergency editions in a remarkable variety of forms—mostly single-sheet or four quarto pages—multigraphed or cyclostyled or printed by volunteer firms. Members of editorial and commercial staffs helped to get out emergency issues; two members of the Walter family worked in *The Times* foundry. An attempt to burn down *The Times* office by pouring a stream of petrol into the machine room and throwing lighted matches on it was unsuccessful, the staff putting out the blaze before the fire-engines arrived. Subsequently there was a hostile demonstration. No employee of the paper—the proprietors were assured—had anything to do with these violent acts.

The Press, while they were anxious that everything possible should be done to defeat the attempt to prevent newspaper production, declined through their official organizations a suggestion that they should co-operate in getting out an emergency news-

[1] During the railway strike of 1919 the father of the *Daily Mail* printers' chapel wrote a letter to Lord Northcliffe strongly protesting against the policy of the paper. Northcliffe replied: "I hope you will understand that I have no intention of allowing newspapers to be influenced in this or any other matter by anyone. I am entirely satisfied with the attitude of my journals towards this national calamity, and rather than be dictated to by anyone, or any body of men, I will stop the publication of these newspapers, and, in view of your letter, I have so informed the Newspaper Proprietors' Association."

sheet, disliking the idea of an official organ with a propaganda purpose. The Government went ahead with their scheme, producing the *British Gazette* from the *Morning Post* office for eight days in succession, with a circulation that rose from nearly a quarter of a million to 2,209,000. It was a four-page newspaper of standard size—with the exception of the first number, which had only two pages. The whole of the news in all the issues of the *British Gazette* was set on the Linotype by one man—Mr. Sydney W. H. Long, now director of production for Express Newspapers, Ltd. Members of the editorial staff of the *Morning Post* volunteered for work in the machine-room. The T.U.C. produced their own newspaper during the strike—the *British Worker*, printed by the *Daily Herald*. The circulation reached 750,000, which was more than double the sale of the *Daily Herald* in those days.

The agreement reached between the Newspaper Proprietors' Association and the unions concerned after the strike contained a clear statement that henceforth there should be no interference by the unions with the contents of a newspaper.

The end of the nineteenth century found some of the leading newspapers—as already noted—in a precarious condition; now, halfway through the twentieth century, the Press as a whole is in a stronger financial position than at any previous time. The enormous growth in the volume of advertising since 1901 may be said to have buttressed the independence of the newspaper. Simultaneously the revolution in technique has rescued journalism from its end-of-the-century stagnation, by improving methods of presentation and widening the scope of its interest.

Cautious adaptation of the Northcliffe formula has brought fresh vitality to serious newspapers. Not only is the modern "quality" journal, with its clean, well-designed pages, a better job technically than in 1901, but it is also better written. Modern journalism has responded to the accelerated pace of life and the general trend towards simplicity by evolving a more lucid and direct style of expression in both news and comment. Pompous journalistic writing has long since vanished.

The popular "nationals," with their restless and heavier make-up, their liberal use of pictures (illustration was confined to occasional line drawings or woodcuts before the half-tone process was invented) and their array of features, and in a few instances an emphatic broadening of appeal, have followed a path of evolution of their own. The principal recent change to be noted in most journals is a greater aliveness and seriousness on the leader (or magazine) page, which reflects in the length of the articles and the choice of subjects the increased public interest in foreign affairs and vital national issues; and in some papers more virile leader-writing has taken the place of "bitty" editorials. Of nearly all the popular daily newspapers it can be said that they are better edited, better written and wider in their outlook than half a century ago. The newspapers of 1901, produced in an age when motoring had not yet become a significant factor and flying still seemed like a dream (or a nightmare) of a remote future, were beginning to reveal more awareness of the world outside Britain;[1] the newspapers of today, produced in the Atomic Age, have been made internationally minded by world-wide wars and by international air services that have shrunk the old conceptions of distance.

The vogue of the columnist, which began between the two world wars, has not developed here to the same extent as in the United States, where in some journals the bold display of regular signed political features tends to reduce the editorial voice to a marginal whisper. Several popular newspapers have signed political commentaries—the leading example is "Spotlight," the feature which A. J. Cummings has contributed to the *News*

[1] The Empire (now Commonwealth) Press Union, founded by Sir Harry Brittain in 1909, has done important work by securing reduced cable rates and increased official facilities that have stimulated the flow of news and information between the countries of the Commonwealth; by organizing Imperial Press Conferences (the seventh of which was held in Canada in 1950); and by arranging training in Britain for Dominion and Colonial journalists—to mention only a few of its valuable activities.

Chronicle for some years—but the majority of British columnists write features that are mainly or wholly non-political. Don Iddon's New York letter and Collie Knox's radio commentary in the *Daily Mail* and Ian Mackay's reporter-at-large articles for the *News Chronicle*—as well as the weekly essays which he has contributed since the death of Robert Lynd—illustrate the rich scope that a signed feature gives to a writer of personality. Best known of the humorous columns in the daily Press is the "Beachcomber" feature which J. B. Morton (succeeding D. B. Wyndham Lewis) has contributed to the *Daily Express* since 1924, during which period he has created many characters of delightful absurdity to serve as vehicles for his satire on the follies of the times. Gossip pages and columns, a persistent feature of popular journalism, were especially prominent in the larger pre-war newspapers, and the most discussed was the late Viscount Castlerosse's "Londoner's Log" in the *Sunday Express*. But there is nothing fundamentally new in the idea of a regular contributed feature: it has even been plausibly suggested that Dr. Johnson, who wrote "The Idler" essays for the *Universal Chronicle* in 1758, was our first columnist. Early in this century Spencer Leigh Hughes, M.P., wrote a daily column for the *Morning Leader* under the title "Sub Rosa" which has never been excelled in the field of humorous commentary; and Oswald Barron's light essays signed "The Londoner," which appeared daily in the London *Evening News* for many years, can be described without exaggeration as the work of a columnist of distinction.

Cartoonists are more numerous today, but few are doing outstanding work. Low (David Low), a New Zealander, is in a class by himself because of his creative genius and the acid bite of his drawing; and for thirty years—working successively on the *Star*, the *Evening Standard* and the *Daily Herald*—he has shown unceasing invention and power of line. "Vicky" (Viktor Weiss), who came to England shortly before the Second World War and joined the *News Chronicle*, is consistently witty and effective. Illingworth (Leslie G. Illingworth), of *Punch* and the *Daily Mail*, does highly original work in the cartoon form and had previously made a reputation as a gifted illustrator. Giles (Carl Giles), of the *Daily Express* and the *Sunday Express*, is a brilliant draughtsman who has created a family of very odd characters, and his work is appreciated in America as well as in this country. Pocket cartoons, which have become a regular feature of most popular dailies in the last decade, have introduced a welcome note of gaiety at a time when the world is hagridden by crises and bad news predominates. Osbert Lancaster's work for the *Daily Express*, in which his pocket cartoons have been appearing for many years, is unfailingly topical and witty. Gilbert Wilkinson (*Daily Herald*), who works to a larger size, is infectiously high-spirited; and there are many more who are daily producing entertainment in miniature that delights hosts of newspaper readers. Tom Webster, whose work has appeared in several newspapers, is generally regarded as the most humorous sporting cartoonist this century has produced.

There are people who prophesy that the newspaper as we know it is doomed to be supplemented by "fax," as the Americans call it—the facsimile newspaper transmitted by radio and printed on a receiving set in the home. Superficially it would seem that newspaper production will be enormously simplified in this way, for printing and delivery costs will be virtually eliminated. But is it in the least probable that facsimile newspapers will be exact copies of existing journals—that, for instance, a twelve-page issue of *The Times* or a forty-eight-page issue of the *New York Times* will be broadcast? Is it not more likely that the facsimile journal will be a special type of newspaper, something rather more ambitious than a news bulletin but essentially compact and not requiring the stocking of large quantities of paper by those who have receivers? The *New York Times* made a five-day test in 1948 to find the answer to the question whether television will put the newspaper out of business. A close analysis of this experience, as given by Mr. Arthur Hays Sulzberger, publisher of the *New York Times*, at a meeting of the New York State Publishers' Association, indicated that the paper is practically untelevizable in its complete form, and that television and radio can never replace the newspaper that devotes itself to the comprehensive publication of news. During those five days the *New York Times* published just over 2,000 individual stories. In making the check, the stock table was counted as one story whereas reports from London and Berlin of the same situation were counted as separate stories. "Of these 2,068 stories we calculate that 207, or 10 per cent., would have lent themselves to some phase of television. ... Fully half of these were in the sports category."

The idea that the facsimile journal will supplant the ordinary newspaper reminds one of the long-exploded notion, once so firmly held, that the broadcasting of news would be fatal to newspapers (which, by the way, have in the meantime increased their daily sales by millions in this country). Newspapers are largely read in trains and buses and other places where they cannot be received in facsimile form, and although the new method of delivery may be partly competitive it is difficult to believe that it will have the revolutionary effect on the newspaper situation that is visualized by some writers on the subject.

CHAPTER FOURTEEN

The Changing Magazine[1]

THERE are fashions in magazines as well as in other things, and periodicals that appear solidly entrenched can suddenly, and sometimes mysteriously, lose their hold on the public. For several decades the favourite monthly magazines of the British public were the *Strand*, the *London*, *Pearson's*, *Nash's*, the *Windsor*, the *Royal* and *Cassell's*; of these not one has survived, though *Nash's* has produced occasional issues in recent years.

Most of these magazines faded out in the nineteen-thirties; last to go was the *Strand*, which issued its final number in March 1950, after being published for some years in pocket size—markedly different in form from the original conception of Sir George Newnes fifty-nine years earlier. The news that the *Strand*, long regarded as a national institution, was to cease publication, despite the fact that it still had a sale of 100,000 and a large advertisement revenue, came as a shock to the public and the Press alike. "The decision to discontinue a magazine with such a past was naturally reached with great reluctance," stated an editorial note in the last issue. "Conditions after the war, however, have not changed at the speed or in the manner expected; indeed, the problems have increased rather than diminished. With paper three times its former price and with all other costs heavily increased, it has become more and more evident that it is not practicable to revert to the traditional character and size of the *Strand Magazine*—a policy deemed essential to maintain its unrivalled prestige throughout the world. Rather, therefore, than mar a glorious record by continuing a policy of

[1] This chapter covers developments in the entire periodical field, including the weekly, monthly and quarterly reviews.

expediency the proprietors, George Newnes, Ltd., have felt compelled to bring its long and distinguished career to a close."

Another group of magazines—the all-fiction monthlies—disappeared almost completely in the 'thirties. Once there must have been about a dozen of them: one of them, the *Red Magazine*, was so popular for a time that it had to publish twice a month to satisfy its public. Opinions differ regarding the explanation of this sudden withdrawal of public favour from these once prosperous classes of magazine, but two causes may be suggested: (1) new types of periodicals (monthly and weekly) had sprung up, giving the public a wider choice; (2) a string of magazines appeared in the 'twenties and 'thirties appealing directly to women, always big magazine buyers, instantly succeeded and within a few years had a combined sale of probably two million copies a month.

To illustrate how the magazine adventure is constantly changing, consider a copy of *Harmsworth's Magazine* for January 1900, recently found in a second-hand bookshop. Modelled on the picture-at-every-opening formula successfully pioneered by the *Strand*, it aimed at a wider public by means of a lower price—threepence halfpenny (originally threepence) instead of sixpence—and the cover proclaims it as "The Magazine with the Largest Sale in the World." The issue contains thirty-four pages of advertisements (the *Strand* of the nineteen-twenties used to carry something like 100 pages in its richly colourful Christmas numbers). Yet this most successful of magazines, later renamed the *London*, has been dead for years. Long since vanished from the bookstalls, too, are names that were widely known early in this century—*Graphic, English Illustrated Magazine, New Review, Gentlewoman, Ladies' Field, Woman at Home, Lady's Pictorial, Throne, Lady's Realm, Land and Water, Temple Bar, M.A.P., Farm, Field and Fireside, Pall Mall Magazine, World's Work, My Magazine, Rapid Review, Cassell's Saturday Journal, Chums, Little Folks, Black and White, Sunday at Home, Penny Pictorial, Great Thoughts,*

Clarion,[1] the *Prize*, *C. B. Fry's Magazine*, *County Gentleman*, *Flora and Sylva* ("Robinson of Gravetye's" superb monthly, with coloured plates) and many more.

But this largely negative picture, taken by itself, would give a misleading impression of what has been happening in this century. The magazine adventure has become much more varied and more prosperous—and far more exacting—than it was fifty years ago. Looked at through modern eyes it might almost be said that the adventure had hardly begun in 1901; there were a few successful popular monthlies and three highly profitable popular weeklies (*Tit-Bits*, *Answers* and *Pearson's Weekly*), as compared with the host of periodicals of today. Layout was unimaginative and many of the articles were flat in subject and treatment, but there was one respect in which several of the magazines—the *Strand* in particular—excelled. They commanded the services of a team of first-class storytellers who cannot be matched today—Rudyard Kipling, H. G. Wells, W. W. Jacobs, Conan Doyle, E. W. Hornung, Cutcliffe Hyne and others.

Two interesting developments came in the first decade of this

[1] The *Clarion*, which survived until the 'thirties, was founded in 1891 by Robert Blatchford (1851–1943)—one of the most popular journalists of his time—in conjunction with his brother, A. M. Thompson and E. F. Fay. At the age of 14 Blatchford was apprenticed to a brush-maker and six years later he ran away and enlisted in the Dublin Fusiliers, attaining the rank of sergeant within a few years. In 1885 he joined the London staff of *Bell's Life*, and the following year he went to the *Sunday Chronicle* in Manchester and continued there until 1891, when he left because of a difference with the proprietor on politics: Blatchford had become a Socialist two years earlier. Then came the founding of the *Clarion*, a Socialist weekly, which achieved an average sale of 30,000. A series of letters addressed to an imaginary working man, giving a plain statement of the case for Socialism, was republished under the title *Merrie England* in 1894 and ran into many editions at prices varying from five shillings to one penny, the total sale being enormous. Blatchford was one of the comparatively few who realized before 1914 that Germany was deliberately planning war, and a series of articles which he wrote for the *Daily Mail* warning the British public of the danger aroused sharp controversy. "I am ready to sacrifice Socialism for the sake of England; but never to sacrifice England for the sake of Socialism," he wrote years later.

century—the starting of *Nash's Magazine* and the upspringing of a number of all-fiction magazines. The former, launched by Eveleigh Nash, a well-known book publisher of those days, was later sold to William Randolph Hearst, who ran it in conjunction with his American *Cosmopolitan* and injected Transatlantic liveliness into the contents and the cover designs, which were changed monthly—then an exceptional policy in this country. Nash's was good value at the then ruling price of sixpence for a first-class magazine and provided brisk competition; but most of the magazines in this group were prospering and their production standard was steadily rising.

The all-fiction magazines, mostly priced at fourpence halfpenny, included the very popular *Storyteller*—planned and edited by Mr. (now Sir) Newman Flower for Cassell & Co., who still had an active periodical publishing department, which about fifteen years later they were to sell to the Amalgamated Press. Among other newcomers in this field were the *Grand* (Newnes), the *New* (Cassell), the *Novel* (Pearson) and the *Premier* and the *Red* (Amalgamated Press). There was a spate of fresh development after the First World War, Hutchinson's producing several all-fiction magazines as well as *Hutchinson's Magazine* (none had a very long life) and the Amalgamated Press issuing, among others, the *Yellow Magazine* and the *Violet Magazine* (the *Red* had started this vogue for colour titles for popular monthlies) and the *Argosy*, a magazine specializing in good fiction that was destined to be the lone survivor of all the short-story monthlies described in this paragraph. *Pan*, an Odhams venture, had a special quality of its own and deserved to live longer than it did. Another Odhams fiction magazine that appeared between the wars was the *Twenty-Story*. Three humorous monthlies, the *Happy Magazine* and the *Sunny Magazine* (Newnes) and the *Merry Magazine* (Amalgamated Press)—caught the popular taste for a time. *Lovat Dickson's Magazine*, a fiction monthly with a discriminating policy that appeared in the 'thirties, did not find a sufficient public.

Two new magazine formulas, both in the field of woman's

journalism, transformed the appearance of the bookstalls in the late 'twenties and the early 'thirties. *Good Housekeeping*, the British edition of an American success, quickly demonstrated that there was a lucrative opening for a first-class women's magazine published at a shilling, and *Woman's Journal*, launched a few years later by the Amalgamated Press, also immediately found favour. Two other shilling magazines, started in 1919 and 1920 respectively—*Homes and Gardens* (originally *Our Homes and Gardens*) and *Ideal Home*—were also shrewdly conceived.

Then came the sixpenny monthlies—one after another. It all began with *Modern Woman*, which on its first appearance in 1925 simultaneously offered a new type of periodical and greater value for money. Within the next few years followed *Woman and Home*, *My Home*, *Wife and Home*, *Woman and Beauty*, *Everywoman*, etc., as well as several that were discontinued or suspended in war-time. A few of these magazines have attained remarkable sales—notably *Woman and Home*, which with a circulation of more than 950,000 now has the largest readership of any monthly. To repeat—new magazines that set a fresh standard of value, plus a strong feminine appeal that obviously made them ideal media for many advertisers, achieved a large circulation within a few years. Undoubtedly the sales of existing magazines, especially the shilling monthlies of general appeal, were affected by this keen competition. Mention must be made, too, of the success gained by the British editions of *Vogue* and *Harper's Bazaar*, both brilliantly edited and produced.

Another interesting chapter of magazine development opened when in 1927 Mr. J. W. Robertson Scott founded the pocket-size *Countryman*. He had been assured by earnest friends that hardly anyone would buy a half-crown quarterly anyway and that any chance of success would be ruined by producing it from a farmhouse deep in the country. But Mr. Robertson Scott, a man of shrewdly practical vision, felt that there was an obvious logic about the idea of publishing a country magazine in the country that would appeal to readers, and he had a clear plan of how to make such a magazine readable and constructive and how to make it pay. He devised a magazine that was agreeable to handle and agreeable to look at, a compactly written magazine that intimately reflected countryside interests and appealed alike to countrymen and to country-loving townsmen. Then he personally interviewed advertisers and advertising agents and having seen the magazine they too yielded to his logic; and soon journalists and others were taking notice of this quarterly from the country that would within a few years swell into an engagingly thick book carrying scores of pages of advertisements and having scores of thousands of readers.

Next to the ubiquitous *Reader's Digest*, no single publication did more than the *Countryman* to focus attention on the possibilities of the pocket magazine. Small-size magazines had been established long before—among them *Printer's Ink* in the United States and the *Overseas Magazine*, *Today* and the *Organiser* in this country—but their shape had not attracted particular attention. Now it began to be realized that the form had something rather friendly and inviting about it and that it was more likely to succeed if given an intimate character—to which in any case its handy size obviously lent itself. Many new "pockets" were started, some of them digests and others magazines that were based on new formulas, including *Lilliput*, *Housewife* (now a large-page magazine), *Men Only* and *My Garden*.

A new creative force in magazine publishing emerged on the other side of the Atlantic in Mr. Henry R. Luce, who followed up the original and highly successful *Time* (produced in collaboration with a college friend in the early nineteen-twenties) with the audaciously conceived, handsomely printed *Fortune*, which in the quality of its production and editorial content became a landmark in magazine publishing. A few years later he made history again with the launching of *Life*, which embodied a novel conception of pictorial journalism with a mass appeal that has stimulated development the world over.

Though the *Time* formula has never gained the same hold over here as in the United States, the *News Review*—founded by the late Tibor Korda in 1936, and later published by Odhams Press—achieved a sale of over 100,000 before it was discontinued and incorporated in *Illustrated* in 1950. *Fortune* has no close parallel in this country, but with the appearance of "Future Books" (now *Future* magazine) a few years ago—and almost simultaneously of "Contact Books" (later *Contact* magazine, which was discontinued in 1951)—we had stimulating evidence that British publishers could match this new type of intelligent magazine journalism in quality if not in volume.

We had not to wait long for the starting of a national pictorial weekly for the British public. In 1938 Mr. Edward Hulton, son of a famous newspaper and magazine publisher, laid the fortunes of another great publishing house when he produced *Picture Post* and sold 750,000 copies of the first issue. The sale is now double that figure. Incidentally, he shattered a venerable superstition that no weekly could achieve a considerable sale at the price of threepence (the price was recently raised to sixpence). Odhams Press developed an attractive weekly pictorial magazine by stages from the former *Passing Show* (founded as a humorous weekly in 1915) and *Weekly Illustrated* (1934). Known since 1939 as *Illustrated*, it has secured a wide readership.

In the weekly field the periodical has reached the scale of big business. Odhams Press alone has built up the sale of three weeklies above the million mark—*Woman* (now over 2,250,000), *Illustrated* and *John Bull*. Other periodicals that have reached seven figures include *Woman's Own* and *Reveille for the Week-End*. In a class by itself is *Radio Times*, which has the world-record sale for a weekly periodical of 8,000,000 copies. Many other papers have circulations ranging from a few hundred thousands to a million, and the aggregate sales of weekly periodicals now reach an astonishing total. Of the weeklies that once dominated this field only the *Tit-Bits* of George Newnes and the *Answers* of Alfred Harmsworth remain. *Pearson's Weekly* ceased publication in 1939 and *Guide and Ideas*—formerly *Ideas*, started by Sir E. Hulton early in the century—in 1941.

The transformation of *John Bull* into a successful weekly

magazine represents one of Odhams most remarkable publishing triumphs. Started in 1906 by Horatio Bottomley, M.P., the notorious financier, as a penny paper featuring "exposures," it achieved a huge circulation, despite the editor's frequent appearances in the law courts and the bankruptcy court. On the eve of the First World War Bottomley caused a sensation by putting out a poster with the message "To Hell with Servia." A former solicitor's clerk and a shorthand writer in the Supreme Court of Judicature for three years, he was well versed in the law; he was also a highly effective orator and advocate and defended himself successfully on so many occasions that he seemed immune from the usual penalties for spurious financial operations; but eventually a fraudulent scheme he had promoted in connection with Victory Bonds brought about his undoing. In 1922, when he was 62 years old, he was sentenced to seven years' penal servitude. Some time before this Odhams Press, who published *John Bull*, had bought out his interest and severed his connection with the paper. The circulation dropped to a low point, but by heavy expenditure and the remodelling of the paper and the engagement of famous contributors *John Bull* was built up into a leading position among the popular weeklies. This was neither Bottomley's first nor his last journalistic undertaking. He founded the *Financial Times*, he owned the *Sun* and the *Sunday Evening Telegram* for a time, and he started the *Sunday Illustrated* a year before his downfall. After he came out of prison he unsuccessfully endeavoured to re-establish himself by starting a new weekly, *John Blunt* (1928); five years later he died in poverty. His first venture into journalism was in 1884, when he published a small suburban weekly called the *Hackney Hansard*, and its success led him to start other papers of the same type. In 1889 he established the Hansard Publishing Union, with a capital of £500,000; two years later it failed and he was bankrupt. Charged with conspiring to defraud, he defended himself and was acquitted. For some years afterwards he engaged in company promoting on a big scale, with unfortunate consequences for many of his shareholders. During the First World War

Bottomley gained wide popularity by his patriotic speeches (for which he received at least £50 each) and by his articles in the *Sunday Pictorial*.

A weekly periodical that courageously endeavoured to find a new public was the *Leader*. Formerly a popular weekly owned by the late Alfred Bates, it was taken over by the Hulton Press in 1944 and produced in an entirely new form as a periodical designed to bridge the gap between the mass newspaper and the serious weeklies with their minority appeal; and the price was raised from twopence to threepence—later fourpence. The paper was again remodelled in 1949, and its policy was defined as giving the public "something better to read"—a policy which on the whole was successfully achieved. At first a circulation of 300,000 was attained, despite an increase of price to sixpence, but after some months the sale fell off and the paper had to cease publication. Simultaneously several popular weeklies published at threepence and fourpence, and mostly offering more reading matter than the forty-page *Leader*, were being vigorously advertised and gaining largely in circulation; and this factor, combined with a shrinkage in income margins at a time of rising prices, was probably the main reason for the failure of a bold experiment.

The most interesting recent accession to the magazine field is *Go*. Started as an international travel magazine just after the Second World War, it was acquired in 1951 by the *Sunday Times*, which has transformed it into a magazine of leisure pursuits—books, art, and music, fashion and beauty, theatre and films, food and flowers, homes and gardens. It sets a new standard in range and quality for the general magazine.

Interesting additions to the periodical field not already mentioned include the *Connoisseur* (1901), which at 10s. a copy is our highest-priced magazine, the *Burlington Magazine* (1903) and *Apollo* (1920)—an exclusive trio; *Science Progress*, a 7s. 6d. quarterly, founded in 1906; the *Tatler*, a witty illustrated weekly which during the Second World War incorporated the *Bystander*, which like itself had been started early in the century; *The Times*

Literary Supplement (1902), the first of several new weeklies from Printing House Square in this century; *Britannia and Eve*, a monthly that incorporates the titles of two magazines, one of which (*Britannia*) made brief and exciting history as a threepenny weekly in the 'twenties; *Music and Letters* (1920), a scholarly quarterly; the *Geographical Magazine* (1935), an attractively designed monthly that has achieved a substantial circulation; the *World Review* (1936), which incorporates the *Review of Reviews*; the *Review of English Studies* (1925), a quarterly; the *London Mystery Magazine* (1949), published from 221b, Baker Street, the traditional address of Sherlock Holmes; *John O'London's Weekly* (1919)—first edited by Wilfred Whitten—a successful re-creation of the *T.P.'s Weekly* formula which earlier in the century had tapped a new market for a literary journal; the *Listener* (1929), which has made striking progress since 1939, in line with several other journals appealing to the serious-minded reader; *Everybody's* (1927), which began life as a competitors' paper and was gradually developed into a new-style weekly magazine that reaches a big public; the *Children's Newspaper* (1919)—started to "make Goodness News"—one of several journalistic inventions of the able and industrious Arthur Mee, whose *Children's Encyclopaedia* and other serial publications had enormous success; and a few dozen county and regional magazines, nearly all of which have sprung up in the last few years.

Something must be said about a few magazines that are rarely seen by the general public but which have an influence out of proportion to their circulation. In the export field alone are to be found several monthlies of importance—among them the beautifully produced *Ambassador*, which firmly controls the standard of the advertisements admitted to its pages. The eight issues of *Alphabet and Image* (now split into *Image*, a fine quarterly of the arts, and *Alphabet*, a journal of typography which it is proposed to publish annually), edited by Mr. Robert Harling, were deservedly admired by native and overseas typophiles for their distinguished production, good writing and well-informed editing. *Signature*, a quadrimestrial of typography and graphic arts, edited by Mr. Oliver Simon, is also stamped with the zest and scholarship and fastidious regard for quality that have characterized several publications in this field in the last quarter of a century, from the days of the *Fleuron* onwards.

When the age of heavy taxation began over thirty years ago and when newspapers began to publish articles of a type that had formerly been found only in the monthlies and quarterlies, there was a general feeling among journalists that the high-priced reviews and literary magazines were doomed. Several have disappeared in the meantime (a loss particularly deplored was that of the *Edinburgh Review*), but fortunately we have still with us the *Quarterly Review*, the *Twentieth Century*, the *Fortnightly*, the *Contemporary Review*, the *National Review*, *Blackwood's Magazine* and the *Cornhill*. Moreover, there have been important additions to the field—among them the *Hibbert Journal* (1902), the *Round Table* (1910), the *Political Quarterly* (1930) and the *Cambridge Journal* (1947).

Murray's *Monthly Review*, started at the turn of the century under the editorship of Sir Henry Newbolt, was discontinued in 1907. The *English Review*, founded by Ford Madox Hueffer (who later changed his name to Ford Madox Ford) in 1908 and now incorporated in the *National Review*, was at its best in the early years. An impressive first issue included contributions by Thomas Hardy, Henry James, Joseph Conrad, W. H. Hudson, Tolstoy and John Galsworthy, together with the opening chapters of H. G. Wells's *Tono-Bungay*. An earlier *English Review*, a literary and political weekly that ran for only four months (1905–1906), was edited and mainly written by T. W. H. Crosland, poet and critic and almost the last of the Bohemians, who achieved notoriety with his books *The Unspeakable Scot*, *The Egregious English* (written under a Scottish pseudonym) and *Taffy Was a Welshman*. Envious, bitter-tongued, aggressively independent—as they would have said in his native Yorkshire, he loved to quarrel with his bread and butter—he vented his sense of frustration on nearly everyone he met without regard to consequences. He made many enemies, but he had good friends who stood firmly by him to the end, seeing in this strange, perverse man a writer of authentic genius whom success had eluded. Before coming to London he worked at Manchester, editing the *Sunday Chronicle*. He held various appointments in London, including assistant editorships on the *Outlook* and the *Academy* and a post under Frank Harris at the time when the latter was vainly trying to convert *Vanity Fair* into a modern version of the *World* of Edmund Yates's days; and at one period he regularly contributed sonnets to the *Sunday Dispatch*.

T. S. Eliot's *Criterion*, a 7s. 6d. literary quarterly, attained a high critical standard during its brief life in the 'twenties and 'thirties. Sir John Squire's *London Mercury* (1919), well printed and discriminating, added an interesting chapter to the history of literary journalism in the same decades and its loss was severely felt. The *Realist* (1929), a handsomely produced review with a humanistic policy, had excellent backing but failed to get a footing—partly, no doubt, because its appearance coincided with the beginning of the Great Depression. The *Adelphi*, founded by John Middleton Murry in 1923, is a quarterly that has survived a variety of changes and is now a review of the arts, under the editorship of B. Ifor Evans; but *Life and Letters*, started about the same time, ceased publication in 1950. *Scrutiny*, founded in 1932, is a critical quarterly that has attracted much attention. Cyril Connolly's *Horizon*, started in 1940, gained a high reputation as a literary magazine, and there was sincere regret when it suspended publication ten years later. *Penguin New Writing*, a quarterly with a fine literary standard, found a wide public during the Second World War and immediately after, but was discontinued in 1950 because of declining sales. Several occasional miscellanies in book-form—notably *Orion* and the *Windmill*—made a considerable impression in war-time and immediately after by the quality and balance of their contents. Though by no means a complete catalogue of the many ventures in this field in modern times, this outline is at least indicative of the enduring interest in the review-form.

Weekly reviews, one of the most difficult of journalistic enterprises, have gained a large new accession of readers, though several famous weeklies had vanished long before the broadening of interest in serious journalism that was noticeable during the Second World War. The *Spectator*, oldest of the weekly reviews, has doubled its sale in the last decade. The *Economist*, now in its second century, has never been more influential than today, when half its copies are sold abroad and its readers include heads of States and governmental ministers and officials. (All the weekly reviews have now a considerable number of air-mail subscribers.) The *New Statesman and Nation*, which topped 100,000 during the war despite its attenuated size of sixteen pages, absorbed in the third and fourth decades of this century three notable weeklies—the literary *Athenaeum*, H. W. Massingham's ably edited *Nation*[1] and Gerald Barry's stimulating *Week-End Review*, which he had swiftly improvised when he and his colleagues departed in a body from the *Saturday Review* in 1930 because of a change of policy. *Time and Tide*, founded by Lady Rhondda in 1920, and the *Tribune*[2] (1937) are additions to our too short list of weekly reviews. The *Saturday Review*, once an influential weekly, died some years ago, after a melancholy period during which it came under the control of the eccentric, well-meaning Lady Houston. Other reviews that have gone include the *New Age*, which, though never prosperous, gained considerable repute during the years it was edited by A. R. Orage; and Hilaire Belloc's *Eye Witness* (later the *New*

[1] Henry William Massingham (1860–1924) edited the *Daily Chronicle* from 1895–1899, when he resigned because of his opposition to the Boer War. After working on the London staff of the *Manchester Guardian* for a time he went to the *Daily News*, for which he wrote the Parliamentary sketch for some years. "The greatest editor whom I have known," wrote H. W. Nevinson in *Fire of Life*. "Though he was so excellent a writer himself, when I look back upon the paper he created and maintained for sixteen years, I can but recall our Fleet Street saying: 'Any bloody fool can write. It needs a heaven-born genius to edit.'" Nevinson himself was a fine journalist and a great humanitarian, who served with distinction as war correspondent and special writer on the *Daily News, Daily Chronicle, Manchester Guardian* and other journals.

[2] The *Tribune* changed to fortnightly publication in 1950.

Witness), in which Cecil Chesterton collaborated—a review that is chiefly remembered for its slashing articles at the time of the "Marconi Affair."

Humour is a branch of journalism which has seen many failures and only rare successes. *Punch*, over a century old, is still without a rival. The *Comic Times*, the *Tomahawk*, *Fun*, *Ariel*, *Judy*, *Moonshine* and *Lika Joko* all failed to establish themselves in the nineteenth century; in recent years *Punch* has had only one potential competitor, *Night and Day* (1937)—modelled on the *New Yorker*, that most potent of influences on modern humour —and this was discontinued after a short life. In *Lilliput* we have a highly successful monthly that blends humour and pictorial originality. Many experiments have been made during the last fifty years in popular humorous journalism. The most noteworthy survivor is *London Opinion*, which began life early in the century as a penny weekly and is now a widely circulated pocket monthly that incorporates another Newnes periodical—the *Humorist*.

Hundreds of periodicals that are rendering valuable and essential service are almost unknown to the general reader—the various trade, technical and professional journals, as well as the numerous papers catering for special interests. Almost every subject is covered, and the leading publications in this important group achieve a high standard of editing and production and are notably constructive and enterprising.

What chiefly emerges from comparison of the magazines of today with those of fifty years ago is the gain in quality and in variety. There are more types of magazine and almost without exception they are better produced. Periodicals of various types have remodelled themselves externally and internally with the happiest results. The *Field*, *Country Life* and the *Queen* are outstanding examples of well-established papers that are attractively up to date in their dress.

Colour, now so lavishly used, was hardly a factor in magazine production at the beginning of the century. Attractive design, both on the cover and in the layout of the pages, has become an essential part of magazine-making. The successful production of a popular magazine, once largely a matter of editorial shrewdness in choosing literary material and requiring the services of only a small staff, now demands the skilful direction of the activities of a team of many talents; and, if the magazine directs its appeal to women, it requires in addition a corps of specialists to deal helpfully with the thousands of questions that are sent in by readers seeking advice on a hundred and one problems. As recent journalistic history reveals, there is still an opening for the exceptional man who has a new idea for a periodical that can be tried out with a moderate capital outlay; but more and more magazine-making calls for immense resources to establish publications of other than specialized appeal.

Three potential competitors of the magazine have appeared in the last quarter of a century—the radio (which has not justified the fears of those who thought that it would reduce the reading public), the popular reprint of the Penguin type (which, though an obvious competitor, has not checked the upward trend in the aggregate sales of magazines) and television. Looking back on the prodigious increase in circulation in this century, it is clear that the magazine, so long as it continues to provide generously the variety implicit in its name and to respond alertly to changing tastes, is unlikely to suffer any permanent setback.

The magazine adventure has become at once more exacting and more stimulating since 1901; it employs thousands where it employed hundreds and attracts an increasing number of talented men and women with glittering prizes as well as by the inherent appeal of the work; and it has now entered a new and sharply competitive stage of development in which the emphasis is on mass appeal.

POSTSCRIPT.—During a severe fuel crisis in February 1947 that cut off the power supply for many industrial firms, newspapers had to revert temporarily to their war-time sizes, and the production of periodicals—which had appeared without interruption throughout six years of war—was banned for a fortnight. The decision to suspend the periodicals was made as the result of a conference between Government representatives and the Periodical Trade Press and Weekly Newspaper Proprietors Association. Briefly, it was laid down that publication of all weekly periodicals and trade and technical journals dated up to Saturday, February 15th, should take place, as printing of sections was in many cases well advanced. After that date, there was to be complete suspension of publication of at least two consecutive issues of all weekly periodicals irrespective of whether they were printed or published inside or outside the restricted areas or from whatever source they drew their paper supplies; but the publication of weekly newspapers would be permitted. A proposal that the *Radio Times* should not be included in the ban was not accepted, and subsequent representations by the weekly reviews that it was in the national interest that they should appear had no success. It was felt that discrimination of any kind was impracticable in the circumstances. The decision of the Government to suspend the periodicals was widely criticized as a needless and panic measure and as an unwarrantable interference with the right to print, and it was argued that the action had no legal justification.

Many daily and weekly newspapers gave space to the reviews and other periodicals. The *Daily Mail*, for instance, twice placed the whole of page 2 at the disposal of the *Spectator*, and the layout evolved to fit review into newspaper was notable for its quiet distinction. The *Manchester Guardian* had *Time and Tide* as its guest, and the *News Chronicle* gave up more than half of its editorial page to the *New Statesman and Nation*. Several periodicals enjoyed the hospitality of the *Evening Standard*—among them the *Spectator* and *Truth*. *The Times* published two *Punch* cartoons. The *Daily Telegraph* gave space to religious weeklies. Trade and technical journals found hospitality in many newspapers. Over 200 provincial weeklies gave space to the *Farmers' Weekly*.

Dozens of periodicals normally printed in London failed to

appear, and many others were produced in skeleton form or by emergency methods, during two stoppages of work in September and October 1950, caused by a dispute between the London Society of Compositors and the London Master Printers' Association. The *Economist* became the first British paper to be produced wholly by Varityper and litho printing. This proportional-spacing typewriter was first employed in the production of a journal by a Florida newspaper, the *Leesburg Commercial Ledger*, a few years earlier, and later several American daily newspapers used this process during printing employees' strikes. In an editorial note the *Economist* wrote: "We are painfully aware that it is only a token issue, but we take some pride in being able to preserve the tradition of unbroken issue in a week that marks our 107th birthday. . . . We have no better friends than the compositors who set our pages week by week. But their union leaders would do well to observe that it is possible to get along without any compositors at all." Other periodicals also made use of the Varityper or produced editions by duplicating processes. The *Kentish Mercury* (Greenwich) printed an issue in typewritten characters photographically reduced and engraved for production.

CHAPTER FIFTEEN

The Press in the Second World War

WHEN the British peoples, with their French and Polish allies, took up the fresh challenge of German militarism in September 1939, the Press of this country faced not only all the uncertainties and difficulties of war-time publication (of which there had been ample experience in 1914–1918) but the grim possibility of the extinction of its printing plant. There had long been warnings that unlimited air warfare threatened large-scale destruction in London and other big cities, and metropolitan newspapers, visualizing the possibility that their offices would be heavily damaged or even completely destroyed, had made elaborate plans to ensure continuous publication, including arrangements for production in the provinces if necessary.

It was not until early in September 1940, when heavy bombing raids on the capital began, that these plans were put to the test. The *Evening Standard* and the *Daily Herald* were the first victims. The former paper's offices received a direct hit from a large-calibre bomb which wrecked a 15,000-gallon tank on the roof and did extensive damage in the composing room. The managing editor and executives were sleeping on the premises and took immediate steps to ensure uninterrupted production. The editorial and composing departments were transferred to the *Daily Express* building and the printing of the paper was done on the south side of the river.

Not long after *The Times* office was seriously damaged by bombing. The building was struck by heavy-calibre bombs at press-time one morning, but the presses continued to turn and the paper appeared as usual. Warned by the roof-spotters that danger was imminent the staff had descended to safety, except for three members of the staff who were sleeping on the lower floors and had fortunate escapes. No one was more than slightly hurt. It was the main building facing Queen Victoria Street that was struck, all the front rooms—which housed the editorial, managerial and advertisement departments—being wrecked. But though internal damage was severe, the fabric itself stoutly resisted the bombardment. Windows were smashed, the famous clock disappeared and the building showed its wounds, but otherwise the solid structure withstood the test. The plant and the machinery escaped damage. The editorial offices of the *Daily Sketch* (now the *Daily Graphic*) were damaged, but publication continued without interruption in the emergency production premises below ground. There was one casualty, a member of the photographic staff being killed while alone in the dark-room developing plates.

Fleet Street was within the area of attack on December 29, 1940—the night of the Second Great Fire of London—when the Germans rained bombs down for hours in a concentrated attempt to destroy the City and set acres of buildings ablaze. St. Bride's Church—the "Cathedral of Fleet Street" and one of Wren's most beautiful churches—was gutted. The fine steeple survived, but the main structure was left a burnt-out shell and many memorials to famous journalists which it contained were destroyed or damaged. A shower of incendiary bombs fell on the *Daily Telegraph* building. The electricity and gas supplies failed for a time; the women's editorial department on the third floor was destroyed by flames; bombs fell in the composing-room and were promptly extinguished; but notwithstanding all these difficulties the paper appeared as usual next day. Advertising agents, printers and others associated with the Fleet Street area had their premises burnt out or seriously damaged. Dr. Johnson's house in Gough Square suffered damage, but the doctor's chair and a number of first editions were saved. Fleet Street itself bore little evidence of the night of havoc, the destruction being in adjoining streets, courts and squares. Paternoster Row, the great centre of publishing which had many associations with journalism, was destroyed, and the Simpkin Marshall building in Ave Maria

Lane was burnt out: altogether millions of books were consumed in the destruction of publishing and wholesale houses in this area. J. Whitaker & Sons, Ltd., lost the offices in Paternoster Row from which for seventy-five years they had issued *The Bookseller*, *Current Literature* and other publications.

Fleet Street was one of many London districts to be heavily attacked in May 1941. The offices of the *Morning Advertiser* were burnt out and publication of one issue was missed. Other structures to be burnt out were the old *Daily News* building in Bouverie Street and the old *News of the World* building across the way. Production of the *News of the World* continued and distribution was effected with a delay of not more than a few hours. The new building of the *News Chronicle* escaped damage, but it was necessary to make temporary arrangements for the production of this paper and its associated journal the *Star*, and Allied Newspapers provided the necessary equipment and accommodation. Some months previously the *News Chronicle* had had its alternative plant at Commercial Wharf destroyed by enemy action. The *World's Press News* lost its equipment, files and part of its records when the building in which it had offices was destroyed. The Odhams Press premises at La Belle Sauvage, which had been used for printing the *Daily Herald* and the *People* until the reduction in newspaper sizes, were severely damaged. These premises at one time formed a part of those occupied by Cassell & Co. and had therefore many interesting associations with journalism and publishing. Serjeants Inn, where Delane of *The Times* lived, was destroyed.

It was reported in January 1941 that the Newspaper Library at Colindale had received a direct hit in a raid. Damaged newspaper files were piled high among the wreckage, and some had been hurled on to neighbouring roofs. The loss was largely irreplaceable, 30,000 volumes of newspapers—British journals of the nineteenth century and some of the eighteenth century—being destroyed.

"Good-neighbour" arrangements made possible continuous publication of provincial newspapers that suffered damage during air raids—when, for instance, the *Midland Daily Telegraph* (Coventry) was printed by the *Birmingham Gazette*; the *Western Mail* and the *South Wales Echo* (Cardiff) by the *South Wales Argus* (Newport), and the *Yorkshire Evening Press* (York) by the *Yorkshire Evening News* (Leeds). The offices of three Belfast newspapers—the *Irish News*, the *Belfast Telegraph* and the *Northern Whig*—were damaged in the spring of 1941. The *Irish News* building was so heavily damaged that production of the paper seemed impracticable. However, the *Belfast News-Letter*, which escaped damage, came to the rescue, and thousands of copies of a single sheet were got out. Later the *Belfast Telegraph*, which suffered damage from blast that threw everything into confusion but which was nevertheless able to appear at the customary time, was also able to help the *Irish News*. The *Northern Whig* building was badly damaged, but with the aid of the *Belfast News-Letter* the paper was on sale as usual next morning. Afterwards it was produced from the offices of the *Belfast Telegraph*. The *Shields Gazette* office received a direct hit in September 1941, but the printing works escaped damage and the paper appeared as usual.

Never since journalism began has there been a reporting job equal to that involved in the covering of the Second World War. Never before had a war required battalions of correspondents and photographers to record it—not to mention the newspapermen actually in the Services who produced Forces newspapers and magazines, and a great number of journalists employed in the compilation of air-borne newspapers and other forms of psychological warfare.

The First World War was far more static and involved only a small number of fronts; in the Second World War there were numerous fronts, some of them fast-moving, stretching right round the globe. Most correspondents saw more than one campaign, and a few, because of the general use of planes by reporters, had the remarkable experience of seeing nearly all of them. Desmond Tighe of Reuters, for instance, travelled more

1896

1914

ATOMIC BOMB: JAPS GIVEN 48 HOURS TO SURRENDER

Radios threaten Tokio. 'You can expect annihilation'

From JAMES BROUGH, Daily Mail Correspondent   New York, Monday Night

JAPAN is faced with obliteration by the new British-American atomic bomb—mightiest destructive force the world has ever known—unless she surrenders unconditionally in a few days

ZERO HOUR CAME ON JULY 16
Blind girl 'saw' the first

CHURCHILL TELLS BRITAIN'S PART
Spies, RAF, commandos
WE BEAT **in battle of wits**
NAZIS
BY FEW

1945

The Daily Mail

THE EVOLUTION OF MODERN HEADLINES

since the founding of the *Daily Mail* in 1896 is illustrated by these reproductions of main news pages.

than 100,000 miles, through fifty countries, and missed only two important fronts. The aeroplane may have been a doubtful gift to civilization, but it has equipped the modern correspondent with seven-league boots.

Except for a few diehards in the "too Silent Service" and elsewhere who could not be made to see that any failure to report British achievement meant that her war effort was underrated by allies and neutrals, most of the Service chiefs realized how vital it was that our own people and the world should be promptly and fully informed of the progress of the war. Gone was the patronizing attitude of Haig's day; gone was the sort of mentality that in 1914 was responsible for giving orders to arrest war correspondents at sight. In this war correspondents were able to get right up to the front among the fighting men and shared their risks—inevitably at a heavy cost in casualties in proportion to their numbers—and were given ample facilities for speeding their reports home. Only in the East was this impossible, none but official Russian reporters being allowed to report the war on that front.

And what a story these war correspondents had to tell in those six tremendous years! They described how in a few short and terrible weeks in 1940 Denmark, Norway, Holland, Belgium and France were conquered; how long lines of panic-stricken refugees fleeing across Belgium and France were machine-gunned by German pilots; how the "miracle of Dunkirk" was followed by the historic victory in the Battle of Britain; how London endured the long ordeal by bombing in the winter of 1940–1941; how the Balkan countries fell and almost the whole of the Continent came under Hitler's rule; how the tide turned and how the Eighth Army poured through the gap they had torn in Rommel's front at El Alamein and began the long chase across North Africa that ended in the complete surrender of the Axis forces in Tunisia. Then came the series of invasions, starting with North Africa and leading up to the supreme adventure of D-Day in June, 1944, when the greatest armada in history crossed the Channel and British, American and Allied forces smashed their way into

Hitler's "Fortress Europe." All these daring operations were swiftly reported by correspondents who sailed in the invasion ships or went ashore with the soldiers or flew in with the paratroops or watched the scene Xerxes-like from observation planes. From the Far East, from Burma and from the many Pacific islands where landings were made, innumerable correspondents sent vivid dispatches describing the tough and bloody warfare against the death-despising Japs; other correspondents (several of whom were not to return) flew in bombers engaged in raiding Germany; and others watched the terrific drama of battles at sea.

Elaborate arrangements were made well in advance for the Press coverage of the greatest of all news stories—the invasion of Normandy. The number of correspondents accredited to SHAEF (Supreme Headquarters Allied Expeditionary Force) was over 550; afterwards women correspondents—18 British, 10 Dominion and 22 American—were given facilities which did not include covering the operational activities of front-line troops. The war reporters were specially trained before D-Day so that they would be able to cope with all the conditions they would be likely to meet. They lived in small groups with the troops "somewhere in England" and were trained to read maps, to pitch tents, to dig fox-holes, to march across country and to take cover. Shortly before the invasion the correspondents met General Eisenhower, the Supreme Commander, who told them: "I believe that the old saw—'public opinion wins wars'—is true; our countries fight best when our people are best informed. You will be allowed to report everything possible, consistent, of course, with military security. I will never tell you anything false."

D-Day 1944 may have been the peak of reporting experience, but there were great moments to come—the stubborn fighting in Normandy followed by the break-through that took the Allies at a breathless pace across France and Belgium; the invasion of Germany and the crossing of the Rhine; the collapse of the once mighty Wehrmacht; the surrender of Nazi chieftains; the entry into ruined Berlin; the surrender of the Japanese aboard the U.S.S. *Missouri* (300 correspondents and photographers watched the ceremony); the landings in Japan. . . . Most British newspapers had only four pages a day in which to cover all aspects of the greatest war in history, and how admirably they told this story of campaigns and events all over the world can be seen in the files for 1939–1945—and how well, too, the correspondents did their exacting and dangerous job. Scores of British and Allied newspapermen were killed or injured in the course of duty.

The majority of daily newspapers reduced their size to eight pages on the outbreak of war, reverting to ten and twelve pages during the winter when there was a lull in the fighting and advertisers regained confidence. Then came the German invasion of Norway in April 1940, and the cutting off of the chief source of wood-pulp. Newsprint rationing was imposed—first, 60 per cent. of pre-war consumption and then, later in the year, a sharp cut to 30 per cent. From July 1940 newspapers were reduced to six pages, returns and contents bills were abolished and a ban was placed on the issue of new publications. Contents bills (also called news-bills, posters and placards) had been used for stimulating newspaper sales for well over a century. Originally they were detailed, listing the principal contents in a dozen or more lines of heavy type, often with a sub-line to each in smaller type; in modern times they have been limited to proclaiming a single important or sensational news story, set in a few bold words that could be read at a distance. In war-time newspaper sellers began the practice—still continued—of chalking the contents on blackboards.

In the spring of 1941, when rationing became even more severe, there was a further reduction to four pages (eight pages for the smaller-size journals), and much ingenuity had to be used to make the most of the limited space in these thin issues. The whole process of editorial selection had to be sharpened, but it was still found possible to relate the story of the greatest of all wars adequately if not fully. There were some casualties among local weeklies, but it was the periodicals that were hardest hit by paper rationing and war conditions, a long list of magazines being either suspended or amalgamated. Later the newsprint ration was reduced to the meagre allowance of $19\frac{1}{2}$ per cent., and some newspapers found it necessary to cut their printing order in order to preserve what was considered to be an adequate minimum size and the continuance of essential features. Readers in 1942 were urged to "Share your newspaper."

In view of the improvement in the shipping situation, the Minister of Supply was able in September 1943 to authorize an increase in the newsprint ration from $19\frac{1}{2}$ to $21\frac{3}{8}$ per cent. of the pre-war consumption. This represented an addition of about 2,000,000 copies a day. It was stated in the House of Commons that the increase was made in order to meet the heavy demand for newspapers, particularly by the Forces, and that the total number of papers available would be about 19,000,000 a day.

Many foreign journals were produced in London during the war, after the German conquest of a number of Continental countries. Dozens of newspapers and periodicals—daily, weekly and monthly—were started by our allies and by various "free" movements. Another interesting development was the printing (from November 21, 1942) of the European edition of the *Stars and Stripes*, the daily newspaper for the United States armed forces, at the office of *The Times*.

During the war one daily newspaper and a newsletter were suppressed by the British Government and another daily was threatened with suppression.

The *Daily Worker*, the Communist organ, was suppressed on January 21, 1941—under Defence Regulation 2D—because of its subversive activities. The leading article in the *Daily Telegraph* on the decision was typical of editorial comment:

> Freedom of opinion and discussion in the Press are at the foundation of democratic institutions; and the long hesitation of the Government to interfere even with the injurious activity of the *Daily Worker* is a recognition of the fact. But this is no case of ordinary criticism of the Government, which is the birthright of any citizen of a democratic country.

This organ of Communism has existed to serve not British but alien ends by the systematic publication of matter intended to prevent the nation's survival by disabling its prosecution of the war. It is propaganda as hostile to this country as that of GOEBBELS himself, and as continuous. Its dominant purpose has been to make mischief, to sow tares at a time when the nation, whose tolerance it has so constantly abused, is engaged in a life and death struggle with an enemy who shows no tolerance himself. If the *Daily Worker* had attempted to carry on its subversive work in Germany, it would not merely have been suppressed. Those responsible for its publication would most likely have been beheaded.

After Russia came into the war (June 1941) numerous attempts were made to have the ban removed, but it was not lifted until September 1942. The ban imposed at the same time on the *Week*, a newsletter issued to subscribers only, was also removed. The statement announcing the decision of the Home Secretary (Mr. Herbert Morrison) pointed out that he had more than once stated in Parliament that the imposition of the ban did not imply the suppression of these papers for the whole duration of the war.

Press opinion was divided on the issues raised by the Home Secretary's threat—on March 19, 1942—to suppress the *Daily Mirror* unless it refrained from the further publication of matter calculated to foment opposition to the successful prosecution of the war. Mr. Herbert Morrison made his statement in the House of Commons after Mr. Spens (Ashford, U.) had asked him whether he had seen a cartoon recently published in the *Daily Mirror* of a distressed seaman on a raft over the words, "The price of petrol has been raised a penny"; and as this suggestion that seamen were risking their lives in order that bigger profits might be made was calculated to discourage seamen and readers of all classes from serving the country in its time of need and was conducive to defeatism, whether action could not be taken to prevent a newspaper from publishing irresponsible matter likely to influence public opinion in a manner prejudicial to the efficient prosecution of the war. Mr. Morrison replied:

The cartoon in question is only one example, but a particularly evil example, of the policy and methods of a newspaper which, intent on exploiting an appetite for sensation and with a reckless indifference to the national interest and to the prejudicial effect on the war effort, has repeatedly published scurrilous misrepresentations, distorted and exaggerated statements, and irresponsible generalizations. In the same issue the leading article stated: ". . . the accepted tip for Army leadership would, in plain truth, be this: All who aspire to mislead others in war should be brass-buttoned boneheads, socially prejudiced, arrogant and fussy. A tendency to heart disease, apoplexy, diabetes and high blood pressure is desirable in the highest posts. . . ." Reasonable criticism on specific points and persons is one thing; general violent denunciation, manifestly tending to undermine the Army and depress the whole population, is quite another. Such insidious attacks are not to be excused by calls in other parts of the paper for more vigorous action. . . .

As it is possible that some of the persons responsible for the publication of such matter have not realised that it is within the ambit of Regulation 2D, it has been thought right in the first instance to take action by way of warning. I have seen those responsible for the publication of the *Daily Mirror*, and I have made clear to them the considerations which I have outlined to the House. A watch will be kept on this paper, and the course which the Government may ultimately decide to take will depend on whether those concerned recognise their public responsibility and take care to refrain from further publication of matter calculated to foment opposition to the successful prosecution of the war.

A few samples will show the division of opinion in the Press on the Home Secretary's warning statement. *The Times* said the journalistic offences cited deserved the castigation they had received, but there was equally a danger in granting them too much importance. Ministers were at all times apt to take the headier flights of the Press too seriously. The *Manchester Guardian* commented: "The least the Government can do in its treatment of criticisms of friendly intent is to rely on the judgment of the courts." The *Daily Telegraph*: "The examples given . . . will be enough for any reasonable mind. They are not to be treated as criticism of the Government; they come under the heading of irresponsible wrecking of morale." The *Glasgow Herald*: "Such alleged offences as Mr. Morrison complains of should be dealt with under some part of the Defence Regulations which permits judicial review, if, indeed, it is not thought to be wiser and politically safer to allow the opinion of a public which is by no means without common sense to deal in its own way with the exaggerations of inveterate grumblers." The *Birmingham Post*: "The Home Secretary's stern warning . . . is almost certain to be represented as a threat to the freedom of the Press. In truth, it threatens nothing but a scurrilous licence that is a public danger in time of war." The *Daily Herald*: "It is a hundred times more sensible to permit a newspaper to write foolishly than to take action which might undermine public faith in the Press as an independent medium."

CHAPTER SIXTEEN

Parliament and the Press

PARLIAMENT decided in 1946 that it had become necessary to look into the state of the British Press and see whether anything could be done to "further the free expression of opinion." The proposal that such an inquiry be instituted was first made at the annual delegate meeting of the National Union of Journalists in the same year, and subsequently the Lord President of the Council (Mr. Herbert Morrison) received a deputation and promised to convey their representations to the Government.

By 270 votes to 157 the House of Commons on October 29th carried a motion asking for the setting up of a Royal Commission. The Government had left the motion to a free vote of the House. Over 100 Labour M.P.s did not take part in the voting. Those who voted against were mainly Conservatives; they also included six Labour M.P.s, two Liberal M.P.s and two Independents. This was the wording of the motion:

> That having regard to the increasing public concern at the growth of monopolistic tendencies in the control of the Press, and with the object of furthering the free expression of opinion through the Press and the greatest practicable accuracy in the presentation of news, this House considers that a Royal Commission should be appointed to inquire into the finance, control, management and ownership of the Press.

The proposer, Mr. Haydn Davies (St. Pancras, S.W., Lab.), said that journalists wanted freedom of the Press, but for years they had watched it being whittled away. The present owners had a virtual monopoly of the field, and the only real freedom of the Press was the freedom of the newspaper proprietors, who had a perfect closed shop with the highest entrance fee in industry.

Sir D. Maxwell Fyfe (Liverpool, West Derby, C.), in opposing the motion, said that what was behind it was not a desire for freedom at all. The movers wanted to saddle the country with a number of papers of their own way of thinking. The British Press shone forth as an example of freedom and independence. He would remind them of the journalists' song:

> The Pope can launch his interdict,
> The union its decree,
> But the bubble is blown and the bubble is pricked
> By us, and such as we.

The Royal Commission, as subsequently set up, consisted of seventeen representative men and women (of whom only two were professional journalists), under the chairmanship of Sir David Ross, Provost of Oriel College, Oxford. It began taking evidence in June 1947, and concluded its hearings twelve months later. One of the persons asked to give evidence before it was Mr. Aneurin Bevan, Minister of Health. The invitation was sent to him after a speech at the Labour Party conference (May 1948) in which, after urging that they should not allow themselves "to be scared by headlines in the capitalist Press," he continued: "It is the most prostituted Press in the world, most of it owned by a gang of millionaires. . . . The national and provincial newspapers are pumping a deadly poison into the public mind, week by week." Lord Winterton raised in the House of Commons the question of the responsibility, both individual and corporate, of Ministers who made serious charges against an institution that was the subject of a Royal Commission. The Home Secretary (Mr. Chuter Ede) replied that the constitutional position was that it did not seem desirable that Ministers who would have to consider the report of the Royal Commission should give evidence in front of that Royal Commission. The Government felt that Mr. Bevan had a perfect right to express in the country his views with regard to the Press. Among the newspapers which made editorial comment on this ruling was the *Manchester Guardian*, which observed: "If Mr. Bevan had evidence to justify his charge his right as a citizen to expose a grave public evil would outweigh his highly contingent responsibility as a Minister. The Prime Minister has saved his trying colleague from the unpleasant necessity of admitting a lie."

The Commission heard evidence on thirty-eight days, and its members asked 13,239 questions. In its report, issued on June 29, 1949, the Commission made only one major recommendation—the setting up of a General Council of the Press, a fifth of whose members should be outsiders. The two journalist members (Sir George Waters and Mr. R. C. K. Ensor) were opposed to the inclusion of the outside element. Other recommendations included:

The present agreement to refrain from "virtually buying readers"—non-journalistic methods of competition by canvassing, free gifts, free insurance and such-like—should be prolonged indefinitely.

Where one company, either directly or through subsidiaries, owned daily newspapers (other than sporting newspapers) in more than two towns, all the newspapers so owned by that company should be required by law to carry on the front page a formula clearly indicating their common ownership.

If local monopolies in a considerable area, whether rural or urban, should be found not to be within the purview of the Monopolies Commission, the Monopolies and Restrictive Practices Act, 1948, should be amended to bring newspaper monopolies in areas of this size within its scope.

The report consisted of 180 pages, with 183 pages of appendices. These were some of the points:

It is generally agreed that the British Press is inferior to none in the world. It is free from corruption: both those who own the Press and those who are employed on it would universally condemn the acceptance or soliciting of bribes.

We have had evidence also that the direct influence of advertisers on the policy of newspapers is negligible. We have had no evidence at all that advertisers are able to influence the treatment of public questions in the Press; on the contrary, we are convinced that the Press is alert to any such attempts by advertisers and ready on all occasions to repulse them. It is undoubtedly a great merit of the British Press that it is completely independent of outside interests and that its policy is the policy of those who own and conduct it.

There is nothing approaching monopoly in the Press as a whole or, with the single exception of the London financial daily, in any class of newspaper: nor is there in those classes of periodical which we have examined.

The largest single aggregation of newspapers in one ownership, that controlled by Kemsley Newspapers, Limited, accounts for 17·18 per cent of the total number of general daily and Sunday newspapers in the country. Concentration of ownership has gone farthest among provincial morning newspapers, 24 per cent. of which are members of the Kemsley chain.[1]

In fifty-eight towns out of sixty-six in Great Britain in which daily newspapers are published there is a local monopoly, in the sense that there is only one daily newspaper or all the dailies are in one ownership. Twelve of these towns neither import provincial dailies published elsewhere nor publish separately owned weeklies. More extensive monopolies in the publication of daily newspapers exist in the extreme North of England, in Devon and Cornwall, and in South Wales. But the importance of any local monopoly is qualified by the fact that national newspapers circulate throughout the country.

The present degree of concentration of ownership in the newspaper press as a whole or in any important class of it is not so great as to prejudice the free expression of opinion or the accurate presentation of news or to be contrary to the best interests of the public.

One of the questions the Commission was asked to consider was this: "Do any other factors in the control, management or ownership of the Press or of the news agencies, or any external influences operating upon those concerned in control, management, or ownership militate against the free expression of opinion and the accurate presentation of news?" These were the main points in their answer:

In considering this question we have taken as our standard two requirements, first that, while the selection of news may be affected by a newspaper's political and other opinions the news it reports

[1] See Appendix B for details of the principal newspaper chains.

should be reported truthfully and without excessive bias, and second that the number and variety of newspapers should be such that the Press as a whole gives an opportunity for all important points of view to be effectively presented in terms of the varying standards of taste, political opinion, and education among the principal groups of the population.

The first requirement is satisfied in very different measure by different papers. A number of quality papers do fully or almost fully meet its demands. But all the popular papers and certain of the quality fall short of the standard achieved by the best, either through excessive partisanship or through distortion for the sake of news value. The provincial newspapers generally fall short to a lesser extent than the popular national newspapers.

As to the second requirement, the Press provides for a sufficient variety of political opinion but not for a sufficient variety of intellectual levels. . . . The failure of the Press to keep pace with the requirements of society is attributable largely to the plain fact that an industry that lives by the sale of its products must give the public what the public will buy. A newspaper cannot, therefore, raise its standard far above that of its public and may anticipate profit from lowering its standard in order to gain an advantage over a competitor. This tendency is not always resisted as firmly as the public interest requires. The Press does not do all it might to encourage its public to accept or demand material of higher quality.

Nevertheless, the Press has considerable achievements to its credit. It provides cheaply and efficiently a mass of information and entertainment for which there is a wide public demand. It acknowledges high standards of public responsibility and service. It is jealous of its own independence and reputation and many of those employed in it have a sense of vocation.

Another question to which the members of the Commission addressed themselves was how freedom and accuracy could best be promoted.

We do not see a solution to the problems we have indicated in major changes in the ownership and control of the industry. Free enterprise is a prerequisite of a free Press, and free enterprise in the case of newspapers of any considerable circulation will generally mean commercially profitable enterprise.

Nor do we see the solution in any form of State control of the Press. We prefer to seek the means of maintaining the free expression of opinion and the greatest practicable accuracy in the presentation of news, and, generally, a proper relationship between the Press and society, primarily in the Press itself.

Accordingly we recommend:

That the Press should establish a General Council of the Press consisting of at least twenty-five members, representing proprietors, editors, and other journalists, and having lay members amounting to about 20 per cent of the total, including the chairman. The lay members should be nominated jointly by the Lord Chief Justice and the Lord President of the Court of Session, who in choosing the other lay members should consult the chairman. The chairman, on whom a heavy burden of work will fall, should be paid.

The objects of the General Council should be to safeguard the freedom of the Press; to encourage the growth of the sense of public responsibility and public service amongst all engaged in the profession of journalism—that is, in the editorial production of newspapers— whether as directors, editors, or other journalists; and to further the efficiency of the profession and the well-being of those who practise it.

The House of Commons had a debate on the report on July 28, 1949, and agreed to this motion, moved by Mr. Herbert Morrison: "That this House, having taken into consideration the report of the Royal Commission of the Press, would welcome all possible action on the part of the Press to give effect to the Commission's conclusions and recommendations."

In 1947, the year in which the Royal Commission began its hearings, a "privilege" case in which journalists were concerned came before the Committee of Privileges of the House of Commons. It arose from the publication of an article in the *World's Press News* of April 3, 1947, and resulted in the expulsion of the journalist M.P. who wrote it—Mr. Garry Allighan (Gravesend, Lab.)—after a debate in the House on October 30th. Mr. Arthur Heighway, editor of the paper, was called to the Bar of the House and reprimanded by the Speaker. The article complained of contained these (among other) statements:

Willy Nally put his foot ankle-deep into it last week when, in Parliament, he accused M.P.s—of whom 21 are his fellow members in the N.U.J.—of taking Beaverbrook money as "bribes." That fascinating grotesquerie caused the Speaker to demand a withdrawal and to contemplate action in respect of a breach of privilege. Complete withdrawal and apology which exonerated his colleagues were forthcoming from Willy Nally willy nilly.

This pool-busting, Co-op.-nominated journalist M.P. was righteously angered by the fact that the *Evening Standard* manages to get what the Parliamentary Labour Party has, for years, referred to as "leaks." . . . How do they get the stuff? Anyone with wide Fleet Street experience would know that there is nothing mystic about this.

Every newspaper in the Street has anything up to half a dozen M.P.s on its "Contacts" list. They always have had—what's the Contacts file for, otherwise? Some of the "contacts" are on a retainer, some get paid for what they produce, some are content to accept "payment in kind"—personal publicity.

That is one way any enterprising reporter gets what the Party calls "leaks." Another way more accurately justifies that description. M.P.s "leak" around the bar. Being no less human than subs., some M.P.s "knock 'em back" at the bar and, being less absorptive than reporters, become lubricated into loquacity.

No worthwhile reporter could fail to get the stuff. If he knew no other way, and had no other contacts, all he would have to do would be to spend his time, and the paper's money, at the bar, and if he did not pick up enough bits and pieces from M.P.s in search of refreshment to make a first-rate "inside" story, he ought to be fired. Herbert Morrison is not half the Party "boss" he's accused of being—if he were he'd put the bar out of bounds to Labour M.P.s, some of whom have succeeded in approaching the fringe of semi-sobriety.

The Committee heard evidence on eight days. Four outstanding incidents in the proceedings were:

> (*a*) Mr. Allighan, who accepted full responsibility for the article and freely admitted that he had made "a grievous mistake in writing it," was later recalled and agreed when questioned that he had received payment for writing reports of Labour Party meetings for the *Evening Standard*.

(b) Mr. Guy Schofield, editor of the London *Evening News*, said that a member of Parliament on the "contacts" list who was paid £5 a week irrespective of what he turned in, was the source of information on which a report of a private meeting of the Labour Party on April 23 was based. Neither he nor the paper's political correspondent (Mr. Stanley Dobson) would disclose the name when giving evidence.

(c) Subsequently Mr. Evelyn Walkden, M.P. (Doncaster, Lab.), made a personal statement in the House revealing that he was the member who had received the payment. The matter was reported to the Committee of Privileges.

(d) Both Mr. Schofield and Mr. Dobson were summoned to the Bar of the House on August 12—when the House considered the report of the Committee of Privileges—and apologized for refusing to disclose the name and thereby committing contempt of the House.

The case came before the House of Commons on October 30th, and after Mr. Allighan had made a statement expressing deep regret and humbly and sincerely apologizing for writing in such a way as to put an affront on the House, Mr. Morrison moved that he be suspended for six months; but after discussion the House accepted—by 187 votes to 75—an amendment that he be expelled. The House also passed a motion directing Mr. Walkden to attend in his place forthwith to be reprimanded by the Speaker.

Later in the year—on December 10th—the House of Commons passed this resolution by 287 votes to 123: "That, if in any case hereafter a member shall have been found guilty by this House of corruptly accepting payment for the disclosure and publication of confidential information about matters to be proceeded with in Parliament, any person responsible for offering such payment shall incur the grave displeasure of this House; and this House will take such action as it may, in the circumstances, think fit." Mr. Morrison, who moved the resolution, said it arose out of the cases of Mr. Garry Allighan and Mr. Evelyn Walkden. They were not going to take action against the journalists or editors concerned in those cases, but it was not in accordance with the laws of natural justice that members should find themselves shattered and ruined and the people who paid them money should get off scot-free. Earl Winterton (Horsham, C.) described the motion as most dangerous and unnecessary. By passing it the House would extend privilege in a way in which it had never hitherto existed. This dangerous resolution might be used by a subsequent Government as an engine of suppression against the Press or members of the House.

In 1939 the Lord Chancellor (Viscount Maugham) appointed a committee "to consider the law of defamation and to report on the changes in the existing law, practice and procedure relating to the matter which are desirable." The meetings of the Committee were suspended during the Second World War, and it was not until October 1948 that the report was presented to Parliament. The recommendations included the following:

If in the case of "unintentional defamation" the defendant publishes a suitable correction and apology, no monetary damages shall be awarded.

The law of libel and slander should not be assimilated. (*Two members dissented.*)

All defamatory statements or images broadcast over the radio should be treated as libels.

The definition of "newspaper" in the Law of Libel Amendment Act, 1888, should be enlarged to include periodicals published at intervals of not more than thirty-six days.

The number of reports entitled to privilege should be extended.

The Committee's report gave this summary of the general criticisms expressed by witnesses of the existing law and practice in actions for defamation: (*a*) Unnecessarily complicated; (*b*) unduly costly; (*c*) such as to make it difficult to forecast the result of an action both as to liability and as to the measure of damages; (*d*) liable to stifle discussion upon matters of public interest and concern; (*e*) too severe upon a defendant who is innocent of any intention to defame; (*f*) too favourable to those who, in colloquial language, may be described as "gold-digging" plaintiffs.

Mr. Bertram Christian, the publisher, one of the members of the Committee, attached a reservation to the report expressing the view that the recommendations did not go as far as they might in remedying defects in the existing law. "Claims in respect of libel are more lightly launched, more difficult to defend and more burdensome in their effects than is the case in other similar actions. I am not satisfied that we have done everything possible to render them less tempting to initiate and costly to resist."

The report made this observation: "Authors, critics, journalists, book publishers, newspaper proprietors, printers and newspaper distributors are particularly liable to become defendants in actions for defamation, and the criticisms of the existing law from their point of view were submitted with skill, lucidity and moderation by their respective representative organizations." The Press especially has for many years urged the need to reform and clarify the existing law, which handicaps the proper discussion of matters of public interest and encourages the money-making type of libel action; and it is to be hoped that Parliament will give effect to the findings of the Committee in the near future.

CHAPTER SEVENTEEN

The Daily Miracle

"A newspaper is one of the most remarkable products of modern society. To gather news from five continents; to print and distribute it so fast that what happens at dawn in India may be read before breakfast in England; to perform the feat afresh every twenty-four hours; and to sell the product for less than the price of a box of matches—this, were it not so familiar, would be recognised as an astonishing achievement."—*From the report of the Royal Commission on the Press* (1947–1949).

THREE centuries and a quarter ago a few now dimly perceived figures made the first tentative steps in the march of journalism —a word that was then unknown—and forty years later evolved the news-sheet out of the newsbook. From these uncertain beginnings, perilously conducted in the chill shadow of the censorship, has sprung the gigantic organization of the modern Press. The daily miracle of the newspaper, which reports happenings in all parts of the world and takes the news quickly to every town and village throughout the country, has long been accepted as part of the natural order of things.

A few facts will make clear the prodigious development since the far-off pioneer days. The newsbooks were mostly written by a single author, as he was then called; the principal daily newspapers of today employ editors, sub-editors, copy-tasters, special correspondents, reporters, specialist writers, staff correspondents at the key capitals of the world and occasional correspondents in every town of importance at home and abroad—altogether an organization of several hundred journalists. In addition, newspapers have at their service the comprehensive coverage of home and foreign news provided by Reuters, the Press Association and other agencies.[1]

[1] See Appendix A.

THE DAILY MIRACLE

The cost of newsgathering is colossal. Take foreign news alone. In 1950 the *Daily Express*, to give one example, spent £225,000 on its foreign news service. Twenty-five staff reporters were engaged on foreign assignments and more than one hundred resident and part-time correspondents were serving the paper from foreign places. The *Daily Express*, like other national dailies, reduces the burden of such expenditure by syndicating its service to Dominion, Colonial and foreign newspapers: two hundred journals were subscribing for the *Express* foreign service in 1950. In striking contrast is the fact that in 1773, long before the age of special correspondents and heavy cable bills, one of the chief dailies of the time—the *Public Advertiser*—spent only £114 in this department: "the entire cost of collecting and translating foreign news, including the purchase of foreign newspapers."[1]

The newsbooks were dependent upon infrequent mails for the news from the provinces and abroad. Today news and pictures from home and abroad are dispatched by the swiftest available means—cable, radio, telegraph and telephone—and no expense is spared to ensure that news reaches the office before the deadline, i.e. the latest time by which it must be received to ensure insertion in the next issue. Within living memory there has been a striking acceleration in news collection and distribution: by comparison with today even the journalism of 1900 seems to belong to a remote and leisurely age. The Press has been constantly quickening its tempo—by the faster printing of newspapers, by simultaneous printing at several centres, by air distribution to the Continent and by the production of lightweight air-mail editions for more distant points (London dailies are now on sale in New York on the day of publication), by the more rapid transmission of news and pictures (for example, by wire or radio across the world or by mobile radio direct from newspoints in this country), and by installing teleprinters (which have supplanted morse) and teletypesetters. But enterprise in news collection and in distribution is no new thing: it is

[1] *English Newspapers* (H. R. Fox Bourne).

only the pace that exceeds anything imagined by the newspaper conductors of the nineteenth century who boldly organized express courier services, engaged express stage-coaches, chartered special steamers and trains, and made early use of the cable service and of special telegraph wires between their London and provincial offices.

The newsbooks were published once a week; today, with newspapers appearing in the morning, the afternoon and the evening, the latest news is available at almost any hour of the day. But it is in the multiplicity of publications that there has been the most remarkable development. Not more than a score of newsbooks were on sale at any one period, and when repression was at its most severe they were limited to a couple of officially produced pamphlets. Now the total number of newspapers and periodicals of all kinds is over 5,000, with aggregate sales per issue of dozens of millions of copies. The combined circulation of the newsbooks probably did not exceed from 10,000 to 20,000 copies.

But to anyone who has had occasion to study the development of journalism since the beginning of things the gain in quality and variety is more interesting, and more impressive, than the statistics of growth and the details of the mechanical triumphs that have made giant circulations possible. In *Pendennis* (written about 1850) Thackeray described the enterprise of the newspaper in oft-quoted words:

> There she is—the great engine—she never sleeps. She has her ambassadors in every quarter of the world—her couriers upon every road. Her officers march along with armies, and her envoys walk into statesmen's cabinets. They are ubiquitous. . . .

The scope of the newspaper has been tremendously widened since Thackeray drew that picture a century ago. Then it was mainly concerned with political events at home and abroad, the law courts and finance, and looked upon the lighter interests of mankind as too trivial for attention; now its purpose is to bring the whole panorama of contemporary activities within its purview. Then the newspaper was for the most part solid and unimaginative in style and presentation; now it aims at ease and lucidity in writing and (in some cases) enlists the aid of brilliant typographers to ensure good design and clear presentation. Take any old-established newspaper and compare its present-day issues with those of a century ago and there can be no question about the transformation in scope and quality; and equally there can be no question that a newspaper of the Victorian type would find no readers in a generation accustomed to the convenient make-up and the comprehensive news and features of the modern journal.

In a typical issue of a serious morning newspaper today may be found, in addition to what may be called the routine news—reports of Parliament, the courts, the Stock Exchange and other market information—a well-balanced portrayal of all the matters that are currently engaging the attention of intelligent people. The leader page, for instance, is no longer limited to politics: there will be at least one article on some lighter topic which in the urbanity of its style as well as in the choice of subject recalls the days when Steele and Addison were daily entertaining their readers with reflections on the passing show. The more important news is supplemented by background articles—well-informed contributions by staff correspondents or by authoritative writers specially commissioned explaining the significance behind some current development reported in the news columns. In every department—home politics, foreign affairs, finance, industry, science, the theatre, radio, the cinema, sport, natural history, and all the other interests, both light and serious, of the reader—there are specialists who combine knowledgeableness with the touch of style that the critical reader expects to find in the treatment of any subject in his favourite journal. Bernard Darwin, Neville Cardus and others have delightfully proved that journalism can be blended with literary grace even on the sports page. At the other extreme we have frequent evidence that foreign correspondents, who rarely unbent in the old days, can bring to their work a freshness and humanness of approach that multiplies their readers without detracting from the value of their political assessments.

Journalism as a field for all the talents—as the wide-ranging record of, and commentary upon, the contemporary scene—is strikingly exemplified in the *Sunday Times* and the *Observer*, two papers that have sprung from the original invention of J. L. Garvin. His was the basic formula, embodied in the new *Observer* of forty years ago, for a Sunday journal that would appeal to serious men and women, and that vision of what makes a civilized newspaper has been constantly enlarged by the heirs of his tradition. Even in the shrunken eight-page and ten-page papers of today—before 1939 the issues ran to thirty-two or forty pages—the *Sunday Times* and the *Observer* cover a great diversity of subjects, each of them treated by a contributor of distinction.

In the many popular newspapers, both London and provincial, which aim to interest everyman without indulging in sensationalism—and most of the "populars" come within this classification—sport may seem to claim an undue share of the available space (until we remember that sport appeals to the majority of readers), but in the rest of the paper the principle of variety is steadily borne in mind and a reasonable balance kept between grave and gay. It was, of course, the popular journal—especially the *Daily Mail* of Alfred Harmsworth—that started the trend towards making the newspaper a more complete reflection of current happenings. Now there are signs that a new and more serious conception of popular journalism is beginning to take hold, that we may be in the first stage of an evolution that will meet the lack expressed in this passage of the report of the Royal Commission: "The Press provides for a sufficient variety of political opinion but not for a sufficient variety of intellectual levels. The gap between the best of the quality papers and the general run of the popular Press is too wide, and the number of papers of an intermediate type is too small."

But the miracle remains. . . . At half the price charged for the simple operation of conveying a letter from place to place, the newspaper gives its readers the news of all the world and punctually delivers every day "one of the most remarkable products of modern society," the compact result of a thousand complex activities and processes crammed into twenty-four hours.

A free Press has made possible the realization of the ideal of government by the people in this and other countries; a fearless, critical free Press is the one indispensable safeguard to ensure the survival of democracy in the present dangerous crisis of civilization.

Journalism is the supreme means of communication. The democratic system can be worked successfully only when there is full play for the expression of public opinion, of the views of minorities as well as of the majority, of fresh and independent currents of opinion as well as governmental hand-outs. Without a prompt and regular service of objective information the unity of the nation would be frequently endangered by suspicion, misunderstanding and doubt. Few journalists would be so uncritical as to assert that this vital informative function is fully and perfectly discharged; the remarkable thing is that the job has been so well done throughout a decade in which the British Press has existed on a meagre ration of newsprint that restricts newspapers to a quarter of their normal size.

Never was the need for alert and vigorously independent journalism greater than today. In this age of uncertainty and crumbling faith and moral nihilism—of old political heresies revived in delusive new forms, of evil masquerading as good—the journalist has the urgent task of defending the spiritual values of civilization and keeping the conception of freedom clear and untarnished. The Press has many enemies, open and unavowed; it has many highly critical friends, too. It cannot be taken for granted in the kind of world we are living in that the march of journalism will continue uninterruptedly. The price of journalistic liberty, as of all human freedoms, is eternal vigilance—to defend this hard-won liberty not only by resisting encroachments but by the steady improvement of standards that provides the surest armour of a free institution.

BIBLIOGRAPHY

The books consulted in the writing of this history include:
ANDREWS, ALEXANDER: *History of British Journalism* (1859).
ASPINALL, ARTHUR: *Politics and the Press c. 1780–1850*. Home and Van Thal.
BENTLEY, E. C.: *Those Days*. Constable.
BLUMENFELD, R. D.: *R.D.B.'s Diary*. Heinemann.
BOURNE, H. R. FOX: *English Newspapers: Chapters in the History of Journalism* (1887). Chatto and Windus.
BROWN, W. SORLEY: *The Life and Genius of T. W. H. Crosland*. Cecil Palmer.
CAMROSE, VISCOUNT: *British Newspapers and Their Controllers*. Cassell.
CATLING, THOMAS: *My Life's Pilgrimage*. John Murray.
CLARKE, TOM: *My Northcliffe Diary*. Gollancz.
Northcliffe in History. Hutchinson.
COLE, G. D. H.: *The Life of William Cobbett*. Home and Van Thal.
CONNELL, JOHN: *W. E. Henley*. Constable.
COOK, SIR E. T.: *Delane of "The Times."* Constable.
COOPER, CHARLES A.: *An Editor's Retrospect*. Macmillan.
COURTNEY, MRS. W. L.: *The Making of an Editor: W. L. Courtney 1850–1928*. Macmillan.
DARK, SIDNEY: *The Life of Sir Arthur Pearson*. Hodder and Stoughton.
DASENT, A. I.: *John Thadeus Delane*. John Murray.
FRIEDERICHS, HULDA: *The Life of Sir George Newnes*. Hodder and Stoughton.
FURNEAUX, RUPERT: *The First War Correspondent: William Howard Russell of "The Times."* Hodder and Stoughton.
FYFE, HAMILTON: *Northcliffe*. Allen and Unwin.
T. P. O'Connor. Allen and Unwin.
Sixty Years of Fleet Street. W. H. Allen.

GARVIN, KATHARINE: *J. L. Garvin.* Heinemann.
GIBBS, SIR PHILIP: *The Pageant of the Years.* Heinemann.
GRAHAM, WALTER: *English Literary Periodicals.* Nelson (New York).
HAMMOND, J. L.: *C. P. Scott.* Bell.
HARRIS, WILSON: *J. A. Spender.* Cassell.
HINDLE, WILFRID: *The Morning Post: 1772–1937.* Routledge.
HUDSON, DEREK: *Thomas Barnes of "The Times."* Cambridge University Press.
HUNT, F. KNIGHT: *The Fourth Estate* (1850).
HYDE, H. MONTGOMERY: *Mr. and Mrs. Beeton.* Harrap.
JONES, KENNEDY: *Fleet Street and Downing Street.* Hutchinson.
KINGSMILL, HUGH: *Frank Harris.* Jonathan Cape.
LANE, MARGARET: *Edgar Wallace.* Heinemann.
LUCAS, REGINALD: *Lord Glenesk and the "Morning Post."* Alston Rivers.
MCKENZIE, F. A.: *The Mystery of the "Daily Mail."*
MILLS, J. SAXON: *Sir Edward Cook.* Constable.
MORISON, STANLEY: *The English Newspaper: 1622–1932.* Cambridge University Press.
Ichabod Dawks and His News-Letter. Cambridge University Press.
John Bell. Cambridge University Press.
MUDDIMAN, J. G.: *The King's Journalist.* John Lane.
Tercentary Handlist of English and Welsh Newspapers, Magazines and Reviews (1920). The Times.
P E P (Political and Economic Planning): *Report on the British Press* (1938).
QUENNELL, PETER: *Four Portraits.* Collins.
RIGHYNI, S. L.: "Provincial Newspapers in Transition" (article in *Alphabet and Image: 6*).
ROBBINS, SIR ALFRED: *The Press.* Ernest Benn.
ROBERTSON SCOTT, J. W.: *The Story of the "Pall Mall Gazette."* Oxford University Press.
SALA, G. A.: *The Life and Adventures of George Augustus Sala* (1895). Cassell.

SCOTT-JAMES, R. A.: *The Influence of the Press.* Partridge.
SHIELDS GAZETTE: *Centenary of the "Shields Gazette"* (1849–1949).
SIMONIS, H.: *The Street of Ink.* Cassell.
SPENDER, J. A.: *Life, Journalism and Politics.* Cassell.
SPIELMANN, M. H.: *The History of "Punch"* (1895). Cassell.
STEED, H. WICKHAM: *Through Thirty Years.* Heinemann.
STOREY, GRAHAM: *Reuters' Century.* Max Parrish.
STRAUS, RALPH: *Sala: The Portrait of an Eminent Victorian.* Constable.
SUTHERLAND, JAMES: *Defoe.* Methuen.
TAYLOR, H. A.: *Robert Donald.* Stanley Paul.
THOMAS, SIR W. BEACH: *The Story of "The Spectator": 1828–1928.* Methuen.
THORPE, JAMES: "Draughtsmen of the Early 'Daily Graphic'" (article in *Alphabet and Image: 2*).
THE TIMES: *History of "The Times"* (Vols. I–III).
WHYTE, FREDERIC: *The Life of W. T. Stead.* Jonathan Cape.
WICKWAR, WILLIAM H.: *The Struggle for the Freedom of the Press: 1819–1832.* Allen and Unwin.
WILLIAMS, J. B. (pseudonym of J. G. Muddiman, *q.v.*): *A History of English Journalism to the Foundation of the Gazette.* Longman.
YATES, EDMUND: *Edmund Yates: His Recollections and Experiences* (1884).
(BY VARIOUS WRITERS): *C. P. Scott: The Making of the "Manchester Guardian."* Frederick Muller.

The *Cambridge History of English Literature*; the *Dictionary of National Biography*; the *Newspaper Press Directory*; *The Romance of the Amalgamated Press*; the *Fleet Street Annual*; the report of the Royal Commission on the Press (1947–1949).

I have also consulted numerous periodicals, and I am especially indebted to the three professional journals—the *Newspaper World* (founded 1898), the *Advertiser's Weekly* (1913), and the *World's Press News* (1929).

APPENDIX A

The News Agencies

SUPPLEMENTING the news service of the daily paper is the comprehensive organization of the news agencies—Reuters with its international network, the Press Association with its 1,500 correspondents in the British Isles, and others. The leading morning newspapers seek to have independent coverage of major events, but even they make frequent use of agency messages, which in any case are vital for checking and supplying additional details. From the agencies, too, come reports of Parliamentary debates, political and other speeches in London and the country, trials, inquests, and so on. Few newspapers have their own Parliamentary reporting staff (apart from sketch writers and Lobby correspondents), and important political meetings as well as big trials normally require only the attendance of a special correspondent to convey the "atmosphere" of the occasion and introduce the detailed agency report. The development of the agency has been of particular advantage to smaller newspapers, enabling them to obtain at moderate cost an efficient service of home and foreign news.

Reuters, the oldest of the agencies, dates back to 1851. Its founder, Julius de Reuter (1816–1899), who was born at Cassel in Germany, gained his first experience of collecting and distributing news in 1850. Then a bank clerk, he saw an opportunity in the fact that there was a 30-mile gap between the end of the recently constructed German telegraph lines at Aix-la-Chapelle and the French and Belgian lines at Verviers. He set up an organization to collect Stock Exchange prices and by using pigeon post from Brussels to Aix he got his news through hours ahead of the stage-coach service. The general establishment of telegraphic communications suggested a wider field of activity—a European news service, with headquarters at Paris. But the French authorities were not co-operative, so Reuter decided to make London his centre and he became a British subject. He took a small office in the Royal Exchange in 1851 and appointed correspondents on the Continent to collect news and share-prices. Some years elapsed before the Press as a whole recognized the value of his service, but afterwards progress was rapid and continuous and the organization was extended to cover the entire world. Typical of Reuter's enterprise was the method he adopted to minimize the delay in the receipt of American news before the laying of the Atlantic cable. This news came by sea, and in order to anticipate a rival organization Reuter chartered a steamer to meet the liner off Ireland and pick up a box containing the American dispatches which was dropped overboard by the purser. This was immediately conveyed to Crookhaven, whence the news was flashed to London over a private telegraph wire. In 1880 Baron Julius de Reuter (the honour had been conferred nine years earlier by the Duke of Saxe-Coburg-Gotha) retired and was succeeded by his elder son Baron Herbert de Reuter. In 1915 Mr. (now Sir) Roderick Jones acquired control of the agency. Holding that Reuters was a national institution, he considered methods of ensuring its independence after his retirement or death, and in 1926 he offered the ownership 50–50 to the Newspaper Proprietors Association, representing the London newspapers, and the Press Association, representing the provincial newspapers. Only the latter accepted. However, in 1941, nine months after Sir Roderick Jones had resigned, the N.P.A. decided that the time had come for them to be associated with the agency. On October 29th of that year it was announced that the Press Association, who were the sole holders of the shares of Reuters, Ltd., had agreed, in co-operation with the Newspaper Proprietors Association, to enter into common and equal partnership in Reuters and that this should be regarded as a trust and not as an investment. In particular the parties agreed to use their best endeavours to ensure:

(*a*) That Reuters shall at no time pass into the hands of any one interest, group or faction.

APPENDIX A

(*b*) That its integrity, independence and freedom from bias shall at all times be fully preserved.

(*c*) That its business shall be so administered that it shall supply an unbiased and reliable news service to British, Dominion, Colonial, foreign and other overseas newspapers and agencies with which it has or may hereafter have contracts.

That arrangement has since been extended to include Australia, New Zealand and India. Reuters operates in every country in the world, bringing news into London for the British Press and the B.B.C. and sending news from London to the newspapers of the world. Half a million words reach Reuters London headquarters daily from these many sources. There it is sifted and condensed and sent out to subscribers—by radio to 3,000 daily newspapers outside Great Britain and by teleprinter to newspapers in this country.

The Press Association, Ltd. (founded 1868) is a co-operative home news organization owned by the provincial newspapers. It pays no dividends: any surplus arising from its operations is applied to the improvement of the services and the strengthening of the organization. As already mentioned, it is part-owner of Reuters, Ltd., and it also owns one half of P.A.—Reuter Photos., Ltd. and P.A.—Reuter Features, Ltd. The P.A.'s home news coverage includes all general news events, Parliament, and descriptive services of every branch of sport, and in addition it supplies to provincial newspapers the Reuter and Associated Press World News Services. It has a multi-channel private telegraph system to practically every morning and evening newspaper in the British Isles, which not only enables the speediest distribution of news, but also carries wired photographs. It co-operates with the Exchange Telegraph Company in the collecting and issuing as a joint service of racing, football and cricket results, Stock Exchange prices and market reports, and reports of cases in the High Courts. Moreover, it owns the Central News Parliamentary Service—separately staffed and competitive with the P.A. Service—which provides most London and some provincial newspapers with daily reports of the proceedings of both Houses. All P.A. services are available to members and non-members alike, the latter being charged 10 per cent. extra. "The basic policy governing the Press Association's circulation of news has never varied since the Association was first formed," the Press Commission was told. "It is to report factually all events of sufficient news interest accurately and without bias, and to circulate the reports to subscribers as speedily as possible without comment or expression of opinion."

The Exchange Telegraph Co., Ltd. (founded 1872) provides a general service of home and foreign news—it has over 1,000 full-time and part-time correspondents at home and nearly 100 abroad—Parliamentary reports, a comprehensive service of Stock Exchange intelligence (prices, dividends and market information) and reports of sporting events, as well as the various services already mentioned which it supplies jointly with the Press Association. Over two-thirds of its income is drawn from private subscribers: it provides clubs, business houses, hotels, etc., with a tape-machine service of news, Stock Exchange prices and sporting results. Between the two world wars, the Exchange Telegraph—in conjunction with the Press Association—acquired the Central News, Ltd., which had been losing ground for many years, and tried unsuccessfully to revive it. First the foreign news service and then the home news of Central News had to be discontinued. Only the Parliamentary and London Letter services remained, and these were taken over by the Press Association. The Exchange Telegraph transferred its advertising agency work to the Central News, which is now purely an advertising agency. "The Central News died because there was insufficient demand for its services," stated the Press Commission in its report. "We have found no feeling among our witnesses that there is need or room for another general news agency to supply either home or foreign news, and very little criticism of those that exist."

The British United Press, Ltd. (founded 1923), a Canadian subsidiary of the United Press, provides an overseas news service to the Press of Great Britain and the British Commonwealth. In addition to supplying the services of the United Press Associations of America, it has its own correspondents in overseas centres to cover news of British interest.

APPENDIX B

The Principal Newspaper Chains

THE Kemsley Group consists of 27 daily and Sunday newspapers (1 national morning, 2 national sporting, 6 provincial mornings, 3 provincial sporting, 9 provincial evenings, 6 national and provincial Sunday papers), 1 national overseas weekly and 9 local weeklies. Kemsley Newspapers, Ltd. (chairman, Viscount Kemsley) owns the *Sunday Times, Sunday Chronicle, Empire News* (Manchester), *Daily Dispatch* (Manchester), *Evening Chronicle* (Manchester), *Sporting Chronicle* (Manchester) and *Chronicle Mid-day* (Manchester), and controls the Daily Graphic and Sunday Graphic, Ltd., Newcastle Chronicle and Journal, Ltd., Scottish Daily Record and Evening News, Ltd., and Kemsley Northern Newspapers, Ltd. The last-named company controls Aberdeen Journals, Ltd., Macclesfield Times, Ltd., Northern Daily Telegraph, Ltd., North Eastern Evening Gazette, Ltd., Sheffield Telegraph and Star, Ltd., Stockport Express, Ltd., Western Mail and Echo, Ltd., and the Yorkshire Herald Newspaper Co., Ltd.

The Rothermere Group comprises 9 daily and Sunday newspapers wholly owned (1 national morning, 1 London evening, 6 provincial evenings and 1 national Sunday journal), 2 provincial evenings in which it has a majority interest, 4 provincial evenings in which it has a minority interest and 6 local weeklies wholly or partly owned. The Daily Mail and General Trust, Ltd. (chairman, Viscount Rothermere) controls Associated Newspapers, Ltd., which owns the *Daily Mail*, the London *Evening News, Sunday Dispatch* and *Overseas Weekly Mail*. Subsidiaries of Associated Newspapers are Northcliffe Newspapers Group, Ltd. (a management company), Cheltenham Newspaper Co., Ltd., Derby Daily Telegraph, Ltd., Gloucestershire Newspapers, Ltd.,

Staffordshire Sentinel Newspapers, Ltd., Swansea Press, Ltd., Hull and Grimsby Newspapers, Ltd., and Lincolnshire Publishing Co., Ltd. Associated Newspapers has a minority interest in News Holdings, Ltd. (which owns the two Leicester evenings and associated weeklies) and Bristol United Press, Ltd. (which owns the two Bristol evenings). Other subsidiaries of Associated Newspapers include the Anglo-Newfoundland Development Co., Ltd., and Empire Paper Mills, Ltd.

The Westminster Press Group consists of 14 daily and Sunday newspapers (4 provincial mornings, 9 provincial evenings and 1 provincial Sunday journal) and 32 local weeklies. Its seventeen subsidiaries include Barrow News and Mail, Ltd., Birmingham Gazette, Ltd., Bradford and District Newspaper Co., Ltd., North of England Newspaper Co., Ltd., Northern Press, Ltd., Nottingham Journal, Ltd., Oxford Times, Ltd. and Swindon Press, Ltd.

The Harmsworth Group, controlled by Consolidated Press, Ltd. (chairman, Sir Harold Harmsworth), owns 1 provincial morning, 3 provincial evenings and 20 local weeklies. Subsidiaries include the Western Morning News Co., Ltd., Western Times Co., Ltd., and the Field Press, Ltd.

INDEX

A. Beckett, G. A., 209 n
Aberdeen Journal, 175
Academy, 202–203, 295
Addison, Joseph, 37, 44, 54, 188, 189, 221, 325; his writings for the *Tatler* and the *Spectator*, 52–54
Adelphi, 295
Advertisements, 65, 128, 276–277; early, 21, 41–42; advertisement tax, 76; nine-page advertisement, 139 n; advertising during railway mania, 140 n, 158–159; advertisement tax abolished, 152
Advertising World, 266
All the Year Round, 164, 208
Allied Newspapers, Ltd., 266, 273, 303
Allighan, Garry, 317–320
Almon, John, 70 n, 72, 75
Alphabet, 293
Alphabet and Image, 263, 293
Alsager, T. M., 140–141
Althorp, Lord, 134–136
Amalgamated Press, Ltd., 233, 249, 262 n, 266, 287, 288
Ambassador, 293
Amhurst, Nicholas, 52
Andrews, W. L., 271
Answers, 46 n, 241, 249, 286, 290; founded, 236–237
Anti-Jacobin (Canning's), 60–63, 106 (Greenwood's), 63 n
Anti-Jacobin Review and Magazine, 106
"Ape" (Carlo Pellegrini), 217
Apollo, 292
Applegarth, Ambrose, 130
Archer, Thomas, 12, 13
Archer, William, 258
Argosy, 287
Ariel, 297
Armstrong, Anthony, 210
Arnold, Sir Edwin, 164
Arnold, Matthew, 213, 224, 227
Associated Newspapers, Ltd., 233, 249, 260
Astor, the Hon. J. J., 270
Astor, 1st Lord, 264–265
    2nd Lord, 265
Athenaeum, 202, 296
Athenian Mercury, 46 n
Athletic News, 264 n
Atlantic Daily Mail, 243
Atlas, 201
Atterbury, Francis, 48
Axon, William E. A., 175

Bagehot, Walter, 191, 202, 214
Baldwin, Edward, 163 n
Baptist Times, 221 n
Barnes, Thomas, 92, 97, 128, 169, 193, 269; as editor of *The Times*, 131–139
Barr, Robert, 220
Barrington-Ward, R. M., 269
Barron, Oswald, 281
Barry, Sir Gerald, 296
Bate, the Rev. Henry, 79–80
Bates, Alfred, 292
Bauer, Andrew, 130
Beaverbrook, Lord, 250, 264, 318; his career, 264 n
Beckford, William, 101
Beerbohm, Sir Max, 215
Beeton, Samuel Orchart, 208
Beeton, Mrs. S. O., 208
Belcher, George, 210
Belfast News-Letter, 175, 304
Belfast Telegraph, 304
Bell, C. F. Moberly, 267, 269
Bell, John, 6, 79–85, 88, 222
Bell, John Browne, 84
Bell, Robert, 83
Bell's Life in London, 83, 92, 286 n
The Bell's New Weekly Messenger, 84
Bell's Weekly Dispatch, 83
Bell's Weekly Messenger, 82–84
Belloc, Hilaire, 296
Bennett, James Gordon, 163, 204
Bennett, James Gordon (II), 252
Bentham, Jeremy, 118, 214
Bentley, E. C., 258
Bentley's Miscellany, 213
Berrow's Worcester Journal, 43
Berry, James Gomer: see *Lord Kemsley*
    William Ewert: see *Lord Camrose*
Berthold's Political Handkerchief, 148 n
Bevan, Aneurin, 313–314
Bicycling News, 236
Biographical Magazine, 173
Birkenhead, Sir John, 19–20
Birmingham Daily Press, 175
Birmingham Gazette, 304
Birmingham Post, 175, 272, 311
Black, John, 90–92
Black and White, 211, 285
Black Dwarf, 120, 121
Blackwood, William, 194, 201
Blackwood's Magazine, 197, 201, 203 n, 294; founded, 194–196
Blanchard, S. L., 157

337

Bland, Hubert, 187
Blatchford, Robert, 187, 286 n
Blowitz, Henri de, 169–170
Blumenfeld, R. D., 252–253
Bombing of newspaper offices, 301 et seq.
Bookman, 221 n
Bookseller, 303
Borthwick, Algernon (Lord Glenesk), 181–182, 217 n
Borthwick, Peter, 181
Boswell, James, 57
Bottomley, Horatio, 264, 291–292
Bourne, H. R. Fox, 7, 8, 33 n, 42 n
Bourne, Nicholas, 12, 13, 15
Bowles, T. Gibson, 217
Boyer, A., 38, 60
Boy's Own Paper, 221
Bradbury and Evans, 157, 209
Bradford Observer, 175
Braille edition of *Daily Mail*, 243
Brailsford, H. N., 258
Bright, John, 153–154, 160, 174, 183
Bristol Evening Post, 273
Bristol Evening World, 273
Bristol Times and Mirror, 43, 273
Britannia, 293
Britannia and Eve, 293
British Academy, 84
British Gazette, 279
British Magazine, 58
  (Smollett's), 59
British Museum Library, 6
British Press, 156
British United Press, Ltd., 334
British Weekly, 221 n
British Worker, 279
Brittain, Sir Harry, 280 n
Brogue, David, 211
Brooks, Shirley, 209
Brougham, Lord, 116, 134, 135–137, 188–190, 206
Buckle, George Earle, 169, 269
Buckley, Sam, 39
Building News, 173
Bulletin, 262
Bulwer-Lytton, Sir Edward, 147–148, 153
Burke, Edmund, 75
Burleigh, Bennet, 164
Burlington Magazine, 292
Burnand, Sir Francis, 209
Burney Collection, 6, 34, 42 n
Burnham, Lord: see *Edward Levy Lawson*
Business and Agency News, 185
Butter, Nathaniel, 13–15
Butterfly, 220
Byrne, Nicholas, edits *Morning Post*, 133; stabbed, 133
Byron, Lord, 118, 190, 191, 192
Bystander, 292

Cadbury family, 258
Caird, Sir Andrew, 248
Caledonian Mercury, 179
Cambridge Journal, 294
Camden, Lord, 75
Campbell, Thomas, 198
Camrose, Lord (William Ewert Berry), 249, 271, 273–274; jointly acquires the *Sunday Times* and other newspaper interests, 265–266; remakes the *Daily Telegraph*, 270–271
Canning, George, 60–62, 105, 120, 192
Cardus, Neville, 325
Carlile, Richard, 120–122; sent to prison, 123; wife and sister imprisoned, 124; his sacrifices for cause of free discussion, 125
Carlyle, Thomas, 196
Carnegie, Andrew, 173
Carr, Sir Emsley, 275 n
Carr, Lascelles, 275 n
Carr, W. Dargarville, 236
Cartoonists, 281–282
Casey, W. F., 269
Cassell, John, 179, 207–208
Cassell and Co., 287, 303
Cassell's Illustrated Family Paper, 208
Cassell's Magazine, 208, 284
Cassell's Popular Educator, 208
Cassell's Saturday Journal, 285
Castlerosse, Lord, 281
Catholic Times, 221 n
Catto, Sir Thomas, 257
Cave, Edward, 55–56
C. B. Fry's Magazine, 286
Cecil, Lord, on C. P. Scott, 183
Central News, 180, 333, 334
Central Press, 179
Chamberlain, Joseph, 259
Chambers, William and Robert, 205–206
Chambers's Encyclopaedia, 205
Chambers's Journal, founded, 205; printed in three centres, 34, 206
Champion, 58, 193
Chapman and Hall, 215
Charles I, report of execution, 18–19
Charles II, coronation of, 23
Charles Knight's Weekly Newspaper, 178
Charlton, Randall, 261
Chatterton, Thomas, 101
Chenery, Thomas, 169
Chester Courant, 43
Chesterton, Cecil, 297
Chesterton, G. K., 258
Children's Encyclopaedia, 293
Children's Newspaper, 293
Chit Chat, 54
Christian, Bertram, 321
Christian, 221 n

INDEX

Christian Herald, 221 n
Christian World, 221 n
Christiansen, Arthur, 253
Christie, J. H., 197
Chums, 285
Church of England Newspaper, 211 n
Church Quarterly Review, 221 n
Church Times, 221 n
Churchill, Winston S., 33 n; novel serialised, 213
Clarion, 286
Clarke, Tom, describes Northcliffe's last days, 248
Classical Review, 221
Cleaver, Reginald, 263
Clement, William, 92
Clerkenwell News, 185
Cobbett, William, 103–106, 118, 119, 120, 121, 191; the Political Register, 107–115; sent to prison, 110–111; becomes popular leader, 112; escapes to America, 113; returns, 114; successfully defends himself against charge of inciting violence, 115–116
Cobbett's Evening Post, 114
Cobbett's Two-Penny Trash, 114
Cobden, Richard, 142, 150, 160, 163
Colburn, Henry, 202
Coleridge, J. T., 193
Coleridge, Lord, 219
Coleridge, S. T., 89, 93–94, 95, 196
Columnists, 280–281
Comic Times, 297
Commonwealth Press Union, 280 n
Connoisseur, 292
Connolly, Cyril, 295
Conrad, Joseph, 294
Constable, Archibald, 189, 190
Constitutional, 157
Contact, 290
"Contact Books," 290
Contemporary Review, 214, 294
Contents bills banned, 307
Continental Daily Mail, 243
A Continuation of certaine Speciall and Remarkable Passages from both Houses of Parliament, 16
Cook, Sir E. T., 231–232, 256
Cook, Dr. F. A., 261
Cook, John Douglas, 203
Cook, Walter, 16
Cooper, Charles A., 180 n
Cornhill Magazine, 212–213, 226, 294
Corral, George, 80
Cosmopolitan Magazine, 287
Country Journal, 52
Country Life, 221, 297
Countryman, 288–289
County Gentleman, 286

Courier, 61, 95–96, 109, 156
Courtney, W. L., 215
Covent-Garden Journal, 58
Cowdray, Lord, 255
Cowen, Joseph, 265
Cowper, William, 130
Cox, Edward, 80
Cox, Harold, 191
Crabbe, George (poem quoted), 69, 78
Croker, John Wilson, 192
Craftsman, 48, 52
Criterion, 295
Critical Review, 59
Cromwell, Oliver, and the Press, 24
Crosland, T. W. H., 294–295
Crouch, John, 24
Crozier, W. P., 183
Cummings, A. J., 280–281
Currant Intelligence, 35
Current Intelligence, 34–35
Current Literature, 303
Cust, H. J. C., 232

Daily Advertiser, 41–42, 74, 82
Daily Call, 262
Daily Chronicle, 231 n, 233, 246, 258, 260, 261, 296 n; acquired by Edward Lloyd, 185; amalgamated with Daily News, 255, 256–257
Daily Citizen, 262
Daily Courant, 39–41
Daily Courier, 235
Daily Dispatch, 264 n
Daily Express (1877), 168 n
(1900), 231, 253, 255 n, 264, 274, 276, 281, 282, 301; founded, 252; pioneers triplicate publication, 243 n; circulation, 263; cost of foreign news, 323
Daily Graphic, 7, 212, 262, 263
Daily Herald, 257, 279, 281, 282, 311; acquired by Odhams Press, Ltd., 262–263; air raid damage, 301, 303
Daily Journal, 41
Daily Mail, 34, 149–150, 166, 203 n, 222, 233, 234, 248, 252, 253, 254, 255, 257, 274, 276, 281, 286 n, 299, 326; its early years, 238–243; Northern edition started, 243; aviation prizes, 244; attacks Lord Kitchener, 244–247; under Rothermere, 249–251; £50,000 damages for libel, 260; the Daily Mail and the General Strike, 277–278
Daily Mirror, started as woman's newspaper, 262; first daily to print news photographs, 262 n; circulation, 263; war-time threat of suppression, 309–311

Daily News, 155, 163, 167–168, 169, 218, 220, 231 n, 232, 245–246, 255, 296 n; Charles Dickens as editor, 157–158; incorporates *Daily Chronicle*, 256–257; under A. G. Gardiner, 258
Daily News and Leader, 258
Daily Paper, 262
Daily Picture Paper, 262
Daily Post, 41, 70
Daily Sketch, 262, 264 n, 266; offices bombed, 302
Daily Telegraph, 94, 158, 169, 222, 226, 239, 253, 258 n, 265, 266, 267, 299, 308–309, 310; founded, 160; becomes penny newspaper, 161, 271; development of, 162–164; famous *Daily Telegraph* men, 164–166; circulation, 166–167; Sunday edition, 242; incorporates *Morning Post*, 254; revival under Lord Camrose, 270–271; air raid damage, 302
Daily Universal Register: see *The Times*
Daily War Telegraph, 175
Daily Worker, 263, 308–309
Dalziel, Davison, 262
Darwin, Bernard, 325
Dasent, G. W., 169
Davies, Haydn, 312
Dawks, Ichabod, 6, 35–36
Dawks's News-Letter, 35
Dawson, Geoffrey, 247; career, 268–269
Day (1798), 156
  (1867), 168 n
Day and New Times, 156
Defamation, law of: Committee's report on, 320–321
Defoe, Daniel, 41, 46–51, 52
Delafield, E. M., 210
Delane, John Thadeus, 167, 169, 181, 244, 267, 269, 303; editor of *The Times*, 139–146
Delane, W. F. A., 140–141
De Quincey, Thomas, 196, 197
Derby Daily Express, 273
Derby Daily Telegraph, 273
Destructive and Poor Man's Conservative, 127
The Devil in London, 209 n
Dewsbury Daily Reporter, 176
Dial, 168 n
Diary, 73, 89
Dickens, Charles, 164, 184; reporter on the *Morning Chronicle*, 92; edits *Daily News*, 157–158; conducts periodicals, 208, 213
Dickens, John, 157
Dictionary of National Biography, 212, 268
Digests, origin of, 7, 59
Dilke, A. Wentworth, 186

Dillingham, John, 17
Dillon, Dr. E. J., 165–166, 215
Disraeli, Benjamin, 151, 156, 227, 240 n
Dobson, Stanley, 319
Dome, 220
Domestick Intelligencer, 35
Donald, Sir Robert, 233, 257
Douglas, Lord Alfred, 203
Douglas, James, 234
Douglas Jerrold's Shilling Magazine, 185
Douglas Jerrold's Weekly Newspaper, 185
Doyle, Sir A. Conan, 235, 286
Doyle, Richard, 210
Du Maurier, George, 210
Dunton, John, 46 n
Dury, Giles, 21, 27

East Anglian Daily Times, 175
East Lancashire Echo, 176
Eastern Morning News, 179, 256
Echo, 7, 172–173, 176 n, 259
Echo and Evening Chronicle, 259
Economist, 30, 202, 296, 300
Ede, Chuter, 313
Edinburgh Courant, 43
Edinburgh Flying Post, 43
Edinburgh Gazette, 43
Edinburgh Monthly Magazine, 194
Edinburgh Review, 156, 192, 194, 196, 294; aims of its founders, 188–189; severity of its literary criticism, 190–191
Edinburgh War Telegraph, 161
Edwards, John Passmore, 173, 186
Egan, Pierce, 83 n
Eglington, William, 179
Eisenhower, General, 306
Eldon, Lord, 120, 189
Eliot, George, 212, 214
Eliot, T. S., 295
Ellenborough, Lord, 110, 114
Ellis, George, 62, 191, 192
Empire News, 276
Empire Press Union, 280 n
Encyclopaedia Britannica, 267
English Chronicle, 81
English Historical Review, 221
English Illustrated Magazine, 213, 285
English Review, 294
Englishman, 54
Englishwoman's Domestic Magazine, 208
Ensor, R. C. K., 258, 314
Erskine, Lord, 75, 76
European Magazine, 89, 91
Evans, B. Ifor, 295
Evans, W. J., 233
Evening Courant, 40
Evening Illustrated Paper, 7, 177
Evening Mail, 75

INDEX

Evening Mercury, 7, 176
Evening News (London), 161, 173, 176, 216, 233, 249, 259, 260, 281; bought and modernised by the Harmsworth brothers, 234, 237–238
Evening newspaper, the first, 74–75
Evening Post, 40
Evening Standard, 259, 264 n, 281, 299, 318; absorbs three evening journals, 232; offices bombed, 301
Evening Star (1788), 75
  (1856), 160, 167 n
Evening Times, 259–260
Evening Times and Echo, 273
Everybody's, 293
Everywoman, 288
Examiner (1710), 44, 48
  (1808), 90, 116–118, 131, 193, 201–202
Exchange Telegraph Company, 181, 333, 334
Express, 155
Eye Witness, 296–297

Facsimile newspapers, 282–283
Farm, Field and Fireside, 285
Farmers' Weekly, 299
Farthing newspapers, 72 n, 173–174
Faulkner, David, 171
Fay, E. F., 286 n
"F. C. G." (Francis Carruthers Gould), 232
Female Tatler, 48
Field, 221, 297
Fielding, Henry, 58
Figaro in London, 209 n
Financial News, 177
Financial Times, 177, 291
Fish, W. G., 248
Fleet Street Annual, 7
Fleuron, 293
Flora and Sylva, 286
Flower, Sir Newman, 287
Flying Post, 36, 36 n, 37, 44, 49
Fog's Weekly Journal, 51
Fonblanque, Albany, 201–202
Forbes, Archibald, 168
Ford, Ford Madox, 294
Foreign newspapers in war-time London, 308
Fortnightly Review, 214–215, 265, 294
Fortune, 289, 290
"Fougasse" (Cyril Kenneth Bird), 209, 210
Fox, Charles James, 75, 76, 192
Francis, Sir Philip, 70
Fraser, Hugh, 195
Fraser, Sir John Foster, 187
Fraser's Magazine, 195–196
Freeholder, 54
Frere, John Hookham, 62, 192

Fun, 297
Furniss, Harry, 210
Future, 290
"Future Books," 290
Fyfe, Sir D. Maxwell, 313

Galpin, T. D., 208
Galsworthy, John, 294
Gardiner, A. G., 245, 256; editor of the *Daily News*, 258
Gardiner, Clive, 256
Garvin, J. L., 203, 229, 231 n, 232, 249; remodels the *Observer*, 264, 267, 326; his career, 265
Garvin, Katharine, 265
Gazetteer, 74, 76, 89, 94, 101
General Advertiser, 74, 88
General Evening Post, 68 n
General Strike, 277–279
Gentleman's Journal, 46 n
Gentleman's Magazine, 54–56, 59, 64
Gentlewoman, 285
Geographical Magazine, 293
German Intelligencer, 14
Gibbs, Sir Philip, 261
Gifford, John, 106
Gifford, William, 62, 192–193
Giles (Carl Giles), 282
Gladstone, William Ewart, 151–155
Glasgow Daily Record, 238, 249
Glasgow Herald, 175, 182, 258 n, 311
Globe, 155–156, 226, 232, 257, 259
Gloucester Journal, 43
Go, 292
Good Housekeeping, 288
Graham, R. B. Cunninghame, 215
Graham, Walter, 60 n
Grand Magazine, 287
Grand Magazine of Magazines, 59–60
Grant, Albert ("Baron Grant"), 173
Graphic, 211–212, 263, 285
Grave, Charles, 210
Gray, James, 89
Gray, Thomas, 60
Great Thoughts, 285
Greeley, Horace, 163
Greenock Telegraph, 177–178
Greenwood, Frederick, 63, 177, 208, 211, 213, 231; creator of the *Pall Mall Gazette*, 225–227
Greenwood, James, 226
Greville, Charles, 138, 145
Grub-Street Journal, 51
Guardian (Steele's), 54
  (1846), 221 n
Guide and Ideas, 290
Guild of British Newspaper Editors, 277 n
Guthrie, William, 56

341

Hackney Hansard, 291
Halfpenny evening newspapers, early London ventures, 172, 176; first provincial halfpenny evening papers, 177–178
Halfpenny morning newspapers, early ventures, 171–172; first provincial halfpenny morning paper, 175 n
Halfpenny Post, 42 n
Halfpenny Sunday newspaper, 186
Hallam, Henry, 189
Hamilton, Archibald, 59
Hammond, George, 105
Hammond, J. L., 183, 258
Hands, Charles E., 234, 243
Hansard Publishing Union, 291
Happy Magazine, 287
Hardman, Sir William, 236
Hardy, Thomas, 213, 294
Harley, Robert (1st Earl of Oxford), 47–49
Harling, Robert, 293
Harmsworth, Alfred: see *Lord Northcliffe*
Harmsworth Group, details of, 336
Harmsworth, Harold Sidney: see *Lord Rothermere*
Harmsworth, Sir Harold, 336
Harmsworth's Magazine, 285
Harper's Bazaar, 288
Harris, Frank, 215–216, 231 n, 295
Harris, Wilson, 256, 257, 258
Harrison, Frederic, 214
Harrison, William, 257
Hawkins, Sir John, 56
Hazlitt, William, 90, 193
The Heads of Severall Proceedings in this Present Parliament (afterwards *A Perfect Diurnall of the Passages in Parliament*), 15
Hearst, W. R., 287
Heighway, Arthur, 317–318
Henderson, James, 236
Henley, W. E., 203
Heraclitus Ridens, 35
Herbert, Sir Alan, 210
Herbert, Sidney, 144–145
Hereford Journal, 43
Herschel, Sir John, 214
Hetherington, Henry, 126–127
Hewart, Lord, 233
Hibbert Journal, 294
Hill, Dr. John, 58
Hobby Horse, 220
Hodgson, Stuart, 258
Home Notes, 231
Homes and Gardens, 288
Hone, William, 120–121, 122
Hood, Thomas, 210
Hook, Theodore, 5, 197–200
Hooper, H. E., 267

Horizon, 295
Horner, Francis, 189
Hornung, E. W., 286
Hour, 168 n
Household Words, 164, 208
Housewife, 289
Houston, Lady, 296
Hudson, W. H., 294
Hughes, Spencer Leigh, 281
Hulton, Edward, 290, 292
— Sir Edward, 263–264, 290
Humorist, 297
Humorous journals, 209–210, 297
Hunt, F. Knight, 95 n
Hunt, Henry, 132
Hunt, John, 116–118
Hunt, Leigh, 84, 131, 164, 193, 198, 202 n; imprisoned, 116–118; attacked by *Blackwood's*, 194–195
Hunt, Thornton, 164, 202
Hutchinson's Magazine, 287
Hutton, R. H., 202, 227
Huxley, Leonard, 213
Huxley, T. H., 213
Hyne, C. J. Cutcliffe, 286

Iddon, Don, 281
Ideal Home, 288
Ideas, 290
Idler, 220
Iliffe, Lord, 266
Iliffe, William, 236
Illingworth, L. G., 210, 281–282
Illuminated Magazine, 185
Illustrated, 290
Illustrated London News, 154, 158, 165, 209, 212; founded, 210–211
Illustrated Mail, 242
Illustrated Newspapers, Ltd., 257
Illustrated Sporting and Dramatic News, 221
Illustrated Sunday Herald, 263, 264 n
Illustrated Times, 211, 218
Illustrations, the first pictorial daily newspaper, 7, 177; eighteenth-century illustrations in newspapers, 38, 74; news photographs, 262 n; draughtsmen of the early *Daily Graphic*, 263; wider use of illustrations, 280
Image, 293
Impartial Protestant Mercury, 35
Imperial Press Conferences, 280 n
Independent Observer, 184 n
Ingram, Sir Bruce, 210
Ingram, Herbert, 158, 210, 211
Ingram, Sir William, 210, 211, 236
Institute of Journalists, 277 n
Insurance, free accident, 235, 274–275
Intelligencer, 29

INDEX

Intertype, 239 n
Inveresk Paper Co., Ltd., 257
Irish News, 304
Iron Times, 158
Ives, Chester, 255 n

Jackson, W. M., 267
"Jacob Omnium," 227
Jacobs, W. W., 286
James, Henry, 213, 294
Jeffrey, Francis (Lord Jeffrey), co-founder and editor of *Edinburgh Review*, 188–191
Jerdan, William, 180, 202
Jerome, Jerome K., 220
Jerrold, Douglas, 185, 210
Jewish Chronicle, 221 n
Johannesburg Star, 269
John Blunt, 291
John Bull (Theodore Hook's), 5, 199–200 (1906), 290–291
John o' London's Weekly, 293
Johnson, Mrs. Elizabeth, 75, 83
E. Johnson's British Gazette, 75, 83–84
Johnson, Henry, 85
Johnson, Dr. Samuel, 56–57, 64, 69–70, 281
Jones, Kennedy, 237–238
Jones, Sir Roderick, 332
Jones's Evening News-Letter, 35 n
Jonson, Ben, 14
Judy, 297
"Junius" (Sir Philip Francis?), letters of, 70–73, 82, 101, 103

Keats, John, 192, 195
Keene, Charles, 210
Kemsley Group, 266, 273, 315; details of, 335
Kemsley, Lord (James Gomer Berry), 249, 335; jointly acquires the *Sunday Times* and other interests, 265–266
Kentish Gazette, 43
Kentish Mercury, 300
King, Dr. William, 48
Kingdomes Intelligencer, 23, 27
Kingdomes Weekly Intelligencer, 17
Kingdomes Weekly Post, 36 n
Kingsmill, Hugh, 216
Kipling, Rudyard, 213, 243 n, 286
Kitchener, Lord, 144 n, 244–246
Knight, Charles, 178, 206–207
Knox, Collie, 281
Knox, E. V., 209
Koenig, Frederic, 130
Korda, Tibor, 290

La Belle Assemblée, 84
Labouchere, Henry, 168, 170, 219–220

Ladies' Field, 285
Lady's Pictorial, 236, 285
Lady's Realm, 285
Lamb, Charles, 89, 93–94, 118, 131, 197
Lancaster, Osbert, 282
Land and Water, 285
Lane, William, 75
Lang, Andrew, 197 n
Latest News, 176
Laughing Mercury, 23
Lawson, Edward Levy (afterwards 1st Lord Burnham), and the making of the *Daily Telegraph*, 162–164; publicly honoured as Father of the Press, 166
Lawson, Lionel, 162
Leader (1850), 202
(Edward Hulton's), 292
Leech, John, 210
Leeds Intelligencer, 149 n, 183
Leeds Mercury, 43, 149 n, 175, 225, 249, 271
Leeds Times, 149 n
Leesburg Commercial Ledger, 300
Le Gallienne, Richard, 233–234
Le Marchant, Sir Denis, 135
Le Mercure Anglois, 17
Lemon, Mark, 209
Leng, Sir John, 262
Le Sage, Sir J. M., 164
L'Estrange, Sir Roger, 11, 28–32
Levy, J. M., 161–162
Lewes, G. H., 202, 214, 227
Lewis, D. B. Wyndham, 281
Lewis, Sir George Cornewall, 153
Licensing Act (1662), 28–29; allowed to lapse (1695), 36
Life, 289
Life and Letters, 295
Lika Joko, 297
Lilliput, 289, 297
L'Illustration, 208
Limbird, John, 207
Lincoln, Rutland and Stamford Mercury, 43
Linotype, 239 n
Listener, 293
Litchfield, Leonard, 34
Literary Courier of Grub-street, 51
Literary Gazette, 180, 202
Literature, 203
Little Folks, 285
Liverpool and Northern Daily Times, 175
Liverpool and Southport Daily News, 176
Liverpool Courant, 43
Liverpool Daily Post, 161, 175, 177, 182, 265
Liverpool Mercury, 271
Lloyd, Edward, 184–185
Lloyd, Frank, 257

Lloyd George, D., 247, 257, 275 n
Lloyd's Illustrated Sunday Newspaper, 184
Lloyd's List and Shipping Gazette, 254
Lloyd's Penny Sunday Times, 184
Lloyd's Weekly News, 184, 185, 275
Lloyd's Weekly Newspaper, 184–186, 267
Lockhart, John Gibson, 193–194, 196, 197, 198
London, 257
London Advertiser, 58
London Chronicle, 67, 68 n
London Courant, 74, 76
London Daily Advertiser, 58
London Daily Chronicle and Clerkenwell News, 185
London Daily Mercury, 7, 176, 178
London Daily Post, 70
London Evening News, 161
London Evening Post, 88, 102
London Farthing-Post, 42 n
London Gazette, 21, 33–37, 39, 43, 52, 66, 68; published daily, 158–159
London Halfpenny Newspaper, 186
London Journal, 118
London Magazine (eighteenth century), 55
  (1820), 196–197
  (1898), 284, 285
London Mercury (seventeenth century), 35
  (1919), 295
London Morning, 255
London Morning Mail, 7, 171–172
London Museum, 59, 70 n
London Mystery Magazine, 293
London News Agency, 181 n
London Opinion, 297
London Post, 36
London Telegraph, 158
Long, Sydney W. H., 279
Longman's Magazine, 196
Louis Napoleon, 143
Lovat Dickson's Magazine, 287
Low (David Low), 281
Loyal Impartial Mercury, 35
Loyal London Mercury, 35
Lucas, E. V., 210
Lucas, Samuel, 160
Luce, Henry R., 289
Lucy, Sir H. W., 210
Lynd, Robert, 281
Lyndhurst, Lord, 134, 138

Macaulay, Lord, 32, 36, 37, 191, 195, 196
Mackay, Ian, 281
Macleod, Gilbert, 119
Macmillan's Magazine, 213
Maddick, George, 172
Magazine of Magazines, 7, 59–60
Maginn, William, 195–196
Mail, 75

Maine, Sir Henry, 227
Majority, 262
Mallet, E., 39
Man in the Moon, 24
Manchester Courier, 271
Manchester Daily Telegraph, 175
Manchester Evening Chronicle, 264 n
Manchester Evening Mail, 176
Manchester Evening News, 176
Manchester Examiner and Times, 161
Manchester Gazette, 43
Manchester Guardian, 175, 258 n, 264 n, 266, 267, 270, 272, 296 n, 299, 310, 313–314; under C. P. Scott's editorship, 182–183
Manchester "newspaper war," 175–176
Manchester Observer, 119
Manchester Weekly Telegraph, 175
Manley, Mrs. Mary de la Rivière, 48
Mansfield, Lord, 70–72, 75–76
M.A.P., 285
Marlowe, Thomas, 233, 242
Martineau, Harriet, 158
Massingham, H. W., 203, 258; edits the Star, 233; the Nation, 296; and the Daily Chronicle, 296 n
Masterman, C. F. G., 258
Maugham, Lord, 320
Mawson, Robert, 51 n
Maxwell, John, 213
May, Phil, 210, 263
Mayhew, Henry, 209 n, 210
Mechanics' Magazine, 173
Mee, Arthur, 293
Melbourne, Lord, 92
Men Only, 289
Mercurius Anglicus, 35
Mercurius Aulicus, 19
Mercurius Britanicus (1643), 19–20
Mercurius Britannicus (1625), 13
Mercurius Civicus, 16
Mercurius Democritus, 23
Mercurius Fumigosis, 23
Mercurius Gallobelgicus, 13
Mercurius Jocosus, 23
Mercurius Mastix, 25
Mercurius Politicus, 21, 27
Mercurius Pragmaticus, 20, 25
Mercurius Publicus, 23, 27
Meredith, George, 213
Merry Magazine, 287
Methodist Magazine, 221 n
Methodist Recorder, 221 n
Middlesex Journal, 76, 101
Midland Daily Telegraph, 304
Mill, James, 91
  John Stuart, 91
Millais, Sir J. E., 211
Milne, A. A., 210

INDEX

Milner, Lord, 229, 268
Milner-Gibson, Thomas, 150–155
Milton, John, 21, 97, 190
Mirror, 207
Miscellany, 51
Mist, Nathaniel, 50–51
Mist's Weekly Journal, 50–51
Modern Society, 216
Modern Woman, 288
Monotype, 239 n
Montague, C. E., 182–183
Monthly Review, 294
Moonshine, 297
Moore, Thomas, 89, 118, 190–191, 192
Morison, Stanley, 6, 7, 35 n, 79, 84 n
Morley, John (Lord Morley), 142, 167 n, 215, 225, 227–228
Morning, 7, 255 n
Morning Advertiser, 153 n, 180, 255; offices destroyed in air raid, 303
Morning Chronicle, 61, 66, 73, 74, 78, 82, 95, 124, 136, 137–138, 163, 193, 203; under James Perry, 88–90; under John Black, 90–92
Morning Herald (1780), 61, 65, 74, 76, 80, 81 n, 163 n
(formerly *London Morning*), 255 n
Morning Latest News, 7, 172, 255 n
Morning Leader, 233, 255, 281
Morning Mail (London), 172
(Manchester), 176
Morning News, 176
Morning newspapers, first London halfpenny, 7, 171–172
Morning Post, 61, 68, 74, 78, 82, 117, 156, 162, 163, 217, 217 n, 228, 236, 257, 279; founded, 79; counterfeit edition, 80; under Daniel Stuart, 92–95; office attacked by mob, 133; editor stabbed, 133; under Lord Glenesk, 181–182; absorbed by *Daily Telegraph*, 254, 271
Morning Star (eighteenth century), 75, 81 (1856), 160, 167
Morning Star and Dial, 167 n
Morris, Mowbray, 140–141
Morrison, Herbert, 309–311, 312, 317, 319–320
Morrow, George, 210
Morton, J. B., 281
Motteux, Peter Anthony, 46
Muddiman, Henry, 7, 21–23, 27–31, 33–35
Muddiman, J. G. (pen-name J. B. Williams), 7, 12 n
Mudford, W. H., 181
Municipal Journal, 257
Murray, E. C. Grenville, 217–218, 220
Murray, John, 156, 192
Murray, John Grey, 213

Murray, Lord, 188
Murray's Magazine, 213
Murry, J. Middleton, 295
Music and Letters, 293
My Garden, 289
My Home, 288
My Magazine, 285

Nally, Will, 318
Nash, Eveleigh, 287
Nash's Magazine, 284, 287
Nation, 202, 203, 233, 296
National Observer, 203
National Press Agency, 179
National Review, 221, 294
National Union of Journalists, 277 n
Nature, 221
Nedham, Marchamont, 19–21, 27, 28
Nevinson, H. W., 182, 258, 296 n
New Age, 296
New Magazine, 287
New Monthly Magazine, 200
New Observer, 184 n
New Review, 285
New Statesman and Nation, 202, 296, 299
New Times, 156
New Witness, 296–297
New York Daily Tribune, 163
New York Evening Telegram, 252
New York Herald, 163, 164, 204, 252; London edition, 253
New York Times, 282–283
New York World, 231 n
New Yorker, 297
Newbolt, Sir Henry, 294
Newcastle Chronicle, 265
Newcastle Evening Chronicle, 273
Newcastle Evening World, 273–274
Newcastle Journal, 43
Newes, 29
Newes from Most Parts of Christendom, 13
Newes from Spain, 13
Newnes, Sir George, 186, 220, 230, 235, 236, 242, 274, 284, 290; starts *Westminster Gazette*, 231–232; *Tit-Bits*, 234–235; *Strand Magazine*, 235
Newnes (George) Ltd., 275 n, 285, 287, 297
News agencies, 179–181, 331
News Chronicle (formerly *Daily News*, q.v.), 155, 255, 270, 280, 281, 299; air raid damage, 303
News of the World, 84, 184, 186, 275; air raid damage, 303
News Review, 289
Newsbooks, 11–26, 322, 323, 324
Newsletters, 30–31, 35–36
Newspaper chains, details of the principal, 335–336

Newspaper funds, 144 n
Newspaper Library, 6, 149, 161, 173, 177; air raid damage, 303
Newspaper Press Directory, 174, 175
Newspaper Press Fund, 277 n
Newspaper Proprietors' Association, 278 n, 279, 332
Newspaper Society, 175
Newspapers, the first, 33–34; simultaneous publication in more than one centre, 34, 243 n; postscripts, 37; first daily, 39–40; the tri-weeklies, 40; farthing newspapers, 42 n, 173–174; provincial weeklies founded, 42–43; stamp tax first imposed, 43; newspaper sales in the eighteenth century, 44, 65; government bribes, 64–65, 88; first evening paper, 74–75; first Sunday paper, 75; development of foreign correspondence during French Revolution, 67–69, 87–88, 89; first evening paper to issue second edition, 95; "silver" and "golden" numbers, 149–150; railway dailies, 158; first penny morning paper, 161; early halfpenny morning newspapers, 171–172; expansion of the Press after the removal of the stamp duty, 174 et seq.; New Journalism, 224 et seq.; passing of the London literary evenings, 232; heavy cost of foreign news services, 254, 323; Lord Rothermere's plan for a chain of evening papers, 273–274; rise in circulations during and after Second World War, 275–276; growth of advertisement revenue, 276, 279; the General Strike and the Press, 277–279; facsimile newspapers, 282–283; newspaper offices damaged by bombs, 301 et seq.; the reporting of the Second World War, 304–306; wartime rationing of newsprint, 307–308; findings of the Royal Commission on the Press, 314–317; wider scope of the newspaper, 324–326
Nicoll, Sir W. Robertson, 221 n
Night and Day, 297
Night Post, 40
Nineteenth Century, 214
Noon Gazette, 74, 76
North and South Shields Gazette, 177
North British Mail, 175
North Briton, 59, 97–101
North, Christopher (John Wilson), 194–196
North, Lord, 100, 103
North Mail, 259
North Times, 175, 176
Northampton Mercury, 43

Northcliffe, Lord (Alfred Charles William Harmsworth), 8, 139, 162, 166, 219, 231 n, 252, 253, 260, 277, 278 n, 279, 290, 326; buys *Weekly Dispatch*, 186, 242; early journalistic experience, 224, 236; buys *Evening News*, 234, 237–238; starts *Answers*, 236; launches other periodicals, 237; early years of the *Daily Mail*, 238–243; his criticism of Victorian editors, 224; and Victorian newspapers, 241; offers big prizes to stimulate development of aviation, 244; violently attacked for blunt criticism of Lord Kitchener, 244–246; becomes chief of British War Mission to the United States, 247; the last days, 248; Spender's estimate of, 249; J. L. Garvin's tribute, 249; the founding of the *Daily Mirror*, 262–263; purchase of the *Observer*, 264; restores prosperity to *The Times*, 267–270
Northcliffe Newspapers, Ltd., 250, 273
Northern Daily Express, 179
Northern Daily Telegraph, 257
Northern Echo, 175, 224–225
Northern Express, 161
Northern Express and Lancashire Daily Post, 175
Northern Star, 149 n
Northern Tatler, 43
Northern Whig, 175, 304
Norwich Mercury, 43
Norwich Post, 42
Norwich Postman, 42
Nottingham Guardian, 175
Nottingham Journal, 43, 175
Nouvelles Ordinaires de Londres, 17
Novel Magazine, 287

Observator (L'Estrange's), 32, 46 (Tutchin's), 32–33, 44
Observer, 84, 92, 137, 149, 186, 210, 232, 253, 258 n, 266, 267, 270, 276, 326; remodelled by J. L. Garvin, 264–265
O'Connell, Daniel, 137, 148
O'Connor, Feargus, 149 n
O'Connor, T. P., 8, 162; founds the *Star*, 233; starts the *Sunday Sun* and the *Sun*, 234
Odhams Press, Ltd., 187, 262 n, 276, 287, 289, 290, 291; air raid damage, 303
Oracle, 82
Orage, A. R., 296
Organiser, 289
Original London Post, 59
Original Star, 75
Orion, 295
Osbourne, Lloyd, 202 n

INDEX

Our Homes and Gardens, 288
Outlook, 203, 265, 295
Outram, George, 182
Overseas Daily Mail, 243, 249
Overseas Magazine, 289
Owl, 217 n
Oxford Gazette: see *London Gazette*
Oxford Magazine, 59

Pagan, Dr. James, 182
Pageant, 220
Paine, Thomas, 121, 122
Palgrave, F. T., 214
Pall Mall Gazette, 60, 63, 155, 176, 177, 203, 212, 218, 231 n, 232, 257, 259, 265; story of its founding, 225–226; John Morley and W. T. Stead in partnership, 227–228; the "Maiden Tribute" campaign, 229–230
Pall Mall Magazine, 285
Palmerston, Lord, 153, 217
Pan, 287
Parke, Ernest, 233
Parliament, reports of proceedings in newsbooks banned at the Restoration, 26; but permitted in newsletters, 30; House of Commons warns newsletter writers, 36; imposes stamp tax, 43; Parliamentary reports in *Gentleman's Magazine*, etc., 55–56; John Wilkes foils attempt to enforce ban on reports, 101–103; Parliament reduces and finally abolishes "taxes on knowledge," 149–155; appoints Royal Commission on the Press, 312–313; debates findings, 317; journalist M.P. expelled and editor reprimanded in "privilege" case, 317–319
Parliament Scout, 17
Parliamentary Intelligencer, 21, 22, 28
Parnell, Charles Stewart, 170, 267
Partly printed sheets for provincial weeklies, 178–179
Partridge, Sir Bernard, 210
Passing Show, 290
Pater, Walter, 213
Paxton, Joseph, 157
Peace Advocate, 173
Pearson, Sir C. A., 255 n; becomes a periodical publisher, 230–231; starts *Daily Express*, 252; buys the *Standard*, 259; "The Blind Leader of the Blind," 259; unsuccessful bid for *The Times*, 267–268
Pearson's Magazine, 231, 284
Pearson's Weekly, 231, 286, 290
Pecke, Samuel, 15
Peel, Sir Robert, 125, 138

Penguin New Writing, 295
Penny morning newspapers, the first, 161
Penny Bell's Life, 83
Penny Cyclopaedia, 207
Penny Illustrated Paper, 211
Penny Magazine, 207
Penny Pictorial, 285
Penny Sunday Times, 184
Penny-a-liners, 181 n
Penny-a-Week Country Daily Newspaper, 173
People, 187, 276, 303
Pepys, Samuel, 28, 32, 33
A Perfect Diurnall of Some Passages in Parliament, 18
Periodicals, 34; beginnings of, 46; eighteenth-century periodicals, 46 *et seq.*; the rise of the quarterlies, 188; other nineteenth-century developments, 188 *et seq.*; Newnes and the Harmsworths, 234–237; changing fashions in magazines, 284–289; mass-circulation periodicals, 290; the reviews and literary magazines, 294–297; when all periodicals were suspended, 298–299; emergency issues during a trade dispute, 299–300
Perry, James, 78, 91, 92; edits *Morning Chronicle*, 88–90; imprisoned, 90
Petter, G. W., 208
Pick-me-up, 220
Pictorial daily, the first, 9, 177
Pictorial Times, 211
Picture Paper, 262
Picture Post, 290
Pigott, Richard, 170
Pike, G. Holden, 179
Pitt, William, 62, 76, 95, 105, 108 (Earl of Chatham), 56
Plain Englishman, 207
Plebeian, 54
Pocket magazines, 288–289
Poetic Magazine, 173
Political Quarterly, 294
Political Register (1767), 59 (Cobbett's), 105, 107–115, 120
"Pont" (Graham Laidler), 210
Poor Man's Guardian, 126, 127
Pope, Wilson, 233
Porcupine, 106
Porcupine's Gazette, 105
Post Boy, 36, 38 n
Post Man, 36
Poster, 220
Pratt, Lord Chief Justice, 99
Premier Magazine, 287
Press agencies, 178–179
Press Association, 322, 331, 332; founding of, 180; scope of its service, 333–334

Press Club Collection, 6, 171, 172, 173, 176 n, 177
Price, G. Ward, describes Lord Rothermere's methods of work, 250-251
Priestley, Dr. Joseph, 104
Prince Regent, attacked in *Examiner* article, 117-118
Printer's Ink, 289
Prior, Matthew, 46 n, 48
Prize, 286
Prompter, 125
Provincial Newspaper Society, 175
Provincial newspapers, the oldest, 43; first penny morning papers, 161; first halfpenny morning paper, 175 n; first halfpenny evening journals, 176-178; expansion of local weeklies, 178; partly printed sheets, 178-179; provincial dailies establish the Press Association, 180; private telegraph wires, 180; growth in the influence of provincial Press, 181, 183-184
Pryor, S. J., 242
Public Advertiser, 65, 66, 67, 70-74, 82, 323
Public Good, 173
Public Ledger, 74, 157, 254
Public Opinion, 7, 221
Publick Adviser, 21
Publique (Publick) Intelligencer, 21, 27
Pulteney, William, 52
Punch, 157, 172, 182, 185, 281, 297, 299; early history, 209; editors and contributors, 209-210
Punchinello, 209 n
Punch in London, 209 n

Quarterly Review, 62, 106, 156, 179, 194, 196, 198 n, 294; founded, 192; first editor's attitude to writers, 192-193
Queen, 208, 226, 297
Queen's Messenger, 218
Quennell, Peter, 213
Quiver, 208

Radio Times, 290, 299
Raglan, Lord, 144, 244 n
Railway Director, 158
Ralph, James, 58
Ralph, Julian, 243
Rambler, 57
Rand Daily Mail, 260
Rapid Review, 285
Ratcliffe, S. K., 258
Reader, 54
Reader's Digest, 289
Reading Mercury, 43
Read's Weekly Journal, 51, 65
The Real Old John Bull, 200
Realist, 295

Record, 221 n
Red Magazine, 285, 287
Referee, 187, 266-267
Reflector, 118
Reformist's Register, 120
Reid, Sir Wemyss, 225
Religious Review of Reviews, 221 n
Representative, 156
Republican, 121, 122, 123, 124
Reuter, Baron Herbert de, 332
    Baron Julius de, 180
Reuters, 163, 180-181, 260, 304, 322; history of, 331-332; trust formed, 332-333
Reveille for the Week-End, 290
The Review, 46, 47, 49
Review of English Studies, 293
Review of Reviews, 7, 59, 235, 293; founded, 230-231
Revue des Deux Mondes, 214
Reynolds, Frank, 210
Reynolds, G. W., 186
Reynolds News and Sunday Citizen, 186, 276
Reynolds's Weekly Newspaper, 186
Rhondda, Lady, 296
Ricardo, David, 89
Riddell, Lord, 275 n
Rintoul, R. S., 201-202
Ritzema, T. P., 257
Roberts, J., 51
Robertson Scott, J. W., 227 n, 288-289
Robinson, Henry Crabb, 68, 129, 130, 131, 132
Robinson, Sir John, 168
"Robinson of Gravetye" (W. Robinson), 286
Rogers, Samuel, 192
Rosebery, Lord, 223, 242
Ross, Sir David, 313
Rotary printing press, when first used, 185
Rothermere, 1st Lord (Harold Sidney Harmsworth), 234, 237-238, 266, 271; buys control of Associated Newspapers, Ltd., and fails in bid for *The Times*, 249; Air Minister, 250; the United Empire Party, 250; campaign for rearmament, 250; his methods of work, 250-251; buys *Daily Mirror*, 263; starts *Sunday Pictorial*, 263-264; unsuccessful attempt to found a chain of *Evening Worlds*, 273-274
Rothermere, 2nd Lord (Esmond Harmsworth), 251, 335
Rothermere Group, details of, 335
Rougemont, Louis de, 220
Round Table, 294
Royal Commission on the Press, 272, 312-317, 322

INDEX

Royal Magazine, 231, 284
Royal Press, 176
Russel, Alexander, 182
Russell, Sir Edward (Lord Russell of Liverpool), 182
Russell, Lord John, 142, 151
Russell, Sir William Howard, 146, 168; Crimean War dispatches to *The Times*, 144–145

St. Bride's Church, gutted in air raid, 302
St. James's Chronicle, 68, 76
St. James's Evening Post, 40
St. James's Gazette, 177, 226, 232, 259
St. James's Post, 40
St. John, Henry (afterwards Lord Bolingbroke), 48, 52
St. Paul's Magazine, 213–214
Sala, G. A., 170, 211, 212, 236; his work on the *Daily Telegraph*, 164; writes for *Illustrated London News*, 165; founds *Sala's Weekly Journal*, 165; edits *Temple Bar*, 213
Sala's Weekly Journal, 165
Salaries, journalists', 277
Salisbury and Winchester Journal, 43
Salisbury, Lord, 155, 240
Salisbury Postman, 43
Sapt, Arkas, 262 n
Saturday Review, 202; its brilliant inception, 63, 203–204; under Frank Harris, 215; the last phase, 296
Saunders, William, 179
Savoy, 220
Say, Mary, 76
Schofield, Guy, 319
Science Progress, 292
Scotish Dove, 17
Scots Courant, 43
Scots Observer, 203
Scots Postman, 43
Scotsman, 167 n, 175, 180 n, 182, 258 n; special trains, 243 n
Scott, C. P., 270; becomes editor of the *Manchester Guardian*, 182; his views on the conduct of a newspaper, 182; on the importance of the Long Leader, 183
Scott, Clement, 164
Scott, John, 193, 197
Scott, Sir Walter, 189–192, 195, 199, 206
Scottish Daily Express, 243
Scott-James, R. A., 258
Scrutiny, 295
Seaman, Sir Owen, 209
Sedley, Sir Charles, 46 n
Selfridge, Gordon, 277

Serials, the first, 59; as feature of a new Early Victorian daily, 158; Northcliffe's faith in circulation-building value of, 240; *The Times* prints a serial, 240 n
Shackell, —, nominal editor of Theodore Hook's *John Bull*, 200
Sharpe, C. K., 192
Shaw, G. B., 215, 216, 233
Sheffield Daily Telegraph, 161, 175
Shepard, Ernest H., 210
Sheppard, the Rev. Samuel, 24–25
Sheridan, R. B., 77, 78, 93
Sherwin's Weekly Political Register, 121, 122
Shields Gazette, 177–178, 304
Shorter, Clement K., 234
Sidebotham, Herbert, 266
Sidmouth, Lord, 96, 120, 128
Signature, 293
Simon, Lord, 256
Simon, Oliver, 294
Simpkin Marshall's building burnt out in air raid, 302–303
Sims, George R., 187
Six-a-Penny, or Country Daily Newspaper, 174
Sleigh, Colonel, 160
Smith, George, founds *Cornhill Magazine*, 212; starts *Pall Mall Gazette*, 225–226
Smith, John, publisher of *Morning Mail*, 172
Smith, Sydney, and the *Edinburgh Review*, 188–190
Smith's Currant Intelligence, 35
Smollett, T. B., 59
Somerset County Gazette, 209
South Wales Argus, 304
South Wales Echo, 304
Southey, Robert, 94, 192–193, 195
Southport Daily News, 176
Southwood, Lord (J. S. Elias), 262 n
Speaker, 203
Spectator (Steele and Addison's), 39, 41, 44, 52–54, 57, 60
(1828), 6, 204, 296, 297, 299; its "entirely new" plan, 201; under Hutton and Townshend, 202
Spender, Edward, 179
Spender, Harold, 258
Spender, J. A., 226, 228, 230, 231; becomes editor of the *Westminster Gazette*, 232; his estimate of Northcliffe, 248–249; as writing editor, 255–256
Sphere, 211, 234
Spielmann, M. H., 209
Spirit of the Union, 119
Sport and Country, 221 n
Sporting Chronicle, 264 n

Sporting Life, 83
Springfield, Lincoln, 233
"Spy" (Sir Leslie Ward), 217
Squire, Sir John, 295
Stamford News, 118
Stampa, G. L., 210
Standard, 162, 163, 181, 196, 222, 262; becomes morning paper, 155, 167; last years of, 258–259
Stanley, H. M., 164
Star (1788), 74–75, 93
  (1888), 173, 176, 257, 259, 281, 303; founded, 233; its brilliant staff, 233–234
Stars and Stripes, 308
Statist, 203
Stead, W. T., 7, 8, 59, 162, 165, 231 n, 234; first editorship, 224–225; becomes assistant editor of the *Pall Mall Gazette*, 225–227; succeeds Morley as editor; "Maiden Tribute" campaign, 229; imprisoned, 230; starts *Review of Reviews*, 230–231; dies in the *Titanic* disaster, 231; the fiasco of the *Daily Paper*, 262
Steed, H. Wickham, 246 n
Steele, Sir Richard, 46, 48, 54, 55, 60, 188, 189, 221, 325; founds the *Tatler*, 52; and the *Spectator* (with Addison), 53
Steevens, G. W., 241–242
Stephen, Fitzjames, 226–227
Stephen, Leslie, 213, 227
Sterling, Edward, 130–131
Stevenson, R. L., 202 n
Stoddart, Dr. John, dismissed from editorship of *The Times*, 131; starts the *New Times*, 156
Stoddart, Dr. J. H., editor of the *Glasgow Herald*, 182
Stop-press device, 37
Storey, Samuel, 173
Storyteller, 287
Strachey, J. St. Leo, 202, 213
Strand Magazine, 235, 284–285, 286
Straus, Ralph, 165
Street, Peter, 95
Stuart, Daniel, 78, 133; buys *Morning Post* and transforms it into influential newspaper, 92–95; buys *Courier*, 95; his independence, 96
Stuart, Peter, 74–75, 82, 93
Stuart's Star, 75
Studio, 220
Sulzberger, A. H., 282
Summary, 171
Sun (1798), 105, 174; the "Golden *Sun*," 149
  (1893), 234, 237, 259, 291

Sunday at Home, 285
Sunday Chronicle, 186–187, 243 n, 264 n, 276, 286 n, 295; absorbs *Sunday Referee*, 266–267
Sunday Daily Mail, 242
Sunday Dispatch (see also *Weekly Dispatch*), 186, 250, 275, 276, 295
Sunday editions, 242
Sunday Evening Telegram, 264, 291
Sunday Express, 234, 264, 276, 281, 282; triplicate publication, 243 n
Sunday Graphic, 263, 267, 276
Sunday Illustrated, 264, 291
Sunday Mail, 276
Sunday Mercury, 276
Sunday Monitor, 83, 185
Sunday News, 267, 275
Sunday newspapers, the first, 75; a halfpenny Sunday journal, 186; remodelling in twentieth century, 186–187
Sunday Pictorial, 250, 263–264, 276, 292
Sunday Post, 276
Sunday Referee, 266
Sunday Sun (T. P. O'Connor's), 234 (Newcastle), 276
Sunday Times, 84, 161, 184 n, 186, 253, 258 n, 267, 276, 292, 326; remodelled, 265–266
Sunny Magazine, 287
Suppression fees, 88
Sutton, Sir G. A., 233
Swift, Jonathan, 43–44, 48
Swinburne, A. C., 215
Syndication, early examples of, 178–180

Tablet, 221 n
Tatler (Steele's), 37, 46, 48, 52–53, 55
  (Leigh Hunt's), 118
  (1901), 292
Taxes on the Press, stamp tax first imposed (1712), 43; raised by Pitt, 76, 95; advertisement tax, 76; Newspaper Stamp Duties Act of 1819 aimed at cheap Radical papers, 113–114; tax on advertisements lowered (1833), 149; stamp tax and paper duty reduced (1836), 149; advertisement tax abolished (1853), 152; newspaper duty removed (1855), 154; paper freed from duty (1861), 155; the campaign for the removal of the "taxes on knowledge," 147–155; proposed purchase tax withdrawn, 151 n
Taylor, Tom, 209
Tea Table, 54
Telegraph, 94
"Telegraphese," 164
Telegraphing of news, 168, 181; private wires, 180, 324

INDEX

Teleprinters, 323
Teletypesetters, 323
Temple Bar, 213, 218, 285
Tenniel, Sir John, 210
Tennyson, Lord, 213
Tercentenary Handlist of English and Welsh Newspapers, 7
Thackeray, W. M., 157, 196, 210, 225, 324; first editor of *Cornhill*, 212-213
Theatre, 54
Thomas, The Rev. David, 167 n
Thomas, G. H., 212
Thomas, J., 15
Thomas, W. L., 211; 212, 263
Thomason Collection, 6
Thomasson, Franklin, 261
Thompson, A. M., 286 n
Thompson, Henry Yates, 231
Thorpe, James, 263
Throne, 285
Tighe, Desmond, 304-305
Time (Edmund Yates's), 219
— (H. R. Luce's), 289
Time and Tide, 296, 299
The Times, 6, 37, 43, 68-69, 70 n, 74, 82, 97, 111, 149, 156, 157, 162, 163, 181, 193, 196, 203, 217 n, 226, 228, 233, 243, 246, 254-255, 258 n, 266, 282, 299, 308, 310; founded, 85-86; subsidised, 65, 88; early foreign correspondence, 87-88; under John Walter II and Thomas Barnes, 92, 128-139; under J. T. Delane, 139-146; exposes railway mania, 140 n; vindicates right of the Press to make disclosures, 142-144; Louis Napoleon attempts to bribe, 143; *The Times* exposes neglect and ineptitude in the Crimea, 144, 244 n; on the newspaper tax, 152-155; effects of new competition, 166-169; the forged "Parnell" letters, 170-171; publishes a halfpenny morning paper, 171; a period of decline, 222; prints a serial, 240 n; resignation of Geoffrey Dawson, 247; renaissance of *The Times* under Northcliffe, 248, 267-270; emergency issues during General Strike, 278; offices damaged in air raid, 301-302
The Times Literary Supplement, 293
The Times Weekly Edition, 75
Tit-Bits, 46 n, 230, 236, 274, 286, 290; how it began, 234-235
Today, 220, 289
Tolstoy, Count Leo, 294
Tomahawk, 297
Tomlinson, H. M., 258
Topham, Captain Edward, 81, 88
Town and Country Magazine, 59

Town Talk, 54
Townsend, Meredith, 202, 227
T. P.'s Weekly, 293
Tracy, Louis, 237
Traill, H. D., 203
Transatlantic edition of *Daily Mail*, 243
Traveller, 156
Tribune (1906), why it failed, 261 (1937), 296
Trollope, Anthony, 212, 214-215, 227; edits *St. Paul's Magazine*, 213-214
True Briton, 105, 106
True Patriot, 58
Trusler, the Rev. Dr., 79
Truth, 170, 219-220, 299
Tutchin, John, 32-33
Twentieth Century, 214, 294
Twenty-Story Magazine, 287
Twyn, John, 31

United Empire Party, 250
Universal Chronicle, 57, 281
Universal Magazine, 59
Universe, 221 n

Vanity Fair, 217-218, 295
Varityper, 300
"Vicky" (Viktor Weiss), 281
Victoria, Queen, 142, 149, 227
Violet Magazine, 287
Virtue, James, 213
Vizetelly, Henry, 211
Vizetelly, J. T., 211
Vogue, 288

Wace, the Rev. Henry, 147
Wakefield Daily Free Press, 176
Wales, Prince of (the Duke of Windsor), 250
Walkden, Evelyn, 319
Walker, Henry, 27
Walkley, A. B., 233
Wallace, Sir Donald Mackenzie, 170
Wallace, Edgar, his journalistic career, 260, 267
Walpole, Sir Robert, 52, 54, 64-65
Walter, John (1739-1812), 68, 70 n, 75, 90, 128, 129-130; founds *The Times*, 85-86; imprisoned, 87; develops foreign correspondence, 87-88; receives subsidies, 88; accepts fees for suppression of scandalous paragraphs, 88
Walter, John (1776-1847), 68, 139, 141, 142, 145, 193, 269; assumes control of *The Times* and refuses Government subsidies, 88, 128; battle with Post Office monopolists, 129; search for an editor, 130-131; Thomas Barnes

takes charge, 132; growth of *The Times* under John Walter II and Barnes, 139; chooses Delane to succeed Barnes, 140
Walter, John (1818–1894), 146, 166, 168–169, 269; manager of *The Times*, 142; influence over leader page, 169; accepts responsibility for publication of forged "Parnell" letters, 170–171; issues halfpenny morning paper, 171
War correspondents, casualties in Second World War, 307
War Cry, 221 n
Ward, Artemus, 210
Waters, Sir George, 314
Watts, G. F., 209
Webster, Tom, 282
Week, 309
Week-End Review, 296
Weekly Budget, 187
Weekly Chronicle, 210
Weekly Dispatch (now *Sunday Dispatch*), 83, 84, 186, 242, 249, 275
Weekly Echo, 186
Weekly Illustrated, 290
Weekly Journal, 51 n
Weekly Miscellany, 51
Weekly Newes from Italy, Germanie, Hungaria, 12
Weekly News Letter, 36
Weekly Review of the Affairs of France, 46–47
Weekly Sun, 234
Weekly Times, 186
Weekly Times and Echo, 186
Weekly Visions of the late Popish Plot, 35
Wellington, Duke of, 138
Wells, H. G., 215, 286, 294
Wells, Mary, 81
Western Daily Press, 273
Western Independent, 276
Western Mail, 304
Western Morning News, 175, 179
Westminster Gazette, 148 n, 176 n, 226, 235, 259; founded, 231–232; becomes morning paper, 232; J. A. Spender's editorship, 255–256
Westminster Press Group, details of, 336
Westminster Review, 214
Whibley, Charles, 203 n
White Dwarf, 120
Whitehall Evening Post, 68 n
Whitten, Wilfred, 293
Wickwar, William H., 119

Wide World Magazine, 220, 235
Wife and Home, 288
Wilde, Oscar, 216
Wilkes, John, 59, 119; conducts *North Briton*, 97–99; ordered to appear before House of Commons but escapes to France, 100; returns and is sent to prison, 100–101; foils attempt to enforce ban on Parliamentary reports, 101–103
Wilkinson, Gilbert, 282
William IV, 148 n
William, Oliver, 27
Williams, J. B., see *Muddiman, J. G.*
Williamson, Joseph, 33–34
Windham, William, 105, 106
Windmill, 295
Windsor Magazine, 284
Winterton, Lord, 313, 320
Woman, 290
Woman and Beauty, 288
Woman and Home, 288
Woman at Home, 221 n, 285
Woman's Journal, 288
Woman's Own, 290
Wood, Sir Charles, 150–151
Wood, Sir Kingsley, 151 n
Wood, Robert, 16
Woodfall, Henry, 73
Woodfall, Henry Sampson, 70–73, 74
Woodfall, William, 73, 89
Wooler, T. J., 120
Wordsworth, William, 94, 95, 190
World (1787), 65, 81, 88
— (1874), 218–219, 295
World Review, 293
World's Press News, 303, 317–318
World's Work, 285

Yates, Edmund, 211, 218–219, 295
Yellow Book, 220
Yellow Dwarf, 120
Yellow Magazine, 287
York Mercury, 43
Yorkshire Evening News, 34, 304
Yorkshire Evening Post, 34
Yorkshire Evening Press, 304
Yorkshire Observer, 175
Yorkshire Post, 175, 183; incorporates *Leeds Mercury*, 249, 271
Young Newspapermen's Association, 277 n
Youth, 236
Yule, Sir David, 257

Kirtley Library
Columbia College
8th and Rogers
Columbia, MO. 65201